VOLUME ONE

# The Shaping of Musical Elements

VOLUME ONE

# The Shaping of Musical Elements

**ARMAND RUSSELL**
**and ALLEN TRUBITT**

University of Hawaii

**SCHIRMER BOOKS**
A Division of Macmillan, Inc.
**New York**
Maxwell Macmillan Canada
**Toronto**
Maxwell Macmillan International
**New York Oxford Singapore Sydney**

Schirmer Books
A Division of Macmillan, Inc.
866 Third Avenue, New York, N.Y. 10022

Maxwell Macmillan Canada, Inc.
1200 Eglinton Avenue East, Suite 200
Don Mills, Ontario M3C 3N1

Macmillan, Inc., is part of the Maxwell Communication Group of Companies

Library of Congress Catalog Card Number: 91-24556

Printed in the United States of America

printing number
1 2 3 4 5 6 7 8 9 10

**Library of Congress Cataloging-in-Publication Data**

Russell, Armand. 1932–
The Shaping of Musical Elements / Armand Russell and Allen Trubitt.
p. cm.
Includes index.
ISBN 0-02-872080-6
1. Music—Theory. I. Trubitt, Allen R. II. Title.
MT6.R963S5 1991
781—dc20 91-24556
CIP
MN

The paper used in this publication meets the minimum requirements of American National Standard for Information Sciences—Permanence of Paper for Printed Library Materials. ANSI Z39.48-1984.
∞

# CONTENTS


Preface ix

1. Notation, Intervals, and Scales 1

Durations 2
- Note and Rest Values 2
- Ties 2
- Dotted Notes and Rests 3

Meter 4
- Basic Durations 4
- Divisions of Basic Durations: Simple and Compound Meters 4
- Time Signatures 4
- Secondary Accents 6
- Subdivisions of the Basic Duration 7
- Grouping in Rhythmic Notation 7

Pitch Notation 11
- Pitch Designation 11
- Pitch Classes 15
- Octave Designations 16

Dynamics 16

The Diatonic System 17

Intervals 18
- Inversion of Intervals 20
- Compound Intervals 21

Scales 22
- Major Scales 22
- Minor Scales 25

Summary 29

2. Melody and Tonality 30

Rhythm 31
- Durations 31
- Accents 31
- Tension 35

Emergent Tones 36
- Phrase 36
- Contour 36
- Combining Pitch with Rhythm 39
- Melodic Analysis 42

Tonic 44
- Scale Degrees and Tonality 44
- The Characteristics of Tonal Melodies 45

Scales 46
- Pitch Complement 46
- Diatonic Modes 48
- Minor Mode 50

Changes in Tonality and Scales 51
- Modulation 51
- Change of Mode 51

Writing Melodies 52

Summary 53

3. Melody and Form 54

The Motive 55
- Cohesion and Differentiation 55
- Rhythmic Motives 55
- Melodic Motives 57
- Motivic Analysis 61

The Phrase 62
- The Concept of the Phrase 63
- Tension within the Phrase 68

Summary 73

4. Chords 74

Chords 75

Triads 75
- Types of Triads 76
- Identifying Chords bv Letter Name 77


97145

Triads in Major Keys 77
Triads in Minor Keys 78
Seventh Chords 79
The Structure of Seventh Chords 79
Types of Seventh Chords 80
Seventh Chords in Major Keys 81
Seventh Chords in Minor Keys 82
Summary 83

5. Chord Progressions 84

The Normal Progression 85
Alternate Progressions 89
Harmonic Cycles 91
Harmonic Cadences 91
Summary 94

6. Chords in Four Voices 95

The Four-voice Choral Setting 96
Ranges 96
Notation 96
Spacing 97
Chord Representation 98
Soprano Positions 99
Writing Chords 99
Bass Given 100
Soprano Given 100
Roman Numeral Given 100
Summary 101

7. Part Writing 102

Texture in Part Writing 103
The Outer Voices 103
The Inner Voices 103
The Relationships between Voices 104
Parallel Motion 104
Similar Motion 104
Oblique Motion 105
Contrary Motion 105
Other Voice Relationships 105
Voice Leading in Four Voices 106
The Independence of Lines 106
The Tendencies of Tones 110
Procedures for Connecting Chords 112
Procedure for Progressions with Complete Triads 112
Procedure for Progressions with Incomplete Triads 114
Resolution of the V7 in Root Position 115
Final Check for Errors 117
Summary 117

8. Introduction to Melody with Harmony 118

Introduction to Nonharmonic Tones 119
Passing Tone 119
Neighbor Tone 120
Melodic Interest in Part Writing 121
Melodic Interest from Contour and Rhythmic Activity 121
Melodic Interest from Nonharmonic Tones 122
The Harmonic Control of Melody 122
Harmonic Rhythm 123
Harmonization 124
Chord Selection 124
The Process of Harmonizing Melodies 125
Summary 128

9. Triads in First Inversion 129

The Figured Bass System 130
The Role of the Bass Line in Baroque Music 130
The Application of Figures: Root Position Triads 130
Triads in First Inversion 132
Major and Minor Triads in First Inversion 133
Diminished Triads in First Inversion 137
Harmonization Using First-Inversion Triads 138
Procedure for Harmonization with First-Inversion Triads 139
Summary 142

**10. Triads in Second Inversion and Inversions of the V7 143**

Six-Four Chords 144
Dissonance in the Six-Four Chord 144
Doubling 145
Types of Six-Four Chords 145

Inversions of the V7 152
Bass Figurations 152
First Inversion 154
Second Inversion 154
Third Inversion 154

The Complete List of Harmonic Cadences 157

Summary 159

**11. Nonharmonic Tones: Analysis 160**

Basic Characteristics 161

Types of Nonharmonic Tones 161
Passing Tone 161
Neighbor Tone 162
Escape Tone 162
Anticipation 162
Suspension 164
Retardation 165
Appoggiatura 165
Pedal Point 166
Double Neighbor Group 167

Special Usage 168
Consonant Nonharmonic Tones 168
Chromatic Nonharmonic Tones 169
Simultaneous Nonharmonic Tones 169
Anomalies 170

Summary 172

**12. Nonharmonic Tones: Writing 173**

Writing Specific Types of Nonharmonic Tones 174
Passing Tones 174
Neighbor Tones 174
Appoggiaturas and Escape Tones 175
Suspensions and Retardations 176
Anticipations 176
Double Neighbor Groups 176
Pedal Points 177

Nonharmonic Tones in Figured Bass 177
Suspensions and Figured Bass 178
Other Nonharmonic Tones in Figured Bass 182

Summary 183

**13. Nondominant Seventh Chords 185**

Types of Nondominant seventh chords 186
Chord Representation 187
Voice Leading 187
Chord Inversions 187
Chord Progressions 187

Nondominant Seventh Chords Considered by Chord Groups 188
Seventh Chords in Group 2 188
Seventh Chords in Group 3 190
Seventh Chords in Groups 4, 5, and 6 193

Summary 196

**14. Harmonic Tension 197**

Identifying Phrases 198

Harmonic Factors 201
Harmonic Rhythm 201
Chord Progressions 202
Sonority 204

The Crest of the Phrase: Harmony and Melody 206

Tension and Interpretation 209

Summary 210

**15. Texture and Two-Voice Homophony 211**

Texture 212
Relative Placement of Pitch 212
Types of Lines 213
Identifying Lines 213
The Relationships between Lines 217
Procedure for Textural Analysis 221

Two-Voice Homophony 224
Chordal Homophony 224
Melody with Accompaniment 229

Summary 234

**16. Two-Voice Polyphony 235**

Types of Polyphony 236
Differentiated Polyphony 236
Unified Polyphony 237
Writing Two-Voice Counterpoint 239
Imitation 240
Basic Concepts 241
Analysis of Imitation 241
Writing Imitation 244
Summary 245

**17. Modulation 247**

Basic Concepts 248
Smoothness of Modulation 248
Key Relationships 248
Common Chord Modulation 250
The Four Stages of Modulation 250
Establishing New Keys 252
Direct Modulation 000
Analysis of Modulation 257
Writing Modulations 259
Summary 261

**18. Secondary Dominants 262**

Secondary Dominants in Major and Minor Keys 264
Normal Treatment of Secondary Dominants 266
Secondary Dominants in the Normal Progression of Chords 266
Secondary Dominants in Root Position 267
Inversions of Secondary Dominants 269
Less Common Resolutions and Successions of Secondary Dominants 272
Analysis 274
Summary 277

**19. Secondary Leading-Tone Chords 278**

Leading-Tone Chords 279
Types of Leading-Tone Chords 279
Part Writing 280
Secondary Relationships 280
Possible Secondary Leading-Tone Chords 282
Progressions 284
Resolutions of Secondary Leading-Tone Seventh Chords 285
Type 1 286
Type 2 287
Problems in Analysis 289
Enharmonic Spelling 289
Successive Diminished Sevenths 291
Summary 292

**20. Borrowed Chords 293**

Borrowed Chords in Major Keys 294
Chord Group 1 294
Chord Group 2 295
Chord Group 3 296
Chord Group 4 299
Chord Group 5 299
Borrowed Chords in Minor Keys 301
Chord Group 1 302
Chord Group 3 303
Problems in Analysis 303
Summary 304

**21. Form: Higher Structural Units 306**

Higher Structural Levels in Melody 307
Second-Level Structural Units: Periods 307
Third-Level Units 311
Units above the Third Level 314
Higher Structural Levels with the Complete Texture 315
Second-Level Structural Units 315
Third-Level Structural Units 322
Summary 323

**22. Two-Part Forms 324**

Simple Two-Part Forms 325
Binary Form 327
Tonal Arch 328
Continuity 329
Binary Form without Repeats 332
Rounded Binary Form 333
Summary 337

**23.** **Three- and Four-Part Forms 338**

Three-Part Forms 339

Ternary Form 339

Introductions, Transitions, and Codas 345

Other Three-Part Forms 353

Four-Part Forms 358

Tonal Coherence 362

Two-Voice Framework 362

Step Progressions 364

Harmonic Cycles 367

Key Cycles 368

Summary 372

**24.** **Tension in Homophonic Music 373**

Sources of Tension 374

Melodic Tension 374

Harmonic Tension 374

Tension from Texture 375

Tension from Dynamics 377

Tension from Timbre 378

Tension at Higher Structural Levels 379

Melodic Tension in Higher Structural Levels 380

Tension in Higher Structural Units of Homophonic Music 382

Procedure for Formal Analysis 388

Tension and Interpretation 389

Dynamic Interpretation 389

Agogic Interpretation 390

Summary 390

**Appendix A: Aspects of Acoustics 392**

Vibration 393

Frequency 393

Resonance 394

Overtones and Timbre 394

Loudness 396

Tuning and Temperament 396

**Appendix B: Guide to Analytical Symbols 399**

**Glossary 402**

**Index 405**

# PREFACE

To be knowledgeable about music theory, a person needs information, a body of concepts and facts that are essential to the understanding of musical structure, and judgment, the ability to make intelligent choices in a variety of musical situations. Information can be learned, but judgment can only be developed. It comes with experience in the application of information in a variety of situations, by comparing differing solutions to a problem, and by arriving at decisions based on informed study. The theoretical material covered in this text conforms to the body of information usually included in the first year of music theory: diatonic harmony, borrowed chords, secondary dominants, and leading-tone chords; melodic analysis and musical forms, from the phrase to the binary and ternary forms and comparable structures; and textural analysis, with an emphasis on two-voice music.

Throughout, this text is concerned with tension, the principal manifestation of the affective nature of music. We will examine each element of musical structure to see how it contributes to or is affected by the growth and relaxation of tension. As the student becomes more aware of how tension is produced and fluctuates in music, judgment will sharpen and insight into new situations will improve.

Tension patterns in music have direct bearing on the interpretation of that music in performance; performers understand this intuitively. It is a major goal of the authors to bring into focus the forces shaping the rise and fall of tension and to provide the musician with analytical tools for understanding the origin and fluctuation of tension in a particular situation.

Standard terminology has been used wherever possible, but even in a text on fundamentals one occasionally finds a concept that has not been widely explored and for which no generally accepted term is available. In such cases the authors have chosen standard English words rather than neologisms.

This text is intended for a typical college-level freshman music theory course meeting regularly with a teacher for lecture and discussion. It assumes that, in addition to doing the workbook exercises, the student will have opportunities to try out some of the sounds and concepts in a laboratory, usually with keyboard instruments and playback equipment available. Suggested laboratory experiences are found at the end of each workbook chapter, but theory teachers may prefer to replace or supplement these suggestions.

The strategy of the authors in presenting the formal organization of music is to explore motives and other aspects of melody up to the phrase (chapter 3), then move to a consideration of harmony and other topics until chapter 21, which deals with the organization of the period and larger units. Those who prefer to cover the entire area of form from the phrase to the double period should skip to the first half of chapter 21 immediately after finishing chapter 3.

VOLUME ONE

# The Shaping of Musical Elements

CHAPTER ONE

# Notation, Intervals, and Scales

**Terms Introduced in This Chapter**

rhythm
tone
note
rest
tie
dot
basic duration (BD)
tempo
measure
bar
meter
divisions
simple meter
compound meter
time signature
meter signature
beat group
secondary accent
subdivisions
staff
octave
clef
great staff
ledger lines
octave signs
half step (semitone)
whole step (whole tone)
accidentals
pitch class
enharmonic equivalents
octave designations
dynamics
diatonic system
interval
inversion
simple interval
compound interval
major scale
scale degrees
- tonic
- supertonic
- mediant
- subdominant
- dominant
- submediant
- leading tone

key signature
minor scale
natural minor scale
relative minor/major scale
parallel minor/major scale
subtonic
harmonic minor scale
melodic minor scale
circle of fifths

Musical tones have physical properties that can be heard: duration, pitch, intensity, and timbre (tone color). Western music has developed an elaborate system for notating duration and pitch and a somewhat simpler method for specifying intensity (dynamics).

## DURATIONS

**rhythm**

A series of durations is *rhythm* in a specific sense. In a broader sense, the term includes all the implications and relationships that durations can imply.

### Note and Rest Values

**tone**

**note**

A distinction is often made between a *tone* (a musical sound) and a *note* (the symbol for a musical sound). Notes are written symbols used for specifying duration and pitch.

**EXAMPLE 1-1.** The parts of a note

head

stem

flag

**rest**

The basis of rhythmic notation is the system of relative note values. Each note value is twice the length of the next smaller value. Silences are represented by a parallel system of *rests* corresponding to each note value. The whole rest may be used to indicate a full measure rest in any meter.

### Ties

**tie**

The durations of several notes may be combined by *ties*. Tied notes are played without interruption. Ties are written so as to connect the note heads, but they are not used to combine rests.

**EXAMPLE 1-2.** Note and rest values

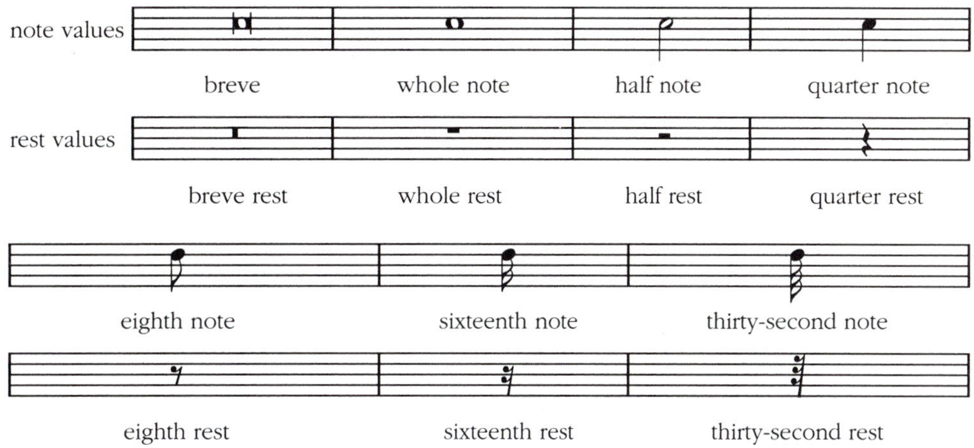


**EXAMPLE 1-3.** Tied notes

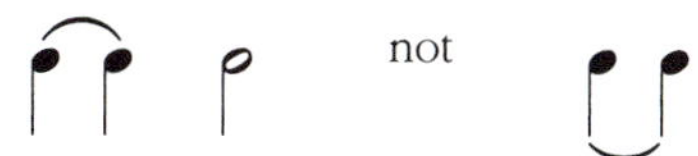


## Dotted Notes and Rests

**dot**

A *dot* increases the value of a note by half of its original value. Each additional dot adds half the value of the preceding dot.

**EXAMPLE 1-4.** Dotted notes

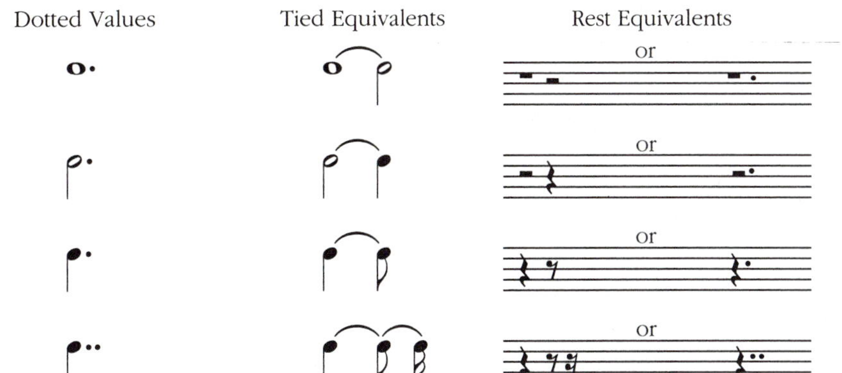

# METER

## Basic Durations

**basic duration**
**tempo**
**measure**
**bar**
**meter**

In most Western music, rhythm is organized by a succession or stream of even pulses, sometimes called beats, but more precisely termed *basic durations* (BD). BD refers to the time that elapses between pulses; the shorter the time between the pulses, the faster the *tempo*.

Certain pulses within the regular stream are perceived as accented or stronger. These stronger pulses appear as the beginning of a group of BDs, called a *measure,* or *bar*. This regular accent pattern is called *meter* and usually consists of groups of two, three, or four beats, called duple, triple, or quadruple meter.

## Divisions of Basic Durations: Simple and Compound Meters

**divisions**
**simple meter**
**compound meter**

Rhythm is further organized by *divisions* of the basic durations, that is, shorter durations within the beat. Basic durations are of two types: those that divide into two equal parts and those that divide into three equal parts. Meters using basic durations that divide into two parts are called *simple meters,* and those using basic durations that divide into three parts are called *compound meters*. In simple meter any undotted note value can be selected to represent the BD; the basic division of the beat is represented by a note one-half the value of the BD. For instance, if a quarter note represents the BD, eighth notes represent the divisions of the beat into two equal parts.

In compound meter any dotted note value may be selected to represent the BD; the basic division of the beat is represented by a note one-third the value of the BD. For instance, if a dotted quarter note represents the BD, eighth notes represent the divisions of the beat into three equal parts.

## Time Signatures

**time signature**
**meter signature**

At the beginning of a piece of music a *time signature* or *meter signature* is given. This consists of two numbers that indicate how the rhythm is notated.

### Time Signatures for Simple Meters

In time signatures for simple meters, the lower number indicates the note value that represents the beat, and the upper number indicates the number of beats in the measure. Once the note value representing the beat has been selected, all the notes and rests in the piece are notated as multiples or divisions of the BD.

In example 1-5a the lower number in the time signature (4) means the quarter note represents the beat, and the upper number (2) indicates the number of beats in the measure. Eighth notes represent divisions of the beat. In example 1-5b the half note represents the beat and quarter notes represent divisions of the beat. In example 1-5c the eighth note represents the beat, and sixteenth notes represent the divisions of the beat. Table 1-1 summarizes the meaning of commonly used time signatures for simple meters. A meter that has two beats per measure is called *duple meter;* three beats per measure, *triple meter;* four beats, *quadruple;* five beats, *quintuple.*

**EXAMPLE 1-5.** Basic durations and divisions in simple meters

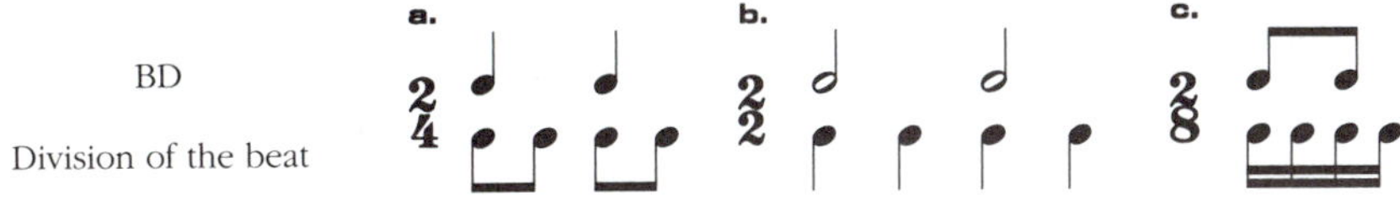


## Time Signatures for Compound Meters

In compound meters the signature must be interpreted differently from simple meters. Signatures for compound meters indicate how many divisions of the beat are contained in each measure. In a measure of compound duple meter, for example $\frac{6}{8}$, the signature will indicate the number of divisions in the measure (six), not the number of beats (two). To determine the number of beats in a measure of compound meter, divide the upper number of the time signature by three.

In example 1-6a the beat is represented by a dotted quarter note, division by eighth notes. There are two beats per measure in examples 1-6b and 1-6c; in each case, however, the BD is represented by different values. In example 1-6b the dotted half note represents the beat and quarter notes represent the divisions; in example 1-6c the dotted eighth note represents the beat, sixteenths the divisions. Table 1-2 summarizes the meaning of commonly used time signatures for compound meters.

| **Note value representing BD:** | ♪ | ♩ | 𝅗𝅥 |
|---|---|---|---|
| 2 beats per measure | $\frac{2}{8}$ | $\frac{2}{4}$ | $\frac{2}{2}$ |
| 3 beats per measure | $\frac{3}{8}$ | $\frac{3}{4}$ | $\frac{3}{2}$ |
| 4 beats per measure | $\frac{4}{8}$ | $\frac{4}{4}$ | $\frac{4}{2}$ |
| 5 beats per measure | $\frac{5}{8}$ | $\frac{5}{4}$ | $\frac{5}{2}$ |

**TABLE 1-1.** Time signatures for basic durations in simple meter

**EXAMPLE 1-6.** Basic durations and divisions in compound meters

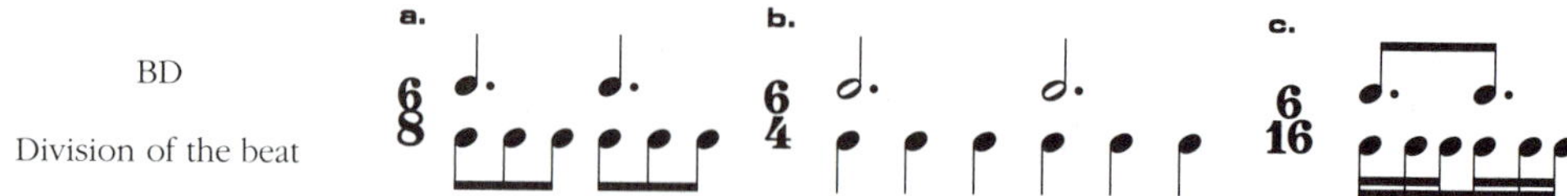


| Note value representing BD: | 𝅘𝅥𝅮. | ♩. | 𝅗𝅥. |
|---|---|---|---|
| 2 beats per measure | 6/16 | 6/8 | 6/4 |
| 3 beats per measure | 9/16 | 9/8 | 9/4 |
| 4 beats per measure | 12/16 | 12/8 | 12/4 |

**TABLE 1-2.** Time signatures for basic durations in compound meter

## Secondary Accents

**beat groups**
**secondary accents**

In meters of more than three beats per measure, the beats are perceived to group into *beat groups* of two or three beats. The first pulse of the first beat group has the primary accent of the measure. The first pulse of succeeding beat groups have *secondary accents,* which, while not as strong as primary accents, are stronger than other beats in the measure. Secondary accents serve to mark divisions within the measure. In examples 1-7a and 1-7b the dashed vertical line marks the place where a secondary accent occurs (on the third beat in $\frac{4}{4}$ and compound meter). In slow tempos, meters with six pulses may exhibit a secondary accent resulting from two beat groups, a three plus three pattern, as in example 1-8.

**EXAMPLE 1-7.** Location of secondary accents

a. In simple meter    b. In compound meter

**EXAMPLE 1-8.** Secondary accents in sextuple meter

Meters with five pulses divide into two beat groups, either three plus two or two plus three. Similarly, meters with seven pulses divide into three beat groups with combinations of twos and three. Wherever possible, the divisions are reflected in the beaming, as shown in example 1-9.

**EXAMPLE 1-9.** Secondary accents in quintuple and septuple meters

## Subdivisions of the Basic Duration

**subdivisions**

When a division is further divided, *subdivisions* of the basic division result. In simple meters there are four subdivisions of the basic duration, and in compound meters, six subdivisions of the basic duration. This is illustrated in $\frac{2}{4}$ and $\frac{6}{8}$ in example 1-10.

**EXAMPLE 1-10.** Divisions and subdivisions

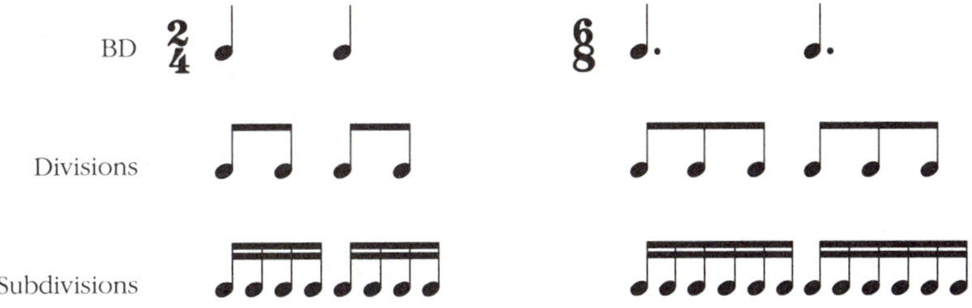


## Grouping in Rhythmic Notation

Music notation is a set of conventions revealed in the practices of the best music publishers today. Musicians learn these conventions through long experience reading music. It is impossible to create rules that fully explain every instance of good rhythmic notation. Notation is designed clearly to reflect beat groups and beats that conform to the metric structure through the application of beams, ties, and rests.

The metric structure is reflected in the beaming of eighth notes and shorter values. Note values that are equivalent to a beat or beat group are beamed together. Example 1-11 shows beamings that reflect beats or beat groups. Some instances of incorrect notation are also shown.

**EXAMPLE 1-11.** Note values beamed in beats or beat groups

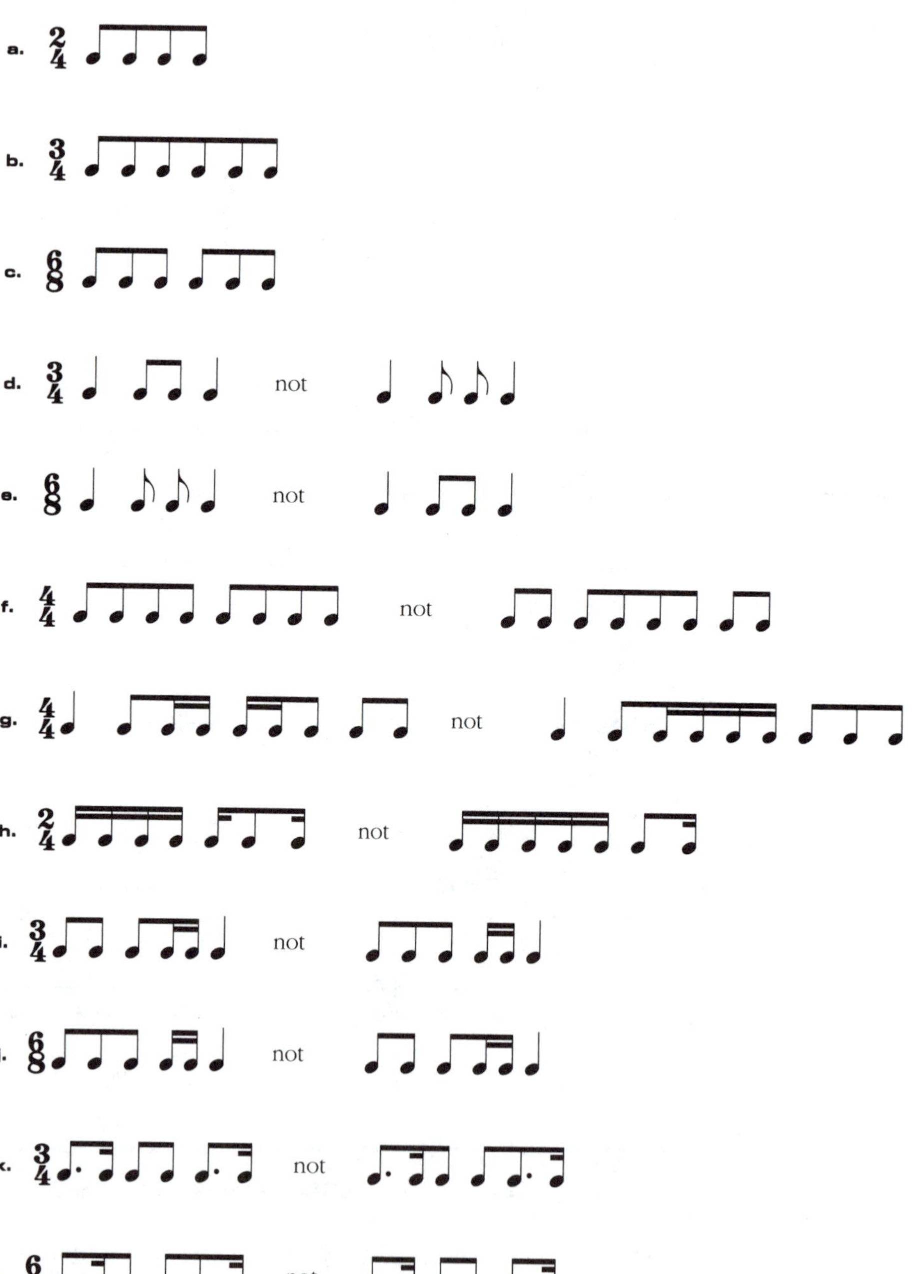

In deciding when to use ties, economy as well as clarity becomes a consideration. The most economical notation is the one that uses the least number of notes and rests. When a complex relationship occurs between durations and metric structure, clarity through the use of ties is preferred and economy sacrificed. Example 1-12 illustrates such cases.

**EXAMPLE 1-12.** The use of ties for clarity

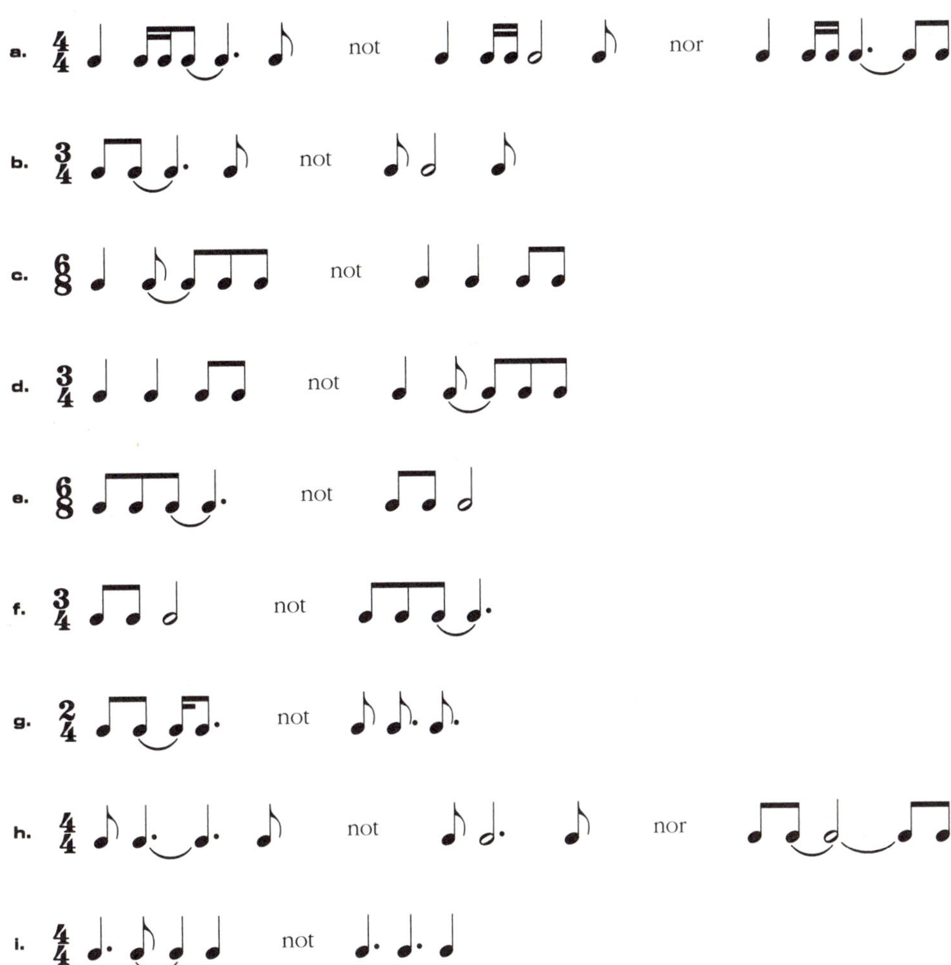


If a simple relationship exists between durations and the metric structure, clarity is not a problem. Use the most economical notation and avoid ties. Example 1-13 illustrates cases typical of this category.

**EXAMPLE 1-13.** Situations where ties are not needed

a.

b.

c. or

d. or

e. or

f.

g.

h.

i.

j.

k.

l.

Clarity takes precedence over economy in the notation of rests as well. Economy is applied in showing beats and beat groups. In compound time dotted rests are used to show basic durations or beat groups, but in simple meters metric structure is made clearer by avoiding dotted rests. Instances of this are shown in example 1-14. Note in examples 1-14e through 1-14i that rests of two beats within a triple beat group are not grouped within a single, larger rest. Similarly, rests of two divisions within a single beat of compound meter are not grouped in a single, longer rest.

**EXAMPLE 1·14.** The use of rests for clarity

a.

b.

c.

d.

e.

f.

g.

h.

i.

j.

## PITCH NOTATION

### Pitch Designation

**staff**

The system for designating pitches employs notes written on or between the lines of a *staff,* which consists of five horizontal lines.

**EXAMPLE 1-15.** The staff

## Note Names

**octave**

The first seven letters of the alphabet are used to designate pitches. If you begin on C and play only the ascending white keys of the keyboard, you will recognize the familiar sound of the seven tones of a major scale. If you stop on eighth tone, you will again be on C, the eighth tone being an *octave* higher than you started. The phenomenon of the octave is one of the most fundamental in music. The relationship between the low C and the high C is unique: the two tones sound almost "identical," yet the distance between them is quite large.

## Clefs

**clef**

The location of specific pitches on the staff is determined by means of a *clef*. Clefs are stylized letters and are often designated by their letter names: the treble clef is a G clef; the soprano, mezzo soprano, alto, and tenor clefs are C clefs; and the bass clef is an F clef. The baritone clef may be written either as a C clef or an F clef. Different clefs are useful in accommodating the ranges of the various voices. In example 1-16 middle C ($c^1$) is given for each clef.

**great staff**

**EXAMPLE 1-16.** $c^1$ on the different clefs

The most frequently used clefs are the treble and the bass, the former for high voices and the latter for low ones. These two clefs are combined with a brace to form the *great staff*. This is useful for notating music in a variety of ranges from high to low.

**EXAMPLE 1-17.** The great staff

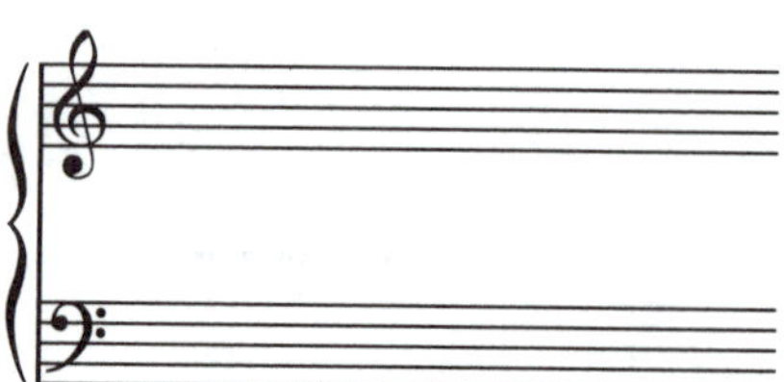

## Ledger Lines

**ledger lines**

*Ledger lines* are short horizontal lines that extend the range above and below the staff to accommodate individual notes that exceed the range of the staff itself. In example 1-16, for example, $c^1$ is notated with one ledger line on both the treble clef and the bass clef.

## Octave Signs

**octave sign**

If the range of a passage moves too far above the treble or below the bass staff, *octave signs* may be used. As shown in example 1-18, $8^{va}$ means *ottava* in Italian (an octave in English), and $15^{ma}$ means *quindicima* in Italian (a fifteenth in English).

**EXAMPLE 1-18.** The use of octave signs

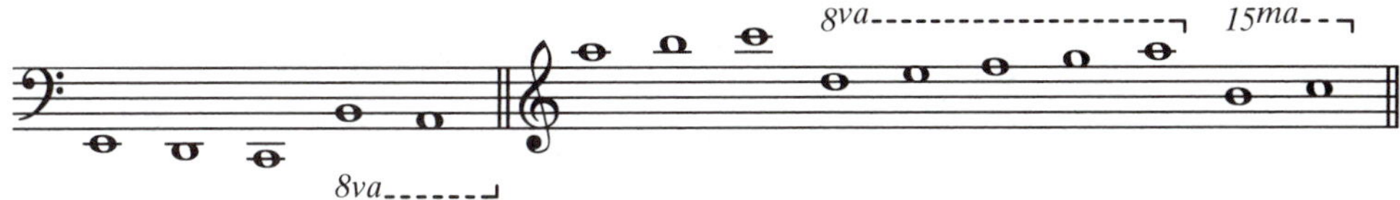


## Accidentals

**half step**

**whole step**

**accidentals**

The distance from any pitch to the next higher or lower pitch is known as a *half step,* or *semitone.* Using the keyboard in example 1-19a as a reference, one can see that C is a half-step higher than B, and F is a half-step higher than E. Two half steps make the distance of a *whole step,* or *whole tone.* Therefore, D is a whole step higher than C and a whole step lower than E.

Symbols written before notes, called *accidentals,* are used to represent all the various pitches on the staff.

♯ sharp: raises the note a half step

♭ flat: lowers the note a half step

× double-sharp: raises the note a whole step

♭♭ double-flat: lowers the note a whole step

♮ natural: cancels previous sharp or flat

Example 1-19b illustrates these.

**EXAMPLE 1-19.** Whole steps, half steps, and accidentals

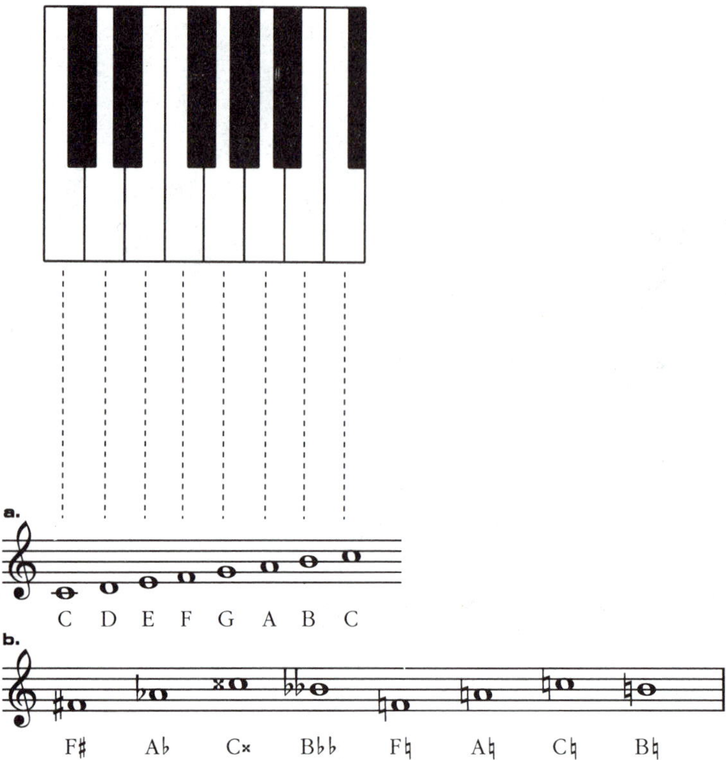


An accidental applies only in the octave given, for the duration of the measure or for the duration of a note tied over into the next measure.

## Stem Direction

When notes with stems occur on or above the middle line of the staff, the stem is written downwards. In such instances, the stem comes down from the left side of the note head. Stems on notes that occur below the middle line of the staff are written upwards; these stems go up from the right side of the note head.

Stems are usually one octave in length. For notes lying more than an octave from the middle line, the stem extends to the middle line, as shown in example 1-20.

**EXAMPLE 1-20.** Length and direction of note stems

## Special Problems in Pitch Notation

When two or more notes are beamed together or use the same stem, the stem direction is determined by the note that is furthest from the middle line of the staff (example 1-21a). If the highest and lowest notes are equidistant from the middle line, the stems go down (example 1-21b). If notes on the same stem are a second apart, the lowest note is on the left side of the stem (example 1-21c).

**EXAMPLE 1-21.** **Direction of note stems and placement of note head and accidentals**

## Pitch Classes

In Western music the octave is divided into twelve parts, each a distinct pitch. Each of these pitches occurs in all octaves, from the highest to the lowest range of the audible spectrum. Each pitch, together with all of its recurrences in other octaves,

**pitch class**

forms a *pitch class.* Thus, all the F-sharps form the pitch class class F-sharp; all the Ds form the pitch class D, and so forth. Each pitch may be spelled in different ways. Notes in the pitch class C-sharp, for example, may be written as D-flat in certain

**enharmonic equivalents**

instances. C-sharp and D-flat are said to be *enharmonic equivalents.* The twelve pitch classes are, in ascending order:

| | | |
|---|---|---|
| C | B♯ | D♭♭ |
| C♯ | B× | D♭ |
| D | C× | E♭♭ |
| E♭ | D♯ | F♭♭ |
| E | D× | F♭ |
| F | E♯ | G♭♭ |
| F♯ | E× | G♭ |
| G | F× | A♭♭ |
| A♭ | G♯ | |
| A | G× | B♭♭ |
| B♭ | A♯ | C♭♭ |
| B | A× | C♭ |

## Octave Designations

**octave designations**

Several systems have been devised to specify the octave in which a particular tone lies. Two systems are shown in example 1-22. The names for the octaves (contra, subcontra, etc.) and the letter forms (c, $c^1$, B, $b^3$, etc.) used to identify a note are shown. In conversation, the octave designation is given first, followed by the letter name of the note, for example, "two-line c" ($c^2$). Hereafter in this text, the first method will be used.

**EXAMPLE 1-22.** Octave designations

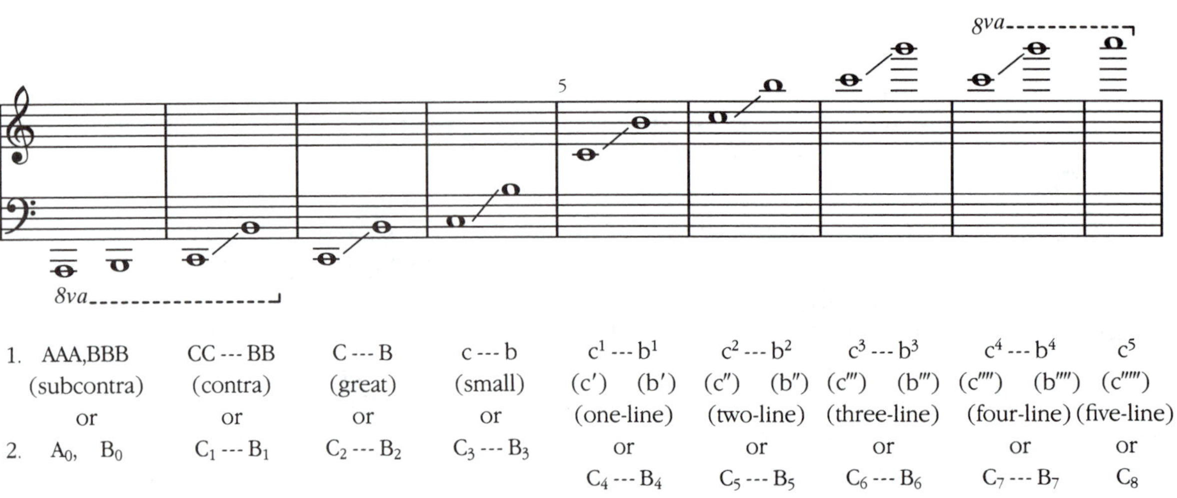


# DYNAMICS

**dynamics**

Dynamics are the degrees of volume or loudness in music. Table 1-3 shows the most commonly used dynamic markings. By extending this system, more extreme possibilities may be derived.

| | Dynamic levels in order of increasing loudness |
|---|---|
| *ppp* | triple piano |
| *pp* | pianissimo (double piano) |
| *p* | piano |
| *mp* | mezzo-piano |
| *mf* | mezzo-forte |
| *f* | forte |
| *ff* | fortissimo (double forte) |
| *fff* | triple forte |

| | Dynamic changes |
|---|---|
| *cresc.* | crescendo (gradually louder) |
| < | crescendo |
| *dim.* | diminuendo (gradually softer) |
| > | diminuendo |
| *decresc.* | decrescendo (gradually softer) |
| *fp* | forte-piano (loud, then immediately soft) |

**TABLE 1-3.** Dynamic levels and changes

## THE DIATONIC SYSTEM

**diatonic system**

Within a particular culture, specific patterns of tones are used in making music. One pattern became established in and around ancient Greece and spread to all parts of the Western world. This pattern is known as the *diatonic system.* It consists of a continuous succession of whole steps (1) and half steps (1/2) in this order: 1/2 1 1 1/2 1 1 1 1/2 1 1 1/2 1 1 1. The pattern recurs every eight notes (an octave higher or lower). Theoretically, the diatonic system may be extended infinitely upward or downward.

## INTERVALS

**interval**

The distance between two pitches is called an *interval.* Intervals are identified in two stages. First, a general numerical description is given, based on the number of notes between and including the two pitches as shown in example 1-23a. In counting the number of steps between two notes, we begin with one, not zero. In example 1-23b (1) the interval is a third. The steps are correctly counted in example 1-23b (2), incorrectly in example 1-23b (3).

**EXAMPLE 1-23.** Identifying intervals numerically

**a.** Interval designations

prime second third fourth 5 fifth sixth seventh octave

**b.** Counting intervals

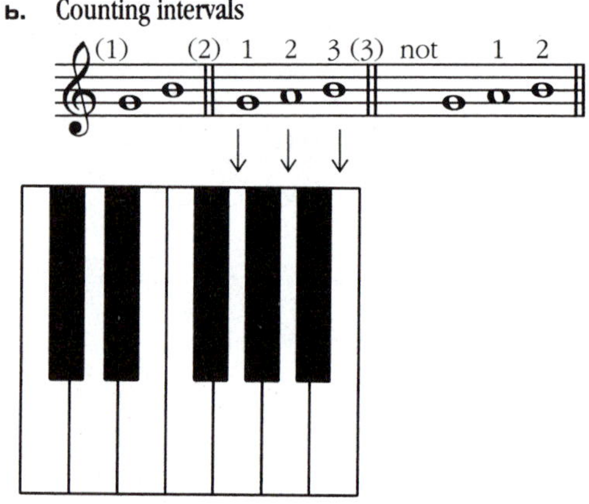


The various intervals have characteristic appearances on the staff. Look at example 1-26a. Note that for the unison (prime), third, fifth, and seventh, the component notes are either both on a line or both on a space, while for the second, fourth, sixth, and octave, one note is on a line and the other is on a space.

Once the numerical size of the interval is known, a more specific designation can be made, depending on the number of whole or half steps between the notes. For this purpose, all intervals are assigned to one of two groups. Group A includes intervals that are capable of being "major" or "minor": seconds, thirds, sixths, and sevenths. Group B includes intervals capable of being "perfect": unisons (or primes), fourths, fifths, and octaves. The intervals in group A may be "major," "minor," "diminished," or "augmented," depending on the number of whole steps they contain.

| | Diminished | Minor | Major | Augmented |
|---|---|---|---|---|
| 2nds | 0 | 1/2 | 1 | 1 1/2 |
| 3rds | 1 | 1 1/2 | 2 | 2 1/2 |
| 6ths | 3 1/2 | 4 | 4 1/2 | 5 |
| 7ths | 4 1/2 | 5 | 5 1/2 | 6 |

**TABLE 1-4.** Steps contained in group A intervals

If a group A interval is a half step smaller than major, it is called *minor;* if it is a half step smaller than minor, it is called *diminished;* if it is a half step larger than major, it is called *augmented.* It is rare to encounter an interval that exceeds these designations, but there are such terms as *doubly diminished* and *doubly augmented* for these cases.

A similar chart can be drawn for the group B intervals (table 1-5). These may be "perfect," "diminished," or "augmented," depending on the number of whole steps they contain. Intervals in this group that are a half step smaller than perfect are called diminished; those a half step larger than perfect are called augmented. (The diminished prime does not logically exist.)

| | Diminished | Perfect | Augmented |
|---|---|---|---|
| primes | --- | 0 | 1/2 |
| 4ths | 2 | 2 1/2 | 3 |
| 5ths | 3 | 3 1/2 | 4 |
| octaves | 5 1/2 | 6 | 6 1/2 |

**TABLE 1-5.** Whole steps contained in group B intervals

The interval shown in example 1-24a (1) is a minor third (m3); the one-and-one-half steps between the tones are shown with the keyboard diagram. Example 1-24a (2) illustrates the two whole steps between the tones of a major third (M3). The interval shown in example 1-24b (1) is a perfect fourth (P4) with two-and-one-half steps between the tones shown on the keyboard. Also included is a perfect fifth (P5) with three-and-one-half steps between the tones shown in example 1-24b (2).

**EXAMPLE 1-24.** Notated intervals and their keyboard locations

a. A minor third (m3) and a major third (M3)

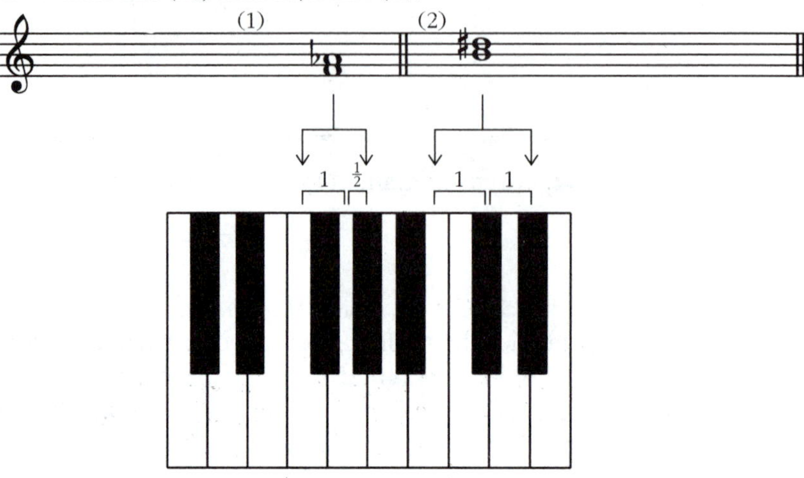


b. A perfect fourth (P4) and a perfect fifth (P5)

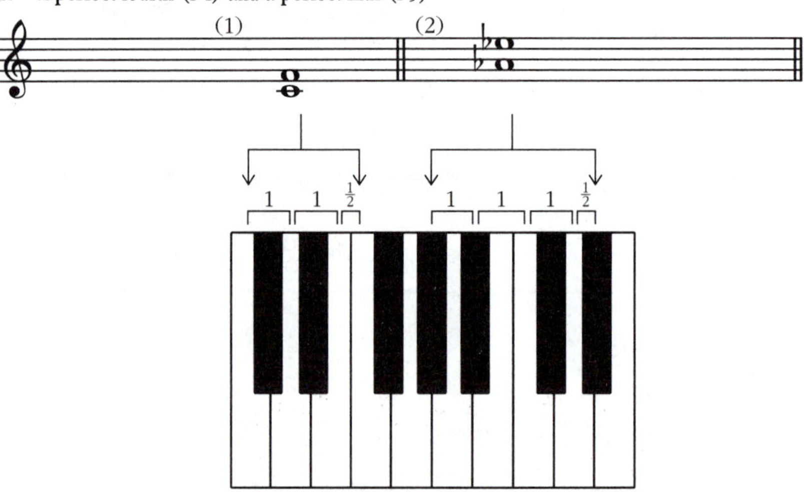


## Inversion of Intervals

Certain intervals have a complementary relationship. For instance, if we start on C and go up a P4, we arrive at F. If from that F we go up a P5, we arrive at the C an octave higher than our starting point. The two intervals, P5 and P4, add up to an octave. Another way of viewing this is through the process of *inversion*. If we move (transpose) the lower tone of an interval up an octave, or the upper tone down an octave, we arrive at a similarly complementary interval. Thus, fourths invert to be-

**inversion**

come fifths, thirds invert to sixths, and sevenths invert to seconds. Notice that a major interval becomes minor when inverted, while a minor interval becomes a major when inverted; likewise, augmented intervals become diminished, diminished intervals become augmented, and perfect intervals remain perfect.

**EXAMPLE 1-25.** Inversion of intervals

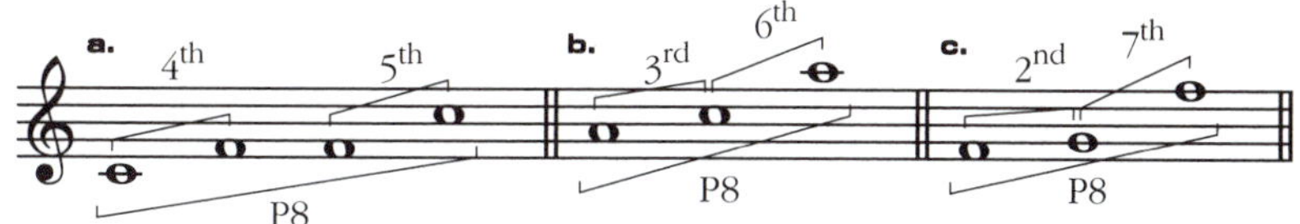


**EXAMPLE 1-26.** Quality of inverted intervals

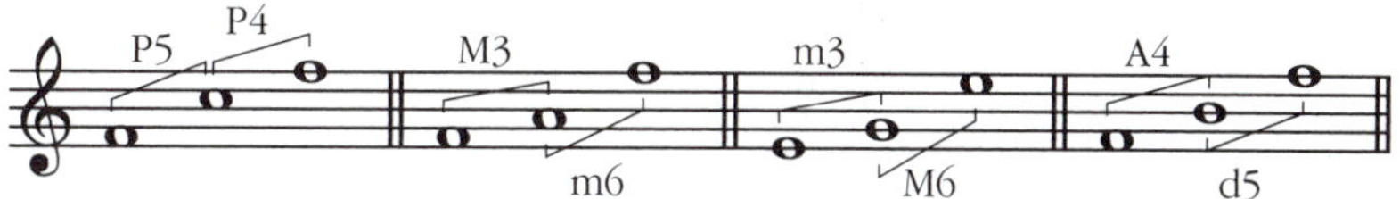


## Compound Intervals

**simple interval**
**compound interval**

Intervals from P1 up to P8 are called *simple intervals.* Those larger than an octave are called *compound intervals.* The numbering system continues after the octave up to the thirteenth: an octave plus a second equals a ninth; octave plus third equals a tenth; octave plus fourth equals an eleventh; octave plus fifth equals a twelfth; and octave plus sixth equals a thirteenth. This is usually as far as compound intervals are reckoned, except occasionally for the double octave (the fifteenth, abbreviated 15$^{ma}$, as mentioned earlier). Compound intervals are often referred to as though they were simple intervals, that is, as though the tones were actually within an octave. Thus a tenth may be called a third if the actual distance between the notes is not pertinent to the discussion.

Compound intervals are named in the same way as their simple interval counterparts, that is, ninths are major or minor (like seconds); elevenths are perfect (like fourths), and so on.

**EXAMPLE 1-27.** Examples of compound intervals

Table 1-6 summarizes the information about the most common intervals from the unison to the octave.

| Name of Interval | Whole steps | Half steps | Abbreviation | Inversion |
|---|---|---|---|---|
| unison or prime | 0 | 0 | P1 | P8 |
| minor second | 1/2 | 1 | m2 | M7 |
| major second | 1 | 2 | M2 | m7 |
| minor third | 1 1/2 | 3 | m3 | M6 |
| major third | 2 | 4 | M3 | m6 |
| perfect fourth | 2 1/2 | 5 | P4 | P5 |
| augmented fourth | 3 | 6 | A4 | d5 |
| diminished fifth | 3 | 6 | d5 | A4 |
| perfect fifth | 3 1/2 | 7 | P5 | P4 |
| minor sixth | 4 | 8 | m6 | M3 |
| major sixth | 4 1/2 | 9 | M6 | m3 |
| minor seventh | 5 | 10 | m7 | M2 |
| major seventh | 5 1/2 | 11 | M7 | m2 |
| perfect octave | 6 | 12 | P8 | P1 |

**TABLE 1-6.** Summary of common intervals

# SCALES

## Major Scales

**major scale**

One of the most important concepts in music theory is the *major scale,* which consists of eight consecutive notes beginning at some point in the diatonic system. It is usually shown in ascending order, the first and last notes an octave apart.

## Major Scale Degrees

**scale degrees**

Each of the eight tones is called a *scale degree* and is given a name depending on where it lies within the scale. The most important scale degree is the *tonic,* or key-note, the scale degree on which the scale begins and ends.

| Scale degree | Name |
|---|---|
| 1 | tonic |
| 2 | supertonic |
| 3 | mediant |
| 4 | subdominant |
| 5 | dominant |
| 6 | submediant |
| 7 | leading tone |
| 8 | tonic |

TABLE 1-7. Major scale degree names

## Major Scale Pattern

The pattern of the major scale may be described as a specific ordering of whole and half steps, as shown in example 1-28.

EXAMPLE 1-28. Major scale pattern

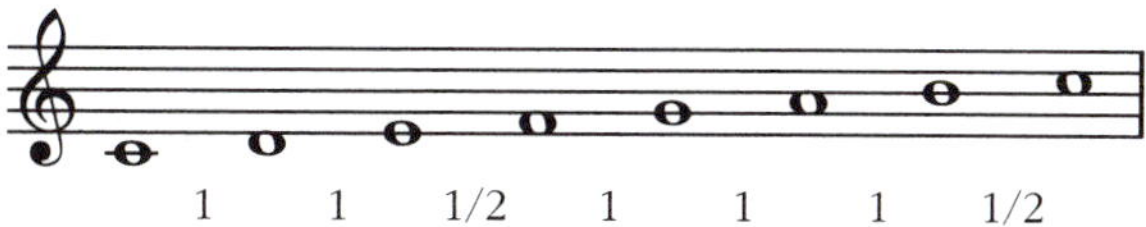


Scales are named according to their tonic: The major scale beginning on C is called the C-major scale, B major begins on B, and so on. We say that we are "in the key of C major," C being the key-note. When learning to write a scale it is usually best to write the scale degrees first, then add the necessary sharps and flats. This will avoid the omission of a scale degree. For instance, example 1-29 shows the steps to be followed in writing the F-sharp major scale.

**EXAMPLE 1-29.** Steps in writing the F-sharp major scale

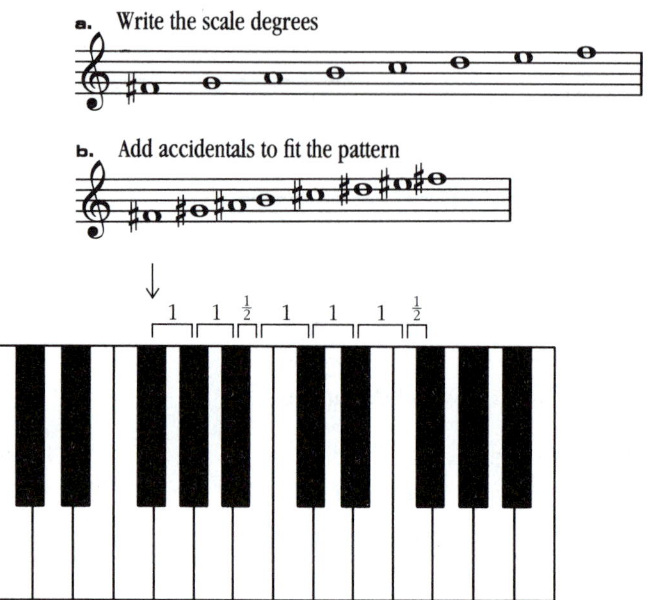


## Major Key Signatures

**key signature**

At the beginning of many compositions there is an indication to the player about the notes to be used. This is given in the form of a *key signature* showing the sharps and flats required for the key of the piece. The sharps and flats are always written in the same order (ex. 1-30), so the performer can tell at a glance which notes are required. Any note not marked with a sharp or flat is understood to be natural.

**EXAMPLE 1-30.** Major key signatures

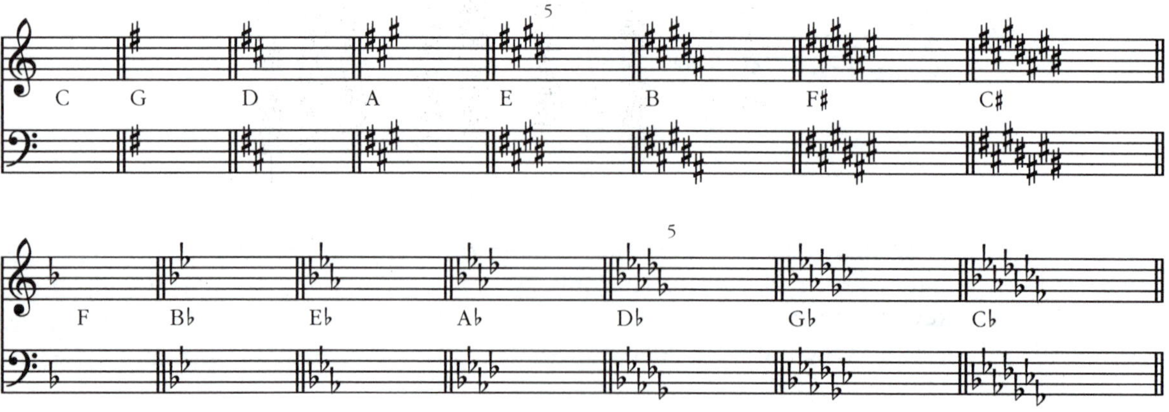

## Minor Scales

**minor scale**

**natural minor scale**

Along with the major scale, the *minor scale* is of great importance in Western music. The minor scale, as we shall see, has some variants, but its basic pattern is shown in example 1-31. This pattern is known as the *natural minor scale.*

**EXAMPLE 1-31.** Natural minor scale

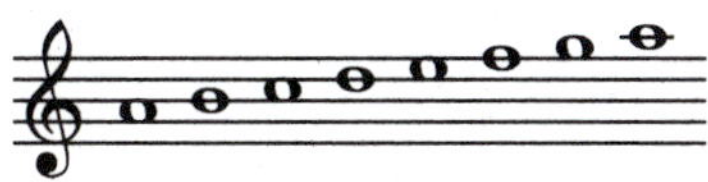

## Relative and Parallel Minor Scales

**relative minor/major scale**

Scales and keys that use the same pitches but have different tonics are called *relative.* The two scales seen in example 1-32 share the same tones. The scale beginning on A is called the A-minor scale. It is said to be the "relative minor" of C major. Conversely, C major is the "relative major" of A minor. The relative minor is found by using the sixth step of the major scale as a tonic.

**EXAMPLE 1-32.** Relative major and minor scale

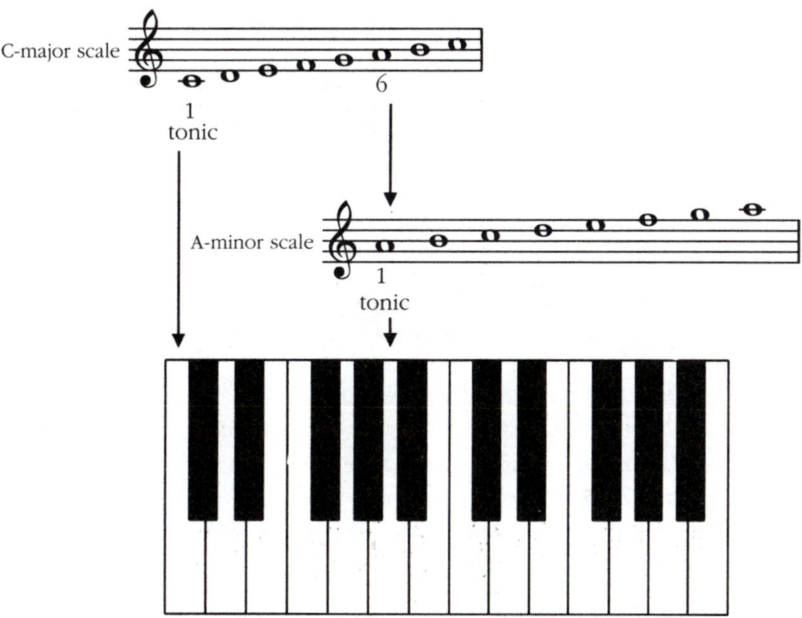

Every major scale has a relative minor scale that may be determined in the same manner. As seen in example 1-33, the relative minor of B-flat major is G minor (G being the sixth degree of the B-flat major scale), and the relative minor of G major is E minor.

**EXAMPLE 1-33.** Examples of relative major and minor scales

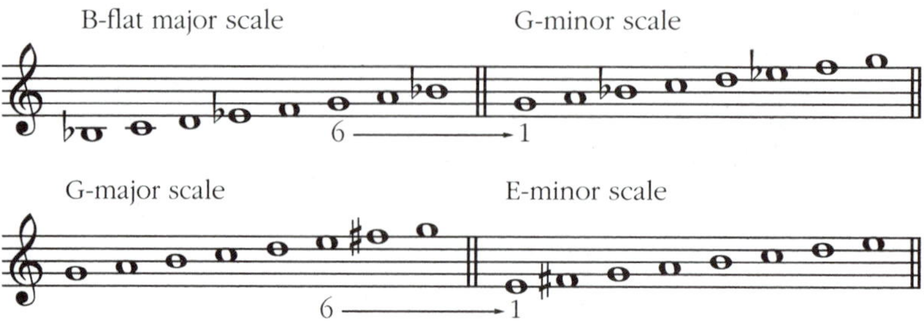


If you begin with the minor scale and wish to determine the relative major, it lies on the third degree, a minor third above the tonic. Thus, the relative major of B-flat minor is D-flat major.

**parallel minor/major scale**

Scales and keys that have the same tonic but use different pitches are called *parallel*. The relationship between B-flat major and B-flat minor is called parallel. B-flat major is the parallel major of B-flat minor. Example 1-34 compares the relative and parallel relationships.

**EXAMPLE 1-34.** Relative and parallel scales

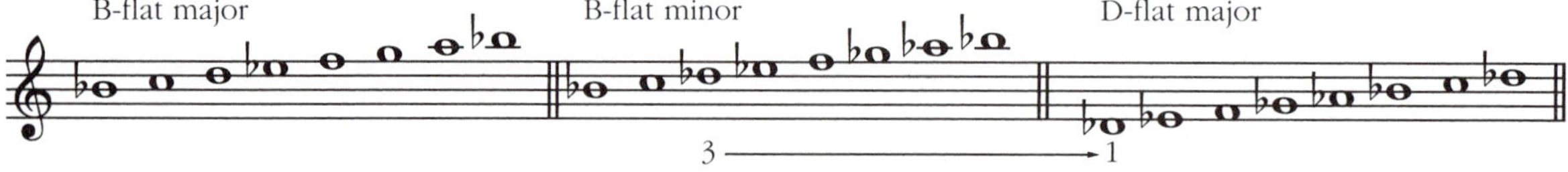


## Harmonic and Melodic Minor Scales

**harmonic minor scale**

**melodic minor scale**

Thus far we have considered only the natural minor scale, which has exactly the same tones as the relative major. There are also two variants of the minor scale: the *harmonic minor scale* (same as the natural minor, with the seventh degree raised a half step) and the *melodic minor scale* (same as the natural minor, except that the sixth and seventh degrees are raised a half step when the scale is ascending; when the scale descends, the unaltered natural minor is shown). Example 1-35 illustrates how the B-flat minor scale and its variants should be written. Note the change in position of the whole and half steps in these variants.

**EXAMPLE 1-35.** The three forms of the B-flat minor scale

a. Natural minor scale

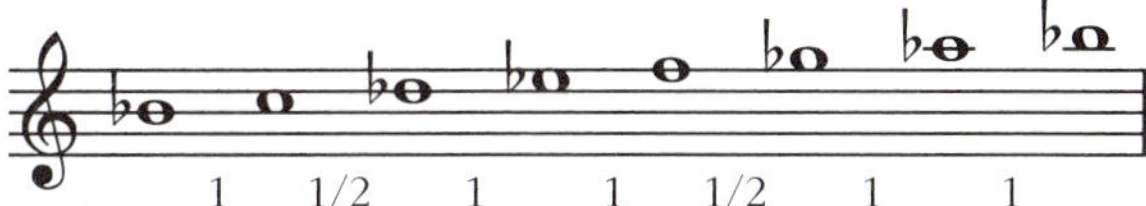


b. Harmonic minor scale (seventh degree raised)

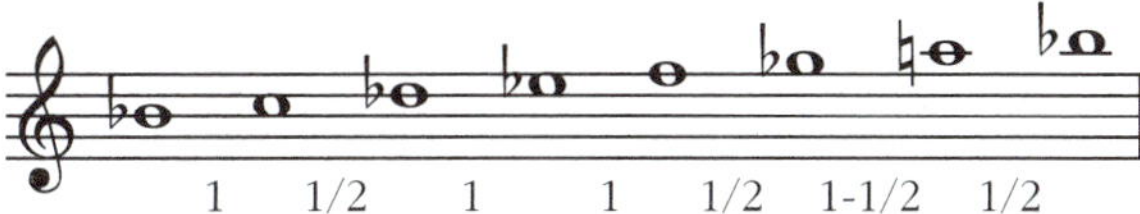


c. Melodic minor (sixth and seventh degrees raised while ascending)

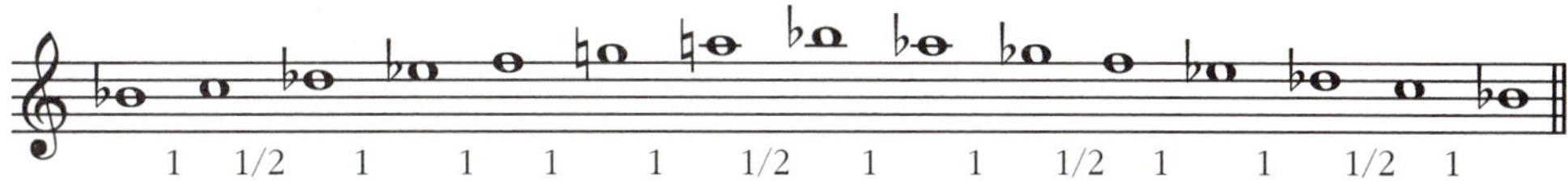


A scale should be understood as a systematic list of pitches, not ascending and descending melodic motion. When deciding to raise or lower the sixth or seventh scale degree in a musical composition, the composer takes into consideration various factors to be studied later.

## Minor Scale Degrees

**subtonic**

The names of the scale degrees are the same in minor as they are in major, except for the variant forms of the seventh scale degree. When 7 is a half step below 8 it is called the leading tone, and when it is a whole step below 8 it is called *subtonic* (see table 1-8).

## Minor Key Signatures

Key signatures for major and minor keys, showing the sharps and flats in their normal order, are illustrated in example 1-36. Notice that for each key signature there is a major and a minor key indicated. Major keys are indicated by a capital letter, as in C major (C). Minor keys are indicated by lower case letters, as in c minor (c).

Alterations in the basic pattern, such as the raising of the sixth and seventh degrees in minor, are not shown in the signature. These alterations must be indicated as accidentals, notes that require sharps or flats not included in the key signature. Therefore, one cannot know from the signature alone which key is intended; only a perusal of the actual notes of the piece can give that information. This will be discussed later. But if you are not already familiar with all of the key signatures in example 1-36, it is wise to memorize them as soon as possible.

| Scale degree | Name |
|---|---|
| 1 | tonic |
| 2 | supertonic |
| 3 | mediant |
| 4 | subdominant |
| 5 | dominant |
| 6 | submediant |
| 7 | subtonic (whole step below 8) |
| | leading tone (half step below 8) |
| 8 | tonic |

**TABLE 1-8.** Minor scale degree names

**EXAMPLE 1-36.** Key signatures

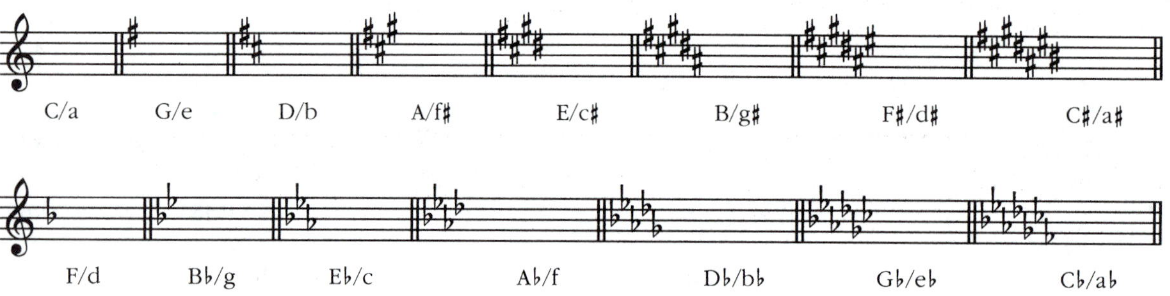


**circle of fifths**

The major and minor keys can be arranged in order of increasing sharps and flats, shown in the form known as the *circle of fifths,* seen in figure 1-1. Beginning with C major at the top of the circle, keys with increasing numbers of sharps are reached by clockwise motion, while keys with increasing numbers of flats are reached by moving counterclockwise. Minor keys with corresponding signatures are shown inside the circle. Notice that three major keys and three minor keys appear with enharmonic equivalents at the bottom of the circle.

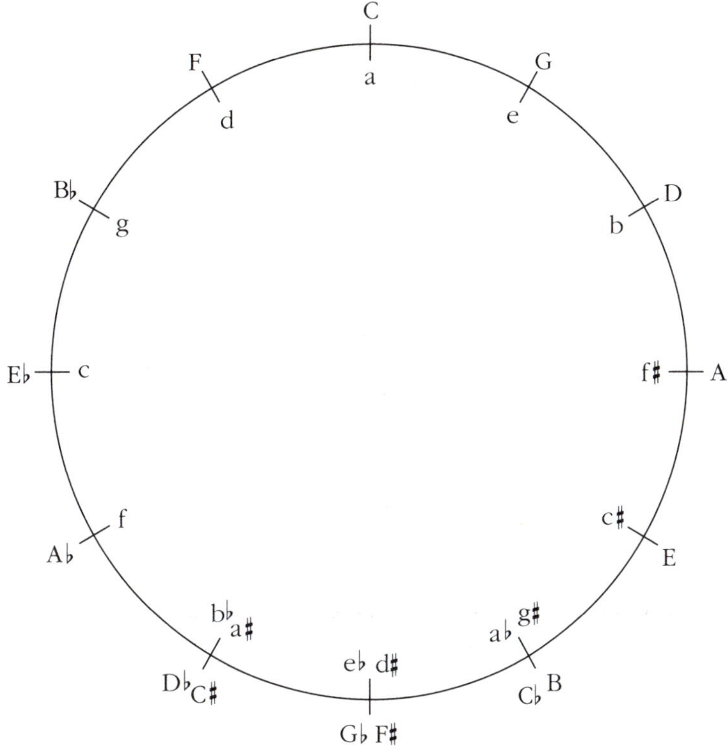


**FIGURE 1-1.** Circle of fifths

## SUMMARY

Music notation employs an array of symbols that indicate rhythmic value by shape and indicate pitch by location on a staff.

The durations of individual tones are heard within a framework of regular beats (equally timed pulses). The rate at which the beats occur is called tempo. The beats tend to group into regular patterns called meter. In a musical work, tones are perceived as multiples, fractional divisions, or subdivisions of the beat.

Letter names are used to identify pitches. The pitch resources used in traditional Western music are embodied in the diatonic system, in which the smallest interval (distance between two pitches) is the half step. Larger intervals may be measured by the number of steps or half steps spanned by the tones. Typically, the pitch resources for a piece can be summarized in a scale, which is a series of ascending pitches with specific intervals between the various scale degrees. The tone on which the scale begins is called the tonic. It is heard as the primary pitch, to which all the other tones are subordinate. The most commonly used of these patterns are the major scale and the minor scale.

CHAPTER TWO

# Melody and Tonality

**Terms Introduced in This Chapter**

attack

release

duration

dynamic accent

agogic accent

metric accent

agogic pattern

arsis

thesis

arsis group

syncopation

subordinate agogic pattern

principal agogic pattern

phrase

cadence

contour

range

tessitura

conjunct and disjunct motion

prominence

change of direction

recurrence

location

emergent tone

step progression

repetition

tonic, tonal center

tonal

atonal

tonality

interval root

scale

pitch complement

diatonic modes

modulation

change of mode

he understanding of melody must include a broad spectrum of concepts that are associated with rhythm and pitch, which leads to further concepts involving tension, tonality, and scales.

## RHYTHM

The organization of melodic rhythm centers on the creation of accents, their relationships, and the tension associated with them.

### Durations

**attack**

**release**

**duration**

Each musical tone has a point of beginning or *attack;* an ending point or *release;* and an elapsed time between the beginning and ending, known as its *duration.* A similar statement may be made for rests in that each has a beginning, an ending, and a particular length.

### Accents

A musical accent is a point of emphasis, an event distinguished from its surroundings by a perceived difference in volume, length, location, or other aspect. It is essential to distinguish between three types of accents, although all three may occur simultaneously.

**dynamic accent**

The *dynamic accent* is produced by an increase in dynamic intensity on the accented tone. It is indicated by various accent marks and by dynamic indications.

**agogic accent**

The *agogic accent* is the natural emphasis attributed to a tone that is longer than the tone(s) preceding it. The agogic accent arises because our minds give greater importance to longer tones.

**metric accent**

The *metric accent* is produced by a pattern of expectations that arises when regularity appears or is suggested by agogic accents, dynamic accents, or other prominent changes in the music. There are traditional assumptions, familiar to all performers, regarding the relative strength of metric points within each meter.

#### Agogic Accents

**agogic pattern**

**arsis**

**thesis**

An agogic accent results from an *agogic pattern* of three components: *arsis, thesis,* and the attack of the thesis, which is the agogic accent itself. The arsis ("lifting") is the unaccented portion of the agogic pattern and consists of the relatively shorter tone or tones that precede the longer tone to come, the thesis. The thesis ("lowering") is the accented portion and is longer than any of the tones in the arsis. The attack of the thesis is the point of accent known as the agogic accent and for analytical purposes will be marked with an upward-pointing triangle as shown in example 2-1. (For a complete list of analytical symbols introduced in this chapter see "Guide to Analytical Symbols," p. 399.)

In example 2-2a, the rhythm resembles that of example 2-2b, except that rests are used for the latter part of the longer note values. Rests extend the effect of the preceding note, so there is little difference between examples 2-2a and b, as far as the agogic patterns are concerned.

**arsis group**

The arsis may consist of a group of durations, all shorter than the thesis to follow. The *arsis group* in example 2-2c illustrates this. Example 2-2d shows the same effect with rests extending the final note. Agogic accents often follow lengthy arsis groups. In example 2-3, the agogic accents are marked with triangles above the thesis tones, while each agogic pattern is indicated by a bracket.

**EXAMPLE 2-1.** The elements of an agogic pattern

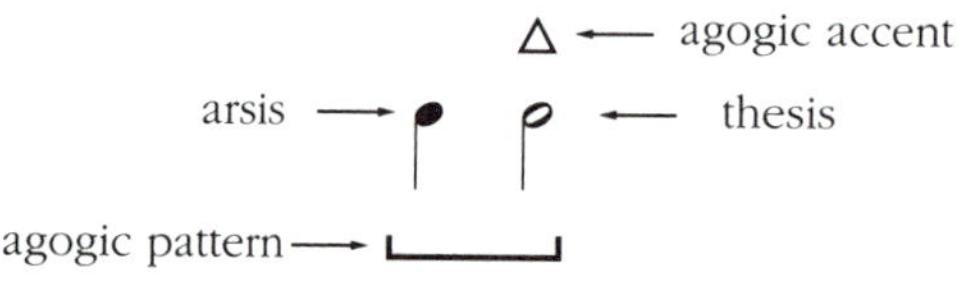


**EXAMPLE 2-2.** Agogic patterns and rests

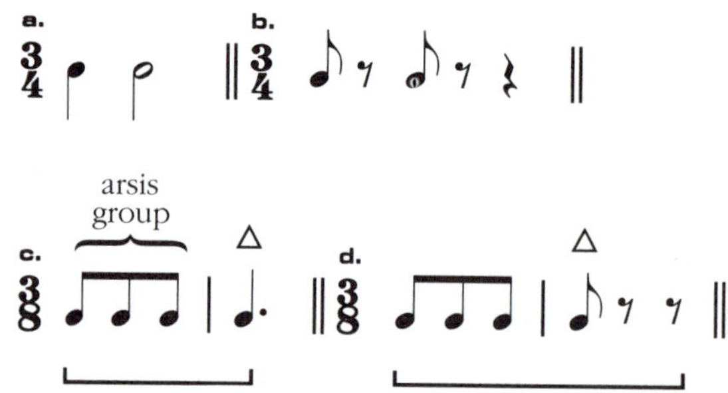


**EXAMPLE 2-3.** Agogic accents and patterns

At times the agogic accents may contradict the metric accents and suggest a meter different from the notated meter signature. In example 2-4a, a meter of $\frac{3}{4}$ is implied by the agogic accents, despite the notated $\frac{4}{4}$ meter. Compare examples 2-4a and b.

**EXAMPLE 2-4.** Implied meter

**syncopation**

The term *syncopation* is used to describe any disturbance of the normal pulse or a rhythm in which the accent is shifted to a normally weak point in the measure. This is illustrated in example 2-4. Syncopations are often less systematic in their suggestion of changes in metric patterns, as seen in examples 2-5a and b. The dynamic accents in measure 3 of example 2-5a will have the effect of disturbing the meter because of the emphasis on what is normally a weak point in the measure.

**EXAMPLE 2-5.** Syncopations

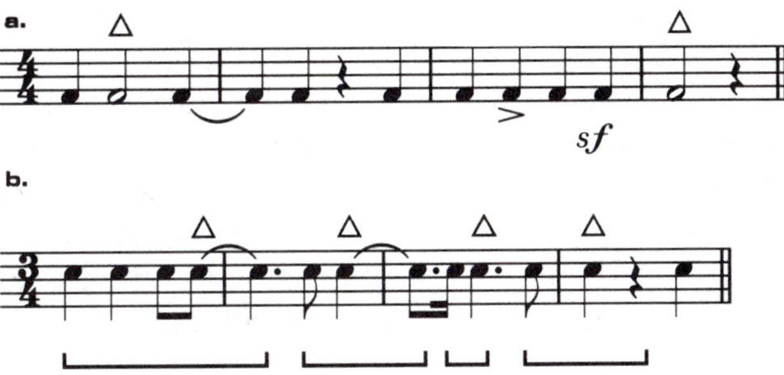


## Subordinate Agogic Patterns

**subordinate agogic pattern**

**principal agogic pattern**

Occasionally an agogic pattern will become part of the arsis of a larger pattern. The imbedded pattern is called a *subordinate agogic pattern,* while the larger pattern is called a *principal agogic pattern.* In example 2-6, each pattern is marked by a bracket, but the agogic accent of the subordinate pattern is marked with a ( △ ). The subordinate pattern, containing no duration longer than the half note, becomes part of the arsis for the principal agogic accent. The quarter note at the beginning is part of the principal agogic pattern, but not part of the subordinate pattern.

**EXAMPLE 2-6.** Elements of subordinate and principal agogic accents

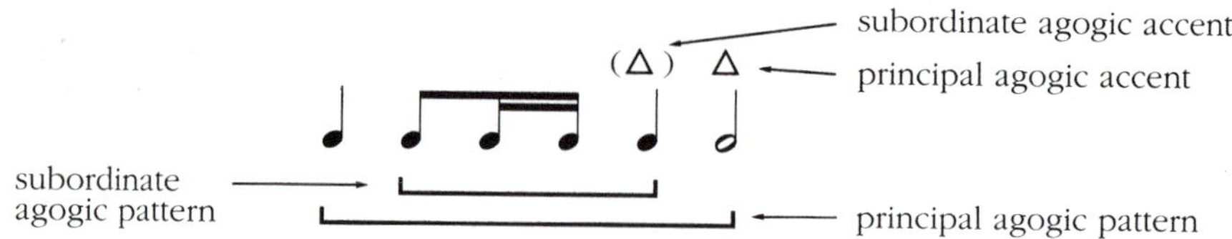


These same concepts and symbols are applied to a more elaborate example in example 2-7. The longest bracket shows the principal agogic pattern, and the arrowhead without parentheses marks the principal agogic accent. Again, subordinate agogic accents are marked with triangles in parentheses, and the upper brackets mark off these patterns.

**EXAMPLE 2-7.** Subordinate and principal agogic patterns and accents

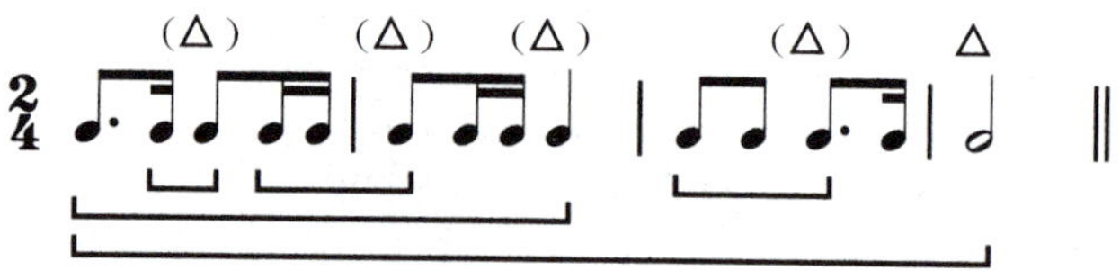


## Metric Accents

Sometimes one finds melodies in which all or most of the notes are of the same duration, so that there may be extended passages where no agogic accents can be found. In analyzing such music, it is often useful to indicate by a ( ∧ ) the metric accent for each measure in which no agogic accent occurs. The metric accent should be marked on the note that begins on the first beat of the measure. If no note begins on the first beat, it is best to mark nothing in the measure. Example 2-8 contains differing note values but no agogic accents.

**EXAMPLE 2-8.** Marking metric accents

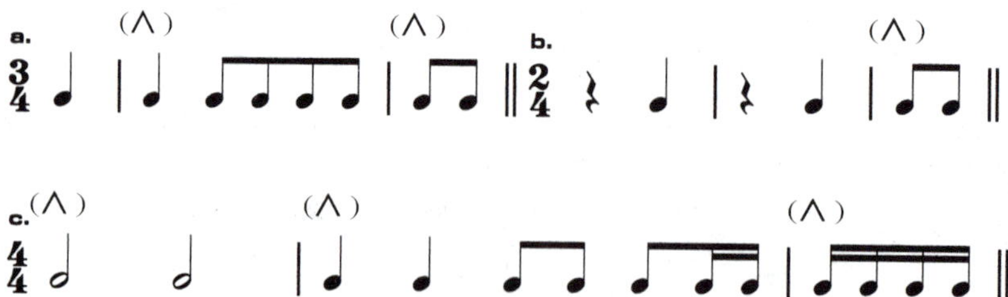

Metric accents are created by our expectations of regularity, while agogic accents are produced by the actual durations of the notes. Agogic accents normally take precedence over metric accents. In most music, of course, there is continual or recurrent agreement between the agogic and metric accents. Often, it is the regularity of the agogic accents that is the primary force in establishing a meter.

## Rhythmic Analysis

Example 2-9 summarizes the method of rhythmic analysis presented thus far. Note these points:

1. Primary agogic accents are found in measures 1, 2, and 4.
2. Measure 1 contains a subordinate agogic accent.
3. Measure 3 has no agogic accent; the metric accent is marked.

**EXAMPLE 2-9.** Handel: Klavier Suite XV, Allemande, HHA iv/6,38

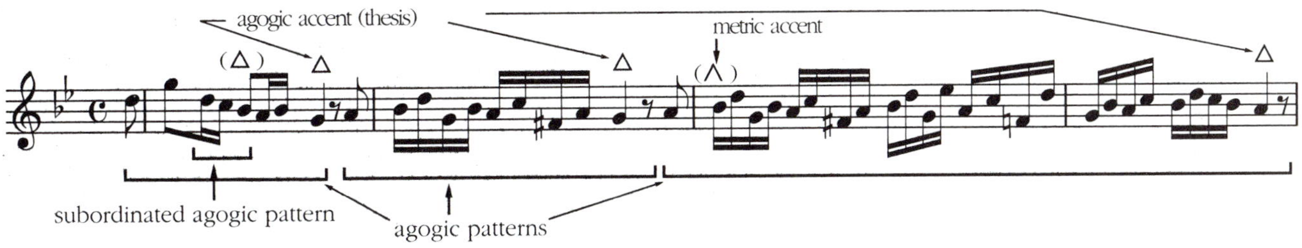


## Tension

Rhythmic patterns, like other aspects of music, give the effect of rising and falling tension. The forces at work are best described in pairs of words expressing opposing elements: stability-instability, continuity-change, sameness-difference. In general, elements of constancy, for example, longer duration, will reduce tension. Elements of change, difference, or instability will increase tension.

The flow of tension is readily seen in an agogic pattern. The arsis generates tension because of its relatively short duration. The more tones in an arsis group, the greater the tension. The tension is at its peak as the thesis begins, at the agogic accent. As illustrated in example 2-10, the moment of the attack of the thesis is the point of greatest tension, after which the tension is released. As the thesis sounds, or continues with rests, the tension reduces.

**EXAMPLE 2-10.** The flow of tension

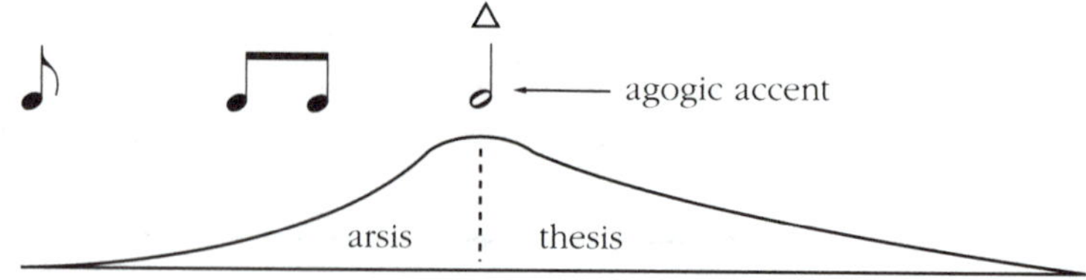


## EMERGENT TONES

As a melody unfolds, the listener's attention is drawn to certain prominent tones. These give a sense of rising and falling tension and become focal points, or peaks of tension. The most prominent tones of a melody may be identified through an understanding of melodic contour and the relationships between melodic pitches and rhythm within the phrase.

### Phrase

**phrase**

A *phrase* is a musical unit with an ending marked by relaxation or a change in treatment. Phrases are typically three to six bars long when the tempo is moderate. If the tempo is rapid, eight-bar phrases may be found; in slow tempos two-bar phrases may occur. The most common length is four measures.

**cadence**

The ending portion of a phrase is called the *cadence*. The cadence is usually perceived as an area of reduced activity or motion, as a pause or breathing point, or as an area preceding change in the kind of activity used. The last pitch in a phrase is called the *cadence pitch*. Rhythmically, a clear cadence usually consists of a strong agogic accent on the cadence pitch.

### Contour

**contour**

The overall shape of the melody is called the *contour*. Although each melody has its own contour, some general observations can be made about a melodic contour's range, motion, and points of prominence.

#### Range and Tessitura

**range**

The *range* of a melody is the distance between the highest and lowest tones. The range of example 2-11 is clearly from $e^1$ to $a^2$.

**EXAMPLE 2-11.** Telemann: Fantasia I, for solo flute

**tessitura**

The *tessitura* of a melody is the average range or the portion of the range that is used most frequently. The range and tessitura of example 2-11 are shown in example 2-12. The range is from $e^1$ to $a^2$, but the most frequently used portion is from $a^1$ to $e^2$.

**EXAMPLE 2-12.** Tessitura and range of example 2-11

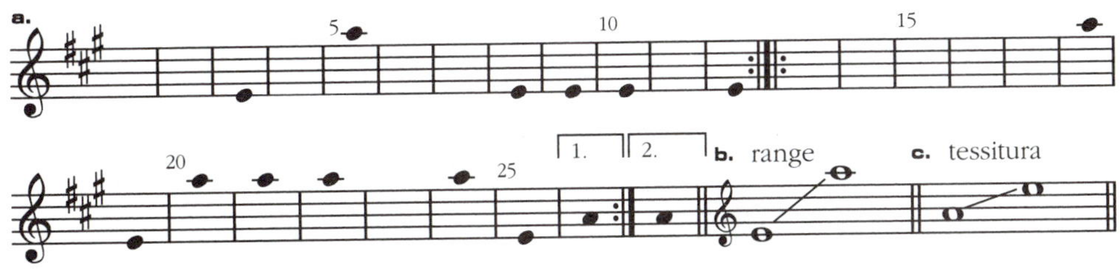


## Melodic Motion

**conjunct and disjunct motion**

Melodic motion will vary in direction and in the degree of smoothness. Melodic motion may ascend (rise), descend (fall), or remain level. It may also be smooth, using steps of primes or seconds, or it may be angular, using skips of thirds or greater. Motion with steps is called *conjunct,* and that with skips is called *disjunct.* Example 2-13 illustrates these ideas. The figure in measure 2 hovers around $a^1$, after which measures 5–6 descend and measure 8 ascends. The music in measure

2 is conjunct and that in measure 7 is disjunct, but most measures combine conjunct and disjunct motion.

**EXAMPLE 2-13.** Telemann: Fantasia I, for solo flute

## Prominence

**prominence**

There are four aspects of contour that produce points of *prominence,* or focal points in the melodic line.

**change of direction**

First, *change of direction* will produce prominence. The tone that gains from this focus is the tone on which the direction changes. (See ex. 2-14. The circles indicate the more prominent tones.)

**EXAMPLE 2-14.** Prominence produced by change of direction

Second, disjunct motion also produces prominence. The tone that is reached by skip will be more prominent; the larger the skip, the greater the prominence. (See ex. 2-15.)

**EXAMPLE 2-15.** Prominence produced by disjunct motion

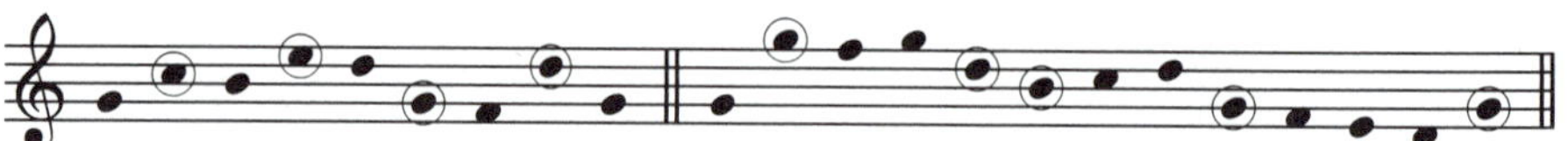

Often a skip will be followed by motion in the opposite direction. It is as though the skip creates a sort of vacuum in musical space, and the natural tendency is to fill this vacuum. This is only a general principle; one can find many exceptions, but there are far more instances where this has been applied. The larger the skip, the more likely that this rule will be followed.

**recurrence**

Third is the use of *recurrence.* A tone gains in significance when it reappears after one or more intervening notes, but it should appear at least three times out of six notes. (See ex. 2-16.)

**EXAMPLE 2-16.** Prominence produced by recurrence

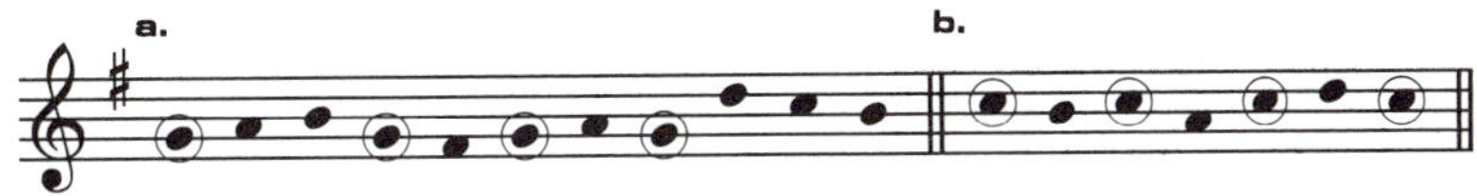


**location**

Fourth, the *location* of notes within a phrase affect their prominence. The first and last notes of the phrase will always have a strong impact on the listener.

## Combining Pitch with Rhythm

**emergent tone**

An *emergent tone* is a melodic tone (typically the most prominent in the measure in which it occurs) that gains prominence from pitch, rhythm, or both. The typical emergent tone will occur on the thesis of an agogic pattern and will have some characteristic contour that reinforces this prominence. Each emergent tone in example 2-17a is shown with an upward arrow including a stem. Less often, an agogic or metric pattern or other aspect of contour will compete as the location of an emergent tone. Judgment will be needed to identify the emergent tones in these cases (see ex. 2-17b).

**EXAMPLE 2-17.** Emergent tones

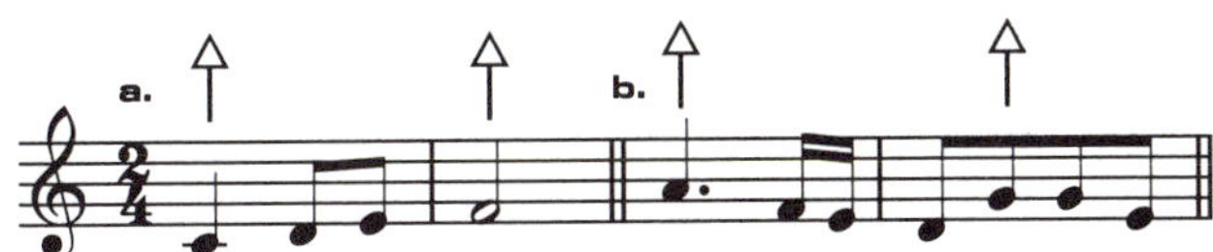


In moderate and quick tempos, a single emergent tone per bar is sufficient; in very slow tempos, such as in example 2-18, it may be useful to select two emergent tones per measure.

**EXAMPLE 2-18.** More than one emergent tone per measure

## Step Progressions

**step progression**

Once we have identified the emergent tones in a melody, we can look for a *step progression,* which is a scale-like pattern formed by two or more emergent tones, usually separated by intervening melodic tones. The method for identifying step progressions is shown in example 2-19. Emergent tones forming a step progression are marked with a number indicating the scale degree and a caret (ˆ); brackets connect the notes that participate in the step progression.

**EXAMPLE 2-19.** Identifying step progressions

**a.** Brahms: Sextet in B-flat, op. 18, second movement

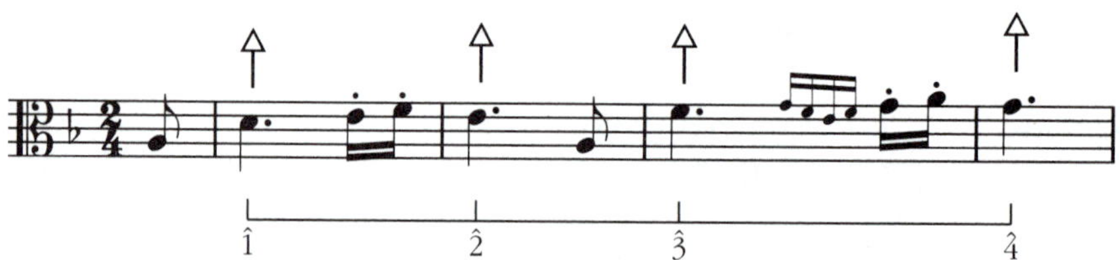


**b.** Brahms: Trio in E-flat for violin, horn, and piano, op. 40, second movement

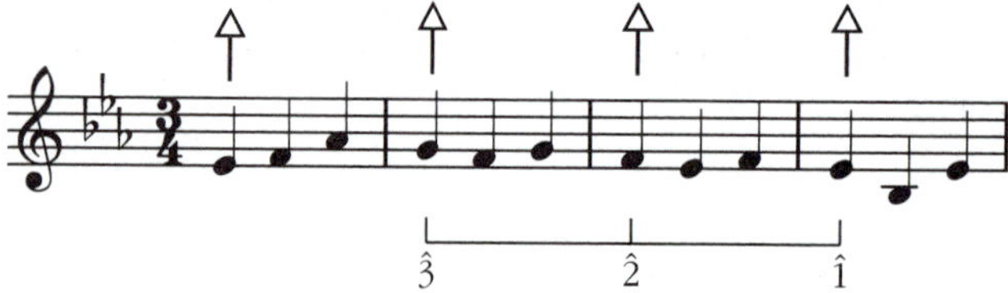


Step progressions often strengthen the sense of which key the piece is in by ending on either $\hat{1}$, $\hat{3}$, or $\hat{5}$, as in example 2-19b and example 2-20a, measure 4. Descending step progressions are found more often than ascending, but both types are common. In example 2-20b, we find two step progressions, both descending.

**EXAMPLE 2-20.** Step progressions

**a.** Dvořak: Piano Trio in F Minor, op. 65, first movement

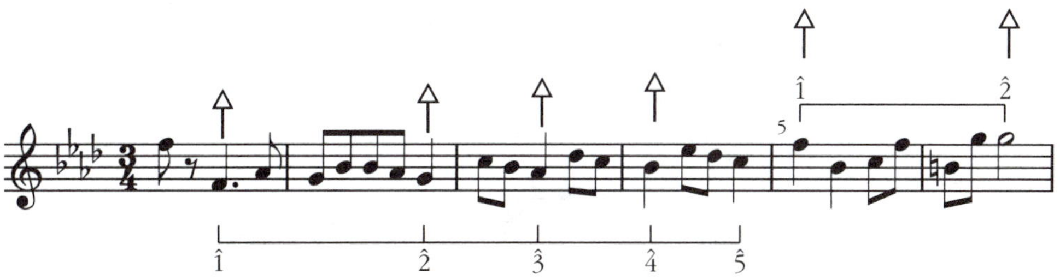


**b.** Handel: Sonata in B-flat, for flute and continuo, HHA iv/18, 15

## Repetition

**repetition**

As we bring together the forces of rhythm and contour, special attention must be given to repeated tones. A tone that is repeated, or repeated more frequently than those around it, will gain prominence, as in example 2-21.

**EXAMPLE 2-21.** Prominence produced by repetition

The total duration devoted to repeated tones also affects prominence. In example 2-22a, measure 1 has greater prominence because the arsis is longer, but in example 2-22b, measure 1 has greater prominence because there is greater activity in the arsis.

**EXAMPLE 2-22.** Prominence produced by duration and repetition

## Melodic Analysis

When analyzing a melody it is best to look first at the rhythm and locate the strongest agogic accents. If agogic accents are weak or lacking, focus on metric accents. Then see if some factor in the contour generates enough tension to offset the agogic or metric accents. Use the following method in analyzing a melody.

First, locate the agogic accents. Where there are none in a particular measure (as in measures 1 and 3 of example 2-23), choose the metric accent as the next strongest rhythmic feature. The notes now identified are the prime candidates for becoming the emergent tones of the melody.

**EXAMPLE 2-23.** Agogic and metric accents in melodic analysis

Second, identify the emergent tones of the melody. Determine if any tone gains sufficient prominence through an aspect of contour (change of direction, disjunct motion, repetition, recurrence, location, or step progression) to offset the rhythmically prominent tones identified in the first step. In example 2-23 we find that the step progression reinforces the first note of measures 1 and 3, both of which have only a metric accent. The final analysis is shown in example 2-24.

**EXAMPLE 2-24.** Emergent tones in melodic analysis

In most instances we will choose one emergent tone per measure. Exceptions to this might be made in the following circumstances:

1. The tempo is very slow and there are many notes per measure.
2. In addition to the most emergent tone, there is another tone in the measure that would continue or complete a step progression previously begun.
3. A new phrase begins in the same measure as that in which the previous phrase ended. Generally in such cases the cadence pitch is more important than the starting tone of the new phrase, but both are emergent tones.

The melodies in example 2-25 give further illustrations of melodic analysis. Example 2-25a is straightforward. In example 2-25b the repeated Gs in measure 3 are strong enough to become emergent, and the B in the same measure forms a step progression with the A in measure 4, so both are emergent tones. In example 2-25c, the step progression and slow tempo justify choosing two emergent tones in some of the measures.

**EXAMPLE 2-25:** Emergent tones in melodic analysis

**a.** Schumann: Symphony No. 2, second movement

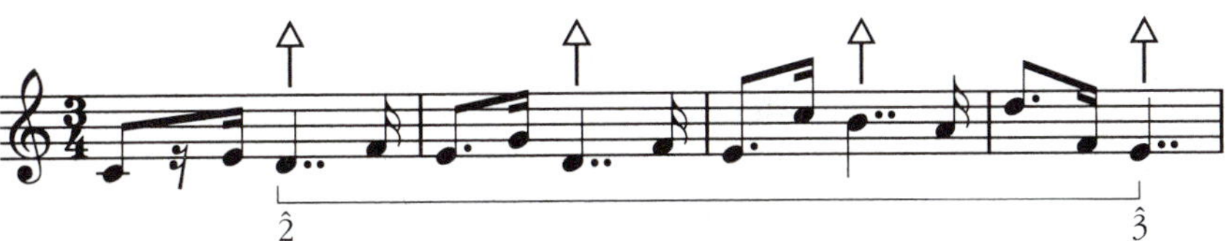


**b.** Cimarosa: *La Astuzie feminili*

**c.** Handel: Sonata in C minor, for oboe and continuo, HHA iv/18,32

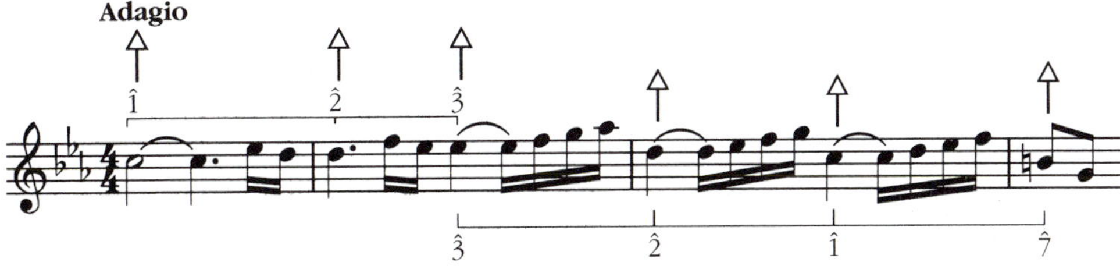


The final check on the accuracy of an analysis is to sing through the melody. The analysis should reflect the way one "hears" the melody. Avoid an analysis that looks good on paper but cannot be "heard."

# TONIC

**tonic, tonal center**

**tonal**

**atonal**

**tonality**

One of the most basic concepts in our traditional music is the *tonic,* or *tonal center.* A tonic or tonal center is one tone or pitch class that is heard as the most important, the other tones relating to it in various supporting or confirming roles. Music that employs such a tonal center is referred to as *tonal.* (Music without a tonal center is sometimes called *atonal.*) *Tonality* is a set of relationships between a tonic and other pitches.

The tonic of a melody is usually perceived intuitively by the listener. A more analytical approach is available through an understanding of the melodic treatment of specific scale degrees.

## Scale Degrees and Tonality

The most important tones of the scale for establishing the tonic or feeling of being in a key are the first, third, and fifth scale degrees ($\hat{1}$, $\hat{3}$, and $\hat{5}$). The importance of these degrees is partly a matter of tradition, but an examination of intervals will reveal other reasons.

### Interval Roots

**interval root**

For acoustical and cultural reasons, when two tones are heard in succession (as a melodic interval) or simultaneously (as a harmonic interval), one of the tones will be heard as "stronger" than the other. The dominating tone is called the *interval root.* In his book *The Craft of Musical Composition,* the composer Paul Hindemith presents the list of interval roots shown in example 2-26. Each interval, together with its inversion, forms a pair in which the interval to the left is more stable, having the stronger, clearer root. The roots are circled.

**EXAMPLE 2-26.** Interval roots

On the left side of the example are those intervals that have the strongest effect in determining tonality. On the right side we find the more ambiguous intervals, with the *tritone* (augmented fourth or diminished fifth) at the far end, very ambiguous in its tonal orientation. In each pair, one interval has the root above and the other has the root below; those with the root below are the more stable.

## Roots of Intervals Using Scale Degrees 1, 3, and 5

In both major and minor keys, scale degrees 1, 3, and 5 combine to form three intervals: a P5 ($\hat{1}$–$\hat{5}$) and two thirds ($\hat{1}$–$\hat{3}$) and ($\hat{3}$–$\hat{5}$). Example 2-27 shows these intervals with the roots circled.

**EXAMPLE 2-27.** Intervals formed by 1, 3, and 5 scale degrees

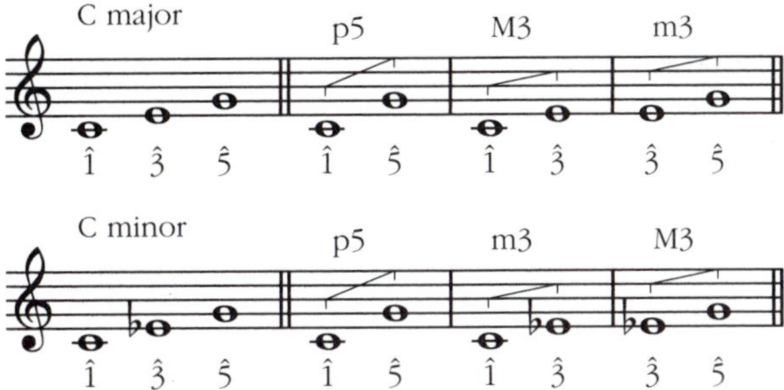


The most important scale degrees for establishing the tonic are $\hat{1}$ and $\hat{5}$. The P5 formed by these scale degrees has the strongest possible root effect on $\hat{1}$. By emphasizing these degrees, a melody strengthens its tonality. The root of the third from $\hat{1}$ to $\hat{3}$ is also $\hat{1}$, so this interval also serves to confirm the tonic, though not as strongly as the P5 ($\hat{1}$–$\hat{5}$). The interval from $\hat{3}$ to $\hat{5}$ does not, by itself, establish the tonic clearly.

## The Characteristics of Tonal Melodies

Several characteristics of tonal melodies will be useful as guides when determining the tonic of a melody.

1. Scale degrees 1 and 5 both appear often among the emergent tones.
2. The first and last tones of a melody (which are often emergent tones) are often either $\hat{1}$, $\hat{3}$, or $\hat{5}$.
3. The highest and lowest emergent tones are often either $\hat{1}$, $\hat{3}$, or $\hat{5}$.
4. Skips are more often between $\hat{1}$, $\hat{3}$, or $\hat{5}$ than between other scale tones.
5. Step progressions often end on $\hat{1}$, $\hat{3}$, or $\hat{5}$.

To identify the tonic of a melody, the melody must be long enough for the tonality to be established. A full phrase is the minimum, but several phrases may be needed in some cases. Special difficulties may arise if tonality is intentionally ambiguous, if a shift in tonality occurs, or if the music relies on harmony to clarify the tonality. These situations will be studied in more detail later.

The characteristics of tonal melodies are illustrated in the melodies of example 2-28. Emergent tones and step progressions are indicated. Each of the two passages in example 2-28 appear at the end of a song; however, the tonic is clearer in example 2-28a, where the step progression leads to tonic at the end. In example 2-28b the step progression ends on $\hat{5}$ and does not lead to the tonic F, which is finally asserted at the end.

**EXAMPLE 2-28.** Characteristics of tonal melodies

**a.** Brahms: *Forty-nine German Folksongs,* No. 13, "Wach Auf, mein Hort"

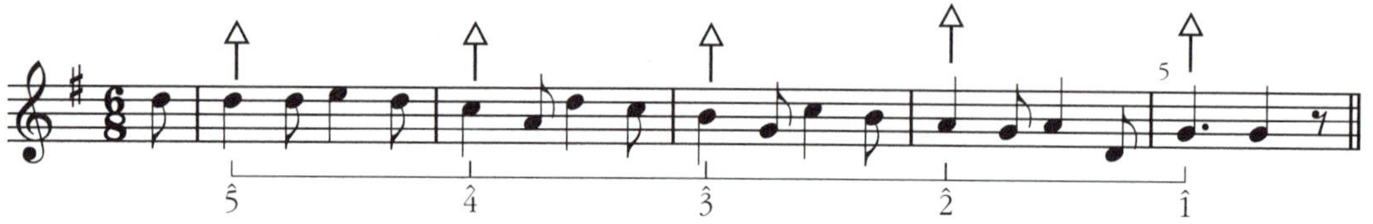


**b.** Brahms: *Forty-nine German Folksongs,* No. 17, "Ach Gott, wie weh tut Scheiden"

# SCALES

**scale**

A *scale* is an ascending succession of tones, beginning on the tonic, with fixed intervals and relationships. (This does not refer to scale "passages" but only to abstract scales displayed for analytical purposes.) Usually scales are shown ascending one octave, but occasionally one finds descending scales or scales that cover less than an octave.

## Pitch Complement

**pitch complement**

A listing of the pitches of a melody in ascending order is called a *pitch complement.* Its purpose is to show the range of a melody, the selection of pitches used, and the intervals between the pitches. The pitch complement of example 2-29 is shown below the melody.

**EXAMPLE 2-29.** A melody and its pitch complement

**a.** Brahms: *Twenty-eight German Folksongs,* No. 12, "Tageweis von einer schönen Frauen"

**b.** Pitch complement

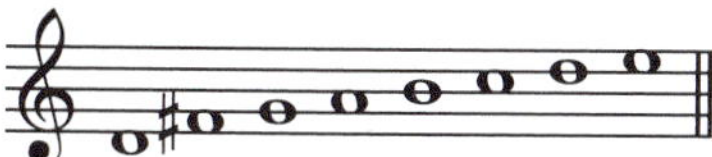

## The Relationship of Pitch Complements to Scales

A scale differs from the pitch complement in several important ways. The scale is presented with the tonic as the lowest tone. It ascends for one octave, indicating pitch classes that are basic to the piece. In example 2-30 notice that tones below the tonic in the pitch complement appear above the lower tonic in a scale.

**EXAMPLE 2-30.** Pitch complements and scales

**a.** Chopin: Piano Sonata, op. 35, third movement

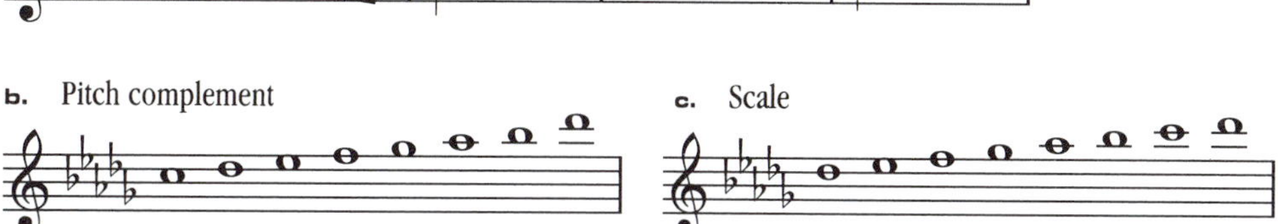


Scales are usually shown occupying a full octave, but many melodies do not actually use that many pitch classes. Some melodies may not include all of the pitches of a major or minor scale, but enough that we can assume the missing notes to complete the pattern. In example 2-31 we find six of the seven pitches of the minor scale in the pitch complement of the melody, but we can assume the missing fourth degree.

**EXAMPLE 2-31.** Schubert: Symphony No. 8, D. 758, first movement

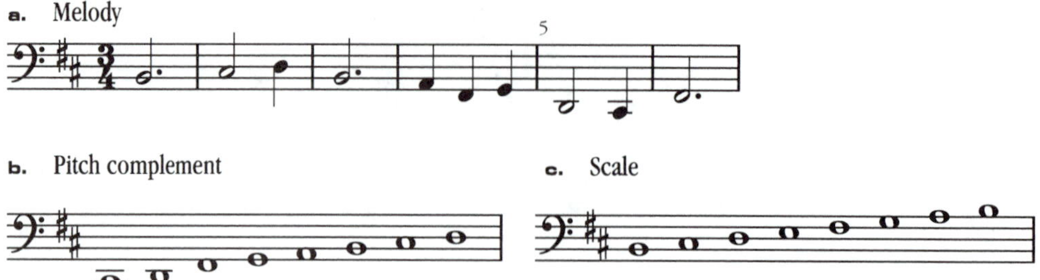


## Diatonic Modes

As seen in chapter 1, the tones of the diatonic system have a characteristic spacing of whole and half steps (see example 2-32a). The pattern of whole and half steps for the major scale is W, W, H, W, W, W, H, or 1, 1, 1/2, 1, 1, 1, 1/2 (see example 2-32b). This pattern can be found within the diatonic system by starting on C.

**EXAMPLE 2-32.** Patterns of whole and half steps

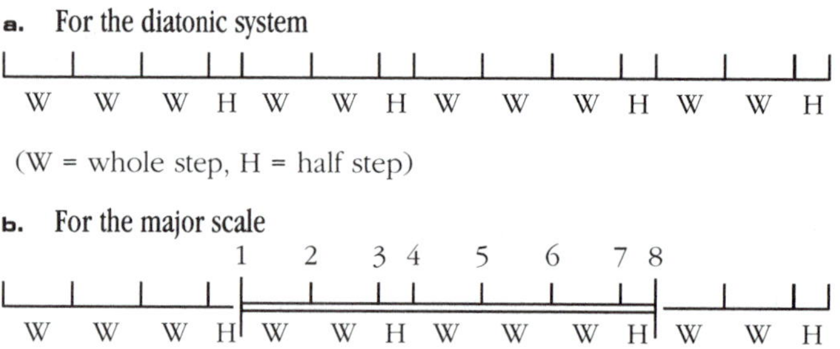


It is possible to start scales in other places as well. Each of these would be a *diatonic scale,* that is, they would all fit within the diatonic system. There are seven different patterns for scales within the diatonic system, each starting at a different place in the system. Each of these is a *diatonic mode* and has been given a Greek name, as shown in table 2-1.

**diatonic modes**

The staff notation of these scale patterns is shown in example 2-33. These scales did not all come into use at the same time. Curiously, the last scales to be recognized were ionian and aeolian, our familiar major and minor scale patterns. These were not recognized by music theorists until the sixteenth century. The locrian mode has been little used because its fifth scale degree is not a perfect fifth above the tonic. This renders the scale unstable, as its tonic is always in doubt.

Each mode has its own interval structure, key signature, and characteristic melodic patterns. Long familiarity with the ionian and aeolian modes makes them seem more "normal" than the others. Compare the effect of the melodies in example 2-34.

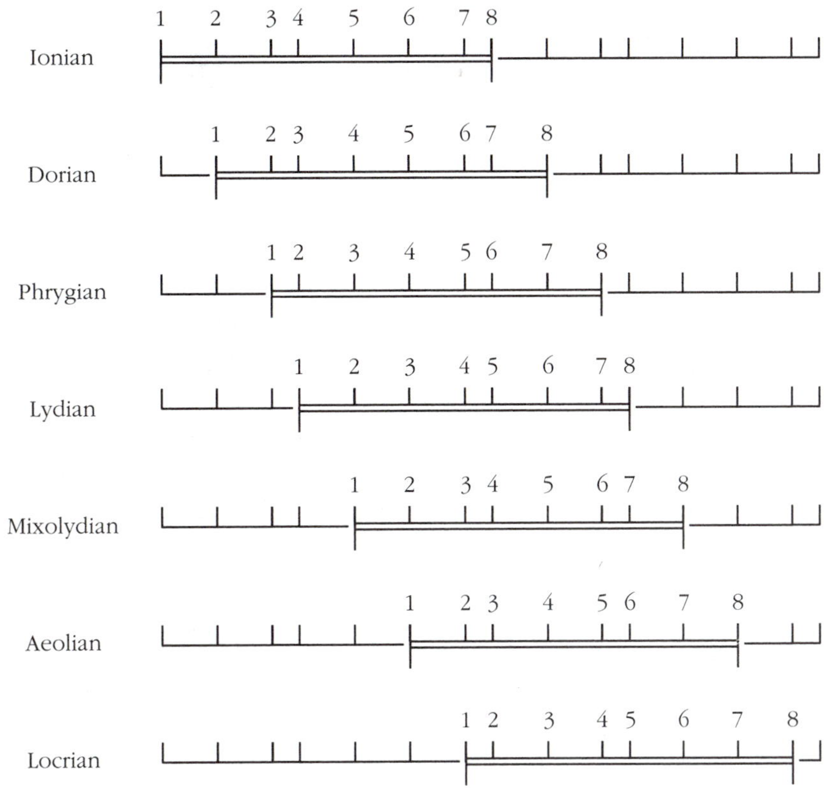


**TABLE 2-1.** Diatonic modes

**EXAMPLE 2-33.** Staff notation of diatonic modes

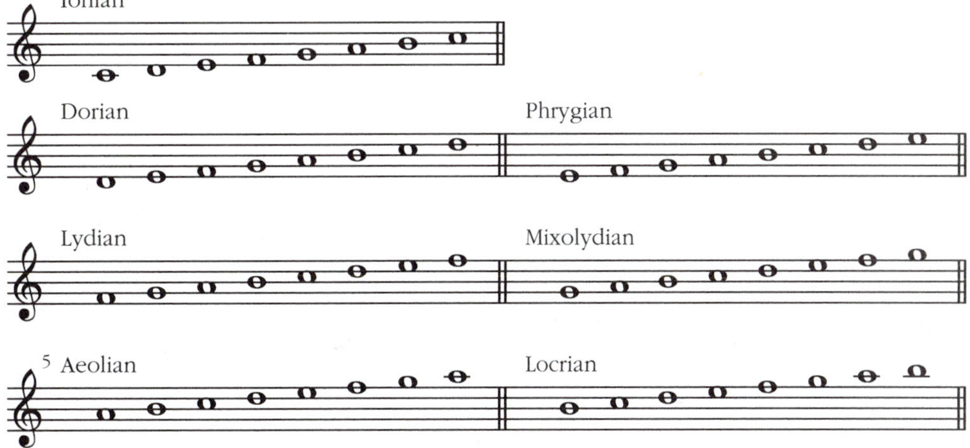

**EXAMPLE 2-34.** Melodies in different modes

## Minor Mode

The minor mode has a basic diatonic pattern to which chromatic alterations are applied, as discussed in chapter 1. It is best to think of the minor mode as simply having variable forms for $\hat{6}$ and $\hat{7}$, the basic scale being the aeolian mode, which is called "natural minor."

The pitch complement and scale of the melody in example 2-35 uses two versions of $\hat{6}$ and $\hat{7}$. It is often said that the raised forms are used in ascending and the lowered forms in descending, but, as example 5 illustrates, there are so many exceptions to this that it can hardly be considered a meaningful rule.

**EXAMPLE 2-35.** J. S. Bach: Passacaglia, BWV 582

## CHANGES IN TONALITY AND SCALES

Only a relatively short musical composition will retain a single tonality or a single scale throughout. To create interest and build tension, a composer may change the tonic, the pitch complement, or both.

### Modulation

**modulation**

A change of tonic is called a *modulation.* The new tonic in a modulation will commonly appear as a strong emergent tone, often near the end of the phrase. When a new tonic is established, a new pitch complement and scale take effect. In example 2-36 the first phrase remains in F major, but the complement changes in measure 6 (B-natural), and the emergent tones in measures 6–10 emphasize C and G, a P5 in which C is the root. The pitch complement of C major is apparent in the second phrase.

**EXAMPLE 2-36.** Haydn: Piano Sonata in C Major, Hob. XVI:9, second movement

In example 2-37 the new tonic arrives as the last tone in a step progression. As was pointed out earlier, step progressions often end on tones that are of unusual significance to the tonality. In example 2-37 the step progression uses the critical tone for the modulation, F-sharp, as a leading tone resolving on G. The strong D in measures 7 and 8 affirms the new tonic with a $\hat{5}$–$\hat{1}$ relationship to the G tonic. A very rapid modulation can produce a startling effect, as seen in example 2-38.

### Change of Mode

**change of mode**

*Change of mode,* sometimes called mutation, is the name given to a change in pitch complement while the tonic remains the same. The most common examples of a change of mode are changes from major to minor and vice versa, but the term may also be applied to changes involving other modes. Often a change of key signature heralds the change of mode to the parallel key, as in the change from A major to the parallel minor in example 2-39.

**EXAMPLE 2-37.** Haydn: Piano Sonata in C Major, Hob. XVI:15, first movement

**EXAMPLE 2-38.** Hartnett: *The Jolly Seven*

**EXAMPLE 2-39.** Rameau: Sarabande

## WRITING MELODIES

In writing a melody, the following points may be useful.

1. It may help to start by composing a rhythm that lies comfortably in the chosen meter, employing agogic accents that usually confirm the meter. Phrases do not often end with a syncopation.
2. In your early efforts, begin on the first, third, or fifth scale degrees of the key you are in. Sing these tones so they are firmly in your ear as you begin selecting pitches.
3. Remember that skips are often followed by motion in the opposite direction.

4. Certain intervals are melodically problematic and should be handled with care. If your ear does not easily guide you in their handling, the following intervals should be avoided: major and minor sevenths, tritones, and intervals larger than an octave. The ascending seventh scale degree has a tendency to move to the tonic, while the descending fourth degree tends to move to the third.

## SUMMARY

Melody consists of the interaction of melodic rhythm and contour, producing a rise and fall of tension and a sense of tonality. Melodic rhythm involves the use of accents (or points of emphasis), of which there are three types: dynamic, agogic, and metric. These accents reveal points in the melody where tension peaks and releases. Various aspects of melody—rhythm and pitch in particular—bring individual tones into prominence, giving them special importance in a melody. These tones are called emergent tones, and they often connect into step progressions and play an important role in establishing a sense of tonality.

A scale is an ascending succession of tones with fixed intervals and relationships beginning on a tonic. Not all melodies use every pitch in a scale, however, and the concept of pitch complement distinguishes those tones used in a melody from those that compose the scale on which the melody is based. Scales include seven diatonic modes, or scales that begin on each of the seven pitches in the diatonic system. Major and minor modes are also a part of the diatonic system. Only a short musical composition will retain a single tonality or scale throughout. The composer may change the tonic upon which the composition is based (called modulation) or may change the pitch complement (called change of mode).

CHAPTER THREE

# Melody and Form

**Terms Introduced in This Chapter**

motive

coherence

differentiation

repetition of motives

recurrence of motives

fragmentation

diminution

augmentation

melodic sequence

leg

member

exact sequence

diatonic sequence

tonal sequence

interval expansion

interval contraction

melodic inversion

retrograde motion

modified recurrence

subphrase

conclusive cadence

inconclusive cadence

interlocking phrase

crest

o understand the structure and overall form of melody, it is necessary to study motives, phrases, and larger units consisting of various groupings of phrases.

## THE MOTIVE

**motive**

A melodic *motive* is a small group of melodic events that may consist of rhythm, pitch relationships, or both. Usually a motive is somewhere between a few notes and two measures in length. Motives make their contribution to coherence through repetition and recurrence.

### Cohesion and Differentiation

**coherence**

**differentiation**

Music includes two basic processes, *coherence* and *differentiation*. Musical events, the tones and rests that compose the work, may be used in such a way that the events draw together or cohere to form groups, or the composer may choose to separate, or differentiate, events from the surrounding material.

The cohering process is basic to the formation of musical structure. Notes combine to form phrases, phrases combine to form melodies, and melodies and phrases form larger sections, all of which combine to form an entire piece. The differentiating process provides an element of contrast and change in music and increases tension. Both processes are essential: Music lacking differentiation would become boring; music in which there was no cohesion would be chaotic.

### Rhythmic Motives

**repetition of motives**

**recurrence of motives**

The significance of a rhythmic motive lies in how it may reappear or contrast with other motives. While contrasting motives produce a sense of differentiation or variety, motives that reappear create unity, either clearly when they involve repetition or recurrence, or less so when they are altered. *Repetition of motives* involves, as in the case of pitches, an immediate reappearance. The *recurrence of motives* is a reappearance after other material has intervened.

A motive usually ends with the thesis of the agogic pattern. For this reason the motive in example 3-1 is best analyzed as shown by the solid brackets and label "a," rather than the analysis shown by the dotted brackets, labeled "x." The restatements of a motive are the best indicators of the motive's identity; hence, in example 3-2 the analysis shown by the dotted brackets in example 3-1 would now be the correct one.

**EXAMPLE 3-1.** Analysis of a rhythmic motive

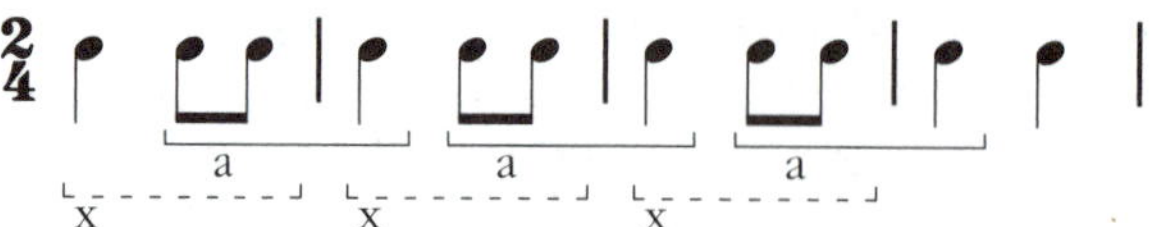


**EXAMPLE 3-2.** Analysis of a rhythmic motive

The last tone of a motive (which is usually the thesis of an agogic pattern) may be varied in length and still be heard as part of the motive. In example 3-3 the motive labeled "a" in measure 1 recurs in measures 2, 3, and 4, each time with changes in the length of the last note.

**EXAMPLE 3-3.** Changes in the last note of a motive

## Rhythmic Variants

Alterations of a motive are called *variants* and can be indicated in an analysis by a "prime" mark after the identifying lower case letter, that is, a′. Three variants are discussed here.

**fragmentation**

The use of only a portion of a motive is called *fragmentation.* The omission of tones must not eliminate essential characteristics of the motive or the identity of the motive will be lost. The motive in measures 1 and 2 of example 3-4 is fragmented in measure 3.

**EXAMPLE 3-4.** Fragmentation

**diminution**

*Diminution* is the term used to describe the recurrence of a pattern with the durations consistently shortened, usually by half. In example 3-5 the durations of motive a are shortened by half in motive a′.

**EXAMPLE 3-5.** Diminution

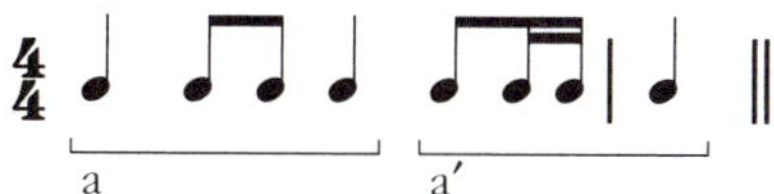


**augmentation**

When the original durations are consistently increased, usually doubled in length, the device is called *augmentation*. The motives marked b and b′ illustrate this in example 3-6.

**EXAMPLE 3-6.** Augmentation

## Analysis of Rhythmic Motives

Example 3-7 illustrates the method of analysis and the techniques discussed thus far. Generally, an analysis of motive structure should identify the largest recurring pattern that does not exceed half the length of a phrase. The lengths of the motives in example 3-7 are determined by the kinds of recurrence and variants used. A high degree of cohesion will be found in measures 1–4 as a result of the recurrence and similarity of motives a and b. In measure 5 a new motive, c, brings differentiation into the picture. Notice the impact of its first appearance.

## Melodic Motives

Melodic motives, including both pitch and rhythmic relationships, give rise to other variation techniques, in addition to those discussed under rhythm.

### Repetition, Recurrence, and Fragmentation

Repetition, recurrence, and fragmentation are used as frequently with melodic motives as with rhythmic motives. Example 3-8 shows the repetition of a melodic motive followed by fragmentation.

**EXAMPLE 3-7.** Analysis of rhythmic motives

1. diminution of a
2. last note of a′ becomes first note of b
3. fragmentation of a′
4. ambiguity of fragmented portions of a leads easily to b′

**EXAMPLE 3-8.** Mozart: Serenade in D, K. 250 ("Haffner")

## Sequence

**melodic sequence**

**leg**

**member**

**exact sequence**

The immediate repetition of a motive on a new pitch level is called a *melodic sequence.* Sometimes there are several such repetitions, each on a new pitch level. The initial statement of the motive is called the first *leg* or *member* of the sequence, and each subsequent leg is numbered in turn. When motives recur on various pitches, the general size of each interval within the motive (thirds, seconds, etc.) is usually maintained, but the exact quality of the interval (major, minor, perfect) may not be. If a sequence copies exactly every interval of the original motive, it is called an *exact sequence.* (See ex. 3-9a.) Notice that the second and third legs of the sequence do not fit in the key (C major). *Diatonic* or *tonal se-*

**diatonic sequence**

**tonal sequence**

*quences,* which remain in the original key, are far more commonly used. (See ex. 3-9b.) The listener has no hesitation in accepting these diatonic variants as virtually identical to the original motive.

**EXAMPLE 3-9.** Sequences

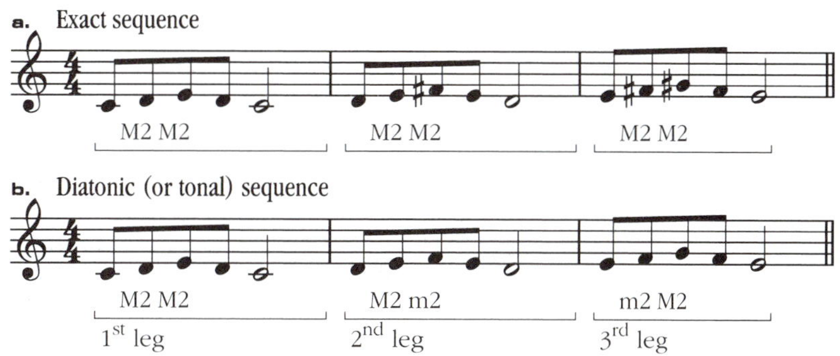


*Modified sequences* are also quite common. Example 3-10 shows a sequence in which the motive recurs twice at the perfect fourth above, with slight modifications.

**EXAMPLE 3-10.** J. S. Bach: Sinfonia 5, BWV 891

## Interval Contraction and Expansion

**interval expansion**

**interval contraction**

If a motive retains its overall characteristic contour and rhythm, it may change in succeeding appearances by an interval expansion technique known as either *interval expansion* or *interval contraction.* In example 3-11, the initial statement of the interval contraction motive occupies the first measure. Notice the changes in the first and last intervals of each succeeding measure.

## Melodic Inversion and Retrograde Motion

**melodic inversion**

In *melodic inversion* a motive is turned upside down, reversing the ascending and descending motion. Typically, melodic inversion uses the tones of the diatonic scale from the passage. In example 3-12, material presented early in the example will sound very different, almost new, offering simultaneous unity and variety.

**EXAMPLE 3-11.** J. S. Bach: Suite No. 5 for violoncello solo, BWV 1011, Sarabande

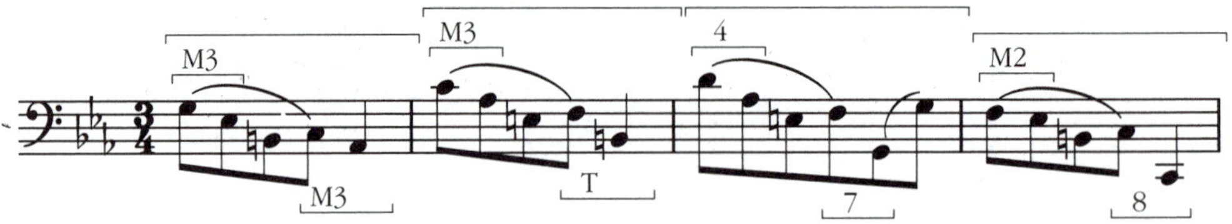


**EXAMPLE 3-12.** J. S. Bach: Suite No. 3, BWV 1068 Overture

**retrograde motion**

Less often encountered is *retrograde motion,* in which a motive is presented backwards. Motives in retrograde motion typically use tones of the diatonic scale. The motives identified in example 3-13a reappear in retrograde form in example 3-13b.

**EXAMPLE 3-13.** C. P. E. Bach: Minuet

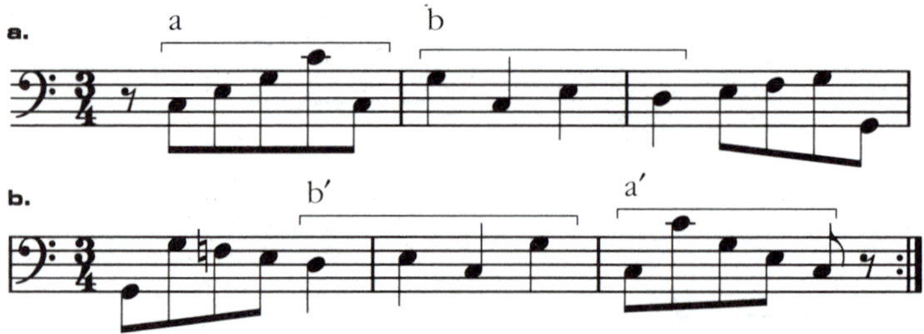


## Modified Recurrence

**modified recurrence**

The term *modified recurrence* refers to any variation that does not fall into one of the categories previously discussed. The number of possible variants of a motive far exceeds our terminology. In example 3-14a, the initial motive appears without an upbeat and is repeated in measure 2 and measure 10 in that form. The recurrence in measure 9, however, is clearly related but has an additional tone, the upbeat. In example 3-14b, the initial motive is retained, but more and more tones are added.

**EXAMPLE 3.14** Examples of modified recurrence

**a.** Beethoven: Piano Sonata, op. 14, no. 1, second movement

**b.** Smetana: *The Bartered Bride,* Overture

Notice the impact of pitch considerations on the rhythmic relationships in example 3-15. The rhythm of motive a is closely related to that of motive b, but the contour of b is very different and actually offers contrast to motive a.

**EXAMPLE 3-15.** Chopin: Mazurka, op. 67, no. 2

## Motivic Analysis

A motive is more important as an element of structure if it is used often, that is, it is more important than a motive that is used only a few times. Patterns that do not recur, recur rarely, or are not very prominent may be omitted in an analysis. While many patterns in a work may be recognized as motives, it may not be practical or necessary to analyze all of them. The analysis of motives is done in two stages, first a study of the rhythm and second a study of pitch to arrive at the final analysis.

The rhythm of figure x in example 3-16 occurs in different fragmentary versions throughout. The figure labeled x′, a fragment of figure x, is used frequently and generates more interest than the initial figure. Two other figures, y and z, are used for contrast.

**EXAMPLE 3-16.** Haydn: String Quartet, Hob. III:24, first movement

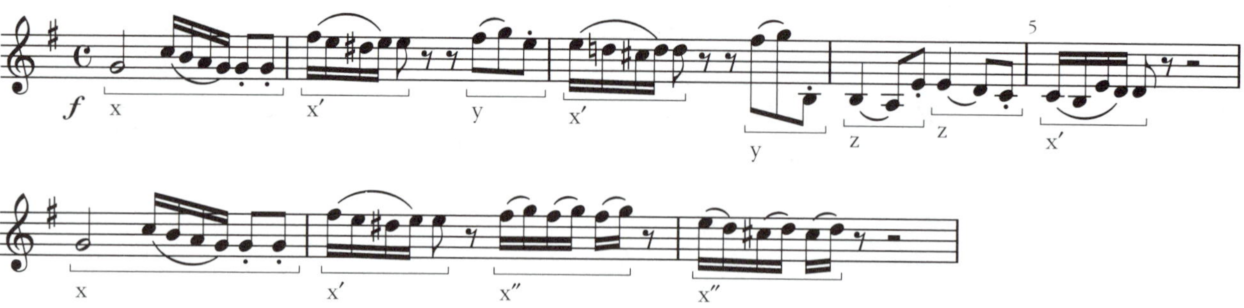


Next, we review the passage with pitch in mind. In example 3-17 four motives are identified after pitch is taken into account. The pitches used with rhythmic figure x have a distinctive contour as well as a distinctive rhythm; these pitches thus become motive a, and it recurs only once, in measure 6. The rhythmic figure x′ is used with a different contour and becomes motive b and its variants. Rhythmic figure y provides contrast with figure x. When pitch is taken into account it is seen that this motive, called c, consists of two eighth notes, a half step apart. Motive c begins innocuously but becomes very striking when subjected to diminution. At two points in this example, motives seem to merge; that is, a group of notes appear to be related to two different motives at the same time. In measure 5, note the contour relationship with motive d in measure 4 (with interval contraction) and the rhythmic relationship with motive b in measure 2. In measure 8 motives b and c seem to merge.

**EXAMPLE 3-17.** Haydn: String Quartet, Hob. III:24, first movement

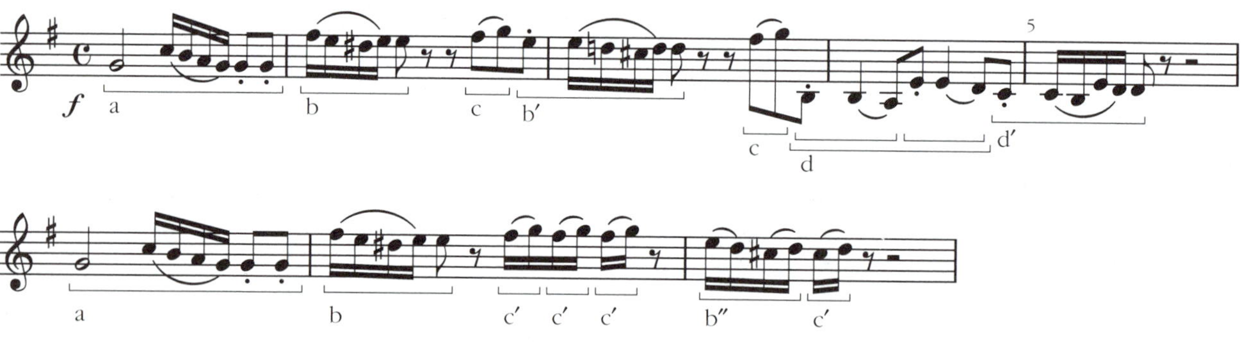


## THE PHRASE

The phrase is of fundamental importance in understanding the role of smaller units, such as motives, as well as larger units for which the phrase is a basic building unit. The phrase has been defined in terms of length and internal treatment. It is necessary now, however, to have a more detailed understanding of the concept of a phrase and the tension associated with it.

## The Concept of the Phrase

As musical circumstances become more challenging, the concept of the phrase is expanded to identify and understand its features in more detail. Specific criteria for identifying and creating melodic phrases are:

1. normal length;
2. strength of cadence;
3. contrast in the content of phrases;
4. reappearance of an opening figure.

### Normal Length

**subphrase**

The normal length of a phrase is between three and six measures, with four measures being the most common. Occasionally one encounters a melody in which the four-bar phrases are clearly divided into two two-bar units. While these two-bar units are important in the structure of the piece, common practice among musicians has been to avoid calling a two-bar unit a phrase unless the tempo is very slow. The term *subphrase* may be applied to such units. Not all phrases have subphrases; however, two-bar subphrases are common in the Classical era. A typical opening phrase from this period (a four-bar phrase composed of symmetrical two-bar subphrases) is seen in example 3-18a; example 3-18b illustrates a two-bar phrase in a slow tempo. A six-bar phrase followed by two four-bar phrases is seen in example 3-18c.

The downward arrows, ↓ , ↓ , and ↓ , separate phrases. (For a complete list of analytical symbols see "Guide to Analytical Symbols," p. 000.) Normally the arrow will be located between notes, separating the notes of the preceding phrase from those of the succeeding phrase. An arrow is also placed before the first note of the work and after the last note so that every note of every phrase may be seen as lying *between* two arrows. Nothing is outside the phrase structure; all portions of the work are considered part of one phrase or another.

The single slashes on the arrows denote beginnings and ends of phrases. The arrow with the slash extending to the right of the shaft denotes the beginning of the phrase ↓ ; the arrow with the slash extending to the left denotes the ending of the preceding phrase ↓ . The first arrow in a piece has no slash on the left side, nor does the last arrow have a slash on the right side. Arrows between two phrases have slashes on both sides ↓ .

**EXAMPLE 3-18.** Examples of phrases

**a.** Mozart: Piano Sonata, K. 282, second movement

**b.** Mozart: Fantasy and a Fugue for Piano, K. 394

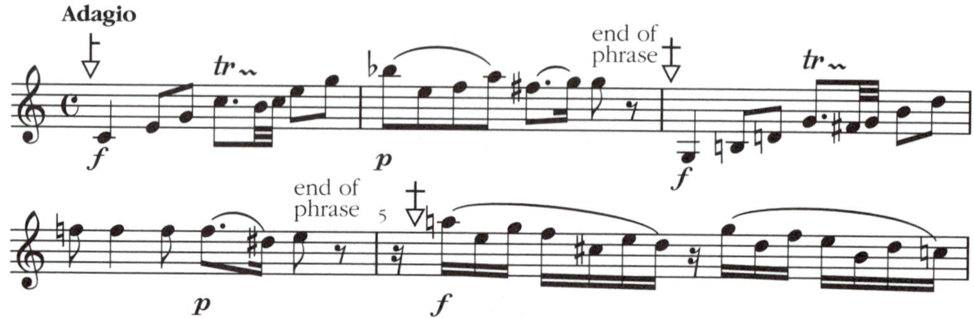


**c.** Haydn: Piano Sonata in C Major, Hob. XVI:15, second movement

## Strength of Cadence

Cadences vary in strength depending on the rhythmic treatment and the scale degree of the cadence pitch. There is often an agogic accent on the cadence pitch; the stronger the agogic accent, the stronger the cadence effect. The strongest cadential effect is when the cadence pitch is the tonic ($\hat{1}$). The cadence pitch is identified as "cadence on $\hat{1}$," or "cad. $\hat{1}$," "cadence on $\hat{5}$," or "cad. $\hat{5}$," and so on.

**conclusive cadence**

**inconclusive cadence**

The strength of a cadence's conclusiveness varies with each scale degree. A cadence on $\hat{1}$ will be considered a *conclusive cadence,* even though it may appear on cadences prior to the final one. Cadences on other scale degrees will be considered *inconclusive.* Cadences on $\hat{2}$, $\hat{4}$, $\hat{6}$, and $\hat{7}$ are the most inconclusive, and those on $\hat{3}$ and $\hat{5}$ less so. Example 3-19 illustrates phrases with cadences on various scale degrees. In examples 3-19 and 3-20, the key is indicated with a colon before each cadence reference; capitals are used for major keys and lower case letters for minor.

**EXAMPLE 3-19.** Cadences on each scale degree

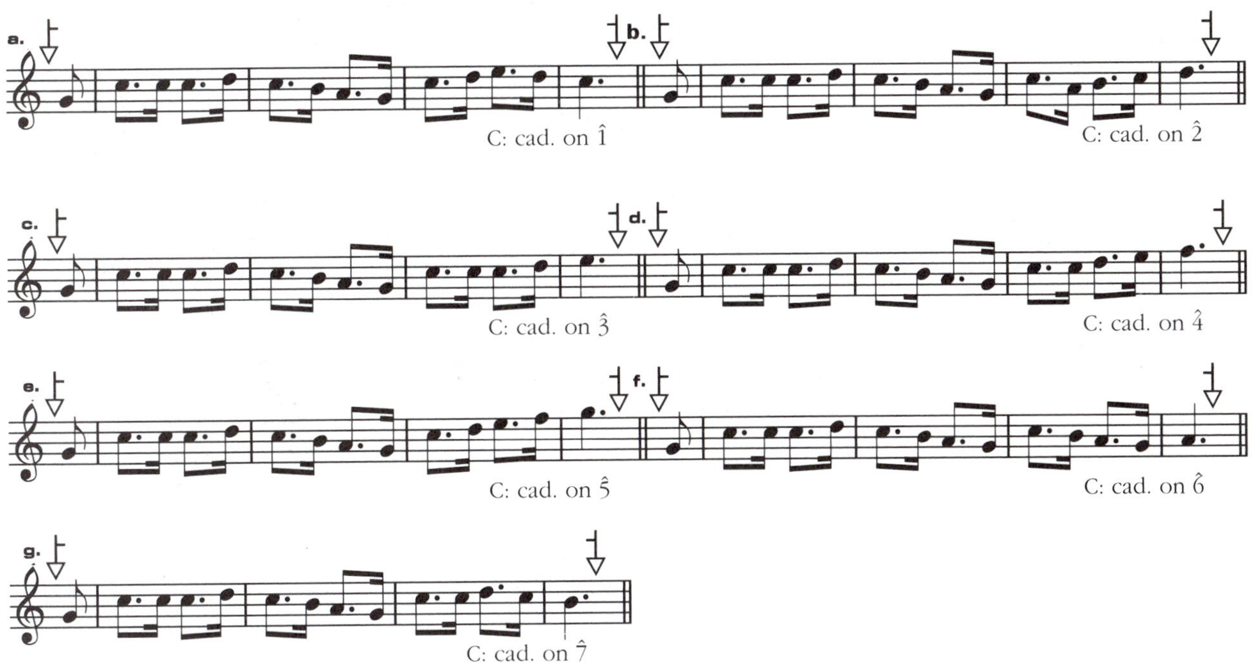


If a modulation occurs, it must be reflected in the analysis of the passage. Example 3-20 shows how the cadences are to be identified in a melodic passage that modulates. The new tonics appear at each cadence.

**EXAMPLE 3-20.** Cadences in modulating passages

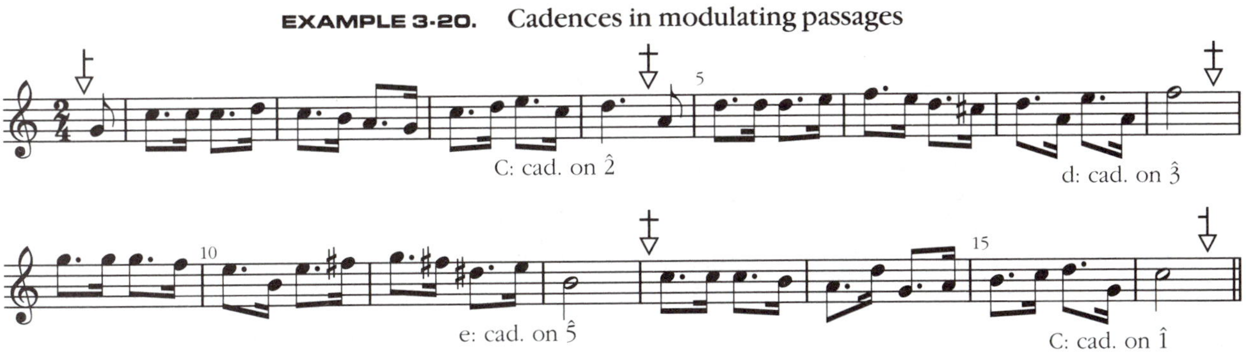


## Contrast in the Content of Phrases

Sometimes a phrase can be easily identified because the material that composes it is markedly different from the material of the phrases before and after it.

Example 3-21 consists of two phrases, each four bars long. Although there is considerable similarity between them, each phrase displays enough inner unity to distinguish it clearly from the other. The overall contour of the second phrase is a free inversion of the first phrase. Subtle differences distinguish the phrases, but at the same time they complement each other beautifully.

**EXAMPLE 3-21.** J. S. Bach: Suite No. 5 for violoncello solo, BWV 1011, Sarabande

A step progression may provide the sense of inner unity that binds a phrase together. In example 3-22 step progressions associated with the melodic sequence extend over several measures.

**EXAMPLE 3-22.** Beethoven: Piano Sonata, op. 2, no. 2, first movement

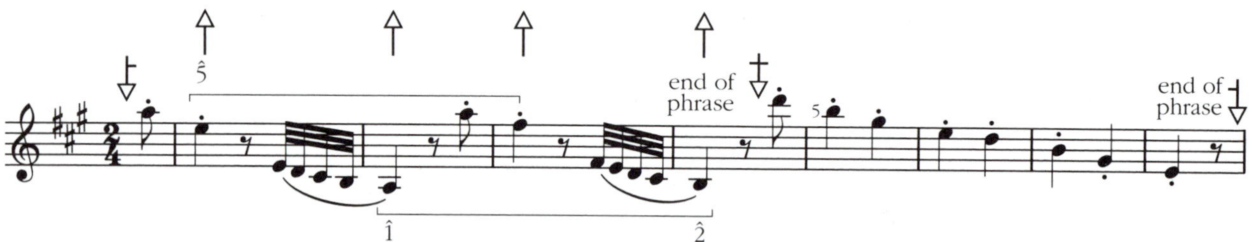


## Reappearance of an Opening Figure

The clear beginning of a new phrase may be the best evidence that the preceding phrase has ended. The clear reappearance of a motive that previously began a phrase serves as a retrospective clue that the previous phrase has ended. In example 3-23, the second phrase begins just like the first.

**EXAMPLE 3-23** Haydn: String Quartet, Hob. III:73, fourth movement

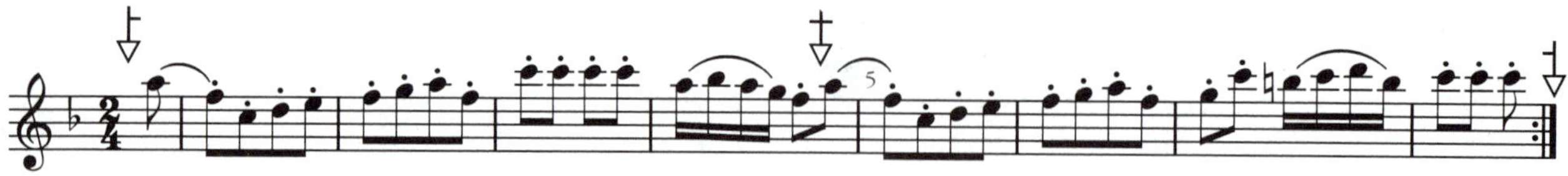

## Interlocking Phrases

**interlocking phrase**

Two phrases are said to be *interlocking* if the last note of the first phrase is also the first note of the following phrase. This occurs when a cadence is so hidden that it can only be heard retrospectively. This is the case in example 3-24a on the first eighth note of measure 4. The evidence that a new phrase has begun may be the appearance of material that is recognized as the beginning of an earlier phrase (see ex. 3-24a), or a substantial change in pattern at a point where a new phrase was expected (see ex. 3-24b). In example 3-24a the reappearance of the opening material is slightly altered by changes in the upbeat notes, but the essential motive is still quite clear.

In identifying interlocking phrases, the arrow is placed directly over the note that is shared by the two phrases. The exact placement of downward arrows is very important. It reflects a careful decision about where the phrase begins and, by implication, which tones belong to each phrase.

**EXAMPLE 3-24.** Interlocking phrases

**a.** Mozart: *Eine kleine Nachtmusik,* K. 525, third movement

**b.** Haydn: Piano Sonata in E minor, Hob. XVI:34, first movement

## Interpretation

Cadence points may be interpreted or delineated through dynamics, rhythmic relationships, or both. A small decrescendo on or during the cadence pitch is often made to emphasize the effect of relaxation at that point. Sometimes the cadence pitch is shortened slightly without altering the pulse. The result is like a singer breathing between phrases. Modifying the tempo at this point by lengthening the last pulse in the phrase is more extreme. Not every cadence needs special treatment or interpretation. The decision of how to handle a particular cadence is complex and should take into account all aspects of the music.

## Tension within the Phrase

The musical experience is a reflection of an emotional experience; common to both is the pattern of the rise and fall of tension. An essential aspect of music's emotional content is tension and relaxation. Within the phrase the main consideration will be the crest of the tension as revealed in rhythm and pitch.

### The Pattern of Tension

Five stages can be identified in a pattern of tension:

1. Starting point, from which tension rises;
2. Period of general increase in tension;
3. Crest, or point of maximum tension;
4. Period of general decline in tension;
5. End point, which also serves as the starting point for the next pattern.

**crest**

These same stages may be observed in the phrase. The beginning of the phrase presents motives and other materials that generate tension. The tension reaches a crest, then declines to the end point following the cadence. The *crest* of a phrase or larger unit is the point at which the tension reaches the maximum level and then begins to release. When a crest occurs on a relatively long note, the tension peaks at the start of the note and releases as the note is sustained. The symbol we will use for the crest of the phrase will be an upward arrow with a slash: ⍏ . Each phrase has only one crest. The upward arrow showing the crest appears between the downward arrows marking the separation between phrases (see ex. 3-25). To determine the crest of a melodic phrase, one must examine both the rhythm and the pitch organization.

**EXAMPLE 3-25.** Symbols showing location of tension in a phrase

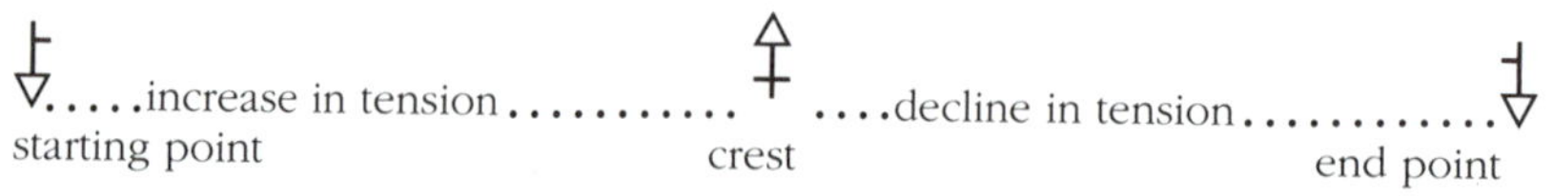

⍖. . . . .increase in tension. . . . . . . . . . . ⍏ . . . .decline in tension. . . . . . . . . . . .⍖
starting point crest end point

### Rhythm and Tension

A rhythmic phrase consists of a number of motives or figures, each of which has an accent, usually agogic. Of the rhythmic accents that appear within a given phrase we want to identify the strongest, as this accent will represent the highest degree of rhythmic tension in the phrase. This will be a point at which a release of tension begins and continues throughout the length of the thesis.

The strength of an agogic accent is determined by three aspects of the agogic pattern: length of the thesis, length of the arsis, and the degree of activity in the arsis. As illustrated in example 3-26, the agogic accent at (2) is stronger than at (1) since the arsis is longer; the one at (3) is stronger than at (2) because the arsis is more active; and the one at (4) is stronger than all the others because both the arsis and thesis are longer.

**EXAMPLE 3-26.** Varying strengths of agogic accents

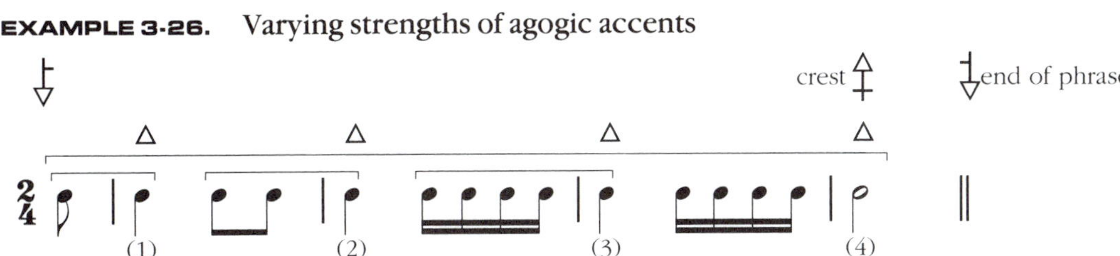


A metric accent that coincides with an agogic accent is far more powerful than an isolated metric accent. In example 3-27 the accent at (1) is considerably weaker than that at (2), where the metric accent is reinforced by an agogic accent. The agogic accent at (3) occurs on a metrically weak beat. The conflict between the accent and the metric scheme creates tension that continues until the next point where the agogic and metric accents coincide, (4). The strongest accent occurs at (4) as a result of the longer thesis, longer arsis, the reinforcement of the metric accent, and the tension created by the metric-agogic conflict in the previous measure.

**EXAMPLE 3-27.** Metric and agogic accents

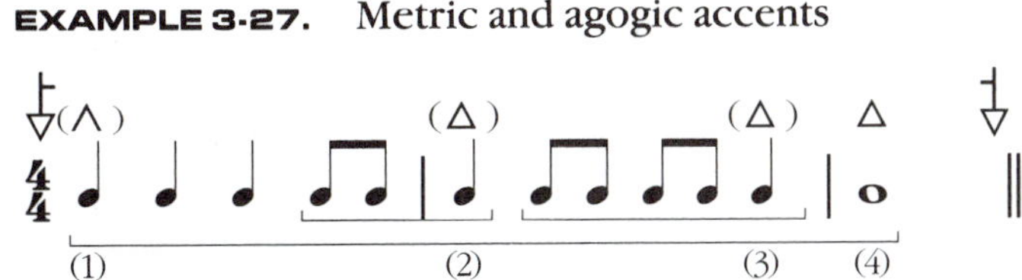


Because tension increases when change occurs, motivic changes between successive agogic patterns generate increases in tension. The last pattern exhibiting motivic difference is usually the strongest. When the accent patterns themselves are about equal, motivic change becomes the most powerful force in developing tension. In example 3-28, these letters indicate the motivic changes: a b b′ c. The differences in these motives build tension culminating on the strongest agogic accent, which occurs in motive c.

**EXAMPLE 3-28.** Mozart: String Quartet, K. 171, third movement

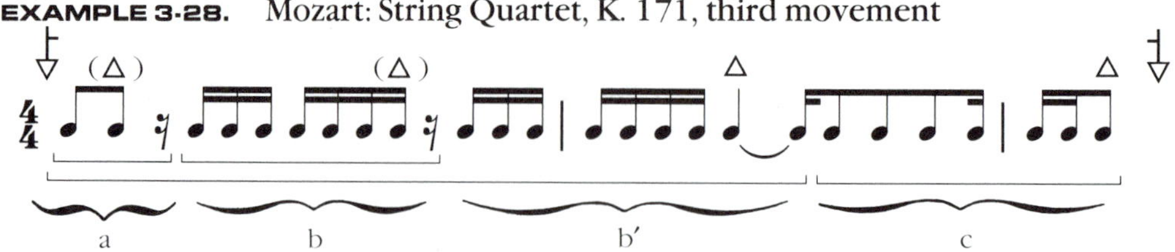


In measure 3 of example 3-29, a new motive brings activity in the arsis. The last motive, in measure 4, has more activity in the arsis and its thesis falls on the beat, but the arsis is rather short. The case is about equal for the strongest accent to be at x or y. Since y presents the last new pattern, it is given priority. As a general principle one should expect tension (and interest) to be sustained until the latest possible point in the phrase.

**EXAMPLE 3-29.** Motivic changes and accent strength

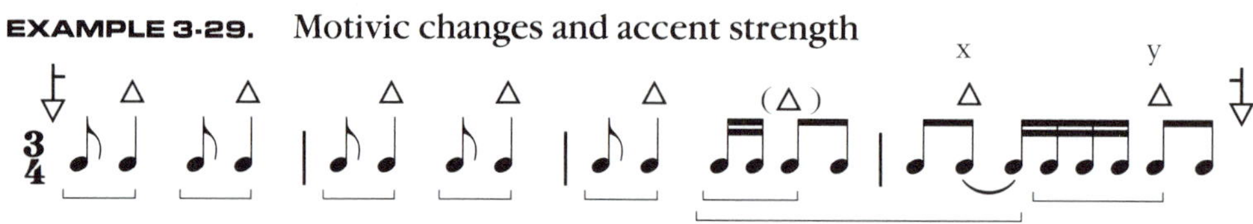


## Pitch and Tension

Rhythm will continue to be the first consideration in determining tension patterns, but pitch, through emergent tones and motives, will influence melodic tension over longer periods.

When an emergent tone occurs on a pitch that has not been emergent earlier in the phrase, the newness adds prominence to the emergent tone. Like other events, new emergent tones that occur later in the phrase often have greater importance and shift our focus toward the cadence.

In example 3-30a, the $g^2$ is accorded extra weight because it appears as an emergent tone for the first time. In example 3-30b, a step progression enhances the increase of tension until the last tone.

We have seen that motivic differences will heighten tension. Reappearing motives reduce tension. In example 3-31 we find a rhythmic motive that repeats, but the second appearance brings a new pitch pattern, thereby increasing tension. In example 3-32 we find a phrase that introduces a new rhythmic motive in measures 3–4 (motive b) and a new emergent tone in measure 4 ($f^1$). While the overall impact of measure 3 is to heighten tension, the new emergent tone at the cadence in measure 4 raises tension even further.

**EXAMPLE 3-30.** Emergent tones and tension

**a.** Beethoven: Piano Sonata, op. 13, third movement

**b.** Mozart: Serenade in D, K. 239, second movement

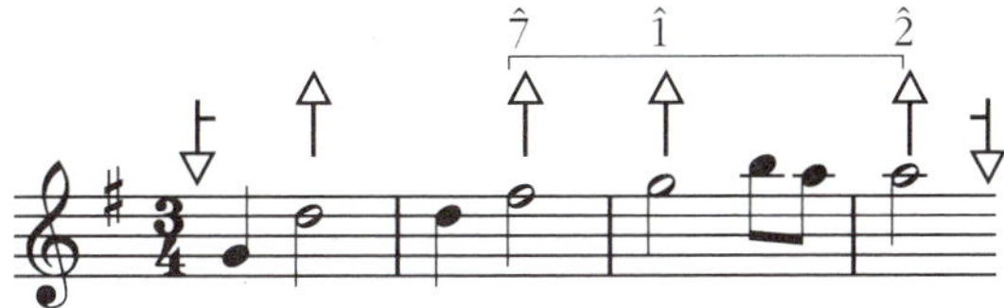


**EXAMPLE 3-31.** Mozart: *The Abduction from the Seraglio,* K. 384

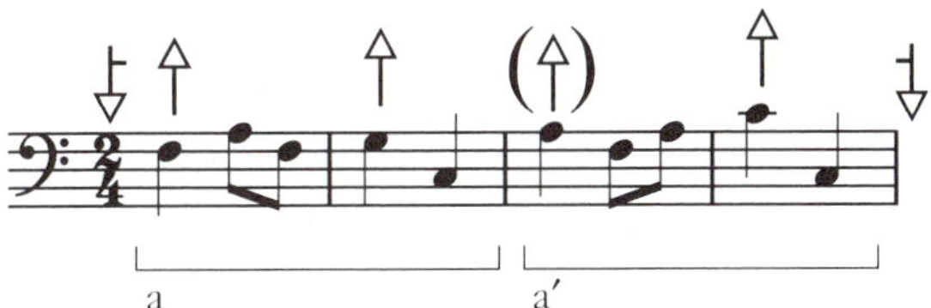


**EXAMPLE 3-32.** Schubert: Entr'acte from *Rosamunde,* D. 797

The issue is not only whether these later motives are inherently more tense than the earlier motives; the change itself produces the tension. The changes may be relatively simple modifications or entirely new material.

## The Crest of the Phrase

In determining the location of a crest or peak of tension within a phrase, rhythm should be considered first and pitch second. The strongest rhythmic accent should be determined, and then emergent tones and motives identified and their relative tension evaluated. In most cases the rhythmic and pitch factors will clearly agree on where the crest of the phrase occurs. In some cases, however, there is more than one alternative for the crest. This would typically occur if there is contradictory evidence or if no one possibility seems stronger than the others. Other things being equal, the last appearance of new or modified pitch or rhythmic material is considered the most emergent.

In example 3-33, the crest is located on the cadence pitch ($b^1$); it bears the strongest agogic accent. The $c^2$ in measure 3 forms a step progression with this tone.

**EXAMPLE 3-33.** Mendelssohn: Violin Concerto, op. 64, first movement

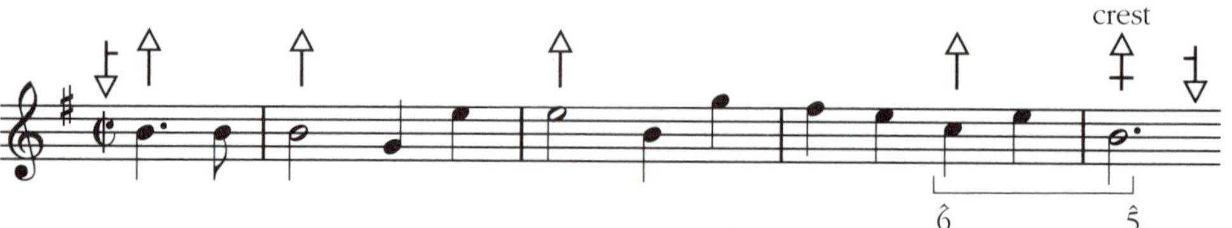


The crest in example 3-34 appears in measure 3, where a new emergent tone arrives simultaneously with a new motive. The final A, despite its prominent location and strong agogic accent, has been heard several times already.

**EXAMPLE 3-34.** Schubert: Piano Quintet, "The Trout," D. 667, fourth movement

The step progression in example 3-35 leads to $\hat{7}$, a new emergent tone. Although the melody descends in the last two measures, the step progression seems to complete its ascent, the anticipated tone being displaced to the octave below.

**EXAMPLE 3-35.** Handel: Sonata in B-flat, for flute and continuo, HHA iv/18, 15, second movement

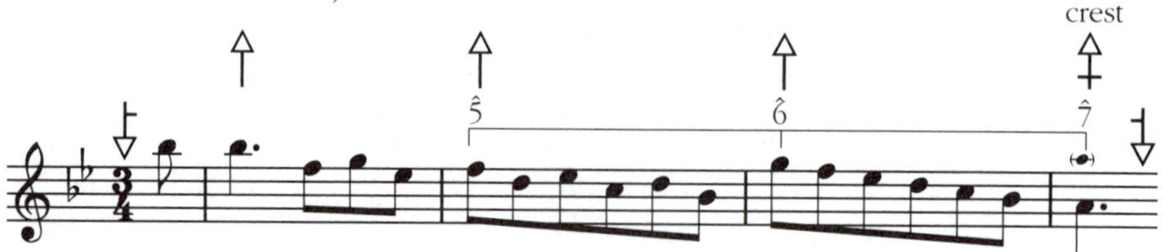

As the more subjective aspects of melody are dealt with, it is inevitable that differences of opinion will arise. The goal is to enable each individual to arrive at a solution best suited to his or her perception of the music.

In some styles of early music the rise and fall of tension may be deliberately dispersed so that no clear crests occur. The above procedure for locating the crest of the phrase will, however, apply to most music now commonly performed.

## SUMMARY

Musical tones and rests tend to come together to form small groups known as motives. Motives may recur quite often in a melody and become a force for coherence. Opposing coherence, however, is the need for differentiation, which helps to provide an aesthetic balance between unity and variety.

The procedure for the motivic analysis of melody consists of: (1) identifying new and recurring motive patterns (rhythmically these are often agogic patterns) and (2) labeling the motives with appropriate letters.

The several concepts are brought together and summarized under the heading of form. This term includes the idea of coherence, by which musical events are grouped, and the idea of differentiation, by which various kinds of distinctions between the grouped events create tension. More narrowly, the term *form* includes motives within phrases, phrases themselves, and the main features of tension that result from differentiation (tension crests). A formal analysis aims at identifying the motives, structure, and tension of the music.

## CHAPTER FOUR

# Chords

**Terms Introduced in This Chapter**

- monophonic
- homophonic
- polyphonic
- chord
- consonance
- dissonance
- triad
- root
- third
- fifth
- triad members
- bass
- root position
- first inversion
- second inversion
- triad types
- major triad
- minor triad
- diminished triad
- augmented triad
- letter names
- Roman numerals
- seventh chord
- seventh chord members
- third inversion

**monophonic**

**homophonic**

**polyphonic**

Our exclusive concern to this point has been with melody and rhythm. We have dealt only with examples consisting of a single line and without accompaniment. Such music is called *monophonic.* Much more familiar to the average listener is music composed of a main melody (salient line) accompanied by chords or other less prominent melodic material (recessive lines). Music that consists of one salient line accompanied by one or more recessive lines is called *homophonic.* Music that involves two or more salient lines (with or without other recessive lines) is called *polyphonic.*

A basic problem in both homophonic and polyphonic music is the coordination of different melodic lines. How can different melodies be brought together without clashing and producing unpleasant discord? The answer is harmony, a musical concept of the highest importance in Western traditional music.

## CHORDS

**chord**

**consonance**

**dissonance**

The basic unit of harmony is the *chord,* the simultaneous sounding of three or more different pitches. To study chords in depth it is necessary to consider harmonic intervals. Music theorists have divided harmonic intervals into two groups: consonance and dissonance. *Consonance* includes sounds that are relatively stable in comparison with the more complex and intense sounds of *dissonance.* Dissonance usually implies tension and instability; consonance implies stability and the release of tension.

Consonant chords contain major thirds, minor thirds, and perfect fifths or inversions of these intervals (minor sixths, major sixths, and perfect fourths). Chords are said to be dissonant if they contain any dissonant intervals, that is, sevenths, seconds, or tritones.

## TRIADS

**triad**

**root**

**third**

**fifth**

**triad members**

Of the many possible chords, one particular configuration has been especially favored over the centuries: the *triad.* In its simplest and most commonly used form, the triad consists of three tones, a root tone plus the third and fifth above it. In the position seen in example 4-1, the lowest tone is called the *root* of the triad, the middle tone, because it is a third above the root, is called the *third* of the triad, and the highest note is called the *fifth* of the triad. These names of the *triad members* are retained regardless of the voicing (placement) or doubling (reinforcement) of tones. Example 4-2 identifies the triad members in some sample situations.

**EXAMPLE 4-1.** Root, third, and fifth of a triad

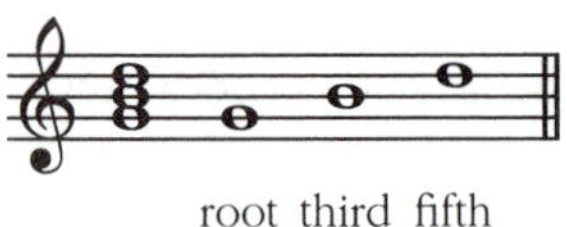


**EXAMPLE 4-2.** Triad members

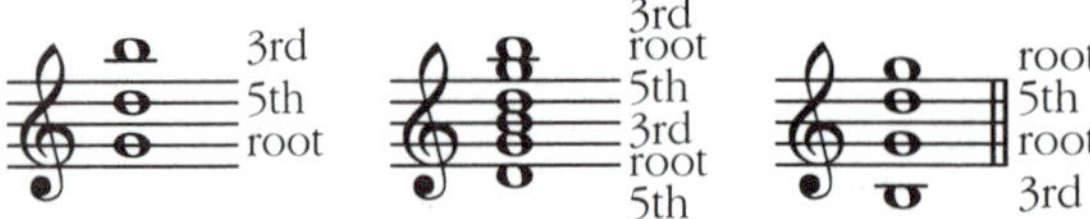


**bass**

Do not confuse the terms *root* and *bass.* The bass is the lowest sounding part; the root is the tone on which the chord is built. In example 4-2, G is the root in every chord, but the bass changes.

**root position**

**first inversion**

**second inversion**

Triads with the root in the bass are said to be in *root position.* When the third or fifth is the lowest voice, the triad is said to be inverted: If the third is in the bass, the triad is in *first inversion;* if the fifth is in the bass, the triad is in *second inversion.* These are illustrated in example 4-3.

**EXAMPLE 4-3.** Triads in root position, first and second inversions

## Types of Triads

**triad types**

**major triad**

**minor triad**

**diminished triad**

**augmented triad**

There are four *triad types.* Each type is defined by the component intervals when the triad is in root position: the interval from the root to the third and the interval from the root to the fifth. The *major triad* has a major third and a perfect fifth, the *minor triad* a minor third and a perfect fifth, the *diminished triad* a minor third and a diminished fifth, and the *augmented triad* a minor third and an augmented fifth. Example 4-4 illustrates the four types. Note the abbreviations (M, m, d, A) used to identify the types of triads.

**EXAMPLE 4-4.** The four triad types

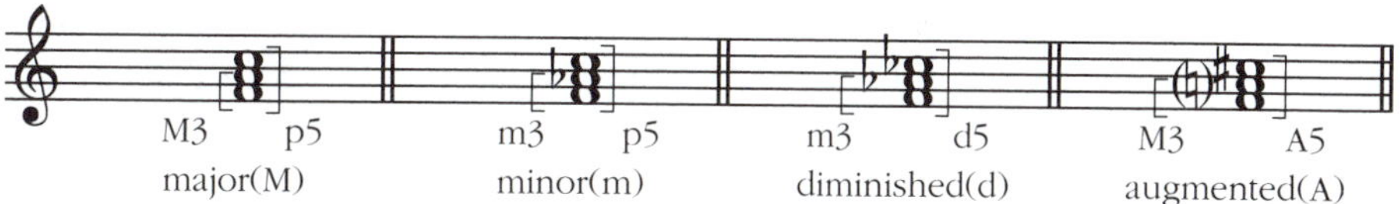


## Identifying Chords by Letter Name

**letter names**

One of the most convenient ways of identifying chords is with a system of *letter names.* If the triad is major, it is simply named after the root pitch, for example, a "C-major chord" (abbreviated C). If the triad is minor, the term "minor" is inserted, for example, a "C-minor chord" (abbreviated Cm or Cmin). Similarly, the terms *augmented* and *diminished* are inserted to identify those triads (abbreviated Caug or C⁺ and Cdim or C°). Example 4-5 illustrates each of these chords.

**EXAMPLE 4-5.** Major, minor, diminished, and augmented chords

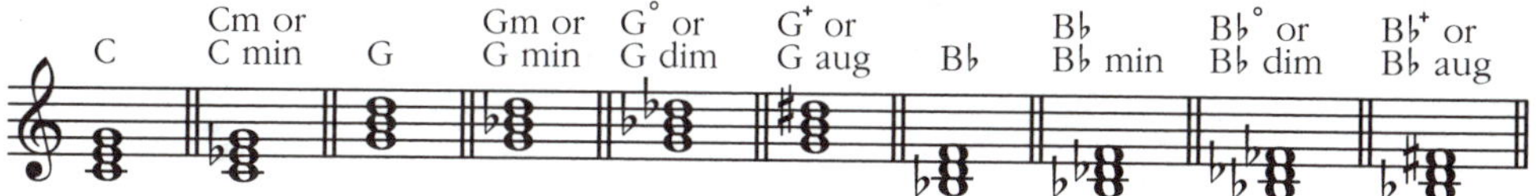


## Triads in Major Keys

A triad may be built on each tone of a major scale and using the tones of that scale only; these are known as diatonic triads. As shown in example 4-6, these triads vary in quality or chord type (M, m, d) depending on the location of the whole and half steps.

**EXAMPLE 4-6.** Triads on each tone of a major scale

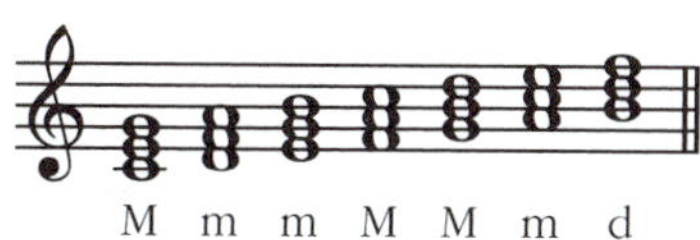


**Roman numerals**

*Roman numerals* are used to identify the scale degree on which the triad is built, as shown in example 4-7. Capital (upper case) Roman numerals indicate a major triad, while lower case numerals indicate minor triads. A small circle to the upper right of a lower case numeral indicates a diminished triad (vii°); a small + to the upper right indicates an augmented triad (III$^{+}$).

Roman numerals can be used to identify a chord only if the key is known. Keys are indicated by a letter followed by a colon. The key is given once before the first Roman numeral in the key, with upper case letters denoting major keys (C:) and lower case letters denoting minor keys (c:).

**EXAMPLE 4-7.** Roman numerals used to identify chords

In addition to the Roman numerals, each chord may be identified by the name of the scale degree on which it is built. The first scale degree is called the tonic, and the triad built on the first degree is called the *tonic triad;* the triad built on the second degree is called the *supertonic triad,* and other chords follow in the same manner.

Notice the distribution of the various chord types within a major key:

| | | | |
|---|---|---|---|
| Major triads: | I | IV | V |
| Minor triads: | ii | iii | vi |
| Diminished triads: | vii° | | |

A particular chord type may appear in different keys on different scales degrees. For example, a C-major triad may be C: I, F: V, or G: IV, as shown in example 4-8.

**EXAMPLE 4-8.** C major triad in different keys

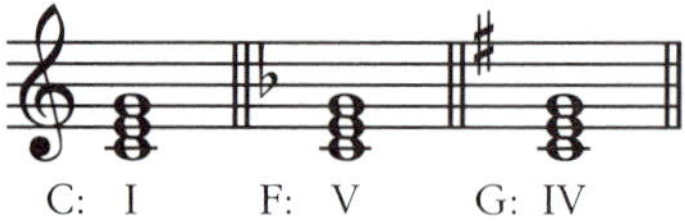


## Triads in Minor Keys

The traditional treatment of chords in minor keys uses the lowered $\hat{6}$ and both the lowered $\hat{7}$ and the raised $\hat{7}$. It is normal to use the raised $\hat{7}$, the leading tone, for V (a major triad) and vii° (a diminished triad). The triad on the third degree often uses the lowered $\hat{7}$, the subtonic, for III (a major triad). One occasionally finds v (a minor triad) and VII (a major triad), which use the lowered $\hat{7}$. It is impossible to make firm rules about which of the variants are used in chord building, but the most commonly used set of chords in a minor key is shown in example 4-9.

**EXAMPLE 4-9.** Most common minor key chords

The distribution of chord types in minor keys is very different from that in major keys:

| | | | |
|---|---|---|---|
| Minor triads: | i | iv | |
| Major triads: | III | V | VI |
| Diminished triads: | ii° | vii° | |

Comparing the triads types in major and minor, we find that only the V and vii° are the same:

| | | | | | | | |
|---|---|---|---|---|---|---|---|
| Major: | I | ii | iii | IV | V | vi | vii° |
| Minor: | i | ii° | III | iv | V | VI | vii° |

## SEVENTH CHORDS

**seventh chord**

By adding a tone lying a seventh above the root to a triad, a *seventh chord* is produced. Seventh chords are found in a wide variety of types and are used in both major and minor keys.

### The Structure of Seventh Chords

**seventh chord members**

There are three different ways to consider the structure of a seventh chord. First, the chord may be considered in terms of *chord members,* in a manner similar to that for triads: root, third, fifth, and seventh (see ex. 4-10a). Second, the chord may be considered a triad plus a seventh above the root of the triad, an approach that will be useful when specifying the exact quality of different types of seventh chords and the preferred way for building the chord (see ex. 4-10b) Third, the chord may be viewed as a "stack" of thirds, an approach that is most useful when a broad overview of traditional chords is desired and specific details need not be addressed.

**EXAMPLE 4-10.** The structure of a seventh chord

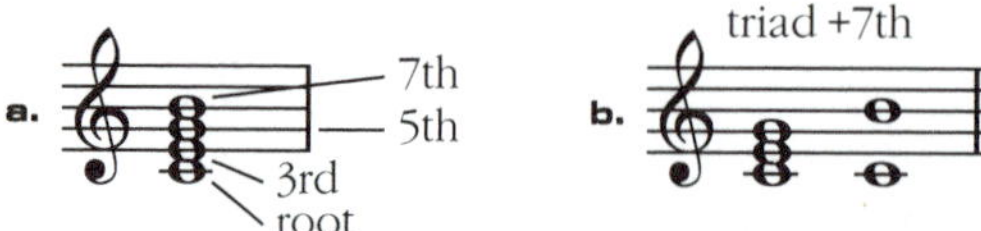


**third inversion**

Seventh chords, like triads, may be inverted by placing different chord members in the lowest voice. Because there are four component tones, there are three possible inversions, including *third inversion,* as illustrated in example 4-11.

**EXAMPLE 4-11.** Inversions of a seventh chord

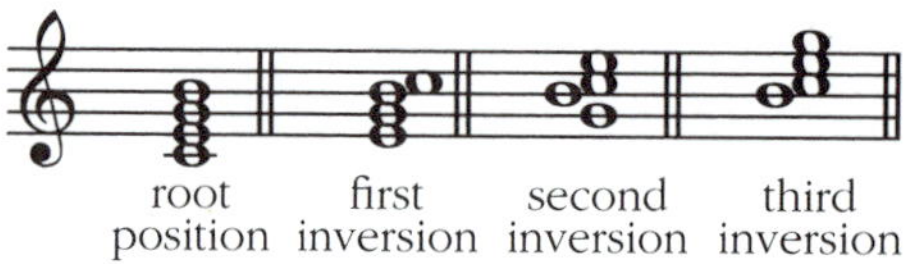


## Types of Seventh Chords

Of the wide variety of possible seventh chords, a limited number have been commonly used and given special names, but a descriptive system is available to describe the less common ones as well. The system for describing the specific structure of different types of seventh chords consists of two letters followed by the number 7. The first letter indicates the type of triad formed by the root, third, and fifth of the chord (either M, m, d, or A) and the second letter indicates the type of seventh as an interval (either M, m, d, or A). The most commonly used types are shown in example 4-12. These may be verbalized respectively as "major-minor seventh," "minor-minor seventh," "major-major seventh," "diminished-minor seventh," and "diminished-diminished seventh."

**EXAMPLE 4-12.** The most common seventh chord types

## Letter Names for Seventh Chords

Letter names may also be given to seventh chords, even though there is no widespread acceptance of a system of letter names for every type of seventh chord. Some of the more common ones are shown in example 4-13. With these symbols, the letter showing the root is followed only by the 7 to designate the Mm7. Therefore, E7 means Mm7 with an E root, Em7 means mm7 on E, Emaj7 means MM7 on E, and Edim7 means dd7 on E.

**EXAMPLE 4-13.** Letter names for seventh chords

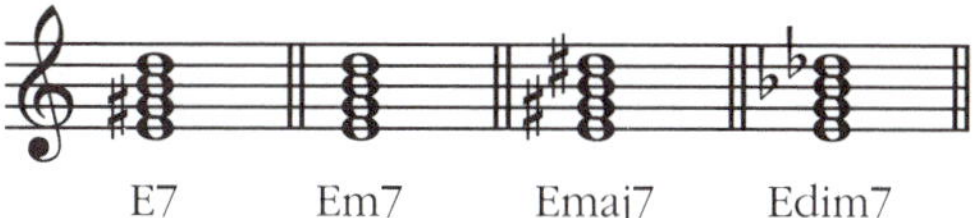


## Other Names for Seventh Chords

Other names are used for some seventh chords; however, such names are not available for all types of seventh chords. An MM7 may be called a "major seventh chord," an mm7 a "minor seventh chord," a dm7 a "half-diminished seventh chord," and a dd7 a "fully diminished seventh chord" or just a "diminished seventh."

## Seventh Chords in Major Keys

Just as Roman numerals are used to identify the scale degree on which a triad is based, a Roman numeral with a 7 added to the right indicates a seventh chord built on that degree. The Roman numeral itself reflects the chord type of the triad of the seventh chord (root, third, and fifth) but the 7 does not reflect the type of seventh that is used. The type of seventh implied depends on the scale degree upon which is is based. Therefore, it is necessary to know the kinds of sevenths that the scale will provide for each seventh chord; for example, a IV7 has a major seventh while a V7 has a minor seventh. In three cases the chord symbol implies a specific type of seventh chord: If the Roman numeral is lower case and appears with a 7, then a mm7 is implied; a lower case Roman numeral with a small circle and a 7 implies a dd7 chord; and a lower case Roman numeral with small circle cut with a diagonal slash and followed by a 7 represents a dm7. Example 4-14 presents all the diatonic seventh chords in a major key. Table 4-1 lists the Roman numerals for diatonic seventh chords together with descriptions of the chord types.

**EXAMPLE 4-14.** Diatonic seventh chords in D major

| Roman numeral | Chord type description |
|---|---|
| I7 | MM7 |
| ii7 | mm7 |
| iii7 | mm7 |
| IV7 | MM7 |
| V7 | Mm7 |
| vi7 | mm7 |
| vii°7 | dm7 |

**TABLE 4-1.** Diatonic seventh chords in major keys

## Seventh Chords in Minor Keys

The seventh chords in a minor key, like the triads, reflect the use of both the lowered and raised variants of $\hat{7}$. Example 4-15 shows the seventh chords in a minor key, with parentheses around the less frequently used chords, that is, those that use the lowered $\hat{7}$. Table 4-2 lists the Roman numerals for seventh chords in a minor key together with descriptions of the chord types.

**EXAMPLE 4-15.** Diatonic seventh chords in D minor

| Roman numeral | Chord type description |
|---|---|
| i7 | mm7 |
| ii°7 | dm7 |
| III7 | MM7 |
| iv7 | mm7 |
| V7 | Mm7 |
| v7 | mm7 |
| VI7 | MM7 |
| vii°7 | dd7 |
| VII7 | Mm7 |

**TABLE 4-2.** Diatonic seventh chords in minor keys

## SUMMARY

The two most commonly used types of chords available in the system of major and minor keys are triads and seventh chords. Chords may be classified into various types depending on the intervals formed by the chord members. Chords are said to be in root position or inverted depending on the bass note. Letter names are used to identify particular chords, while Roman numerals describe the type of chord and its relation to the scale in which it appears. A descriptive system using two letters is used to identify specific types of seventh chords.

CHAPTER FIVE

# Chord Progressions

**Terms Introduced in This Chapter**

chord progression

normal progression

chord group

alternate progression

irregular progression

functional harmony

harmonic cycle

authentic cadence

plagal cadence

half cadence

deceptive cadence

**chord progression**

A succession of two or more different chords is called a *chord progression.* The melody will influence the choice of chord at any particular moment. Melodic patterns that work especially well become clichés, as do the series of chords that accompany them. Throughout the period 1700 to approximately 1900, the preferences of composers for using certain chord progressions became so pronounced that a chart may be drawn showing the normal treatment of chord progressions.

## THE NORMAL PROGRESSION

**normal progression**

**chord group**

Works with clear tonality often begin with a tonic chord, after which other chords appear, progressing in a systematic order toward a return to the tonic chord. This systematic order of chords in tonal music is termed the *normal progression.* This is summarized in table 5-1, in which chords normally progress in a cyclic manner. The normal progression begins with the tonic chord on the right side of the chart (chord group 1), after which the harmony proceeds to any other chord group. Thereafter, the progression moves one chord group at a time from left to right until chord group 1 is reached, whereupon the process begins again.

**In major keys**

| | group 5 | group 4 | group 3 | group 2 | group 1 |
|---|---|---|---|---|---|
| | iii | vi | ii | V | I |
| | | | IV | vii° | |

**In minor keys**

| group 6 | group 5 | group 4 | group 3 | group 2 | group 1 |
|---|---|---|---|---|---|
| VII | III | VI | ii° | V | i |
| | v | | iv | vii° | |

**TABLE 5-1.** The normal progression of chords

Example 5-1 illustrates normal progressions using all chord groups in a major key (examples 5-1a and b) and a minor key (examples 5-1c and d). Diminished triads in first inversion (the most common treatment for these chords) are shown in examples 5-1b, 5-1c, and 5-1d. Diminished triads will be discussed in more detail in chapter 9.

Chord groups 3 and 2 contain two chords each. When the progression arrives at group 3, either the ii or IV chord may be used, and thereafter the progression moves to group 2. A similar choice is available when the progression arrives at chord group 2: Either the V or vii° may be used. Example 5-2a–h shows these options.

**EXAMPLE 5-1.** Normal chord progressions using all chord groups

**a.** Major key

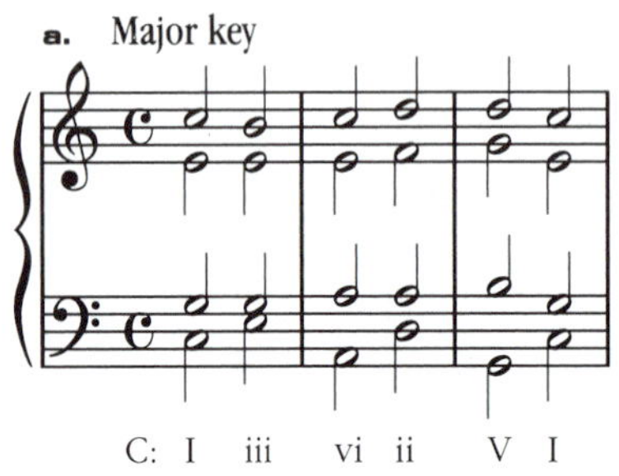


**b.** Major key

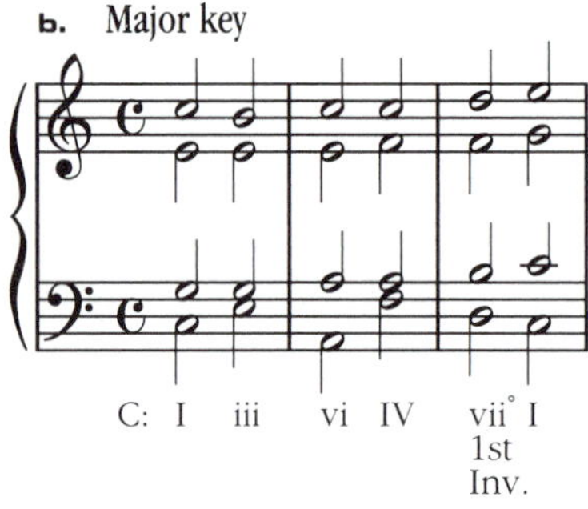


**c.** Minor key

**d.** Minor key

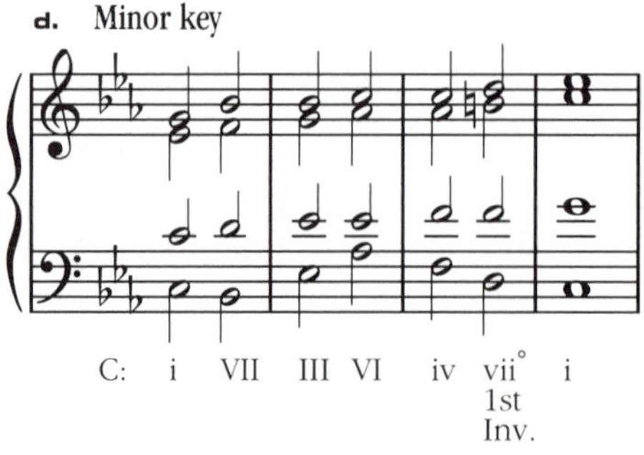

**EXAMPLE 5-2.** Chord progressions using groups 3 and 2

The normal progression includes the possibility of moving between the two chords of a single chord group. The two chords in chord group 3 may be used in succession, in which case IV, the lower option in the chart, normally appears before the ii. Similarly, when the chords in chord group 2 are used in succession, the vii° usually precedes the V. These possibilities are shown in example 5-3a–d. Note that the relationship of a fifth is found between the roots of the chords in each horizontal line of table 5-1: iii vi ii V I (or VII III VI ii° V i) and between IV and vii° (or iv and vii°).

**EXAMPLE 5-3.** Chord progressions using more than one chord from a group

In minor keys the use of the lowered $\hat{7}$ (subtonic), gives rise to some chords that require special notice.

In chord group 5, the III chord uses the lowered $\hat{7}$. In normal usage the raised $\hat{7}$ is used with chord group 2, where there is a strong expectation that the tonic (group 1) will follow. As III does not normally progress to the tonic, the lowered $\hat{7}$ is used.

In chord group 5, the v chord uses the lowered $\hat{7}$. The minor dominant chord that results from using the lowered $\hat{7}$ is also rather remote from the tonic. In comparison to the forceful V of group 2, in which the raised $\hat{7}$ points decisively to group 1, the minor v, with the lowered $\hat{7}$, is rather indecisive and weakens the tonality.

In chord group 6, the VII chord uses the lowered $\hat{7}$. The subtonic chord is very remote from the tonic, requiring the creation of an additional chord group. VII is a major chord that progresses very nicely to III. Because VII–III–VI consists entirely of major triads, this progression may temporarily give the impression of being in the key of the relative major. The appearance of the raised $\hat{7}$ (leading tone) in V (group 2) is necessary to refocus the orientation to A minor rather than C major. In example 5-4, compare the analysis of VII–III–VI in the key of A minor with the same chords analyzed in the key of C major.

**EXAMPLE 5-4.** A progression with the tonic chord

As we continue our studies in harmony, we will be adding many variations to the chart of normal progressions, but we point out in advance that the addition of a seventh does not alter the position of a chord within the chart; that is, V7 and vii°7 or viiø7 are in group 2, along with V and vii°.

## ALTERNATE PROGRESSIONS

**alternate progression**

It is important to emphasize that table 5-1 reflects the "normal," most commonly used progressions. Of course, any chord may be used at any time, but within the tradition with which we are presently concerned, these progressions are indeed normal and are encountered far more frequently than any exceptions. There are, however, a few other progressions that occur with considerable frequency (see table 5-2). Though they do not exhibit the normal motion from group to group, they occur often enough that they cannot be considered exceptional. These *alternate progressions* typically appear with normal progressions, as shown in example 5-5a–d. Table 5-3 is a version of table 5-1 incorporating alternate progressions. It may be easier to remember the alternate progressions this way.

| Major keys | | Minor keys | |
|---|---|---|---|
| IV | I | iv | i |
| vi | V | VI | V |
| V | vi | V | VI |
| iii | IV | III | iv |

**TABLE 5-2.** Frequently encountered alternate progressions

**EXAMPLE 5-5.** Alternate progressions used with normal progressions

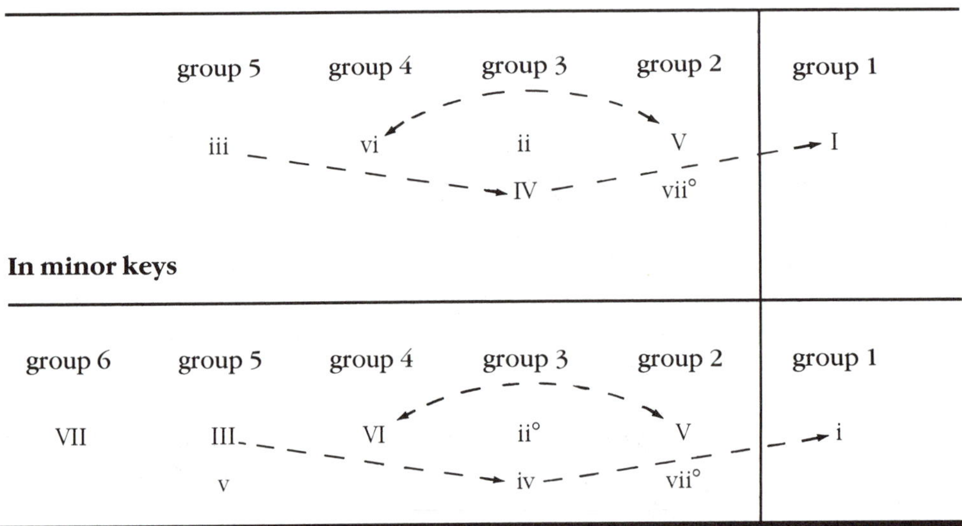


**TABLE 5-3.** The normal and alternate progressions of chords

It is advisable to memorize the chart of normal progressions as well as the list of alternate progressions. Both will be useful tools for analysis, composing, arranging, or other musical efforts.

**irregular progression**

**functional harmony**

The concept of normalcy of progression is based on the clear preference of composers for these successions of chords. This does not mean that all chords always progress normally. A progression that does not follow the normal or alternate patterns is called an *irregular progression.* Such progressions are not to be viewed as wrong but merely unusual or irregular. When composers choose chord progressions that operate according to the patterns defined as normal, they are using *functional harmony.* In functional harmony an irregular progression may occur, but infrequently and singly, not several in succession. Music that contains many irregular progressions is said to contain "nonfunctional" harmony. Our concern for the present is with functional harmony; nonfunctional harmony can be found in many pieces written before 1600 and after 1900, but these dates are only approximate, and instances of nonfunctional harmony can be found between these dates as well.

## HARMONIC CYCLES

**harmonic cycle**

Harmonic progressions in tonal music are organized in cycles: A *harmonic cycle* is a series of chords beginning with a tonic chord, moving to one or more other chords, and ending with the next appearance of the tonic chord. The chords between tonics may or may not be normal progressions. The succeeding cycle begins with the last tonic chord of the preceding cycle so that, as the music unfolds, the harmony becomes a series of cycles beginning and ending with the tonic chord. In example 5-6, the brackets in the chord progression mark off four harmonic cycles. Notice that these cycles vary in size. The first two use chord groups 1 to 4 in the normal progression, while the last two use only groups 1 and 2.

**EXAMPLE 5-6.** Harmonic cycles

Because shorter cycles are more common than long ones, and because the chords in the lower-numbered chord groups play a more direct role in establishing and confirming the tonality, the lower-numbered groups are used more frequently than the higher-numbered groups.

## HARMONIC CADENCES

Cadences are as important in harmony as they are in melody. As with melodic cadences, harmonic cadences are of two types: conclusive and inconclusive. Harmonic cadences are codified into types based on the treatment of harmony at the end of the phrase. A conclusive cadence ends on I; inconclusive cadences do not. To identify more specific types of harmonic cadences, we need additional criteria.

**authentic cadence**

**plagal cadence**

Conclusive cadences may be either authentic or plagal. *Authentic cadences* end with a tonic chord preceded by a chord in group 2. Cadences ending with a tonic chord preceded by a IV chord are called *plagal cadences.* These cadences are illustrated in example 5-7a–f with a few preparatory chords included in each case. The abbreviation AC refers to authentic cadence and PC to plagal cadence.

**EXAMPLE 5-7.** Conclusive harmonic cadences

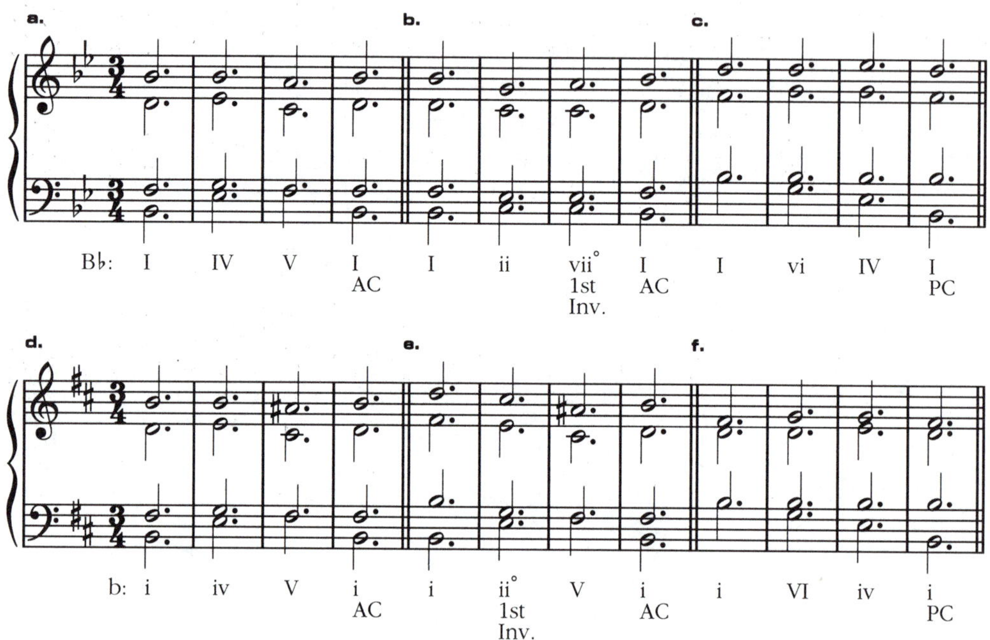


**half cadence**

**deceptive cadence**

There are two types of inconclusive cadences: half cadences and deceptive cadences. A *half cadence* ends the phrase with a chord in group 2 (V or vii°), but there are no restrictions on the preceding chord, although it is usually a chord in group 1 or 3. A *deceptive cadence* ends the phrase with a vi (VI in minor keys) preceded by V or V7. Inconclusive harmonic cadences are illustrated in example 5-8a–f, with the abbreviation HC referring to half cadence and DC to deceptive cadence.

**EXAMPLE 5-8.** Inconclusive harmonic cadences

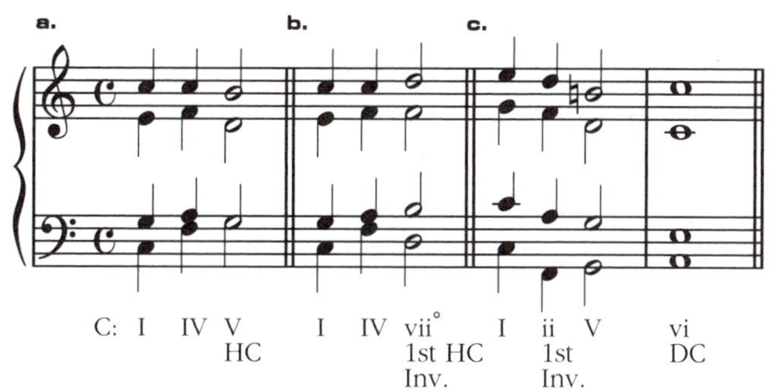


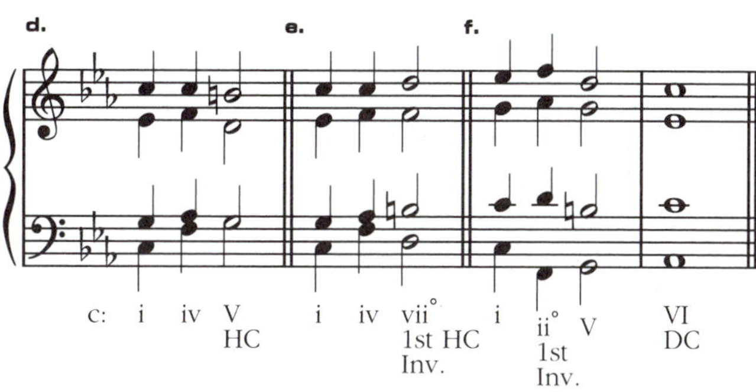


Table 5-4 illustrates these cadences in major and minor keys. The same names are used in minor keys, with necessary changes in the Roman numerals to indicate the different qualities of the chords.

| **Conclusive cadences** | **Major keys** | | **Minor keys** | |
|---|---|---|---|---|
| authentic cadences | V(7) | I | V(7) | i |
| | vii° | I | vii° | i |
| plagal cadence | IV | I | iv | i |
| **Inconclusive cadences** | **Major keys** | | **Minor Keys** | |
| half cadences | | V(7) | | V(7) |
| | | vii° | | vii° |
| deceptive cadence | V(7) | vi | V(7) | VI |

**TABLE 5-4.** Cadences in major and minor keys

A conclusive cadence occurs when a harmonic cycle ends at the close of a phrase; a cycle ending in the middle of a phrase is not a cadence. In example 5-9, a phrase is shown with two harmonic cycles, only the last of which is cadential. The cadence is authentic.

**EXAMPLE 5-9.** Phrase with two harmonic cycles

## SUMMARY

Successions of different chords are called chord progressions. The normal progressions are those that are most frequently used, while the short list of the most common departures from the normal are called alternate progressions. The relatively rare progressions that are neither normal nor alternate are called irregular. Functional harmony uses normal and alternate progressions and nonfunctional harmony uses irregular progressions.

Harmonic cadences are determined by the chords at the end of the phrase. Conclusive cadences end on I and are either authentic, ending with V–I or vii°–I (V–i or vii°–i in minor keys), or plagal, ending with IV–I (iv–i in minor keys). Inconclusive cadences end on a V or vii° and are called half cadences, or V–vi (V–VI in minor keys) and are called deceptive cadences.

CHAPTER SIX

# Chords in Four Voices

**Terms Introduced in This Chapter**

- mixed choir
- soprano
- alto
- tenor
- bass
- SATB
- voicing
- voice range
- crossed voices
- spacing
- close position
- open position
- doubling
- incomplete chord
- soprano position

ecause the customary approach to teaching harmony uses the choral medium, it is necessary to begin by exploring the four-voice choral setting and the application of its features to individual chords.

## THE FOUR-VOICE CHORAL SETTING

**mixed choir**
**soprano**
**alto**
**tenor**
**bass**
**SATB**
**voicing**

The traditional medium for learning harmony is the *mixed choir,* that is, a choir consisting of two women's parts (high: *soprano;* and low: *alto*) and two men's parts (high: *tenor;* and low: *bass*), abbreviated *SATB.* Choral settings in four voices must take into account vocal ranges, notation, and *voicing,* that is the distribution of the tones of a chord above the bass.

### Ranges

**voice range**

**crossed voices**

Example 6-1 shows the ranges of the four voices. Whole notes indicate the normal *voice ranges,* while the black notes show notes that should be used sparingly. Notes at the extremes of the range are difficult for the untrained singer. The highest notes may be strained or shrill, and they may be difficult to sing softly. The lowest notes may be weak and lack definition. In writing exercises, use the middle range of each voice most of the time. Four-part harmony usually does not specify whether the writing is for a large or small choir; the only requirement is that the four parts are balanced. Generally, all voices are kept in the same tessitura, that is, if the soprano is high, the other voices will likely also be high. Normal voice ranges are also maintained, except in rare cases of *crossed voices,* where a lower voice sings above a higher voice.

**EXAMPLE 6-1.** Ranges of the four voices

### Notation

For harmony examples and exercises, the two-stave arrangement shown in example 6-2a is commonly used. Notice that the soprano and alto are written in treble clef, while the tenor and bass are written in bass clef. Soprano and tenor note stems always go up, and alto and bass stems always go down. Example 6-2b shows an alternative notation occasionally used to facilitate keyboard performance: the upper three voices are written in treble clef, leaving only the bass in bass clef. Stemming rules as explained in chapter 1 apply.

**EXAMPLE 6-2.** Notation of four-part harmony

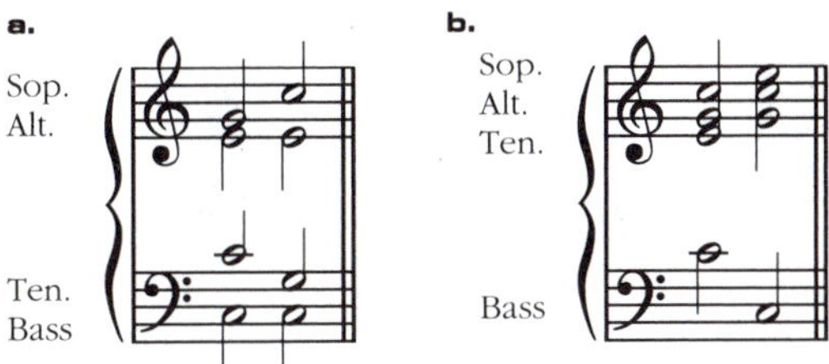


## Spacing

**spacing**

One principle in the distribution of the tones of a chord that has been quite regularly observed by all composers is that of *spacing,* the distance between the parts. There should not be a distance of more than one octave at any given moment between soprano and alto and between alto and tenor. As seen in example 6-3a–b, any distance between the bass and tenor is permissible.

**EXAMPLE 6-3.** Acceptable and unacceptable spacing of voices

a. Acceptable

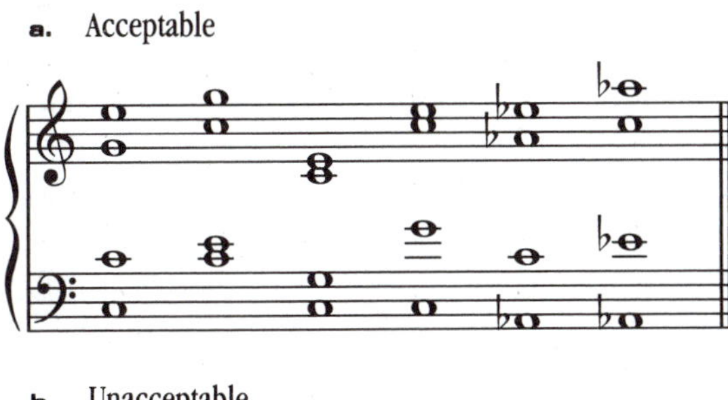

b. Unacceptable

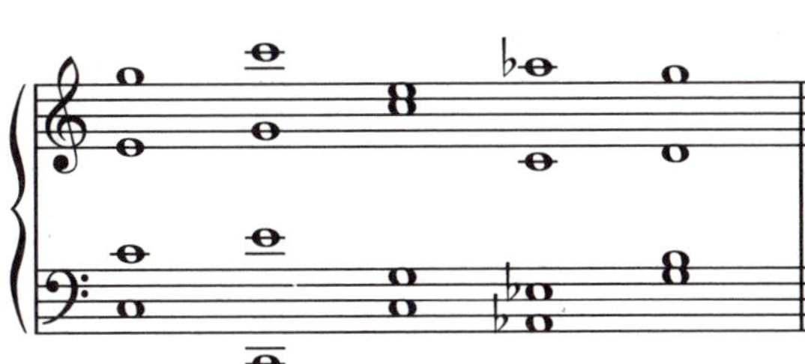

## Open and Close Positions

**close position**

**open position**

A chord is said to be in *close position* if the distance between the soprano and tenor is an octave or less (see ex. 6-4a); if the distance is greater, the chord is in *open position* (see ex. 6-4b). Notice in example 6-4 that the bass plays no part in determining if a chord is in open or close position.

**EXAMPLE 6-4.** Close and open positions

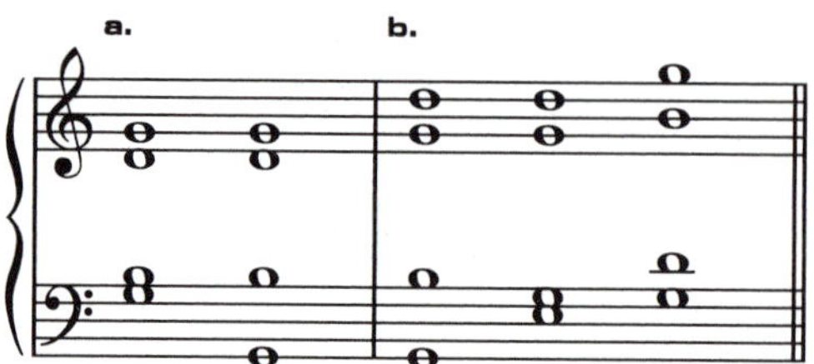


# CHORD REPRESENTATION

**doubling**

The representation of chords in a four-voice setting, that is, the way the three members of the chord appear in the four voices, requires an understanding of the doubling and omission of chord tones. *Doubling* is the appearance of the same chord member in two voices simultaneously. Since there are four voice parts but only three pitch classes represented in the common triad, one of the tones must be doubled. For major and minor triads in root position, the usual tone to be doubled is the root. This reinforces the relatively solid and stable effect of the chord. Notice that in example 6-4 the G is doubled in every chord.

**incomplete chord**

On some occasions the smoothest connection between chords requires the omission of one of the chord tones. In these cases the tone usually omitted is the fifth. A chord in which one or more members are omitted is called an *incomplete chord.* When the fifth is omitted, as in example 6-5a–b, the root of the triad is "tripled," or, in the case of a seventh chord with the fifth omitted, the root is doubled.

**EXAMPLE 6-5.** Incomplete chords

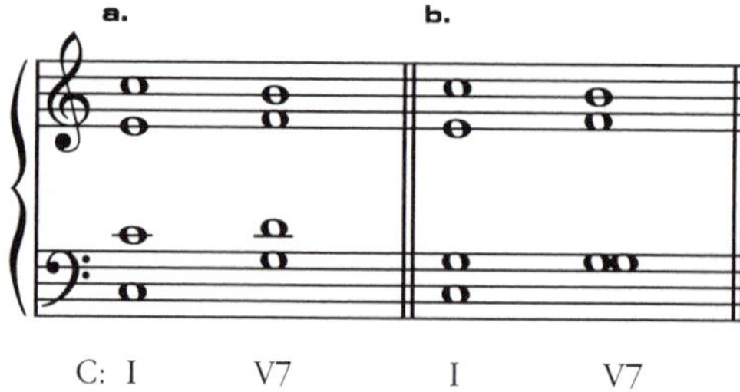

## SOPRANO POSITIONS

**soprano position**

Depending on which tone of the chord is in the soprano, the chord is said to be in the "position of the octave" (ex. 6-6a), "position of the third" (ex. 6-6b), or "position of the fifth" (ex. 6-6c). All of these are known as *soprano positions.* Be sure to keep separate the different uses of the term *position.* They are illustrated in example 6-7a–d.

**EXAMPLE 6-6.** Soprano positions

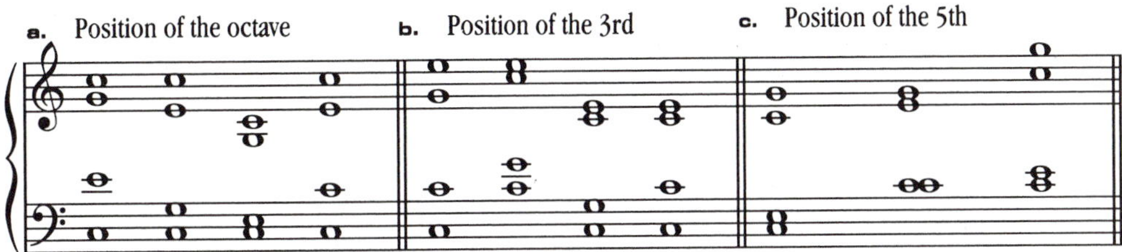


**EXAMPLE 6-7.** Different uses of the term *position*

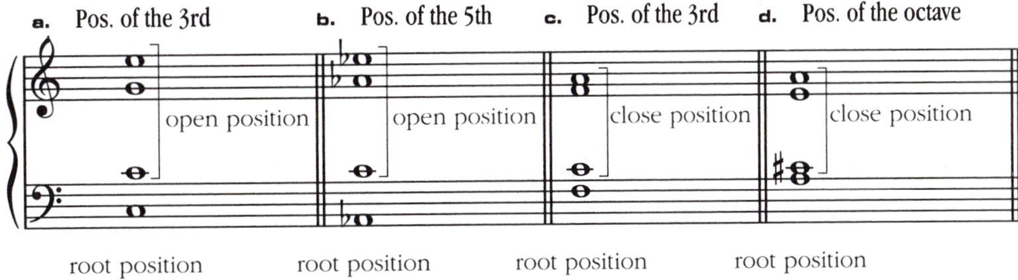


## WRITING CHORDS

The exercises you will do to learn harmony are presented with differing amounts of specificity. In some cases, the bass of a chord will be specified, in others the soprano may be given, and in still others only the chord name will be indicated. Whichever elements are specified, one generally writes a chord for SATB from the outside in, that is, beginning with the outer voices (soprano and bass). The examples that follow will demonstrate how you will be asked to do such exercises in the workbook.

## Bass Given

In example 6-8a–c the requirement is to write an F-major triad with the bass given (root position), the soprano in the position of the third, and the chord in open position. The procedure follows the steps shown: In example 6-8a the bass is given, then the soprano is determined (ex. 6-8b), after which the inner voices are written (ex. 6-8c).

**EXAMPLE 6-8.** Steps in writing four-part harmony

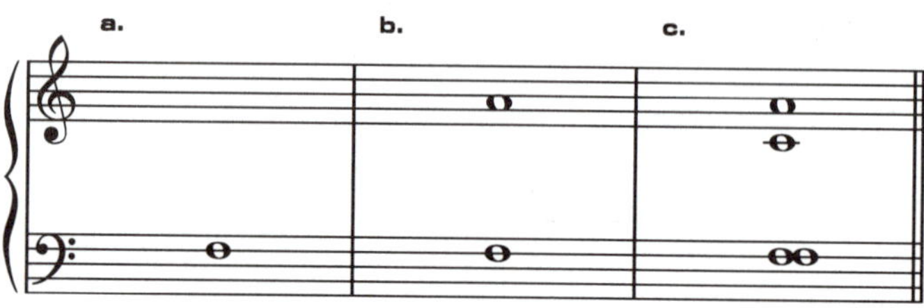


## Soprano Given

In harmonizing a melody one might be confronted with the opposite situation, as in example 6-9a–c, where the intent is for the student to write a D-flat major triad in root position, with the soprano note specified, and the chord in close position. The soprano is specified in example 6-9a. The bass is decided next (ex. 6-9b), and the inner voices last (ex. 6-9c).

**EXAMPLE 6-9.** Steps in harmonizing the soprano

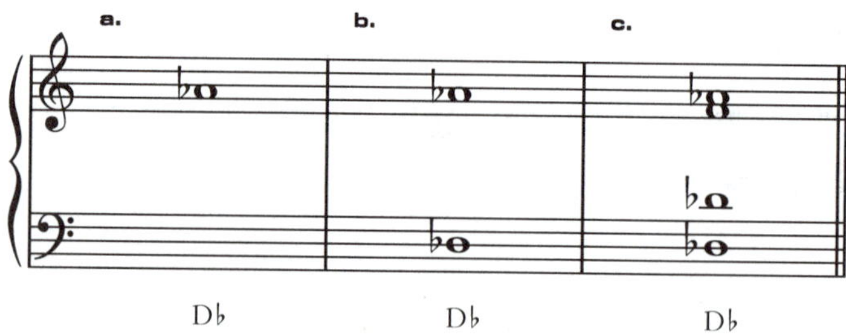


## Roman Numeral Given

If the key and Roman numeral are given, the root of the chord must first be determined, then written in the bass. Bear in mind the key signature and any altered notes (in minor keys). If the soprano note is not specified, choose it before writing the inner voices. In example 6-10, the key and iii chord are specified. The voices should be written in this order: bass, soprano, alto, and tenor.

**EXAMPLE 6-10.** Writing four parts with Roman numeral given

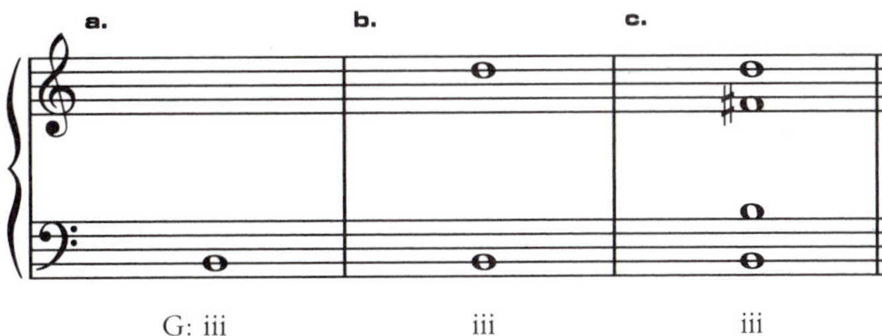


In example 6-11a, the key and the soprano are given. Choose a root-position chord that includes the soprano. The soprano may be the root, third, or fifth of the triad. In the key of F the soprano note $d^2$ could be the root of a vi chord, the third of a IV chord, or the fifth of a ii. Example 6-11b indicates that the IV chord has been chosen and the bass note has been written. Example 6-11c shows the inner voices in place.

**EXAMPLE 6-11.** Writing four-part harmony with soprano note and key given

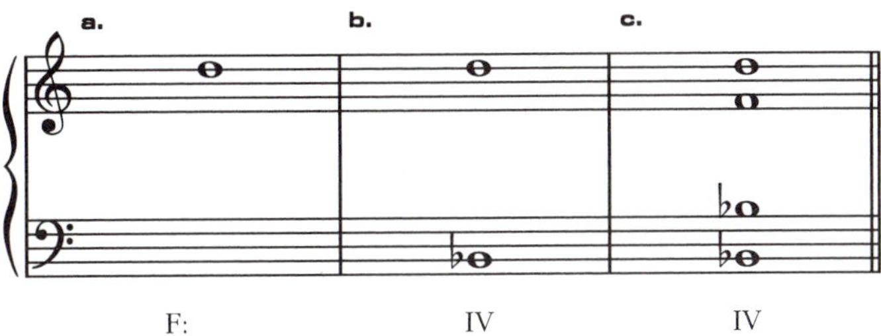


## SUMMARY

As the four-voice choral setting is the primary medium used in the study of harmony, it is important to know the conventions relating to the vocal and notational aspects of the SATB setting. When chords are represented in a four-voice setting there may be a need to double or omit chord members. The four-voice setting of a single chord may also be described in terms of open or close position and soprano position.

CHAPTER SEVEN

# Part Writing

**Terms Introduced in This Chapter**

- part writing
- voice leading
- chordal homophony
- melody with accompaniment
- relative motion
- parallel motion
- similar motion
- oblique motion
- contrary motion
- crossed voices
- overlapping voices
- common tone
- parallel fifths and octaves
- hidden fifths and octaves

**part writing**

**voice leading**

Musical fabric may be conceived of as a combination of simultaneous lines or parts or as a succession of harmonic events. The interrelationship of these two aspects, the horizontal and the vertical, is the concern of part writing. *Part writing* (also called *voice leading*) is the way that simultaneous parts or voices are treated as their harmonic relationships change. The study of part writing requires an understanding of texture, the relationships between voices, and the way in which voices move or "lead" from one chord to the next.

## TEXTURE IN PART WRITING

**chordal homophony**

**melody with accompaniment**

The role of the voices in four-part writing may vary with the type of texture intended. The overall texture that will be considered here is homophonic; that is, there is a single important melodic line to which the other voices are all subordinate. The subordinate voices are unified by rhythmic similarity: They may be rhythmically similar to the melody, in which case the resulting texture is called *chordal homophony,* or the principal melody may have a separate rhythm that is in contrast with the rhythm of the subordinate voices. This texture is known as *melody with accompaniment.* Chordal homophony is the texture that will be emphasized here; the roles of the four voices must be examined in this light.

### The Outer Voices

The outer voices (soprano and bass) are the most conspicuous and therefore have special importance in part writing. The soprano will have the main melodic line, which will move by conjunct or disjunct motion, or a mixture of the two. However, because a disjunct melody is more difficult to use with chordal homophony, a more conservative melody will be encouraged. It is not unusual for the soprano to have a few skips, such as a third, a fourth, and occasional larger skips.

Of the subordinate voices, the bass is the most important. Its chief function is to provide the foundation for a clear and attractive harmonic effect, and for this reason the roots of chords are often assigned to the bass. Because of the nature of the normal progression this means the bass will often have skips of a fourth or fifth, as well as an occasional octave. For the present, stepwise motion in the bass will be used when it is available, but only when using chord inversions can this be fully explored.

### The Inner Voices

The alto and tenor parts are the most subordinate, therefore the most restricted in motion. They are normally limited to stepwise motion and repeated tones with a few skips of a third or a perfect fourth.

## THE RELATIONSHIPS BETWEEN VOICES

**relative motion**

The relationships between voices have been codified with concepts involving pairs of voices and their *relative motion.* When we deal with several voices it is necessary to be aware of the motion of the voices relative to each other. There are four possibilities for relative motion between two voices.

### Parallel Motion

**parallel motion**

*Parallel motion* is the term used to describe the relative motion of two voices moving in the same direction and maintaining the same interval. The intervals between the voices need not be *exactly* the same interval—notice that in example 7-1 the thirds are of different sizes, but the fact that they are all thirds is enough to make this parallel motion.

**EXAMPLE 7-1.** Parallel motion

### Similar Motion

**similar motion**

*Similar motion* is the term used to describe the motion of two voices moving in the same direction but with changes of interval. Example 7-2 shows this type of motion.

**EXAMPLE 7-2.** Similar motion

## Oblique Motion

**oblique motion**

*Oblique motion* is the term used to describe the relative motion between two voices, one of which repeats or sustains its pitch while the other moves, either up or down. This is seen in example 7-3.

**EXAMPLE 7-3.** Oblique motion

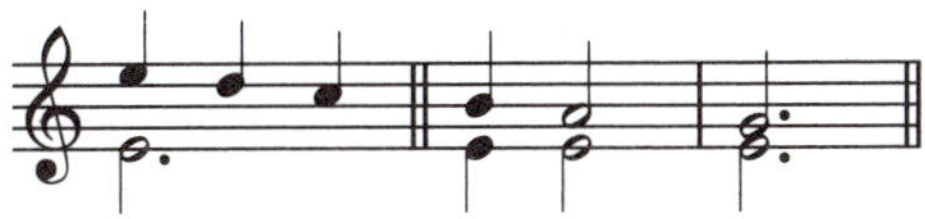

## Contrary Motion

**contrary motion**

*Contrary motion* refers to the motion of two voices moving in opposite directions. This is shown in example 7-4.

**EXAMPLE 7-4.** Contrary motion

The effects of these types of motion are very important in writing independent lines. Parallel and similar motion tend to suggest dependence, while contrary motion promotes independence in the lines. When dealing with more than two voices, the motion of each voice relative to all others must be taken into account.

## Other Voice Relationships

**crossed voices**

Two simultaneous voices normally have a clear relationship of an upper and a lower voice. When this relationship is temporarily reversed it is called *crossed voices.* This is seen in example 7-5a.

**overlapping voices**

When two voices move so that the upper voice goes to a tone lower than that which the lower voice just left it is termed *overlapping voices.* Similarly, overlapping may occur when the lower voice moves to a tone higher than the tone the upper voice just left (see exx. 7-5b and c).

**EXAMPLE 7-5.** Crossed voices and overlapping voices

## VOICE LEADING IN FOUR VOICES

The principles of voice leading result from melodic considerations and the effect of relative motion in four-voice setting of chords. The aim is to have each chord sound even and full and to allow the individual lines to play an effective role in the musical texture. Although our present focus is on the harmonic effect of each chord, one must keep in mind the idea that a series of chords is the product of individual lines.

When connecting chords there are two important principles of voice leading that must be taken into account. These are: (1) the appropriate independence of lines and (2) the tendencies of certain tones to move in particular ways.

### The Independence of Lines

It is a general principle of voice leading that each voice must maintain a level of independence consistent with its role in the texture and harmony. The voice must be neither excessively nor insufficiently independent. Several specific guidelines and rules have been developed to help avoid these extremes and achieve the intended goal.

#### Positive Goals

The following guidelines will help produce the desired results.

**common tone**

1. Move the shortest distance. When moving from one chord to another, a tone in an upper voice should move the shortest distance possible. If the tone is a member of both chords it is called a *common tone* and is usually retained in the same voice for both chords. If there is no common tone, motion by a step is preferable to motion by a skip, and a smaller skip is preferable to a larger one. Examples 7-6a and 6b illustrate this.

**EXAMPLE 7-6.** Moving the shortest distance

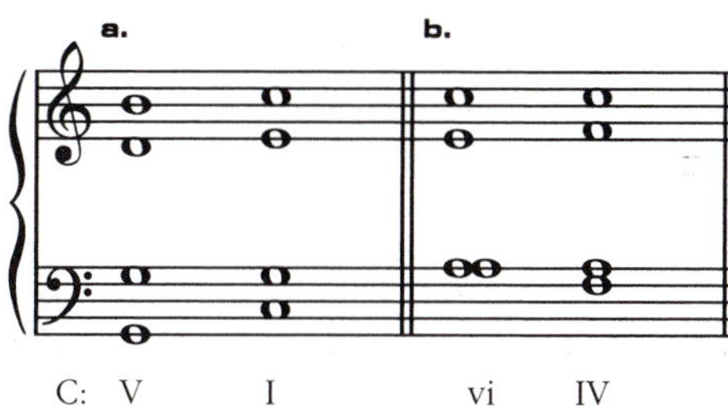


2. Use Contrary motion between outer voices. It is most desirable to have contrary motion between outer voices. Similar and oblique motion are acceptable; parallel motion appears only occasionally between outer voices.
3. Use a mixture of types of motion. It is desirable to mix types of motion between the four voices when moving from one chord to the next; in almost all cases at least two different types of relative motion are found.

In almost all cases in example 7-7, at least two different kinds of relative motion are found as the four voices move from one chord to the next. Note the contrary motion between the lower voices in measure 8. The parallel sixths between soprano and bass (marked x in the example) are balanced by contrary motion in the tenor. A rare instance of all voices moving in similar motion can be seen at the end of the example, in the cadential pattern V–I. Circles in the example indicate tones that are not members of the chord in effect at the moment.

**EXAMPLE 7-7.** J. S. Bach: *Du Friedenfürst Herr Jesu Christ*

## Insufficient Independence

The following points are designed to avoid lines that lack independence and are melodically weak as a result.

**parallel fifths and octaves**

Parallel fifths and octaves. No two voices should move in consecutive (parallel) unisons, octaves, fifteenths, or perfect fifths or twelfths. Such parallelism gives the impression of one reinforced voice and robs one voice of its independence. The sound of *parallel fifths* and *octaves,* as in examples 7-8a and b, is quite obtrusive in some styles. J. S. Bach referred to parallel octaves and fifths as the "greatest error in music." Consecutive or successive octaves and fifths occurring in contrary motion should also be avoided, as shown in examples 7-8c and d. Octaves and fifths that remain on the same tones while a chord changes are not considered parallel (see ex. 7-8e).

**EXAMPLE 7-8.** Parallel fifths and octaves

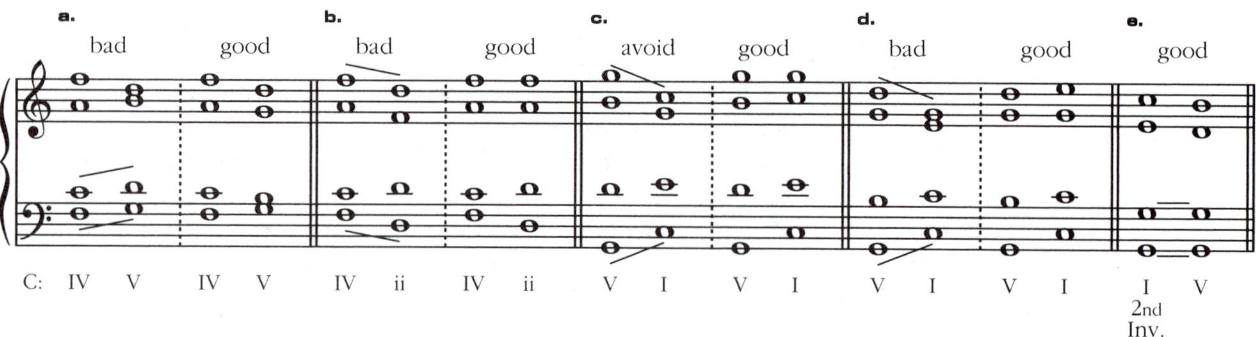


Consecutive unequal fifths. A diminished fifth followed by a perfect fifth between the outer voices is to be avoided, as shown in example 7-9a.

**hidden fifths and octaves**

Hidden fifths and octaves. The approach by similar motion to a fifth or an octave in the outer voices when the soprano skips is termed a *hidden fifth* or *hidden octave,* and both should be avoided, as found in example 7-9b. Note that the fifth is omitted in the I chord to avoid the hidden fifth in this case. Similar motion in all parts. Simultaneous similar motion in all parts, as seen in example 7-10a, is rarely found, except in the conventionalized cadence pattern shown in example 7-10b, where the soprano moves from $\hat{2}$ to $\hat{1}$.

## Excessive Independence

The following points are designed to avoid excessive independence of voices, that is, melodic interest inappropriate for the texture.

Needless skips. Skips of a fourth or more are to be avoided in upper voices, as illustrated in examples 7-11a–e. The soprano may occasionally have larger skips if needed for the melody.

Awkward intervals. Melodic motion with augmented or diminished intervals is avoided when possible. Some of these are seen in examples 7-11b–e.

**EXAMPLE 7-9.** Consecutive unequal fifths and hidden fifths

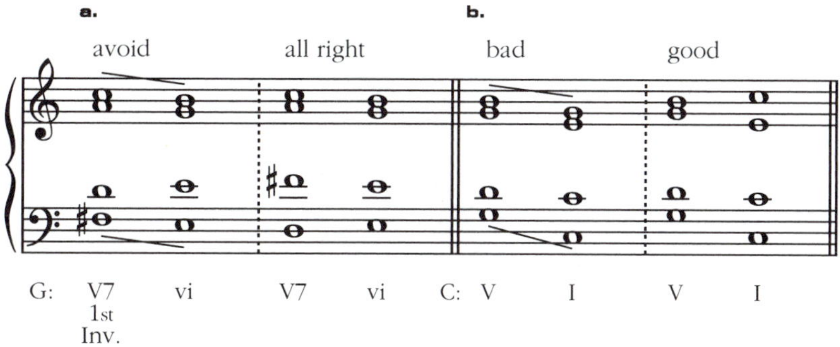


**EXAMPLE 7-10.** Similar motion in all parts

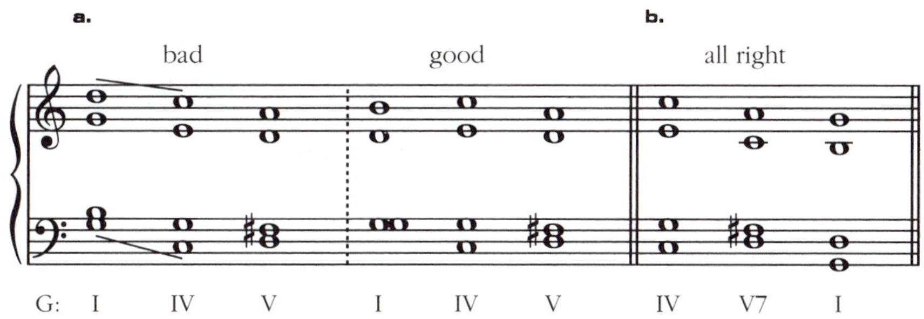


**EXAMPLE 7-11.** Needless skips and awkward intervals

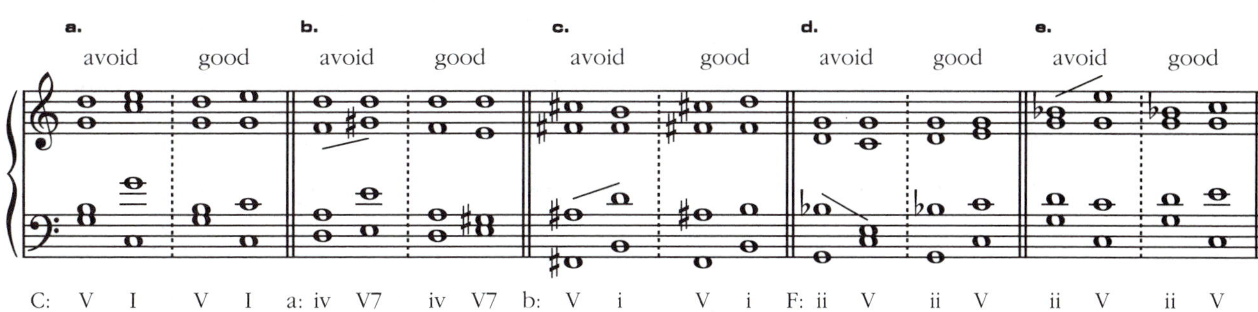

Overlapping voices. Overlapping of voices, as seen in example 7-12a, should be avoided.

Crossed voices. Also to be avoided is the crossing of voices, shown in example 7-12b.

**EXAMPLE 7-12.** Overlapping and crossed voices

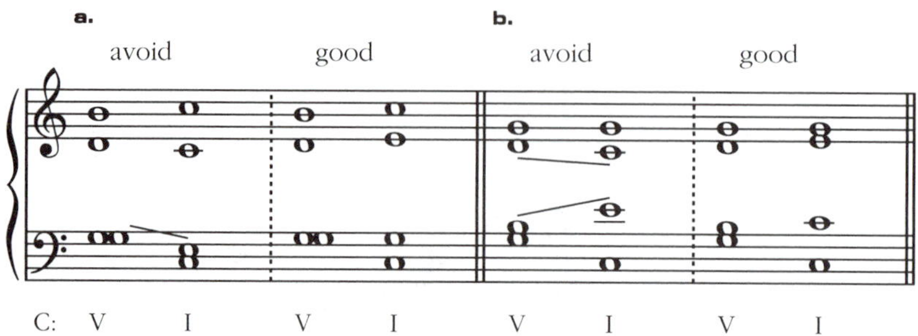


## Three Basic Situations

When applying concepts of voice leading to progressions using triads in root position, there are three basic situations in terms of the number of common tones. A particular melody could complicate the voice leading and require an unusual treatment of the writing, but given only the Roman numerals and the roots in the bass, these three basic situations have well-established solutions that take into account the number of common tones available.

1. Connecting triads with roots a perfect fourth or perfect fifth apart. In this situation there is one common tone. The other voices move to the closest chord tones consistent with good chord representation. Example 7-13a shows the progression I–IV, which may serve as a model for I–V, iii–vi, vi–ii, ii–V, and V–I.
2. Connecting triads with roots a third apart. These progressions have two common tones. Example 7-13b shows the progression I–iii, but the comparable situation arises with I–vi, vi–IV, and IV–ii.
3. Connecting triads with roots a second apart. These progressions have no common tones. The upper voices move in contrary motion to the bass to the closest chord tones available. Example 7-13c illustrates I–ii; these progressions are comparable: IV–V and iii–IV.

## The Tendencies of Tones

Certain scale degrees and chord tones have melodic tendencies that affect voice leading. Scales degrees $\hat{2}$, $\hat{4}$, $\hat{6}$, and $\hat{7}$ have a tendency to move by the shortest distance, to $\hat{1}$, $\hat{3}$, $\hat{5}$, and $\hat{1}$, respectively. In major keys, scale degree $\hat{4}$ tends to move downward to $\hat{3}$ and $\hat{7}$ tends to move upward to $\hat{1}$ ($\hat{8}$). The dissonant interval of the tritone between $\hat{4}$ and $\hat{7}$ usually resolves inward to a third when the tritone is a diminished fifth, as in example 7-14a, and resolves outward to a sixth when the tritone appears as an augmented fourth, as in example 7-14b. The tritone formed by $\hat{4}$ and $\hat{7}$ is found in two chords: V7 and vii°. V7 is of more concern since it is used more often. Example 7-15 illustrates the resolution of the tritone in the common progression V7–I. Note that the fifth is omitted in the I chord.

**EXAMPLE 7-13.** Connecting triads, roots a fourth, third, or second apart

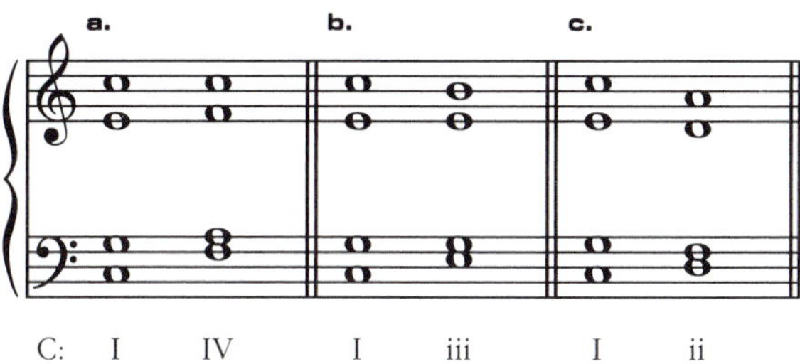


**EXAMPLE 7-14.** Resolutions of the tritone

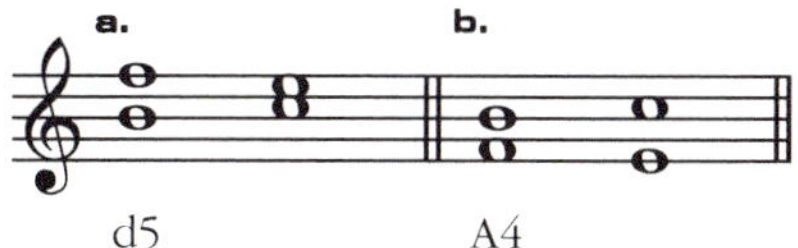


**EXAMPLE 7-15.** Tritone resolution in V7–I progression

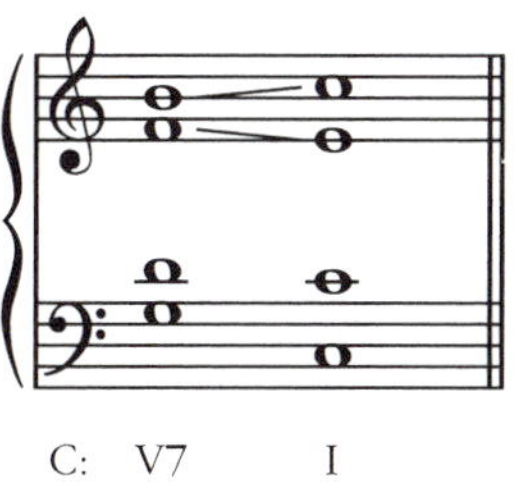


The seventh of a seventh chord is perceived to have a tendency to resolve downward by a step. The seventh of the V7 chord is $\hat{4}$, which has a particularly strong tendency to resolve. The tendency for $\hat{7}$ to resolve is not as strong, and sometimes (especially when $\hat{7}$ is in an inner voice) it is not resolved according to its tendency.

Doubling must now be reassessed as a series of priorities to allow for flexibility in solving problems in voice leading. The strongly preferred candidate for doubling for major and minor triads in root position is the root; if the fifth is omitted, the root is almost always tripled. If considerations of voice leading require it, the third is occasionally doubled as an alternative, but the fifth is doubled only as a last resort.

In this chapter, diatonic chords in root position are used with examples primarily in major keys. The same principles generally apply to progressions in minor keys. Diminished triads have been omitted from this chapter since they are rarely used in root position. This applies to vii° in major and minor keys and to ii° in minor keys. These will be dealt with in chapter 9, when first inversions are considered.

## PROCEDURES FOR CONNECTING CHORDS

When melody and harmony are brought together it is inevitable that there will be moments when the horizontal (melodic) aspect will overshadow the vertical (harmonic) and vice versa. Our goal will be to learn to reconcile these two sometimes opposing forces, but for the present we will focus on the principles that will produce the greatest smoothness. Setting aside for the moment, then, the customary special attention given to the soprano and bass, here are the procedures for connecting consecutive chords with smooth voice leading and minimal possibilities for error:

1. Write the bass notes.
2. Complete the first chord.
3. If there are any tones common to both chords, retain them in the same voices.
4. Move the other parts the shortest distance to the remaining chord tones.

### Procedure for Progressions with Complete Triads

The procedure in the list above can now be applied to the three situations discussed earlier, that is, progressions with varying numbers of common tones.

#### Situation 1: Roots a Perfect Fourth or Perfect Fifth Apart

The intent is to write the progression I–V in the key of A-flat major. Example 7-16 shows the steps. In writing this progression, it is decided in step 2 that the first chord is in the position of the third and in open position. Note in step 3 that there is one common tone.

**EXAMPLE 7-16.** Writing a progression with roots a perfect fourth or fifth apart

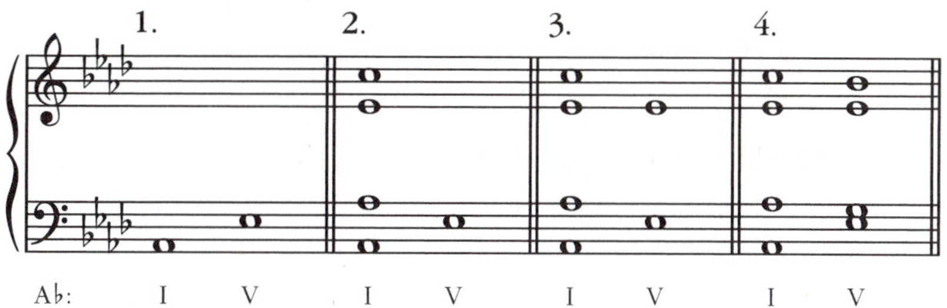


Notice at step 4 that the tenor is a step away from two chord tones, G and B-flat, but the distance from A-flat to G is shorter than A-flat to B-flat. Had the tenor taken the B-flat, the soprano would have had to skip a fourth to $g^1$, making the voice leading much less smooth.

## Situation 2: Roots a Third Apart

The intent is to write the progression I–iii in the key of B-flat major. In step 2 of example 7-17 the first chord is in the position of the octave and in open position. At step 3 we retain two common tones. Step 4 shows the resulting smooth progression.

**EXAMPLE 7-17.** Writing a progression with roots a third apart

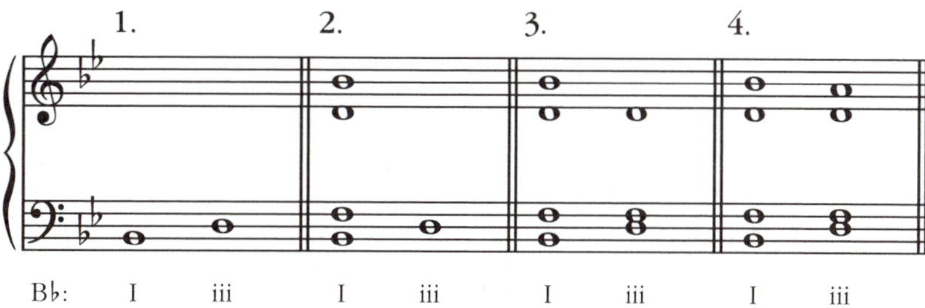


## Situation 3: Roots a Second Apart

The intent is to write IV–V in the key of E-flat major, position unspecified. At step 2 of example 7-18 it is decided to use the position of the third, in close position. Step 3 is omitted because there are no common tones: Therefore, in step 4 the upper three voices must move in *contrary motion* to the bass in order to move the shortest distance without forming parallel fifths or octaves.

**EXAMPLE 7-18.** Writing a progression with roots a second apart

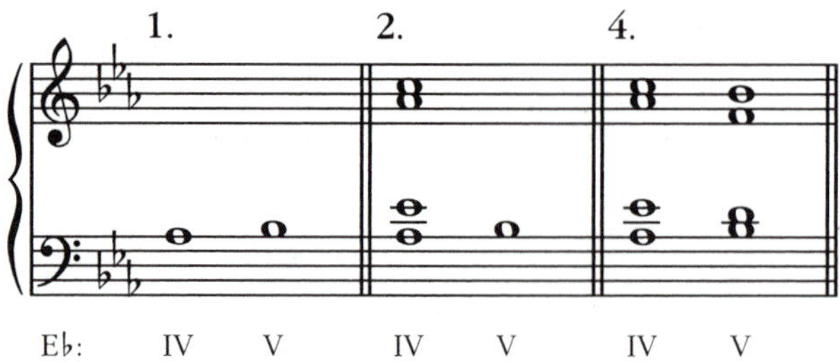


## Procedure for Progressions with Incomplete Triads

Sometimes the demands of voice leading make it impossible to have all members of the triad present. The composer frequently faces the choice between smooth voice leading and harmonic fullness. When this happens, the fifth of the chord is usually omitted. This is seen in example 7-19 with one of the most commonly used progressions. The intent is to write the progression V–I in the key of E-flat major. At step 2 it is decided to use the position of the fifth, in close position, for V. Limiting the soprano to the strong movement from $\hat{2}$ to $\hat{1}$, two possible versions are shown. Example 7-19a achieves harmonic completeness for the I chord at the expense of smooth voice leading: The $\hat{7}$ does not resolve to $\hat{8}$ (acceptable when $\hat{7}$ is in an inner voice), and the available common tone in the tenor is not retained. Example 7-19b, with the same strong $\hat{2}$–$\hat{1}$ in the soprano, also compromises the voice leading: The $\hat{7}$ moves to $\hat{8}$, but the available common tone is not retained. Here harmonic completeness has been sacrificed with an incomplete I chord. Steps 1 and 3 have been omitted in both versions of the example.

**EXAMPLE 7-19.** Harmonic completeness versus smooth voice leading

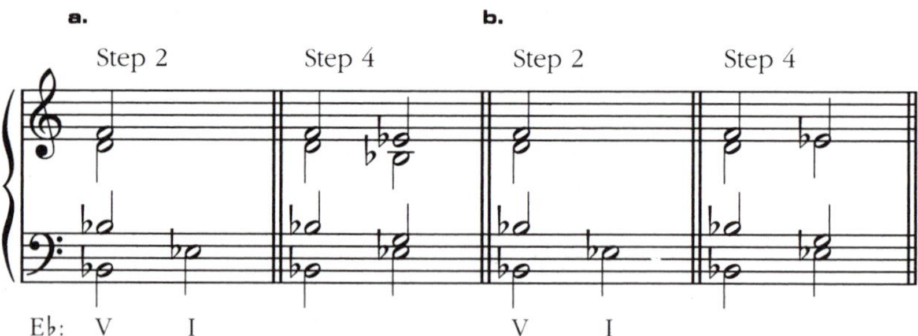


In four-part writing there are many different situations since there are so many variables: soprano position, spacing, chord progressions, chord representation, and inversions. It is impractical to establish a model solution for every problem that may arise. A case in point is the connection of an incomplete triad to a following chord. Examples 7-20a–g illustrate several possibilities that require the application of the principles of voice leading with various progressions and chord representations. In examples 7-20a, b, and c, the voice leading is relatively smooth, with no skip larger than a third; however, in 7-20d and e a skip of a fourth is found in an upper voice in order to avoid forbidden parallels or poor chord representation.

**EXAMPLE 7-20.** Various possibilities in voice leading

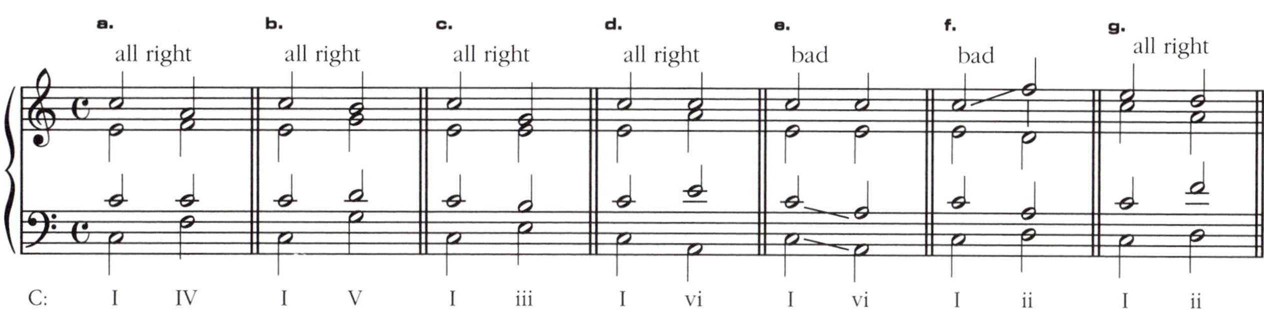


There are many points that could be mentioned about these examples, but we will touch on some of the main ones. Example 7-20a presents no problem, but in example 7-20b the common tone is not held in the progression I–V. In examples 7-20c and d only one common tone is usable. A similar progression in example 7-20e led to unacceptable parallel octaves. Example 7-20f has poor spacing, but there are no good solutions to this problem, given the progression I–ii and this version of the tonic chord. An inversion of ii could solve this problem, but, as we are restricted to root position chords for the present, a change in the placement of I provides the solution shown in example 7-20g.

## Resolution of V7 in Root Position

The procedure for writing the progression V7–I is somewhat different from progressions involving chords that are not dissonant:

1. Write the bass.
2. Complete the first chord.
3. Resolve the seventh of the chord ($\hat{4}$).
4. Resolve $\hat{7}$ upward if it is in the soprano or, if it is in an inner voice, either upward or downward to the closest chord tone.
5. Move the remaining voice to the closest chord tone, retaining a common tone, if possible.

Examples 7-21a and b illustrate the complete resolution of the tritone of the V7 between $\hat{7}$ and $\hat{4}$ (the seventh of the chord). The final I is incomplete as a result. In example 7-21c, the leading tone is not resolved upward, allowing the final tonic chord to be complete. Note that steps 4 and 5 in the list above can be decided at almost the same time to get an effective soprano line.

**EXAMPLE 7-21.** Different ways to resolve the progression V7–I

In example 7-22, the fifth in the V7 has been omitted so that the I chord can be complete.

**EXAMPLE 7-22.** Omission of the fifth in the V7 chord

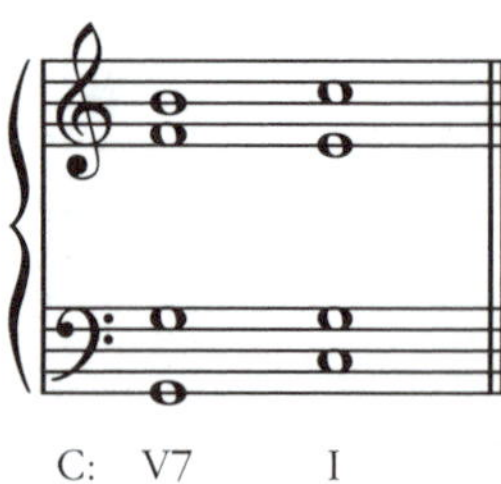

### Final Check for Errors

Following established part-writing procedures will usually minimize the possibility of errors in voice leading, such as parallel octaves or fifths, but one must be able to locate such errors. To do this, check the motion of each voice against every other voice. There are six pairs to be checked: S and A, S and T, S and B, A and T, A and B, and T and B. Check these pairs in the progression in example 7-23 to see if there are any errors.

**EXAMPLE 7-23.** Example for checking voice leading errors

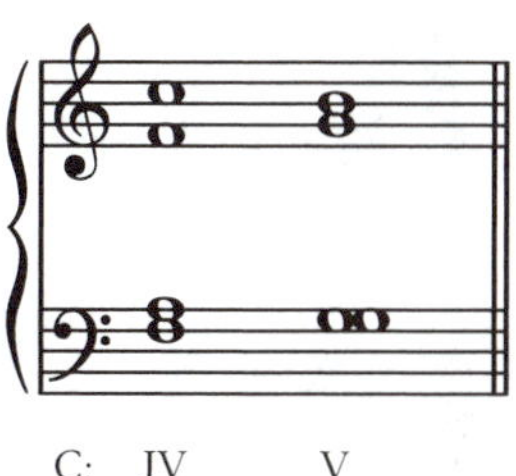


There are parallel octaves between the alto and bass in example 7-23. This process may seem tedious at first, but as one becomes more fluent in writing, the time required will diminish greatly. It is best to work slowly and carefully until you become fluent with the procedure.

## SUMMARY

The study of part writing requires an understanding of appropriate texture, the relationships between voices, and the way in which voices move or "lead" from one chord to the next. With chordal homophony as the texture, the appropriate roles of each of the four voices within this texture must be examined. The relationships between voices are codified with concepts involving pairs of voices and their relative motion.

The principles of voice leading result from melodic considerations and the effect of relative motion in four-voice settings of chords. It is a general principle of voice leading that voices must maintain a level of independence consistent with their role in the texture and harmony. Several specific guidelines and rules have been developed to help avoid the extremes of excessive or insufficient independence and achieve the intended goal. Certain scale degrees and chord tones have melodic tendencies that affect voice leading. For first attempts at connecting chords in root position, detailed procedures should be followed to assure smoothness of voice leading and to minimize the possibility of errors.

CHAPTER EIGHT

# Introduction to Melody with Harmony

**Terms Introduced in This Chapter**

- nonharmonic tone (NHT)
- nonchord tone
- preparation
- resolution
- passing tone (PT)
- accented passing tone
- neighbor tone (NT)
- harmonic rhythm
- harmonization

The intent in this chapter is to develop an understanding of the interaction of melody with harmony. At this introductory stage, it is necessary to maintain limitations on both melody and harmony. Melodies will be used that may easily be related to the harmonic context and the prevailing texture of chordal homophony. Further, the harmonic study will emphasize diatonic triads (excluding vii° and ii°) and the dominant seventh chord, all in root position. As the understanding of harmony is expanded in succeeding chapters, so also will the relationship of melody and harmony be considered in increasing depth.

To deal with melody in a harmonic context and find an appropriate harmony for a given melody, it is necessary to consider melody from a harmonic point of view, using such concepts as voice leading and nonharmonic tones. Good voice leading encourages a minimal degree of melodic independence. On the other hand, the use of nonharmonic tones tends to develop melodic interest.

## INTRODUCTION TO NONHARMONIC TONES

**nonharmonic tone (NHT)**

**nonchord tone**

In tonal music using harmony, all tones are not typically chord tones. A *nonharmonic tone* (*NHT*) or *nonchord tone* is a tone that is not a member of the chord in effect at the time the nonharmonic tone appears. All tones must be either a chord member or a nonharmonic tone. Nonharmonic tones have specific characteristics that identify each nonharmonic tone as belonging to one of several established types. It is difficult to generalize about the types, however. Many of them appear to be decorative and subordinate. Nonharmonic tones typically are not emergent tones. They are often shorter and occur on weaker metric points than the surrounding chord tones. These features, although typical, are not characteristic of all types of nonharmonic tones.

**preparation**

**resolution**

There are nine types of nonharmonic tones, all of which will be discussed in detail in chapter 12, but the two most commonly used types will be defined here and used in the following chapters. To define and understand nonharmonic tones, we must identify three features: the nonharmonic tone itself, the preceding tone in that voice, known as the *preparation,* and the succeeding tone, known as the *resolution*.

### Passing Tone

**passing tone (PT)**

The *passing tone* (*PT*) is a nonharmonic tone that is prepared by a chord tone a step or half step below and is resolved to a chord tone a step or half step above (see ex. 8-1a: This pattern is sometimes called an *ascending passing tone*), or it may be prepared by a chord tone a step or half step above and resolved to a chord tone a step or half step below (see ex. 8-1b, sometimes termed a *descending passing tone*). Passing tones are typically found on metric points weaker than the preparation or resolution; however, if the passing tone occurs on a metric point stronger

**accented passing tone**

than that of the resolution it is called an *accented passing tone* (see ex. 8-1c). Occasionally two passing tones may appear in succession between the tones of preparation and resolution. These are sometimes called *double passing tones* (see ex. 8-1d). Like the other varieties of passing tones, the configuration of preparation, nonharmonic tones, and resolution all appear as a continuous scale-wise ascending or descending line. Example 8-1 illustrates these ideas. The different varieties of passing tones are all labeled simply as PT and circled.

**EXAMPLE 8-1.** Varieties of passing tones

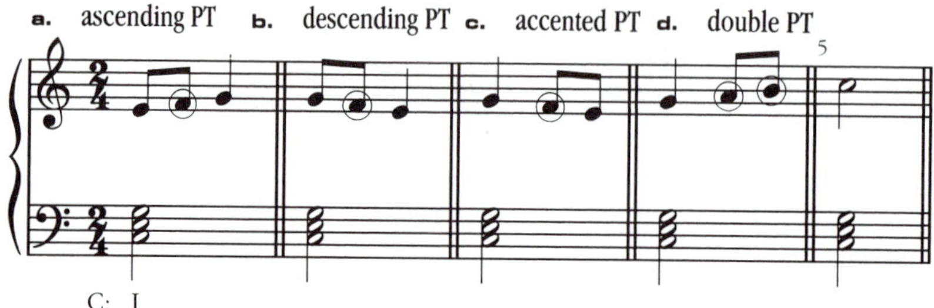


## Neighbor Tone

**neighbor tone (NT)**

The *neighbor tone (NT)* is a nonharmonic tone found a step or half step away from and between chord tones of the same pitch. A neighbor tone below the chord tones is called a *lower neighbor tone* (see ex. 8-2a), and a neighbor tone above the chord tones, an *upper neighbor tone* (see ex. 8-2b). Like the passing tone, the neighbor tone is typically unaccented, but it may be accented (see ex. 8-2c).

**EXAMPLE 8-2.** Neighbor tones

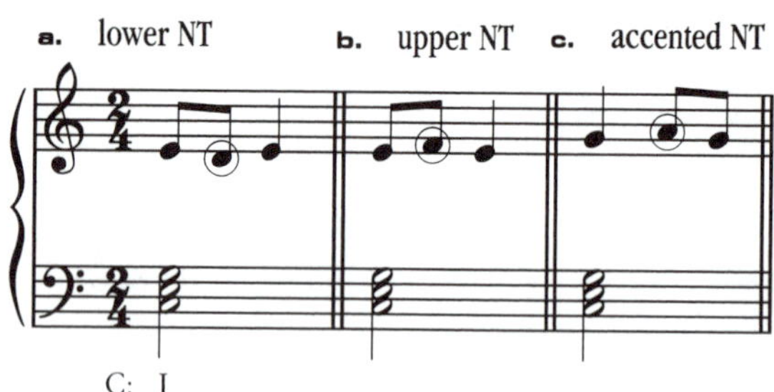

# MELODIC INTEREST IN PART WRITING

Melodic interest and independence can be developed through active melodic contour and rhythm, but nonharmonic tones can also be used for this purpose.

## Melodic Interest from Contour and Rhythmic Activity

In four-part writing, the soprano line is often more interesting than the other voices because the general shape and direction of the line is clearer and stronger. Inner voices, in particular, are often more static and enjoy less clarity in the direction of their lines. Example 8-3 illustrates these differences.

**EXAMPLE 8-3.** Differences in the interest level in the four voices

Melodic interest can be increased by using chord tones that enhance the contour with additional skips or by adding rhythmic figures unique to the line. Example 8-4 shows a few small skips in the soprano using various chord tones during the tenure of a chord. This also entails rhythms that depart modestly from that of the subordinate voices.

**EXAMPLE 8-4.** Skips and rhythmic variations used to create melodic interest

## Melodic Interest from Nonharmonic Tones

The melodic line may gain a considerable amount of attention and interest from the use of nonharmonic tones. Example 8-5 illustrates this with a soprano part that is much more interesting than the other voices. In producing such an abundance of nonharmonic tones, the rhythm of the soprano part also becomes more interesting. Note that nonharmonic tones gain further melodic interest by the use of chromatic alterations, as seen in measure 3.

Used in a restrained manner consistent with the chordal texture used with part writing, a few nonharmonic tones add melodic interest to a voice. This can be applied to any voice, but at this stage of study the soprano will be the only voice so enhanced (see ex. 8-6).

**EXAMPLE 8-5.** Melodic interest from nonharmonic tones

*f* *p* *f* *sf*

F: I V7 I IV V I

**EXAMPLE 8-6.** Enhancement of the soprano with nonharmonic tones

# THE HARMONIC CONTROL OF MELODY

When united with harmony, the tonality and cadences of the melody are controlled by the harmonic organization. The tonality is so strongly established by harmony through the normal progression that the melody is heard within the framework of the harmony. This is particularly apparent at cadences. Melodic and harmonic cadences may be considered conclusive or inconclusive depending on different criteria (scale degrees for melodic cadences versus Roman numerals for harmonic cadences). A harmonic cadence may be conclusive while the associated melodic cadence is inconclusive. One may have an inconclusive melodic cadence on $\hat{3}$ with a conclusive harmonic cadence with an I chord. A conclusive melodic cadence on $\hat{1}$ could appear with an inconclusive vi chord. In these cases, the harmony dominates and is used to describe the cadence. Example 8-7 illustrates such a conclusive cadence.

**EXAMPLE 8-7.** Inconclusive melodic cadence and conclusive harmonic cadence

## HARMONIC RHYTHM

**harmonic rhythm**

The duration of chords is termed *harmonic rhythm*. The chord symbol is placed exactly below the point in the music where the chord takes effect and remains in force until the next chord symbol appears. In example 8-8, the harmonic rhythm begins slowly and moves more quickly toward the end.

Harmonic rhythm is usually closely related to the meter so that important changes in the harmony and longer durations in the harmonic rhythm often begin at important metric points. This tends to reinforce and affirm the meter. This is illustrated in the last measure of example 8-8.

**EXAMPLE 8-8.** Beethoven: Symphony No. 5, fourth movement

# HARMONIZATION

**harmonization**

The creation of harmony for a preexisting melody is called a *harmonization*. To harmonize a melody one must understand its harmonic implications and also understand the way in which harmony should be planned and written. At the heart of the process of harmonizing is chord selection, the choice of appropriate chords at particular times.

## Chord Selection

A melody may imply harmony so clearly that there are few alternatives when harmonizing it, but most simple, conjunct melodies have several alternatives. This means that different factors must be taken into account to provide a harmonization that accommodates the melody appropriately and is at the same time harmonically effective.

### Appropriate Nonharmonic Tones

The chord selection for a harmonization must be such that any nonharmonic tones fall clearly within the description of one of the established types of nonharmonic tones. The full array of types will be introduced at a later point; however, they are not all used with equal frequency. An overabundance of unusual nonharmonic tones creates an abnormal effect. The two types that have been studied up until this point, the passing tone and the neighbor tone, are the most common. We will limit the harmonization to these for now.

### Voice Leading in the Melody

The harmonization must take into account the tendencies of tones to move or resolve in a particular direction that may result from the selection of a particular chord. This situation arises most conspicuously in the case of a V7 with the seventh of the chord in the melody. If the seventh in the melody does not resolve downward by a step in the next chord, the V7 was a poor selection for that situation. Alternatives might include the use of a different harmonic rhythm, the selection of IV, ii, or another chord that would allow the tone in question to become a correctly handled nonharmonic tone. The leading tone ($\hat{7}$) in the soprano is less restricted in its resolution than the seventh of a chord, but, if $\hat{7}$ is the penultimate note of the phrase, it is highly desirable to resolve the $\hat{7}$ to $\hat{8}$.

### Chord Progressions

Whenever possible, a harmonization should follow a normal or alternate progression. Sometimes a particular melody makes this difficult, but usually the options are sufficient to allow for this. The selection of chords in a harmonization can remain normal and still allow enough variety so that redundant and repetitive progressions can be avoided.

## Harmonic Rhythm

The rate at which chords change must be carefully determined so that the harmonization offers the least number of problems and still maintains interest. The harmonic rhythm most often supports and confirms the meter rather than contradicting or conflicting with the metric structure. When there is a choice of equally good options, personal preference may be exercised. At this early stage of study, regular, moderately paced chord changes are appropriate. The kinds of melodies that will be emphasized now will be most effective with a chord change on almost every beat.

## The Process of Harmonizing Melodies

The harmonization of a melody, whether simple or complex, with or without nonharmonic tones, requires a systematic approach to chord selection prior to the actual part writing. It is recommended that the planning phase be done in three steps.

**Step 1.** Determine the tonality and establish it with an opening I chord or V–I, as implied by the melody.

**Step 2.** Decide on the cadence type and choose the last two chords accordingly.

**Step 3.** Determine the intervening chords.

During the planning phase of any harmonization, one is confronted at some point with the task of determining which chord should be chosen for a particular tone: A melody note could be the root, third, or fifth of a chord or even the seventh of a dominant seventh. One then reviews the possibilities (I, ii, iii, IV, V(7), vi in major or i, III, iv, V(7), VI in minor) and decides which harmonization will meet the needs of the various melodic and harmonic factors.

Part writing, the second phase of harmonizing, is accomplished by following the procedures established in the preceding chapter.

The two-phased procedure of planning the chords and writing the parts will be applied to two sample harmonizations. In each case the harmonic rhythm is about the same: one chord for every beat or two. In the first example there are no nonharmonic tones; in the second a few simple nonharmonic tones are included.

## Harmonizing a Melody without Nonharmonic Tones

The melody without nonharmonic tones is shown in example 8-9. The steps used in the planning process are as follows.

**Step 1.** The initial tone $b^1$ could be the root of a iii chord, the fifth of a vi chord, or the third of a I chord. The I is best for establishing the key of G major at the beginning.

Step 2. The melodic cadence on $g^1$ is conclusive. The harmonization could confirm this with a I chord or make the overall cadence inconclusive by using vi. If the cadence were to be conclusive, it would be authentic, not plagal, as the next to the last note, the $a^1$, could be harmonized with V but not IV. The progression V–vi has been chosen, creating an inconclusive (deceptive) cadence.

Step 3. The short harmonic cycle completed early in the phrase firmly establishes the key, allowing the longer (incomplete) cycle that follows to employ a variety of chords in normal and alternate progressions.

**EXAMPLE 8-9.** Steps in harmonizing a melody without nonharmonic tones

Example 8-10 shows the completed harmonization. Note that the voice leading does not always conform to the models that were considered in the last chapter. When a melody is harmonized (as opposed to part writing a bass line or progression), the procedures for connecting chords are frequently compromised to accommodate the melody.

**EXAMPLE 8-10.** Harmonization of example 8-9

## Harmonizing a Melody with Nonharmonic Tones

The melody with nonharmonic tones is shown in example 8-11. The steps used in the planning process are as follows.

**EXAMPLE 8-11.** Steps in harmonizing a melody with nonharmonic tones

**Step 1.** The V–I progression serves to establish the key of D major at the beginning.

**Step 2.** The melodic cadence on $\hat{2}$ can be harmonized only with a half cadence. The V chord can be preceded by IV, making a normal progression.

**Step 3.** The harmonic rhythm of the completed harmonization uses a I chord for two beats and then proceeds with a long harmonic cycle through the middle of the phrase. The first pair of eighth notes uses IV (the $a^1$ is a passing tone), while the second pair uses the I chord (the $g^1$ is an accented passing tone), which completes a harmonic cycle, the only complete cycle in the phrase.

Example 8-12 shows the completed harmonization. The change of position for the I chord in measure 1 facilitates the voice leading. Note that no common tones are retained when IV moves to ii with the passing tones.

**EXAMPLE 8-12.** Harmonization of example 8-11

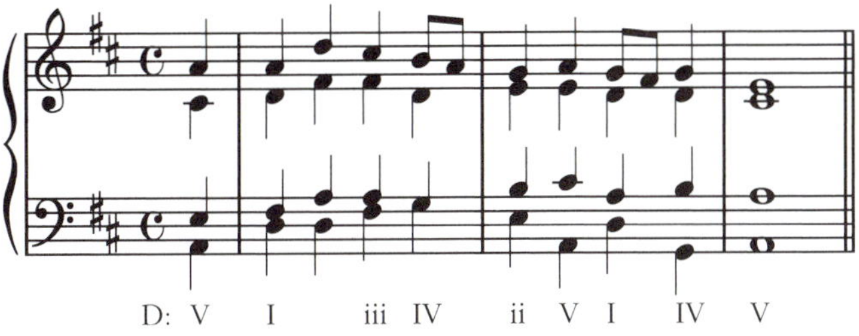


Part writing with nonharmonic tones can lead to parallel fifths or octaves between a nonharmonic tone and a concurrent chord tone or between two simultaneous nonharmonic tones. These should be avoided. Example 8-13a illustrates several of these possibilities. In Example 8-13b a new chord selection has been used to avoid the parallels.

**EXAMPLE 8-13.** Avoiding parallel fifths caused by nonharmonic tones

## SUMMARY

The intent of this chapter is to develop an introductory understanding of the interaction of melody with harmony. To deal with melody in a harmonic context and find an appropriate harmonization for a given melody, it is necessary to consider melody from a harmonic point of view, using such concepts as voice leading and nonharmonic tones. Greater melodic interest and independence can be achieved by increased activity in the melodic contour and rhythm and the use of nonharmonic tones.

When melody is united with harmony, the tonality and the cadences are controlled by the harmony. Harmonization always requires a two-phase process: planning the chords, then completing the part writing. To harmonize a melody one must understand its harmonic implications, plan the chords, and write the progressions. The important factors affecting chord selection are: appropriate nonharmonic tones, voice leading in the melody, chord progressions (normal or alternate), harmonic interest, and harmonic rhythm.

CHAPTER NINE

# Triads in First Inversion

**Terms Introduced in This Chapter**

- figured bass
- continuo
- basso continuo
- thoroughbass
- realization
- chord of the sixth

Triads in first inversion are an important resource in developing the bass line, the most valuable voice in organizing and controlling harmony. In exploring first inversions in depth, the system of "figured bass" will be used and related to the previous study of root position chords.

## THE FIGURED BASS SYSTEM

**figured bass**

The *figured bass* was the fundamental concept underlying the harmonic structure of ensemble music in the Baroque period (1600–1750). The figured bass system was a shorthand method of telling a player not only what chord should be sounding, but also indicating some nonharmonic tones and chord inversions along with the complete bass voice.

### The Role of the Bass Line in Baroque Music

**continuo**

**basso continuo**

**thoroughbass**

**realization**

In the Baroque period, the bass line was especially important, often played by several performers in an ensemble. The typical Baroque texture contains a strong, independent bass line, which, in addition to its melodic interest, had a major influence on the organization and control of the harmony. In the figured bass system a keyboard player in an ensemble was given a part consisting of a bass line with Arabic figures below certain bass notes to indicate which chords were to be played as the harmonic background for the ensemble. Because this bass ran through the entire piece, this part was sometimes called the *continuo, basso continuo,* or *thoroughbass.* The continuo line, that is, the bass line, was played by a keyboard player and one or more melodic bass instruments–cello, string bass, and so on. The continuo keyboard player (usually playing a harpsichord, although any instrument capable of playing chords could have been used) improvised above the figured bass, with a degree of elaboration, brilliance, or subtlety that depended on the skill of the performer. This improvisation is called a *realization* of a figured bass. Although the realization was improvised in the Baroque period, modern practice is to write it out.

### The Application of Figures: Root Position Triads

The Arabic numbers below the figured bass notes indicate intervals counted upward from the bass note. These imply chords that are dealt with according to established principles of voice leading (part writing). The number or numbers make no restrictions on the octave, spacing, or positions of the upper voices.

## Figures for Root Position Triads

The triad in root position is made up of a third and a fifth, counted from the bass upwards. (The inversions of the triad have a different pattern of intervals, to be considered later.) Example 9-1 shows the figured bass for a root position triad. Other numbers could be used also. Here are other possible figured bass indications for a triad in root position (note the absence of 6 or 4):

$$\begin{matrix} 8 & 8 & 8 & 5 & 5 & 3 \\ 5 & 3 & & 3 & & \\ 3 & & & & & \end{matrix}$$

A bass note without any figure also indicates a triad in root position based on that note. The intervals of a fifth and a third above the bass note are "understood" (see ex. 9-2). This is the preferred method.

**EXAMPLE 9-1.** Figured bass for a triad in root position

**EXAMPLE 9-2.** "Understood" figured bass with sample realizations

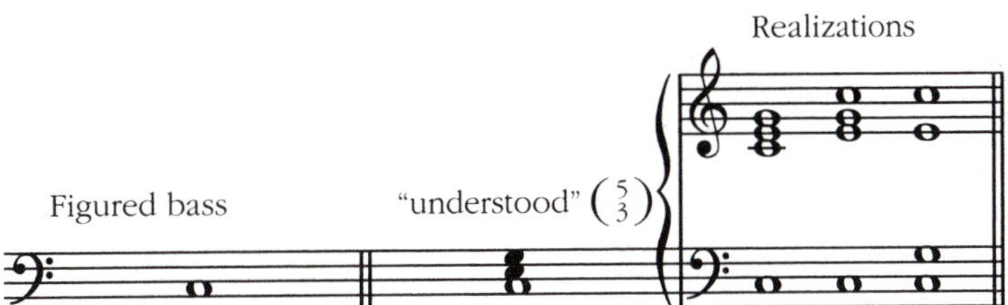


An interval may be altered by a sharp, flat, or natural normally written after the number (although some Baroque music has been published with the accidentals to the left of the numbers). A flat standing by itself indicates a lowered third above the bass; a sharp by itself indicates a raised third. A slash on any part of a number also means it is raised a half step: 4̸, 5̸, 6̸. These accidentals do not always agree with the key signature or the name of the note actually played, as when a raised $\hat{7}$ (leading tone) in C minor might be indicated by a sharp under a G, as in example 9-3. It is understood that B-natural is intended, not b-sharp.

**EXAMPLE 9-3.** Use of accidentals in figured bass

## Realization and Part Writing

When connecting chords in keyboard notation, the procedures are for the most part the same as in vocal music. One difference is that in keyboard notation one usually places the soprano, alto, and tenor parts in the treble staff, using close position. The tenor part is higher than in a choral setting, but in keyboard notation the voices need not adhere to vocal ranges. This arrangement is referred to as "3 + 1," as opposed to the usual "2 + 2" distribution of voices between the staves in choral writing. Both 3 + 1 and 2 + 2 arrangements will be used in exercises.

The principles of part writing all apply to the realization of figured bass. In writing a figured bass where the soprano is not given, these steps are recommended:

**Step 1.** Complete the first chord.

**Step 2.** If there are one or more common tones, keep them in the same part (see ex. 9-4a). If there are no common tones, move the upper voices in contrary motion to the bass to the nearest tone of the new chord (see ex. 9-4b).

**Step 3.** Move the remaining voices the shortest distance to the other chord tones.

# TRIADS IN FIRST INVERSION

The way in which composers use first inversions varies depending on the chord type; major, minor, and diminished triads are each treated differently. Figured bass is a useful approach to understanding the treatment of first inversions.

The possible figurations for a triad in first inversion are as follows.

8 8 6 6
6 6 3
3

(The 6 is necessary; note the absence of 5 and 4.)

The preferred figured bass abbreviation for triads in first inversion is the single number 6; however, sometimes additional numbers are used. The intervals are, as

**chord of the sixth**

always, counted from the bass upwards. The chord implied by the number 6 (sometimes called *chord of the sixth*) is shown in example 9-5. The number 6 is also placed to the right of the Roman numerals in order to show first inversion.

**EXAMPLE 9-4.** Part writing from figured bass

**EXAMPLE 9-5.** Figured bass for first-inversion triads

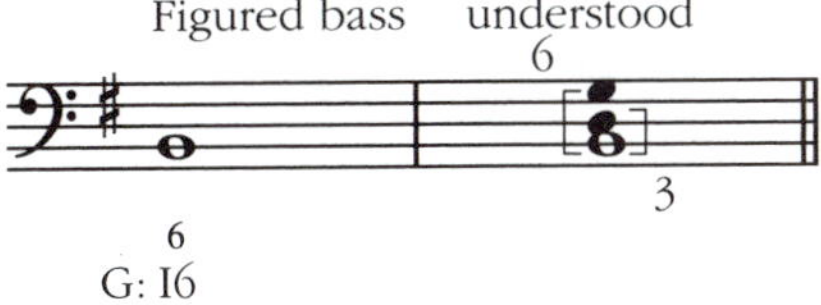


## Major and Minor Triads in First Inversion

While the part writing of major and minor chords in first inversion is basically similar, there are some important distinctions in doubling. Major triads in first inversion normally double the soprano, which should be limited to the root or fifth (see ex. 9-6). The exigencies of voice leading may make this difficult, so alternatives of the third or an inner voice, though rare, are possible. The tendency of the third of the V6, the leading tone, is so strong that it is never doubled. (The leading tone is almost never doubled in any case.)

**EXAMPLE 9-6.** Doublings of first-inversion major triads

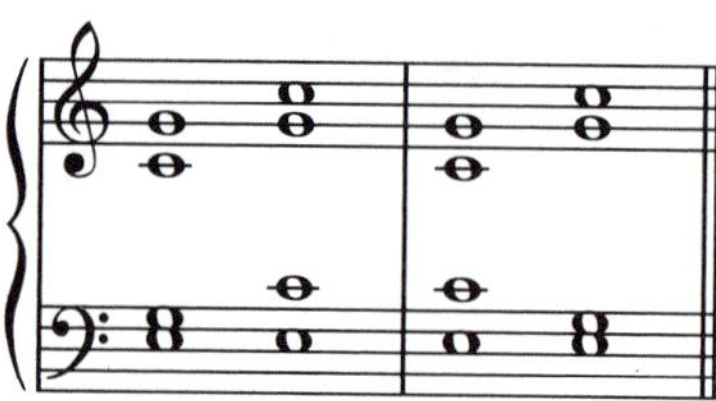


Minor triads in first inversion normally double the soprano or the bass, so the doubled note may be either the root, third, or fifth (see ex. 9-7a). In rare cases justified by voice leading, inner voices may be doubled (see exx. 9-7b, c, and d).

**EXAMPLE 9-7.** Doublings of first-inversion minor triads

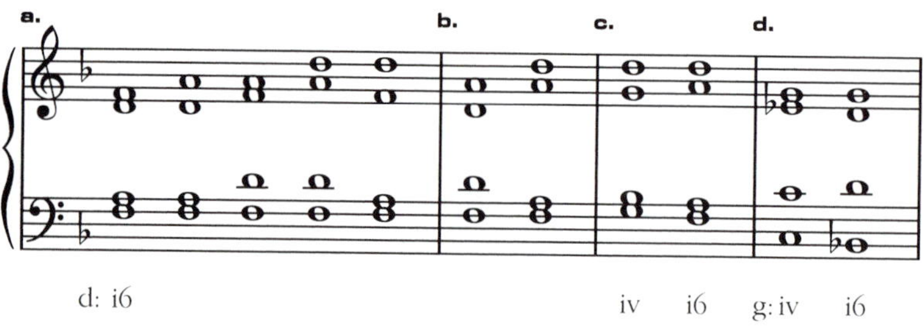


## Part Writing

Bearing in mind the alternative doublings for triads in first inversion, the part writing procedures are applied in example 9-8. The example illustrates a variety of voice leading problems and doublings. Note in example 9-8b the use of the common tones leads to parallel octaves, so steps 3 and 4 are changed to eliminate the common tone.

**EXAMPLE 9-8.** Part writing with first-inversion chords

Examples 9-8a, b, and c are easily arrived at by following the procedures given earlier. Example 9-8d presents a special problem, though by no means an unusual one—the lack of common tones. In example 9-9 (which is the same problem as example 8-8d) we see the iv6 chord with a different doubling. In moving to the V chord the upper D-flat$^1$ in the tenor cannot move in parallel octaves with the bass and so moves up to the E-natural$^1$, which causes the awkward interval of the augmented second. Good voice leading normally avoids the melodic interval of an augmented second. Faced with two poor choices, the solution shown in example 9-8d(4) is preferable. The solution in example 9-9 is not "wrong"; it might be used in some instances, more likely in keyboard writing than in vocal.

**EXAMPLE 9-9.** Alternative solution to example 9-8d

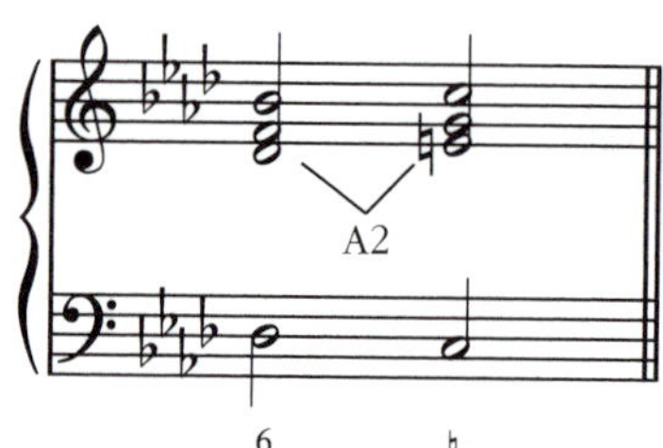


Some further examples of voice leading with first inversions are shown in example 9-10. The ii chord is used more often in first inversion than in root position, especially when nearing a cadence, as shown in example 9-10a, where the ii6 moves to a V7. In example 9-10b and c the successive first-inversion chords require some use of the rarer alternative doublings.

**EXAMPLE 9-10.** Voice leading with triads in first inversion

## Diminished Triads in First Inversion

Because they do not have a perfect fifth, diminished triads are especially unstable and require care in both doubling and voice leading. The vii° in major keys and the ii° and vii° in minor keys are most often found in first inversion. The reason for preferring this inversion is that in this arrangement the dissonance of the diminished fifth is not formed with the bass note.

### Doubling

In four-voice settings, composers have consistently avoided doubling the leading tone, preferring to double the third of diminished chords, as this is the tone that is not part of the dissonant tritone. Thus, in example 9-11, the doubling in c is considered more desirable than the doubling in a or b.

**EXAMPLE 9-11.** Doublings of diminished chords in first inversion

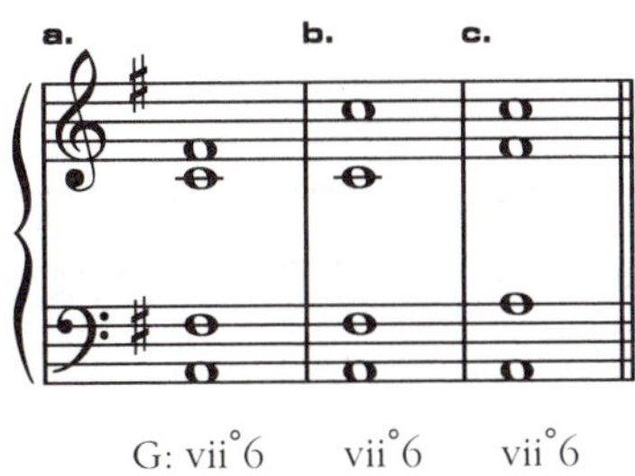


### Part Writing

The preferred voice leading for the progressions vii°6–I and ii°6–V is the same as that for chords with roots a step apart: The upper three voices move stepwise in contrary motion to the bass (see ex. 9-12a, b, and c). Example 9-12a shows the progression in major, example 9-12b in minor. A resolution to I6 is shown in example 9-12d. In minor keys, the bass figuration for vii°6 must show that the leading tone (a sixth above the bass) has been raised. Notice the use of the natural in the figured bass of example 9-12e and the slash in example 9-12f. Four-part realizations are shown below the figured basses in examples 9-12e and 9-12f.

**EXAMPLE 9-12.** Part writing with diminished chords in first inversions

## HARMONIZATION USING FIRST-INVERSION TRIADS

When the first inversions of triads are included in the harmonization of a soprano line, new possibilities arise in the selection of chords and for the melodic character of the bass line. The main reason for using first-inversion triads is to make possible a more conjunct bass line. Notice how much smoother the bass line becomes when inversions are used in example 9-13. The bass has many steps and no skips larger than a third. Compare this with the bass line using the same chords, but in root position, as shown in example 9-14. The parallel octaves and fifths that arise when only roots are in the bass make this chord selection unusable.

**EXAMPLE 9-13.** Conjunct bass line by use of first inversions

**EXAMPLE 9-14.** Bass line with root-position chords

## Procedure for Harmonization with First-Inversion Triads

As with root-position chords, the procedure for harmonization has two phases, planning the chords and part writing. In the first phase, planning the chords, it is wise to look for possible advantageous voice leading in the bass using first inversions. The three steps remain the same, but the inversions broaden the options at each step. The second phase, part writing, is now divided into two steps:

Step 1. Write the bass, using some first inversions to create a strong melodic line with a clear shape including periods of conjunct motion.

Step 2. Complete the part writing of the inner voices, making revisions in the chord selection to arrive at the best possible voice leading.

### First Inversions without Nonharmonic Tones

Example 9-15a shows the steps of the first phase below the melody. In deciding the final version, the possibilities for a smooth bass with first inversions were explored.

Example 9-15b shows a first attempt at writing the bass line. This attempt uses all roots, which results in unacceptable parallels. Example 9-15c shows the use of first inversions, a more acceptable solution. Example 9-15d adds the inner voices to complete the harmonization.

### First Inversions with Nonharmonic Tones

A further increase in the melodic strength of the bass line may be obtained by including some nonharmonic tones such as passing and neighbor tones. These may be added at the first or second step of part writing, but one should avoid parallel fifths or octaves between nonharmonic tones and chord tones, even if, as in example 9-16, unusual doubling is employed.

**EXAMPLE 9-15.** Steps in harmonizing with first-inversion chords and nonharmonic tones

Step 1.

Step 2.

**EXAMPLE 9-16.** Doubling to avoid parallel fifths

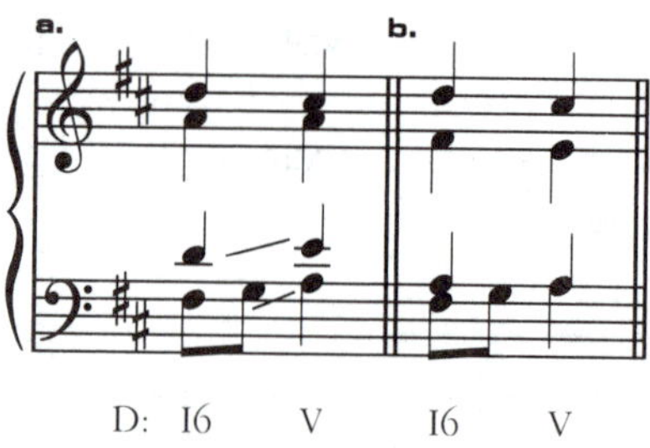


The harmonization of the melody in example 9-17 illustrates the use of a few nonharmonic tones in the final version of the bass (shown in example 9-20). Planning the chords is shown in example 9-17.

**EXAMPLE 9-17.** Planning the chords

In the first step of part writing, the bass is written without nonharmonic tones. This first version of the bass appears in example 9-18, where skips of a third are used. These may be filled in later with stepwise motion of eighth notes to create passing tones, if no parallel fifths result in the final version.

**EXAMPLE 9-18.** Step 1 of part writing: write the bass without nonharmonic tones

Step 2 of part writing is shown in example 9-19, still without the nonharmonic tones in the bass. Finally, after screening for parallels, the passing tones can fill in the thirds in the bass. The result (ex. 9-20) is a harmonization with a strong melodic bass.

**EXAMPLE 9-19.** Step 2 of part writing: fill in inner voices

**EXAMPLE 9-20.** Final harmonization with passing tones in the bass

The melody and bass first shown in example 9-13 are fully harmonized in example 9-21 with nonharmonic tones, which strengthen the bass line. Note that the repeated tones in the original bass line provide an opportunity for a neighbor tone that, when combined with the passing tone, yields a strong descending line.

**EXAMPLE 9-21.** Harmonized version of example 9-13

G: I IV6 V6 I vi6 IV6 ii6 V vi

## SUMMARY

Triads in first inversion are an important resource in developing the bass line, which is the most valuable voice in organizing and controlling harmony. Figured bass was the fundamental concept underlying the harmonic structure of ensemble music in the Baroque period. In figured bass the Arabic numbers below bass notes indicate intervals counted upward from the bass note. The chords thus implied are dealt with according to established principles of voice leading (part writing).

Triads in first inversion offer special problems in doubling and part writing, depending on the type of triad. The practice of composers in dealing with first inversions differs, depending on the chord type; major, minor, and diminished triads are each treated differently. While the part writing of major and minor chords in first inversion is basically similar, there are some important differences in doubling. Because they do not have a perfect fifth, diminished triads are especially unstable and require care in both doubling and voice leading.

When the first inversions of triads are included in the harmonization of a soprano, new possibilities arise in the selection of chords and for the melodic character of the bass line. The main reason for using first-inversion triads is to make possible a more conjunct bass line. As with root-position chords, the procedure for harmonization has two phases, planning the chords and part writing.

CHAPTER TEN

# Triads in Second Inversion and Inversions of the V7

**Terms Introduced in This Chapter**

six-four chord

cadential six-four chord

passing six-four chord

neighbor six-four chord

arpeggiated six-four chord

perfect authentic cadence

imperfect authentic cadence

Phrygian cadence

riads in second inversion and inversions of the dominant seventh are relatively common. They are handled in special ways, however, due largely to their dissonance.

## SIX-FOUR CHORDS

**six-four chord**

The second inversion of a triad is called a *six-four chord,* a term taken from the bass figuration for this chord. These numbers are written to the right of the Roman numerals. Example 10-1 shows the figured bass and the implied tones that would appear in the upper voices. On rare occasions one might also find the numbers $\begin{smallmatrix}8\\6\\4\end{smallmatrix}$.

**EXAMPLE 10-1.** **Figured bass for a triad in second inversion, or six-four chord**

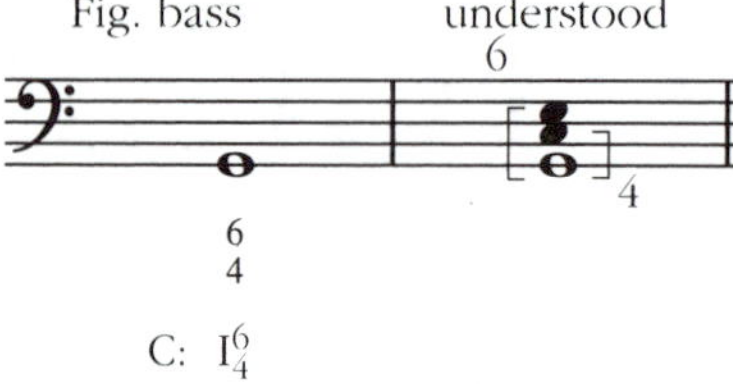


### Dissonance in the Six-Four Chord

The second inversions of major and minor triads are considered dissonant, so they are subject to a treatment different from that of root-position and first-inversion triads. A perfect fourth formed by the bass and an upper voice is considered dissonant (see ex. 10-2a), while a perfect fourth between upper voices is consonant (see ex. 10-2b). The diminished triad in second inversion (see ex. 10-2c) is also dissonant because of the tritone between the root and the fifth. Since the second inversion is dissonant, it requires a resolution with careful voice leading to a relatively stable chord.

**EXAMPLE 10-2.** Dissonance in the six-four chord

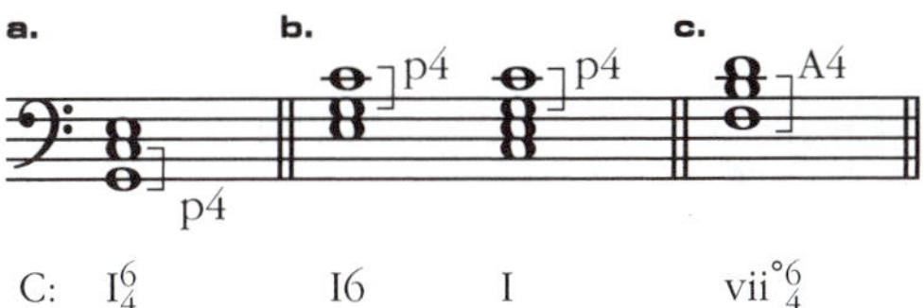


## Doubling

All major and minor six-four chords have the same doubling: The fifth (bass note) is always doubled. In the case of the diminished triad, the third is doubled, as it is the only tone not involved in the tritone. Example 10-3a–e shows four-voice settings of several six-four chords.

**EXAMPLE 10-3.** Four-voice settings of six-four chords

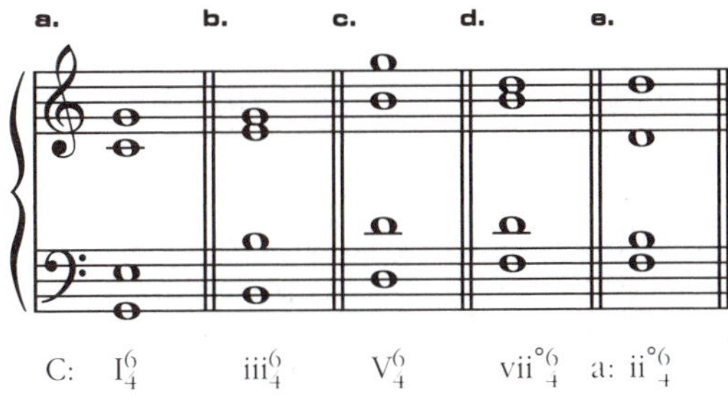


## Types of Six-Four Chords

The uses of six-four chords are so specialized that they may be described in a series of usage types, each with specific characteristics.

### The Cadential Six-Four Chord

**cadential six-four chord**

The most common and important use of a six-four chord is the tonic six-four chord at cadences, just before the dominant. This use of the $I^6_4$ is known as the *cadential six-four* chord. Notice in example 10-4, the smooth voice leading in the upper voices from the $I^6_4$ to V7 (see ex. 10-4a) and $I^6_4$ to V (see ex. 10-4b). The octave skip on the dominant ($\hat{5}$) in the bass is common in this resolution.

**EXAMPLE 10-4.** The cadential six-four chord

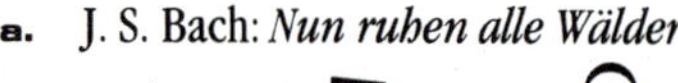

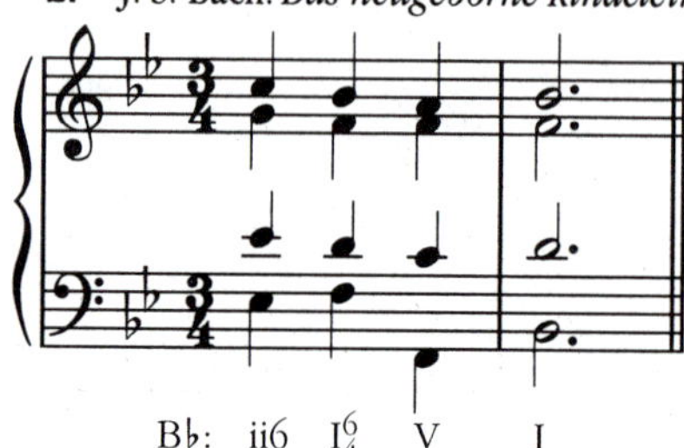


Several important points must be made in conjunction with the cadential six-four:

1. The bass is usually approached by step, from above or below. In the following chord, it is kept as a common tone or skips down an octave.
2. The cadential tonic six-four is usually in a stronger metric position than the V that follows. It may appear on the second beat of a $\frac{3}{4}$ measure, followed by the V on the third beat.
3. The upper voices move conservatively, avoiding skips.

These points, which reflect typical usage, are illustrated in examples 10-5a–d.

In example 10-6 the cadential six-four is shown in figured bass. This common pattern is interesting because it shows how figured bass symbols may be read vertically (as chord) and horizontally (as melodic lines). Notice in the voice leading that the 6 of the $\frac{6}{4}$ moves to the 5 while the 4 moves to the 3. Notice, too, that the 6 need not be in the soprano.

Because the cadential six-four is so clearly attached to the V, it is often considered not a true chord but rather a pattern of decorative nonchord tones leading to the V. In deciding where it fits in a normal progression, it cannot be considered a conventional I chord because of its instability. It is best to view the cadential tonic six-four as an expansion of the V. For purposes of analysis, it therefore belongs in chord group 2.

Other than the cadential I$^{6}_{4}$, the only other second-inversion triad found in a metrically strong position is the IV$^{6}_{4}$, as seen in example 10-7. It appears only as the penultimate chord at a cadence and then only rarely.

**EXAMPLE 10-5.** Typical use of the cadential six-four

**EXAMPLE 10-6.** Cadential six-four in figured bass and in realization

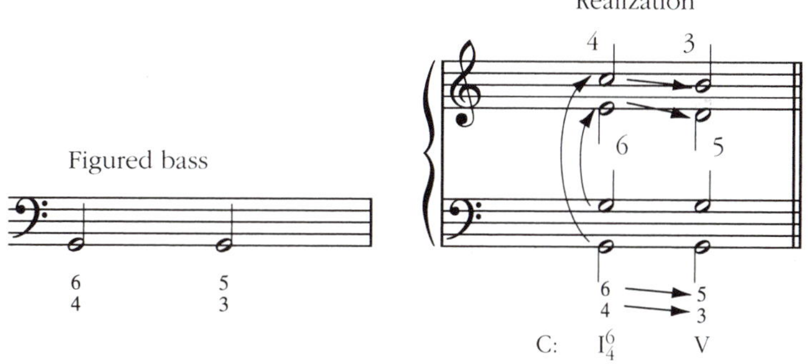


**EXAMPLE 10-7.** The $IV^6_4$ chord

Examples 10-8a–c show several different instances of cadential six-four chords in figured bass. Note the stepwise approach to the bass note of the six-four, the resolution into the V chord, and the various kinds of bass treatment: repeated bass note (in ex. 10-8a), octave skip in bass (in ex. 10-8b), and bass sustaining while the chord changes to $\begin{smallmatrix}5\\3\end{smallmatrix}$ (in ex. 10-8c).

**EXAMPLE 10-8.** Cadential six-four chords in figured bass and in realization

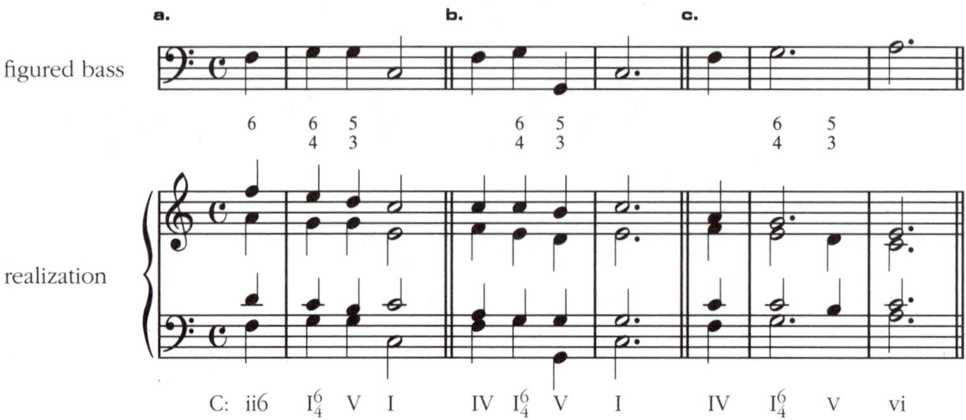


Similar examples of cadential six-four chords in minor are seen in examples 10-9a–c. Note the use of accidentals in the figured bass to indicate the leading tone (raised $\hat{7}$).

**EXAMPLE 10-9.** Cadential six-four chords in minor keys

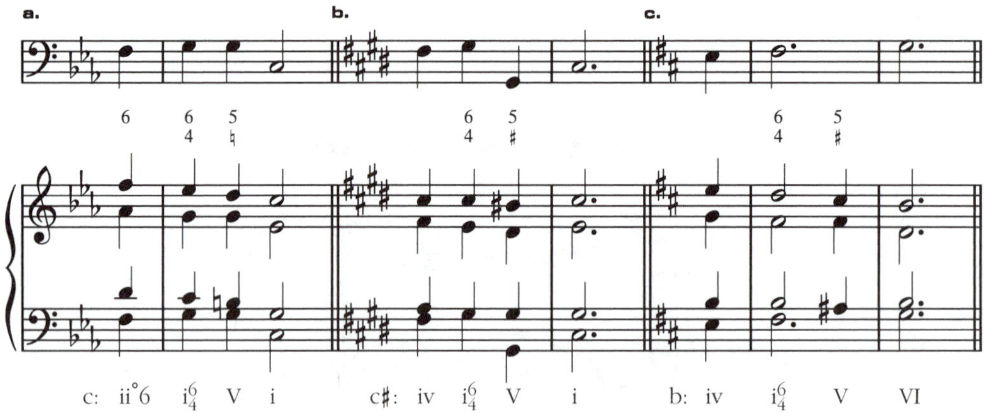

## The Passing Six-Four Chord

**passing six-four chord**

A less common type of triad in second inversion is the *passing six-four chord,* a six-four chord in which the bass tone is treated as if it were a passing tone. Such a case is seen in example 10-10a, where the $V^6_4$ appears between I and I6. Note the very smooth voice leading that produces this chord. This type of chord is always prepared and resolved with very conservative voice leading. Example 10-10b illustrates the same pattern with a descending bass line. In a figured bass the passing six-four would appear as seen in examples 10-11a–b.

**EXAMPLE 10-10.** Passing six-four chords

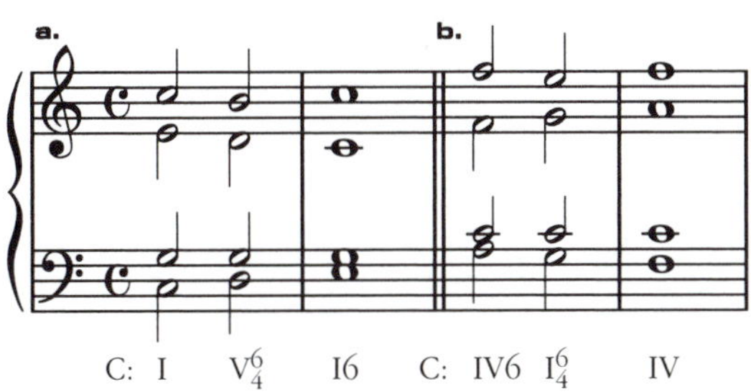


**EXAMPLE 10-11.** Passing six-four in figured bass and in realization

## The Neighbor Six-Four Chord

**neighbor six-four chord**

A *neighbor six-four chord* is a six-four chord in which two of the upper tones are treated like neighbor tones, while the bass is a common tone with the preceding and following chords. The same chord appears before and after it, in root position. The definition of the neighbor six-four chord ensures extremely conservative voice leading, as in example 10-12.

**EXAMPLE 10-12.** The neighbor six-four chord

Example 10-13 demonstrates the neighbor six-four chord in figured bass. Notice that the figured bass numbers resemble those for the cadential six-four; however, the progression is very different.

**EXAMPLE 10-13.** Neighbor six-four in figured bass and in realization

## The Arpeggiated Six-Four Chord

**arpeggiated six-four chord**

The *arpeggiated six-four chord* is a six-four chord that is preceded or followed by the same chord in root position or first inversion. The chord is arpeggiated to some degree in the bass, that is, the notes of the chord are presented singly, in melodic fashion. In such cases, there may be momentary appearances of an inversion or root position, but these will not necessarily all be heard as individual inverted chords. In analysis it is best to select the strongest emergent tone of the arpeggio to serve as representative for all versions of the chord in the passage. Example 10-14a shows this in a chorale, while example 10-4b is more typical of instrumental music. The $^{6}_{4}$ chords are marked with x above the staff but do not appear in the harmonic analysis, since the roots are emergent in the bass.

**EXAMPLE 10-14.** The arpeggiated six-four chord

## The Diminished Triad in Second Inversion

The diminished triad in second inversion may also appear as a neighbor, passing, or arpeggiated six-four, but it occurs in other situations as well. The vii$^{\circ}{}^{6}_{4}$ has a tritone between the bass, $\hat{4}$, and the root above, $\hat{7}$. The bass is usually approached either by step or as a common tone with the preceding chord. The chord typically resolves to I6, the bass descending to $\hat{3}$. The upper voices have some flexibility but are generally handled with conservative voice leading. Example 10-15a shows some approaches to the vii$^{\circ}{}^{6}_{4}$, while example 10-15b gives sample resolutions.

**EXAMPLE 10-15.** The diminished triad in second inversion

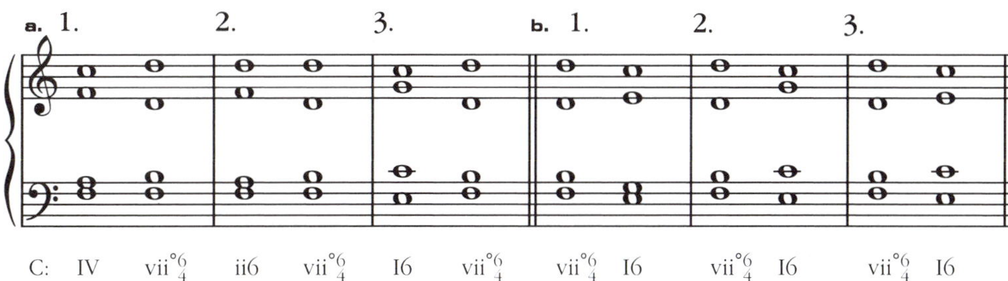

The ii°$^6_4$, like the vii°$^6_4$, is treated with conservative voice leading. The progression is usually normal, with the bass resolving down from $\hat{6}$ to $\hat{5}$. In example 10-16a, some sample preparations are shown. Example 10-16b shows sample resolutions. On rare occasions a six-four chord may appear with the bass prepared by skip, as in example 10-16a(3), but it should then move into the next chord by step or as a common tone.

**EXAMPLE 10-16.** Voice leading with the ii°$^6_4$ chord

## INVERSIONS OF THE V7

The V7, previously studied in root position, may contribute to a more varied bass line if inversions are used. To facilitate the study of these chords, we will survey bass figurations for seventh chords.

### Bass Figurations

The Arabic numbers used with Roman numerals to designate inversions are derived from the figured bass system. Example 10-17 shows the standard figurations and the application to Roman numerals, the "understood" pitch classes implied above the bass, and some possible realizations in four voices.

**EXAMPLE 10-17.** Bass figurations for seventh chords

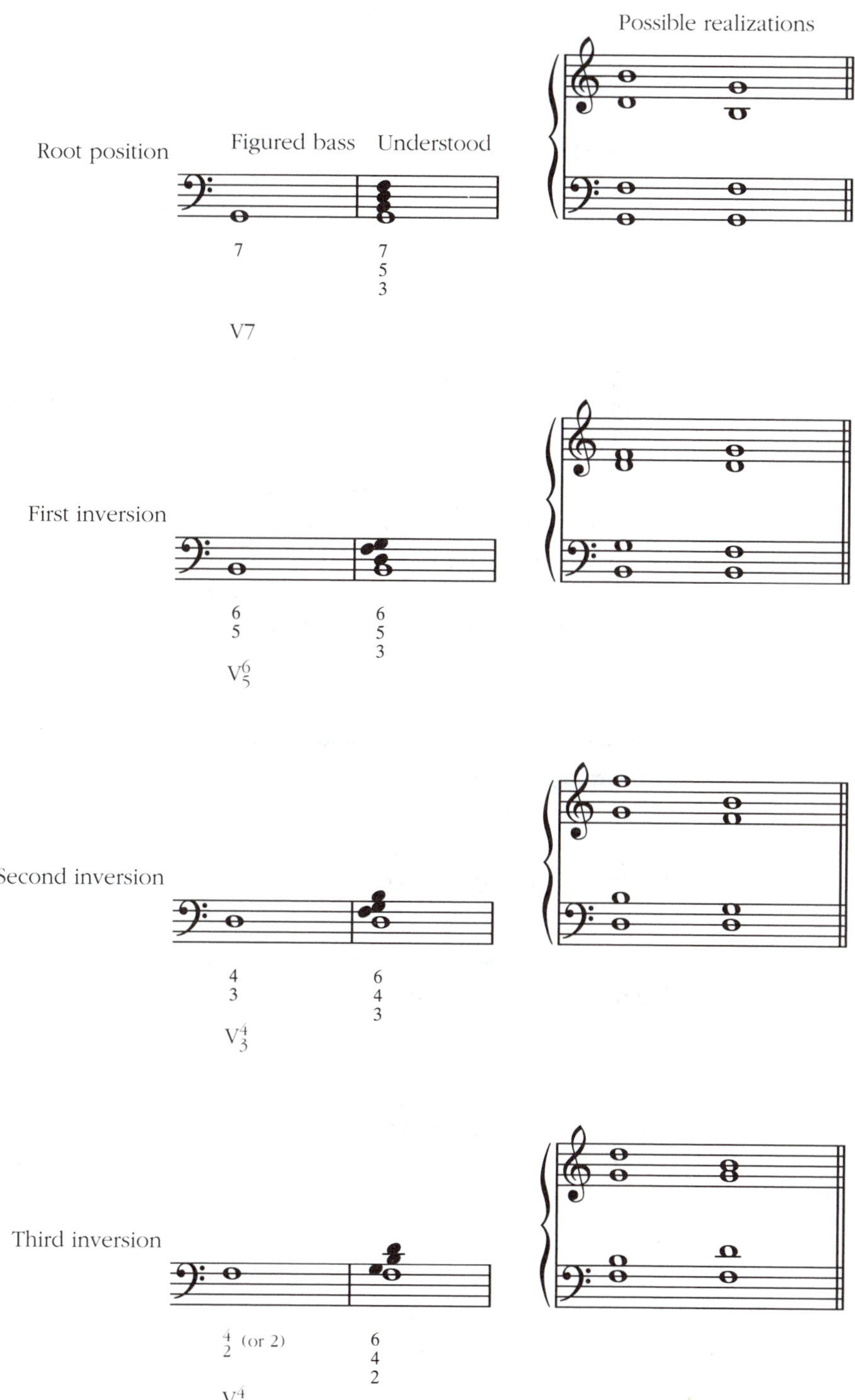

There are several related versions of these figurations that may appear in a figured bass, including versions in which the number 3 is replaced by an accidental and the numbers 6 and 4 are altered to indicate a raised $\hat{7}$ in minor keys. The additional figurations are:

root position: 7

| 7 | 7 | 7 | 7 | 7 | 7 | 7 |
|---|---|---|---|---|---|---|
| 5 | 5 | 5 | 5 | 3 | ♯ | ♮ |
| 3 | ♯ | ♮ | | | | |

first inversion: $^6_5$

| 6 |
|---|
| 5 |
| 3 |

second inversion: $^4_3$

| 6 | 6 | 6♯ | 6♮ |
|---|---|---|---|
| 4 | 4 | 4 | 4 |
| 3 | 3 | 3 | 3 |

third inversion: $^4_2$

| 6 | 6 | 6 | 6 |
|---|---|---|---|
| 4 | 4+ | 4♯ | 4♮ |
| 2 | 2 | 2 | 2 |

Inversions of the V7 share many features in their treatment. Since chord members are normally not omitted in four-voice settings, no doublings appear. The progressions before and after do not differ fundamentally from those for the root-position V7. The voice leading is very conservative in each case, the tritone resolving with the $\hat{7}$ ascending and the $\hat{4}$ descending. Details of the preparation and resolution differ in specific ways, however.

## First Inversion

When the $V^6_5$ resolves to I in root position, the seventh of the chord descends and the third of the chord moves up a half step, as shown in examples 10-18a–c.

## Second Inversion

When the second inversion, $V^4_3$, resolves, it may move to either I or I6. Again, the voice leading is smooth, as in example 10-19a; however, notice the accommodation made in example 10-19b, where the seventh of the $V^4_3$ chord does not descend. This is acceptable when the seventh of the chord is in an inner voice. It is also possible to resolve the seventh and double the third in the I6, as in example 10-19c.

## Third Inversion

The third inversion, $V^4_2$, always resolves to I6. The seventh of the chord in the bass is very prominent. The third inversion is often prepared with conjunct motion or a common tone in the bass, as shown in examples 10-20a–d. Notice in example 10-20e the optional doubling for the tonic triad in first inversion to accommodate the voice leading.

**EXAMPLE 10-18.** Resolution of the V$^6_5$

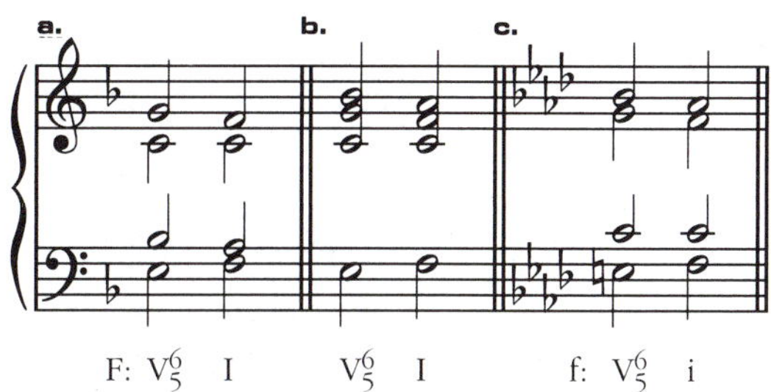


**EXAMPLE 10-19.** Resolution of the V$^4_3$

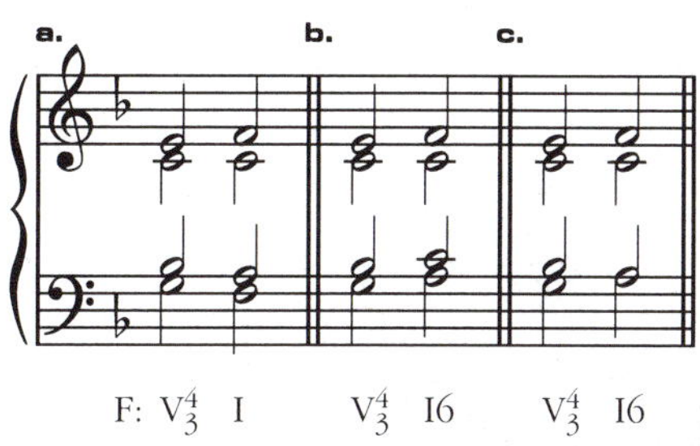


**EXAMPLE 10-20.** Resolution of the V$^4_2$

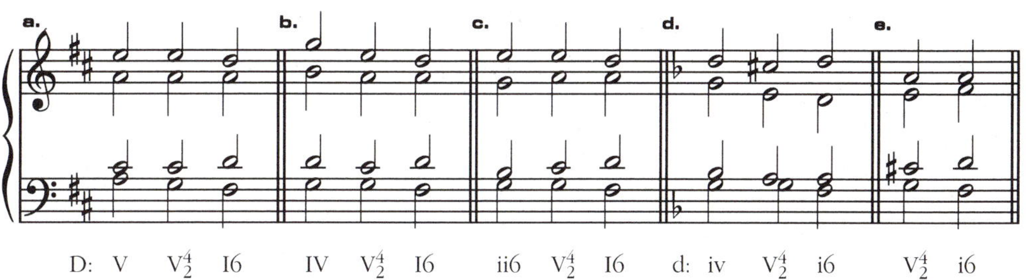


Examples from the literature illustrate the use of inversions of the V7 and their resolutions. Example 10-21 shows how useful inversions are in providing variety in the appearances of the frequently used V chord. Mozart uses the first and second inversions earlier in the phrase, saving the more solid root position V for the cadence. Notice that V$^4_3$ resolves here to I6, allowing the bass to pursue a short scale in parallel tenths with the melody. This resembles the treatment of a passing six-four chord.

**EXAMPLE 10-21.** Mozart: Horn Concerto No. 3, K. 447, second movement

Example 10-22 shows $V^4_3$ moving equally well to I.

**EXAMPLE 10.22.** Mozart: Piano Sonata, K. 545, first movement

The third inversion, $V^4_2$, must resolve to I6. The chord seventh in the bass is rather striking in this case because it is approached by a leap, which is somewhat unusual.

**EXAMPLE 10-23.** Beethoven: Piano Sonata, op. 13, second movement

# THE COMPLETE LIST OF HARMONIC CADENCES

Now that all inversions of all diatonic triads and the V7 have been considered, the list of harmonic cadences can be refined to a greater degree. In particular, features of the soprano and bass may be taken into account in order to distinguish between two types of authentic cadences.

**perfect authentic cadence**

**imperfect authentic cadence**

A cadence is said to be a *perfect authentic cadence* if it meets these conditions: The final chord is I in root position with the tonic ($\hat{1}$) in the soprano, and the penultimate chord is V(7) in root position. If the cadence moves from chord group 2 to group 1 and these exact conditions are not present, the cadence is less conclusive and called an *imperfect authentic cadence.* British writers sometimes refer to the perfect authentic cadence as a "full close." Example 10-24a shows the perfect authentic cadence, and example 10-24b, the imperfect authentic.

**EXAMPLE 10-24.** Authentic cadences

**a.** Perfect authentic cadences

**b.** Imperfect authentic cadences

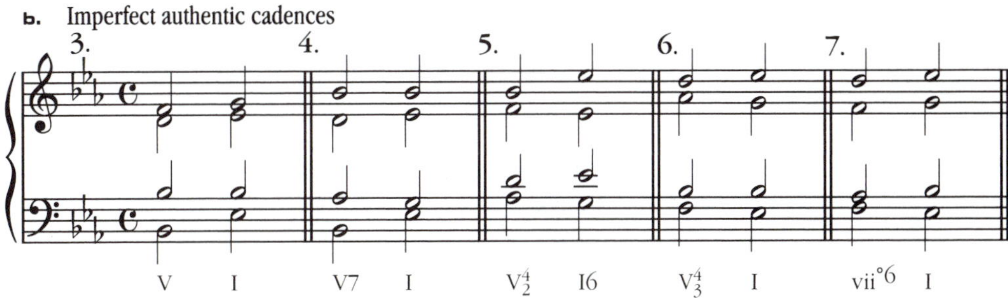


**Phrygian cadence**

Special mention should be made of the *Phrygian cadence,* a half cadence in a minor key in which iv6 moves to V. This is seen in example 10-25, with a smooth preparation coming from a minor dominant chord.

**EXAMPLE 10-25.** Handel: Concerto Grosso, op. 3, no. 4, second movement

For the deceptive cadence, introduced earlier, it is best to have the dominant chord in complete form (see ex. 10-26a). If the fifth is omitted, the voice leading becomes problematic; that is, it may be difficult to avoid parallel octaves or an unusual doubling (see ex. 10-26b). The third is often doubled in the vi, as in example 10-26c. In example 10-26d, the doubled third in the VI avoids an augmented second in the tenor.

**EXAMPLE 10-26.** Deceptive cadences

Following is a complete list of the cadence types with abbreviations that may be useful in analysis.

Conclusive cadences (ending with I or i)
- perfect authentic cadence (PAC)
- imperfect authentic cadence (IAC)
- plagal cadence (PC)

Inconclusive cadences (not ending with I or i)
- half cadence (HC)
- deceptive cadence (DC)

Note that the plagal and deceptive cadences are formed by alternate rather than normal progressions. Irregular progressions almost never occur at cadences. When used, they are usually placed earlier in the phrase and are used to obtain smooth voice leading.

## SUMMARY

Because they are dissonant, triads in second inversion and inversions of the dominant seventh require special treatment. The second inversion of a triad is called a six-four chord, a term taken from the bass figuration for this chord. The fifth is always doubled in major and minor six-four chords.

The uses of six-four chords are so specialized that they may be described in a series of types, each with specific characteristics: the cadential six-four, the passing six-four, the neighbor six-four, and the arpeggiated six-four. The diminished triad in second inversion requires special treatment to allow proper resolution of the tritone.

Inversions of the V7 may contribute to a more varied bass line. Certain sets of Arabic numbers derived from figured bass are used with Roman numerals to designate the inversions of triads (6 $^{6}_{4}$) and of seventh chords ($^{6}_{5}$ $^{4}_{3}$ $^{4}_{2}$).

The complete list of harmonic cadences includes three conclusive cadences: PAC, IAC, and PC; and two inconclusive cadences: HC and DC.

CHAPTER ELEVEN

# Nonharmonic Tones: Analysis

**Terms Introduced in This Chapter**

- escape tone (ET)
- anticipation (Ant)
- suspension (Sus)
- retardation (Ret)
- appoggiatura (App)
- pedal point (Ped)
- double neighbor group (DNG)
- consonant nonharmonic tone
- chromatic nonharmonic tone

Harmonic analysis with Roman numerals appears to emphasize chord relationships and chord characteristics. Other significant aspects of music, however, are also part of harmonic analysis. A particularly important aspect of analysis is the identification of nonharmonic tones and the special features that characterize each specific type. Before clarifying these types, we will consider the general characteristics of nonharmonic tones.

## BASIC CHARACTERISTICS

Typically, nonharmonic tones are dissonant, creating short-term tension as they "clash" with the relatively stable, consonant chord tones. While this image is only a generalization, initially it is valuable in considering the features typical of most nonharmonic tones. Nonharmonic tones are melodic events with essential harmonic relationships. This is revealed in the three basic identifying features for all nonharmonic tones.

1. *Preparation.* This is the preceding chord tone in the voice in which the nonharmonic tone will appear.
2. *Nonharmonic tone.* This note is not a member of the chord, is usually dissonant with the sounding chord, and is perceived as unstable.
3. *Resolution.* This is the succeeding chord tone in the same voice. The chord may be different from the chord during preparation.

## TYPES OF NONHARMONIC TONES

The three basic identifying features are used to describe the nine specific types of nonharmonic tones. The passing tone (PT) and the neighbor tone (NT) were explained in chapter 8 and will be only briefly reviewed here.

### Passing Tone

The passing tone (PT) is always prepared by step and resolved by step, continuing in the direction from which it was approached; that is, if it were approached from below, it will resolve by continuing upward. As explained in chapter 8, a passing tone may be accented or unaccented, ascending or descending, or there may be double passing tones.

## Neighbor Tone

The neighbor tone (NT) is prepared by step, either from above or below, and resolves in the direction opposite to that by which it was prepared, so it returns to the note from which it came. Examples 11-1a–b illustrate neighbor and passing tones in music literature. In example 11-1b, passing tones appear in all four voices.

**EXAMPLE 11-1.** Neighbor and passing tones

**a.** Mozart: Piano Sonata, K. 284, third movement

**b.** Bach: *Allein Gott in der Höh' sei Ehr'*

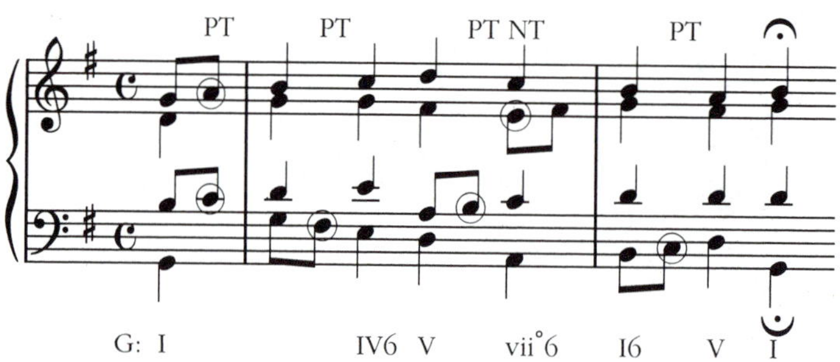


## Escape Tone

**escape tone (ET)**

The *escape tone* (ET) is normally unaccented. It is prepared by step and resolved by skip, usually in the direction opposite to that from which it was approached. It is typically prepared with upward motion and resolved downward by a third. Example 11-2 illustrates the typical treatment. Example 11-3 shows the handling of escape tones in a four-voice setting.

## Anticipation

**anticipation (Ant)**

The *anticipation* (*Ant*) is prepared by step and resolved with a repeated tone, or holds while the chord changes. It "anticipates" the change of harmony. It is always unaccented, usually anticipating a downbeat, as in example 11-4. Typical treatment of the anticipation in four-part writing is seen in example 11-5.

**EXAMPLE 11-2.** Mozart: *Don Giovanni*

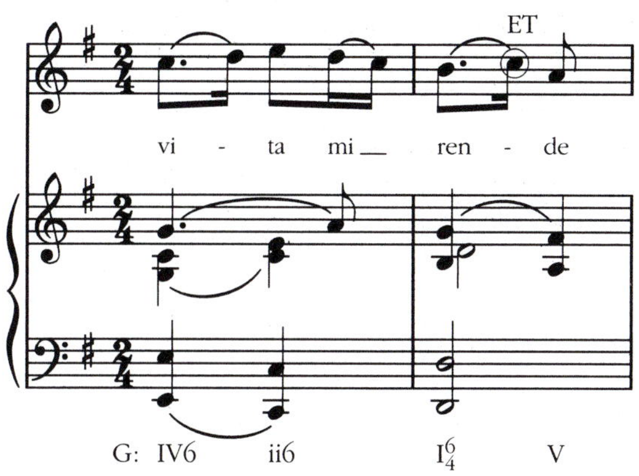


**EXAMPLE 11-3.** Escape tones in four-voice settings

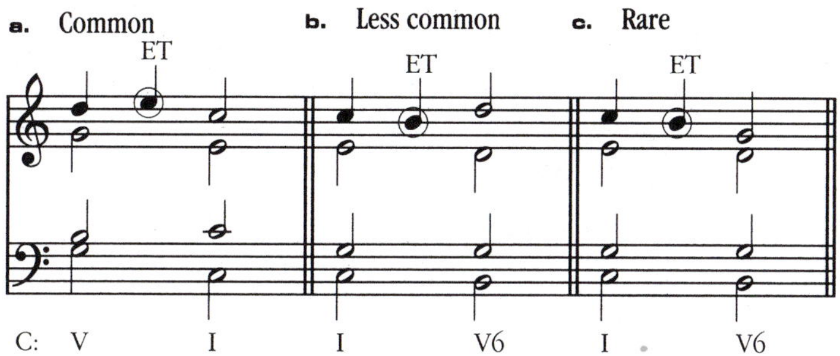


**EXAMPLE 11-4.** J. S. Bach: French Suite V, BWV 817, Gavotte

**EXAMPLE 11-5.** Anticipations in four-voice settings

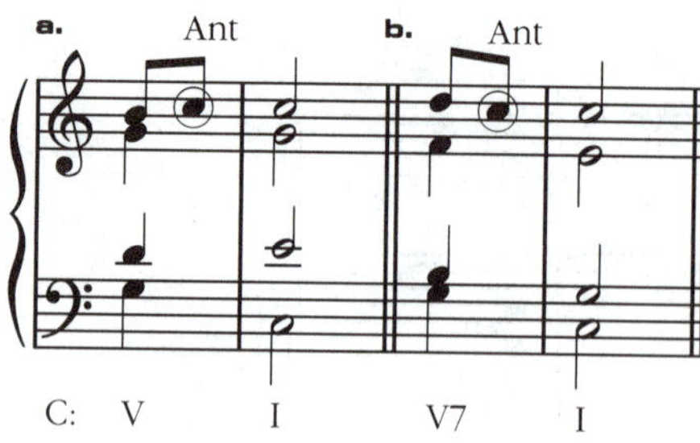


## Suspension

**suspension (Sus)**

The *suspension* (*Sus*) is prepared with a repeated tone or a held tone that becomes a nonharmonic tone when the harmony changes. Thus, it becomes a nonchord tone without moving. It resolves by step downward while the new chord continues to sound. The suspended note occurs on a stronger metric point than the resolution. Typical suspensions are seen in example 11-6a at (1), (2), (3), and (4); and in example 11-6b at (5) and (6). In example 11-6b the suspensions are not tied but articulated. Suspensions in four-part writing are illustrated in example 11-7.

**EXAMPLE 11-6.** Suspensions

a. J. S. Bach: French Suite III, BWV 814, Sarabande

b. Haydn: Piano Sonata in G major, Hob. XVI: 27, second movement

**EXAMPLE 11-7.** Suspensions in four-part writing

## Retardation

**retardation (Ret)**

The *retardation* (*Ret*) is like the suspension in every way except that it resolves upward. Note in example 11-8 the brief preparation and the strong dissonance with the nonharmonic tone.

**EXAMPLE 11-8.** Mozart: Menuet, K. 15

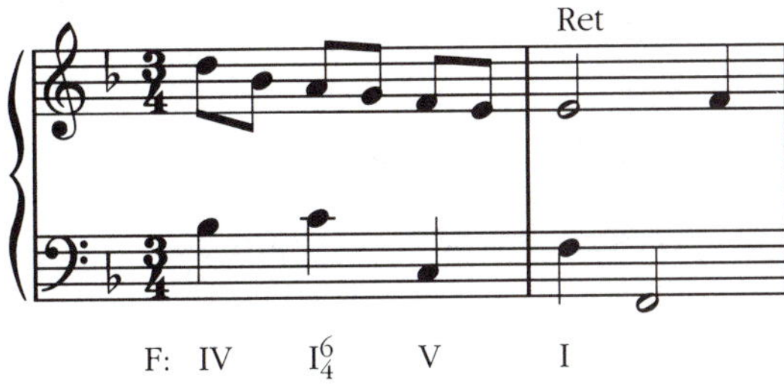


## Appoggiatura

**appoggiatura (App)**

The *appoggiatura* (*App*) is prepared by leap and resolved by step, usually in the direction opposite to that from which it was approached. In example 11-9a, there is a typical appoggiatura and an accented passing tone. Example 11-9b illustrates an unusual type of appoggiatura: It resolves in the same direction as its approach. The term *appoggiatura* means "leaning tone" in Italian. The quality of leaning is a result of being accented, but occasionally an unaccented appoggiatura will be found, as in example 11-10c. Often the appoggiatura is longer than its resolution, as in example 11-9b. Other typical treatments of the appoggiatura are shown in examples 11-10a–c.

**EXAMPLE 11-9.** Appoggiaturas

a. Mozart: *Wie unglücklich bin ich nit,* K. 147

b. J. C. Bach: Piano Sonata, op. 5, no. 3, first movement

**EXAMPLE 11-10.** Treatments of appoggiaturas

## Pedal Point

**pedal point (Ped)**

The *pedal point* (*Ped*) is prepared with a chord tone that is held or repeated through one or more changes in the harmony. At some point the tone does not belong to the sounding chord. It continues to hold or repeat until it is resolved once again by becoming a chord tone. It usually occurs in the bass, but it may appear in any voice. Pedal points are usually on the tonic or dominant tone. They are often used by a composer to give particular emphasis to a tone through its apparent persistence. In example 11-11a, the tonic in the bass begins by being a chord tone, but it becomes dissonant with the harmony until the final I chord. Note that the inversions are not indicated when the harmony is dissonant with a pedal point in the bass. The nonharmonic tone is described below the staff as "I pedal" (tonic pedal).

The pedal point effect may fluctuate in the course of a sustained tone; that is, the pedal tone may alternate between being a chord tone or a nonharmonic tone. Two repeated tones are seen in the tenor and bass of example 11-11b, but notice that only one tone at a time is functioning as a pedal point, the tenor on the second beat of measure 1 and the bass on the first beat of measure 2. This example might be described as a "double pedal point," but, since only one tone at a time is dissonant with the harmony, this is not a very exact description. Note that inversions are shown when the bass is a chord tone, as in the second beat of measure 2 in example 11-11b.

**EXAMPLE 11-11.** Pedal points

**a.** Beethoven: Piano Sonata, op. 14, no. 1, first movement

**b.** Schumann: *Album for the Young,* op. 68, no. 18, "The Reaper's Song"

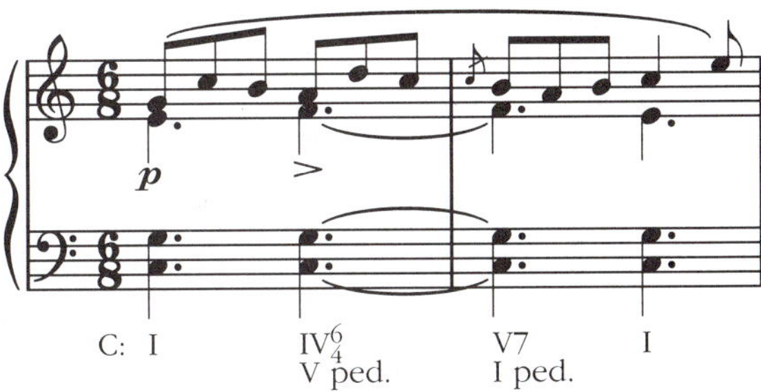


## Double Neighbor Group

**double neighbor group (DNG)**

The *double neighbor group* (*DNG*) consists of two successive nonharmonic tones between two chord tones of the same pitch. The nonharmonic tones are a step below and a step above the surrounding chord tones; they appear like a lower neighbor tone followed by an upper neighbor tone without a chord tone between them. Example 11-12a shows this in simple form, and 11-12b shows an example in music literature. Notice that the preparation is stepwise, as is the resolution.

**EXAMPLE 11-12.** Double neighbor groups

**a.** Example

**b.** Beethoven: Rondo, op. 51, no. 2

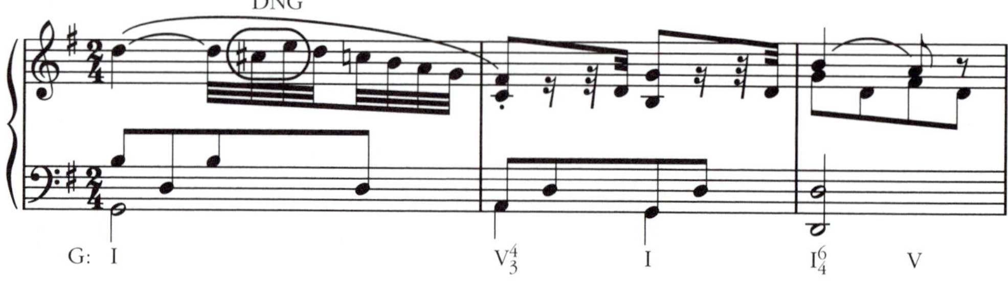


# SPECIAL USAGE

Not all nonharmonic tones are used equally. A broad generalization about the frequency of use of various types of nonharmonic tones might divide the types into three groups:

Very common: passing tones, neighbor tones

Common: appoggiatura, anticipation, suspension

Less common: escape tone, retardation, pedal point, double neighbor group

Occasionally, nonharmonic tones are used in ways that depart from typical models.

## Consonant Nonharmonic Tones

**consonant nonharmonic tone**

Sometimes the effect of a nonharmonic tone can be heard even when there is no dissonance, so as to create a *consonant nonharmonic tone.* Whether a passage should be analyzed as having a consonant nonharmonic tone or as having a new chord depends on the duration and the prevailing harmonic rhythm. At letter x in example 11-13a, there is the possibility of a brief ii chord, but it is unlikely that one will hear this as a real chord: It forms a very irregular progression. The E circled in the alto has so much the character of a neighbor tone that one hears it as nonharmonic. The x in example 11-13b indicates an unaccented, consonant neighbor tone.

**EXAMPLE 11-13.** Consonant nonharmonic tones

**a.** J. S. Bach: *Allein Gott in der Höh' sei Ehr'*

**b.** J. S. Bach: *Meinem Jesum lass ich nicht*

## Chromatic Nonharmonic Tones

**chromatic nonharmonic tones**

Nonharmonic tones that are chromatic alterations of the diatonic pitches are *chromatic nonharmonic tones.* Such alterations are occasionally found with passing tones or neighbor tones. Example 11-14 illustrates this in the first and third beats of measure 2 and the third beat of measure 3. Successive passing tones are also used. Chromatic nonharmonic tones (circled in example 11-14) have the same characteristics as diatonic nonharmonic tones, except that the chromatic nonharmonic tones are more prominent.

## Simultaneous Nonharmonic Tones

Occasionally, two or more nonharmonic tones occur simultaneously. Each nonharmonic tone is described according to its preparation, resolution, and rhythmic position. In example 11-15a, there are simultaneous neighbor tones; in example 11-15b we find a "double suspension."

**EXAMPLE 11-14.** Haydn: Piano Sonata in E minor, Hob. XVI:34, second movement

**EXAMPLE 11-15.** Simultaneous nonharmonic tones

**a.** Brahms: *Variations on a Theme of Haydn,* op. 56b

**b.** Mozart: Piano Sonata, K. 284, third movement

## Anomalies

Occasionally, one encounters a nonharmonic tone that is difficult to categorize because it eludes established definitions. The listener's ear is usually quick to perceive the intent of such passages, despite any difficulties with terminology that may confront the analyst. In example 11-16 the A in the alto at (1) is a suspension, but the F-sharp at (2) intrudes before the resolution at (3). The F-sharp has the contour of an appoggiatura, but it is not preceded by a chord tone. The effect is of a suspension decorated with an appoggiatura.

**EXAMPLE 11-16.** J. S. Bach: *Nun danket alle Gott*

The resolution of a nonharmonic tone is usually consonant, but it sometimes happens that the chord of preparation and resolution is dissonant, for example, V7. In example 11-16, the neighbor tone in the tenor is prepared by and resolves to the seventh of the V7 chord.

In example 11-17 two nonharmonic tones appear in succession in an atypical way. An escape tone does not follow the escape tone nor does a chord tone precede the appoggiatura. The typical contours for these two types of nonharmonic tones are preserved, however.

**EXAMPLE 11-17.** Mozart: Piano Sonata, K. 545, second movement

## SUMMARY

A particularly important aspect of analysis is the identification of nonharmonic tones and the special features that characterize each specific type. The nature of nonharmonic tones as melodic events with essential harmonic relationships is revealed in the three basic identifying features for all nonharmonic tones: the preparation, the nonharmonic tone itself, and the resolution.

The three basic identifying features are used to describe the nine specific types of nonharmonic tones: passing tone, neighbor tone, appoggiatura, escape tone, anticipation, suspension, retardation, pedal point, and double neighbor group. The most commonly used nonharmonic tones are passing tones and neighbor tones, while the least used are escape tone, anticipation, and pedal point.

Sometimes the effect of a nonharmonic tone can be heard even when there is no dissonance, as when a tone forms a new chord that is heard as irregular in progression. Nonharmonic tones may be altered tones, that is, chromatic alterations of the diatonic pitches. Occasionally, two or more nonharmonic tones occur simultaneously, or one encounters a nonharmonic tone that is difficult to categorize because it eludes established definitions. Such cases are defined as combinations of nonharmonic tones with modified features.

CHAPTER TWELVE

# Nonharmonic Tones: Writing

Nonharmonic tones generate special melodic interest in relation to a harmonic context. In writing nonharmonic tones, one must consider the harmony that appears with and around them, whether in a four-part setting or with figured bass.

## WRITING SPECIFIC TYPES OF NONHARMONIC TONES

To aid you in writing nonharmonic tones, we will consider the typical treatment of each type, with particular emphasis on the chord tones around it, to see where a particular type might be introduced.

### Passing Tones

Tones lying a third apart may be connected by a passing tone, or tones a step apart may be connected by a chromatic passing tone. Example 12-1 illustrates this.

**EXAMPLE 12-1.** Typical treatment of passing tones

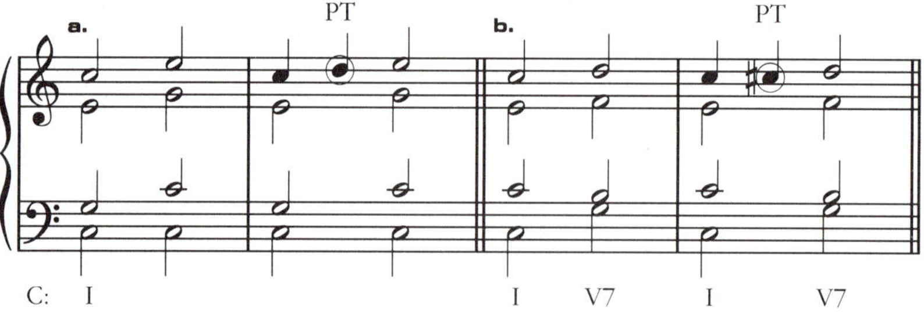


### Neighbor Tones

Repeated tones may be separated by a neighbor tone. Example 12-2 shows both lower and upper neighbor tones.

**EXAMPLE 12-2.** Treatment of neighbor tones

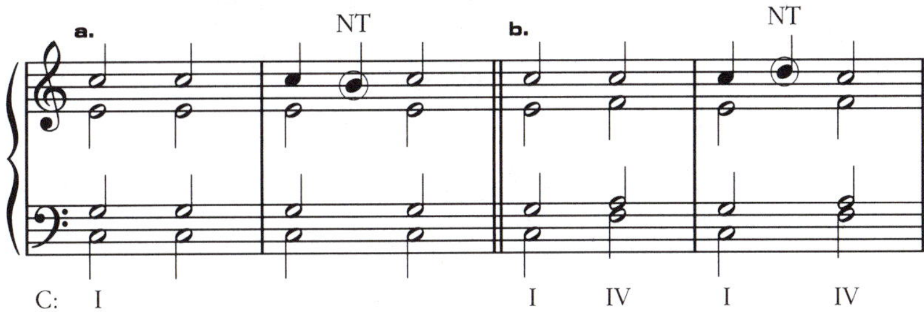


## Appoggiaturas and Escape Tones

The chord tones on each side of an appoggiatura and an escape tone are often a step apart. In examples 12-3a and b, notice the location of the nonharmonic tone relative to its resolution. As is usual, the appoggiaturas are metrically accented, and the escape tones are unaccented.

**EXAMPLE 12-3.** Appoggiaturas and escape tones

**a.** Appoggiatura

**b.** Escape tones

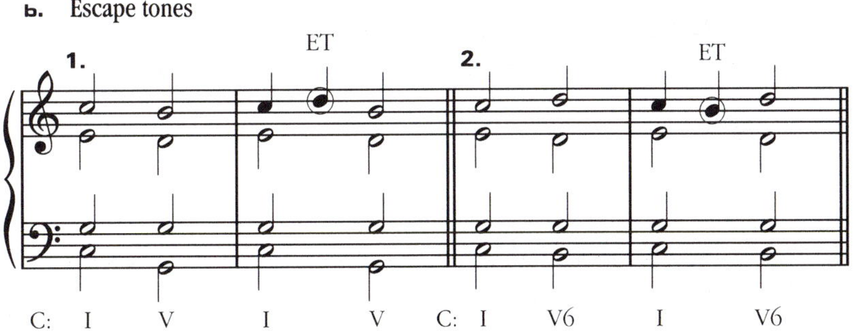

## Suspensions and Retardations

Suspensions may be used to delay a downward stepwise movement, as shown in example 12-4a. Retardations delay an upward stepwise movement, as shown in example 12-4b.

**EXAMPLE 12-4.** Suspensions and retardations

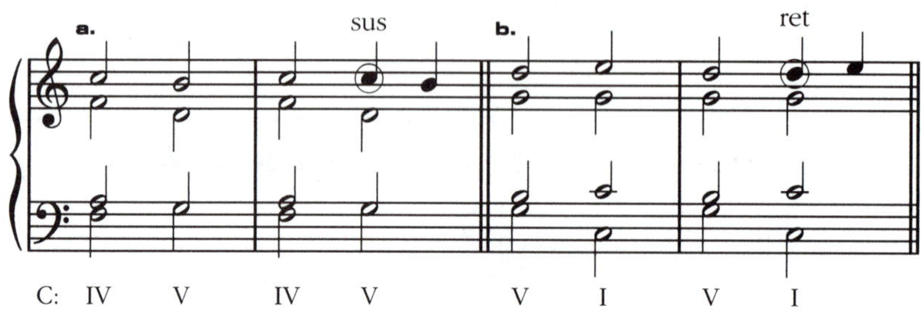


## Anticipations

Anticipations occur at points of stepwise motion. The new chord tone appears prematurely before the chord changes, as in example 12-5.

**EXAMPLE 12-5.** Anticipations

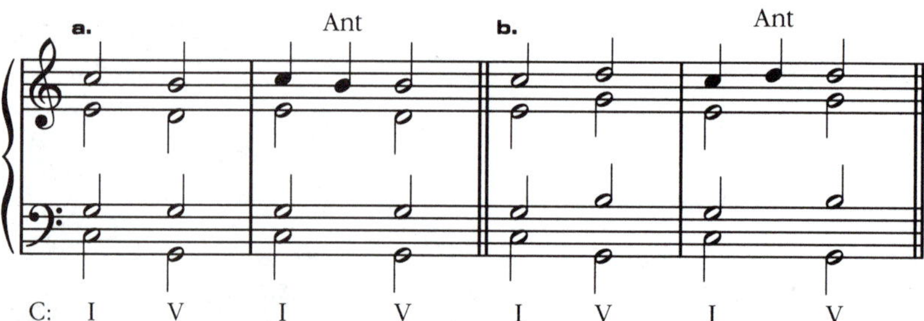


## Double Neighbor Groups

Repeated tones may be separated by a double neighbor group. Example 12-6a shows the upper tone followed by the lower, and example 12-6b shows the reverse.

**EXAMPLE 12-6.** Double neighbor groups

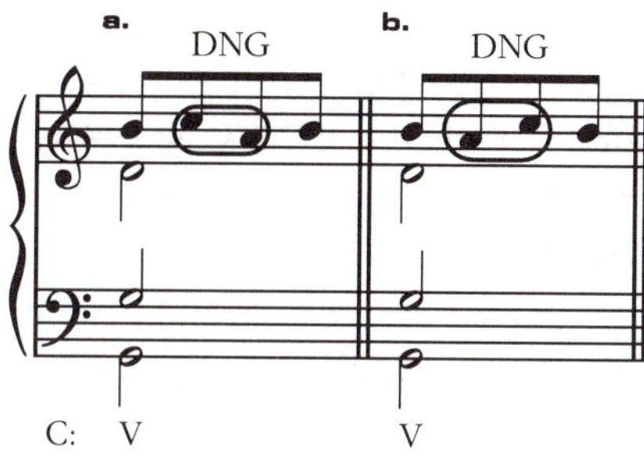


## Pedal Points

Repeated tones, usually in the bass, may be combined with a change of chord in the upper voices, creating a pedal point. Example 12-7a shows a pedal point on the dominant, while example 12-7b has a tonic pedal point.

**EXAMPLE 12-7.** Pedal points

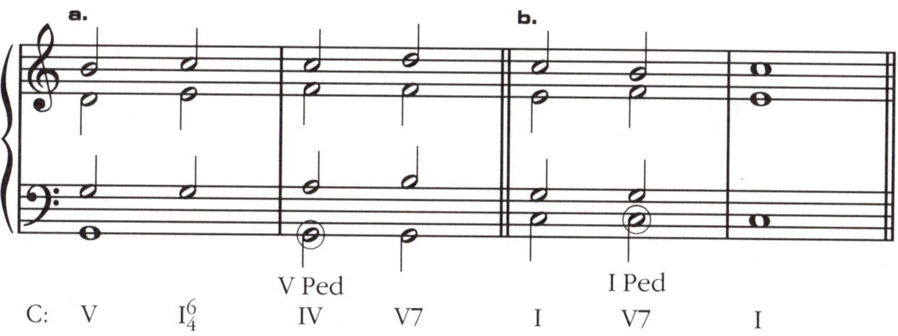


# NONHARMONIC TONES IN FIGURED BASS

Since figured bass symbols represent intervals above the bass note, it is possible to indicate horizontal movement as well as vertical sonorities. This is done by placing the appropriate numbers close together horizontally. The motion indicated by these symbols is always stepwise. Thus, if you find 4–3, the implication is that the voice that has the 4 will move to the 3. The suspension is the nonharmonic tone most commonly shown with figured bass. Suspensions may be understood in more detail by considering their application in figured bass.

## Suspensions and Figured Bass

Because the suspension is accented it gains prominence, but, since the preparatory tone is the same pitch, it has a particularly smooth effect. A suspension may occur whenever a voice descends by step, moving into a new harmony. If the descent is delayed while the other voices move to the new chord tones, the delayed voice will be "suspended" until it descends to its new chord tone. The suspension must be "prepared," that is, that pitch must be a chord tone in the preceding chord.

### Suspensions in Upper Voices

There are three intervallic situations in which suspensions in the upper voices work best: 4–3, 7–6, and 9–8. The most common suspension is 4–3. In example 12-8a, only chord tones are shown, while example 12-8b adds the 4–3 suspension. The figured bass in example 12-8b shows that the other voices hold (indicated by the short dashes) while the 4 moves to 3.

**EXAMPLE 12-8.** Suspension shown in figured bass

In examples 12-9a–e, different suspensions are compared. Typically the elaborate figured bass numbers shown in examples 12-8 are not used. Example 12-9 shows the more common simpler figuration. The tone of resolution is not usually heard with the suspended tone in 4–3 or 7–6 suspensions. In the 9–8 suspension, however, the 8 is often doubled.

In example 12-10 you see a figure that has become known as a suspension with a decorated resolution. The resolution includes a lower neighbor tone.

**EXAMPLE 12-9.** Various suspensions in figured bass

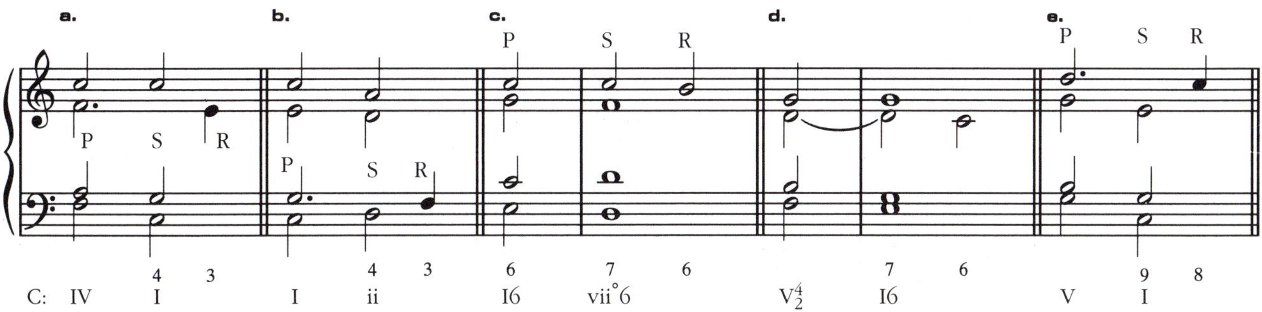


**EXAMPLE 12-10.** Suspension with a decorated resolution

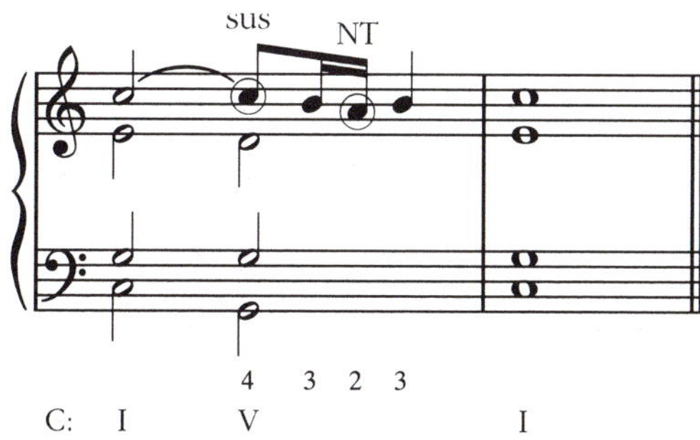


Example 12-11 illustrates a chain of suspensions. Example 12-11a shows the figured bass, while example 12-11b shows the realization. These are a series of successive 7–6 suspensions. The voice leading must avoid parallel octaves, since the prevailing motion of the voices is downward. The suspensions are kept in a single voice because each tone of resolution becomes the preparation for the following suspension. In the alto part the first D resolves one suspension while preparing another.

**EXAMPLE 12-11.** A chain of suspensions

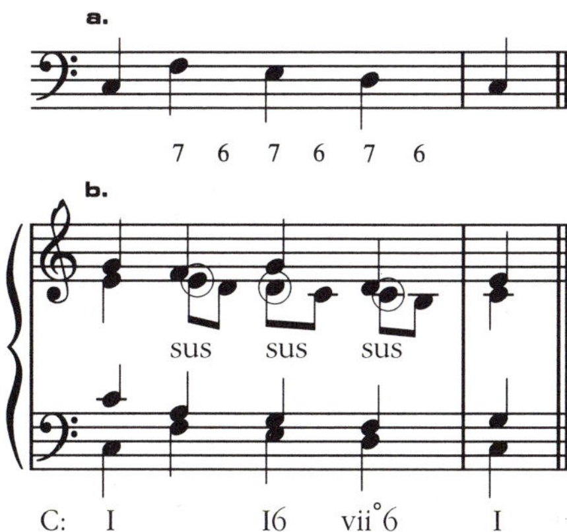

## Suspensions in the Bass

The 2–3 suspension occurs in the bass. The numbers appear to suggest that an upper voice ascends, but that is not so. These numbers refer to an upper voice that is not changing when the bass moves down a step. The second becomes a third as the bass resolves downward. (Remember, all suspensions resolve downward.) In example 12-12a, the suspension resolves to the third of the chord. This is somewhat more common than example 12-12b, where the suspension resolves to the root of the chord. The figured bass in example 12-12 may look formidable because there are so many numbers, but when more figures are given it is actually easier to determine which notes to include in the chord.

**EXAMPLE 12-12.** Suspensions in the bass

a. b.

| | | | | | | |
|---|---|---|---|---|---|---|
| | | 5<br>2 | 6<br>3 | 6 | 7<br>4<br>2 | 8<br>5<br>3 |
| | prep | sus | res | prep | sus | res |
| C: | IV | I6 | | IV6 | V | |

## Realizing Suspensions

In writing a suspension, or any nonharmonic tone, the harmonic background must always be clear. When nonharmonic tones are indicated by the figured bass, the best practice is to determine first the chord of resolution.

There are four steps in writing a suspension:

First, study the figured bass to determine the type of suspension. Example 12-13 is a suspension in an upper voice, 4–3.

**EXAMPLE 12-13.** A 4–3 suspension

Second, plan the chords, using Roman numerals. The 4 is the dissonance, so 3 is the resolution. The 3 standing alone under a bass note indicates a triad in root position: In example 12-14, a V chord in D major appears with a 4–3 suspension.

**EXAMPLE 12-14.** Planning the chords

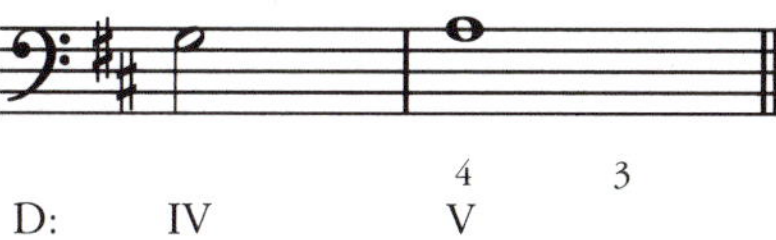


Third, make a provisional sketch of the chord tones. The members of the chord of resolution (V) are A, C-sharp, and E. The preparatory chord can now be decided, as in example 12-15. From that, the voice leading to the chord of resolution is planned. Since C-sharp is the third above the A (the third of the 4–3), the fourth will be the D (the 4 of the 4–3). The D is a common tone from the preceding chord. The suspension should be in the voice that had the D in the preceding chord: the tenor.

**EXAMPLE 12-15.** Sketch of chord tones

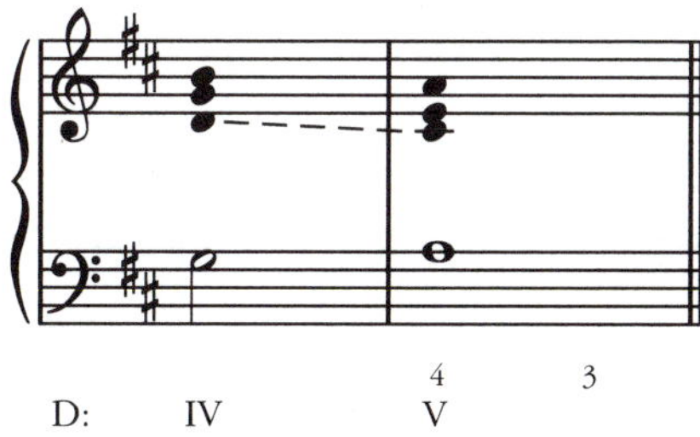


Fourth, complete the suspension and chords. Example 12-16 shows the D held over to become the 4 during the V chord. The suspension may be tied or repeated. The resolution of the 4–3 suspension is not doubled.

**EXAMPLE 12-16.** Completion of the chords and suspension

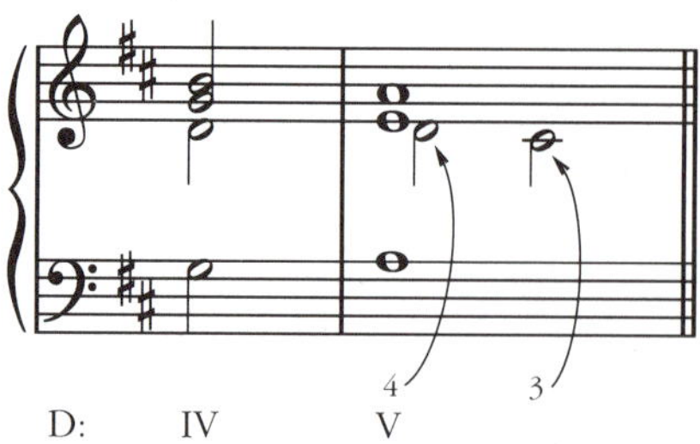


The suspensions in example 12-17 are shown in four parts with two sets of figures. The sets of figures labeled a and b are sufficient to identify the progressions, but the b set relies more on certain intervals being understood, that is, assumed. Sometimes it may seem that there are more figures than necessary, but as you gain experience you will be able to see why the composer sometimes wrote an 8 or 5 where a root position triad seems obvious. The lowest row shows the key and the chord progressions.

**EXAMPLE 12-17.** Different figured bass sets for suspensions

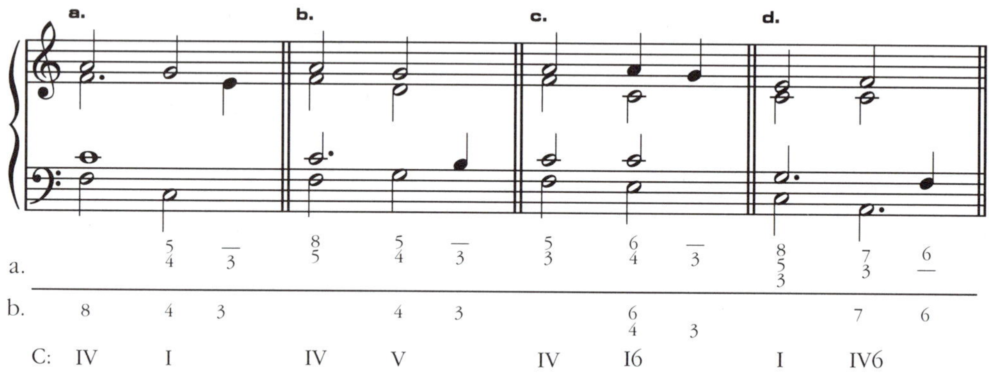


## Other Nonharmonic Tones in Figured Bass

The Arabic figures in figured bass do not specify the exact type of nonharmonic tone to be used in a given situation, but certain combinations strongly suggest particular types. For instance, 4–3, 7–6, 9–8, and 2–3 imply suspensions. In addition, 8–7 is likely to be a passing tone. In realizing the figured bass, remember that most nonharmonic tones resolve by step downward. Example 12-18 illustrates passing tones represented by 8–7.

**EXAMPLE 12-18.** Figured bass and realization of passing tones

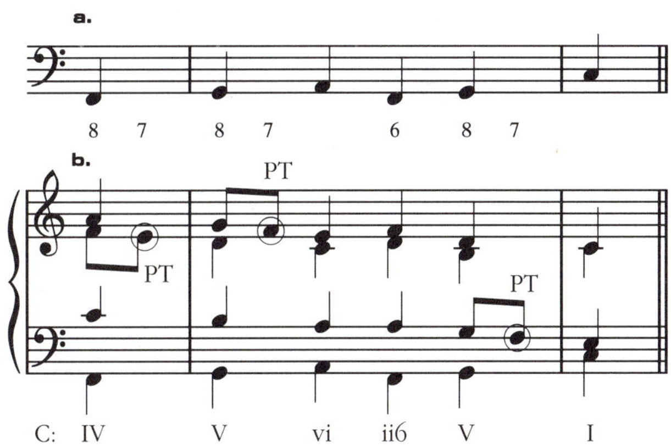


## SUMMARY

| Type | Accented | How Approached | How Resolved | Comments | Other Names |
|---|---|---|---|---|---|
| PT | not usually | step | step | continues in direction of approach | |
| NT | not usually | step | step | returns to approach tone | auxiliary, returning tone |
| ET | no | step | skip | skip usually in direction opposite approach | changing tone, *échappée* |
| Ant | no | step | holds or repeats | | |
| Sus | yes | holds or repeats preparatory tone | step | resolves downward | |
| Ret | yes | holds or repeats preparatory tone | step | resolves upward | |
| App | usually | leap | step | usually resolves in direction opposite approach | leaning tone, unaccented-unprepared NT |
| DNG | not usually | step | step | returns to approach tone, two nonharmonic tones, a 3rd apart | neighbor tone group |
| Ped | variable | holds or repeats preparatory tone and resolution | | chord must change to create dissonance | |

**TABLE 12-1.** Review of nonharmonic tones

### Triads and inversions

| root position | | | 1st inversion | | 2nd inversion |
|---|---|---|---|---|---|
| 5 | 5 | 3 | 6 | 6 | 6 |
| 3 | | | 3 | | 4 |

### Seventh chords and inversions

| root position | | | | 1st inversion | | 2nd inversion | | 3rd inversion | | |
|---|---|---|---|---|---|---|---|---|---|---|
| 7 | 7 | 7 | 7 | 6 | 6 | 6 | 4 | 6 | 4 | 2 |
| 5 | 3 | 5 | | 5 | 5 | 4 | 3 | 4 | 2 | |
| 3 | | | | 3 | | 3 | | 2 | | |

### Nonharmonic tones

**Suspensions**

In upper voices: 4 3   7 6   9 8
In the bass: 2 3

**Passing tones**

In upper voices: 8 7
In bass: usually understood from context

**TABLE 12-2.** Review of figured bass

In the context of melody and harmony, nonharmonic tones serve two essential functions: they endow a voice with greater melodic identity and linear strength, at the same time generating harmonic interest as the dissonance they produce challenges the harmonic background. Both functions have an important role in enhancing the overall tension level and the expressive result. Nonharmonic tones and figured bass are reviewed in table 12-1 and table 12-2.

CHAPTER THIRTEEN

# Nondominant Seventh Chords

Diatonic seventh chords other than the dominant follow many of the previously established principles for the treatment of other chords. These nondominant sevenths offer harmonic interest and variety in chord quality and share several related features and similarities in their treatment.

## TYPES OF NONDOMINANT SEVENTH CHORDS

As explained in chapter 4, the quality of a seventh chord is indicated by a two-letter abbreviation. The dominant seventh chord normally appears in major and minor keys as a Mm7, which means that the dominant triad is major but the interval of the seventh is minor. Other seventh chords have different combinations of major and minor triads and intervals. Compare the chords in examples 13-1a and b. Note that the minor dominant seventh has been included (ex. 13-1b) since it departs significantly from the normal dominant. The types of nondominant seventh chords are somewhat more varied in minor keys than in major keys, as shown in table 13-1.

**EXAMPLE 13-1.** Nondominant seventh chords

**a.** Nondominant seventh chords in major keys

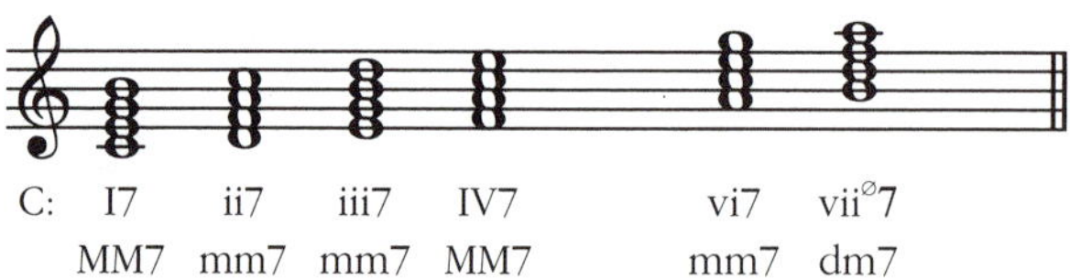


**b.** Nondominant seventh chords in minor keys

| Chord types | In major keys | In minor keys |
|---|---|---|
| MM7 | I7 IV7 | III7 VI7 |
| mm7 | ii7 iii7 vi7 | i7 iv7 (v7) |
| dm7 | viiø7 | iiø7 |
| dd7 | | vii°7 |
| Mm7 | | (VII7) |

**TABLE 13-1.** Nondominant seventh chord types

## Chord Representation

Since all seventh chords have four tones, there is no need for doubling in a four-voice setting. Very rarely, to allow for adjustments in the voice leading, a tone may be omitted, usually the fifth, in which case the root is doubled.

## Voice Leading

The chord's seventh resolves downward one scale degree. The other tones resolve conservatively but differently, depending on circumstances.

## Chord Inversions

All seventh chords and their inversions have the same figured bass symbols and abbreviations. They resolve with conservative voice leading and do not usually omit tones.

## Chord Progressions

Normally all seventh chords resolve to a chord in the next lower-numbered chord group. Deviations from this are rare. Adding a seventh to any chord in table 13-2 does not change its position in the table, except for I7, which, because it is dissonant, does not serve in chord group 1. Group 1 is reserved for the stable form of the tonic, a consonant termination point for harmonic cycles. I7 is in group 4, where it relates to chord group 3 as IV7 relates to group 2.

**Major keys**

| group 5 | group 4 | group 3 | group 2 | group 1 |
|---|---|---|---|---|
| iii iii7 | vi vi7 | ii ii7 | V V7 | I |
| | I7 | IV IV7 | vii° viiø7 | |

**Minor keys**

| group 6 | group 5 | group 4 | group 3 | group 2 | group 1 |
|---|---|---|---|---|---|
| VII VII7 | III III7 | VI VI7 | ii iiø7 | V V7 | i |
| | v v7 | i7 | iv iv7 | vii° vii°7 | |

**TABLE 13-2.** Normal progressions

## NONDOMINANT SEVENTH CHORDS CONSIDERED BY CHORD GROUPS

By viewing nondominant sevenths in chord groups, the emphasis is placed on their normal usage in progressions and part writing. Chord groups 2 and 3 are the most important because of their close relationship to the tonic and their usefulness in harmonization. Chords in the higher-numbered groups, groups 4, 5, and 6, are more remote from the tonic and less frequently used.

### Seventh Chords in Group 2

Besides the V7, chord group 2 contains leading-tone seventh chords that are very different in major and minor keys. The leading-tone seventh in a major key is vii°7, dm7, and progresses normally to the tonic. The seventh resolves down by step and the root ascends by step, as shown in example 13-2.

Parallel fifths must be avoided in the resolution of the third and seventh of the chord, as in example 13-3a. This situation is best handled by having the seventh below the third, as in example 13-3b, or, if the third ascends, to double the third in the tonic chord, shown in example 13-3c.

**EXAMPLE 13-2.** Resolution of vii°7 to I

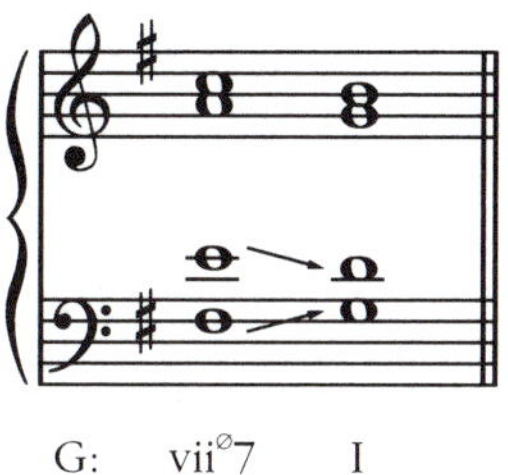


**EXAMPLE 13-3.** Avoiding parallel fifths

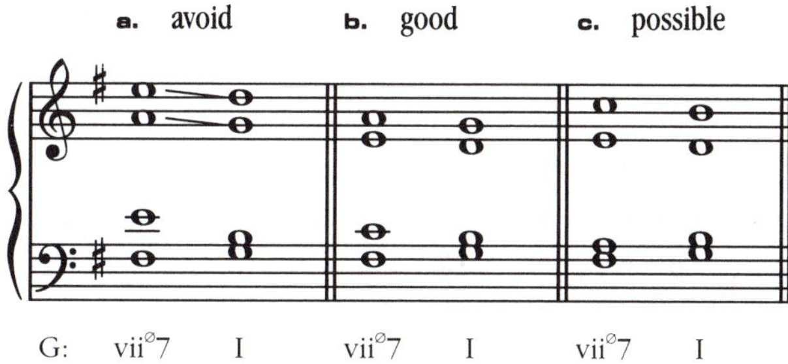


Inversions are rare but possible. First inversion (ex. 13-4a) is restricted to a resolution in which the bass moves up to I6 in order to avoid parallel fifths with the resolving seventh. Example 13-4b illustrates the resolution of the second inversion.

**EXAMPLE 13-4.** Resolutions of inversions

The leading-tone seventh chord in a minor key is the fully diminished seventh chord, vii°7 (dd7), hence it contains two tritones. The seventh must resolve downward a half step and the root upward a half step (ex. 13-5a). Usually the upper voices descend as the root ascends, so the tonic chord is complete, with the root doubled. In a few instances the third ascends, resolving the tritone with the seventh and producing a doubled third in the tonic chord (ex. 13-5b). Inversions of vii°7 are not difficult to resolve since the normal voice leading follows the same principles as vii°7 in root position. Examples 13-5c and d show the most typical resolutions. The third inversion is avoided since the resolving seventh would lead to a tonic six-four chord.

**EXAMPLE 13-5.** Resolutions of leading-tone seventh chords

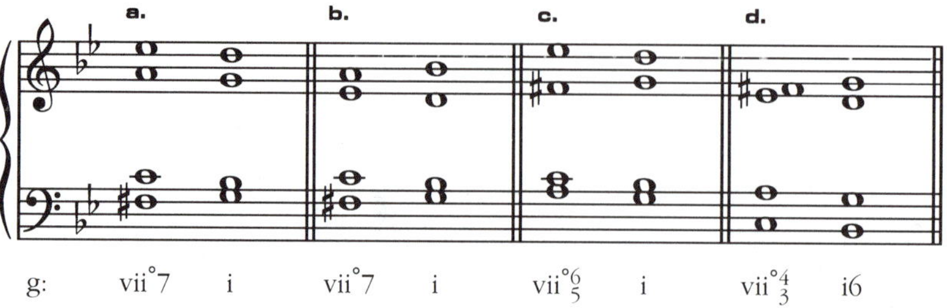


## Seventh Chords in Group 3

The subdominant seventh and supertonic seventh chords are very different in major and minor, but in both modes it is the supertonic that is the most frequently used, and most often in first inversion. Both chords progress to group 2, with or without an intervening tonic six-four.

The supertonic seventh appears occasionally in root position, but it is used most often as ii$^6_5$, which is particularly effective in leading to V7. The ii$^6_5$ offers the mild dissonance of the minor-minor seventh chord moving smoothly to the sharper dissonance of the V7 or I$^6_4$ (see exx. 13-6a–c). In example 13-7, the arrival of the V7 is delayed by the appearance of the cadential six-four, but the voice leading is more flexible and free, since the instrumental setting lacks the performance limitations of a vocal medium, the model for four-part writing.

**EXAMPLE 13-6.** Resolutions of supertonic seventh chords

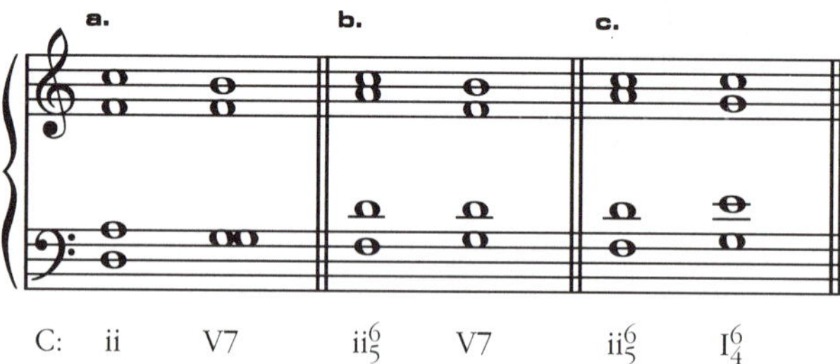

**EXAMPLE 13-7.** Mozart: Piano Sonata, K. 333, third movement

In a minor key, the half-diminished ii°7 is used. As in a major key, the first inversion is the common treatment of the chord. Example 13-8 illustrates the resolutions to V7 and $\text{I}^6_4$. In example 13-9, the supertonic seventh appears in a third inversion, resulting in a bass that is almost a pedal point; the voice leading is so smooth that the chords seem almost incidental to the component lines.

**EXAMPLE 13-8.** Resolutions of $\text{ii}^{\circ 6}_{5}$ chords

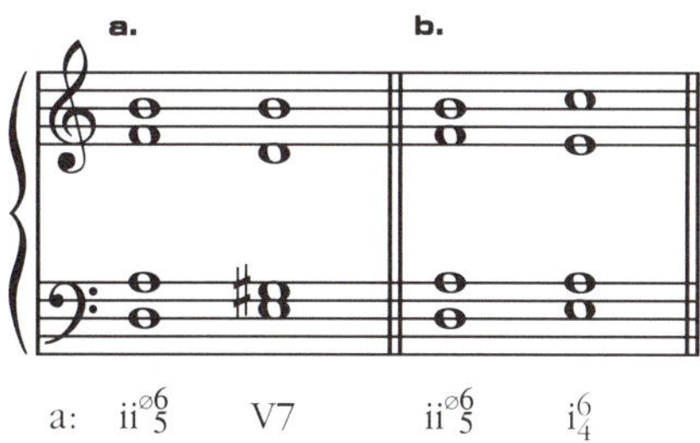


The subdominant seventh is used less often in approaching V. While this progression may be satisfactory harmonically, there is a problem with the voice leading. Note the resolution of IV to V with the leading tone doubled in example 13-10a. This would prevent parallel fifths between soprano and alto, but such doubling is avoided. The progression to V7 will correct this, as in example 13-10b, or the chord seventh may be placed below the third so the parallel fifths become acceptable parallel fourths, as in example 13-10c. The progression to the tonic six-four delays the resolution of the seventh, as shown in example 13-10d.

**EXAMPLE 13-9.** Schubert: *Hektors Abschied*, D. 312

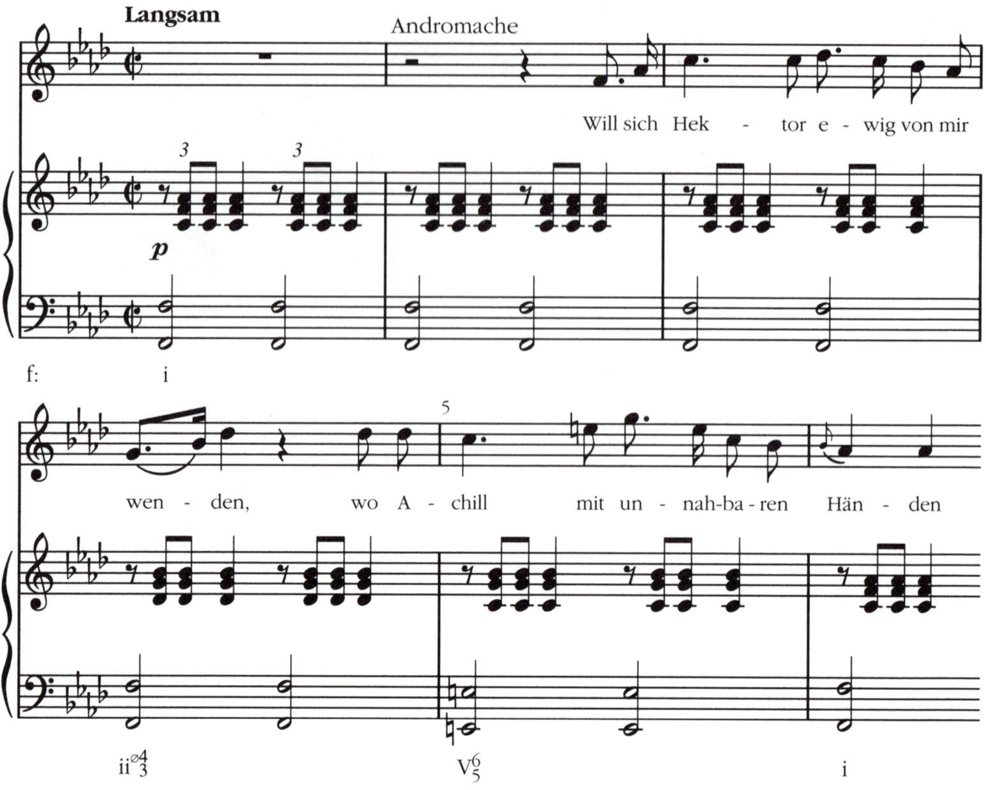


**EXAMPLE 13-10.** Resolutions of IV7 chords

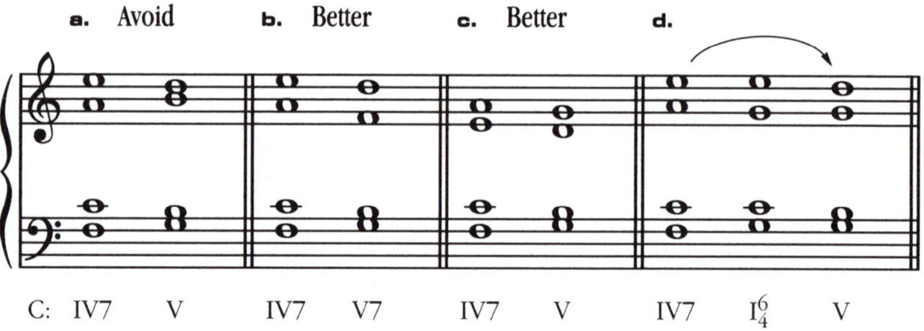


Example 13-11 illustrates a passage for which differing analyses are possible. Is the chord on the first beat of measure 3 a IV7 or a ii$^6_5$ with the F-sharp suspended? Most listeners would probably favor the analysis with ii$^6_5$. While the IV7 appears with a metric and agogic accent, the milder sonority of ii$^6_5$ gives it the quality of a resolution, making the F-sharp on the downbeat sound "nonchordal."

**EXAMPLE 13-11.** Loewe: *Max' Abschied von Augsburg,* op. 124, no. 3

## Seventh Chords in Groups 4, 5, and 6

Seventh chords in groups 4 and 5 are handled in ways comparable to chords in group 3, but they are used less because they are more remote from the tonic. In group 4, vi7 and I7 are used in major keys and VI7 and i7 in minor. There are several possibilities for progressions to chords with and without sevenths in chord group 4. Example 13-12 shows some of these.

**EXAMPLE 13-12.** Resolutions of seventh chords from group 4

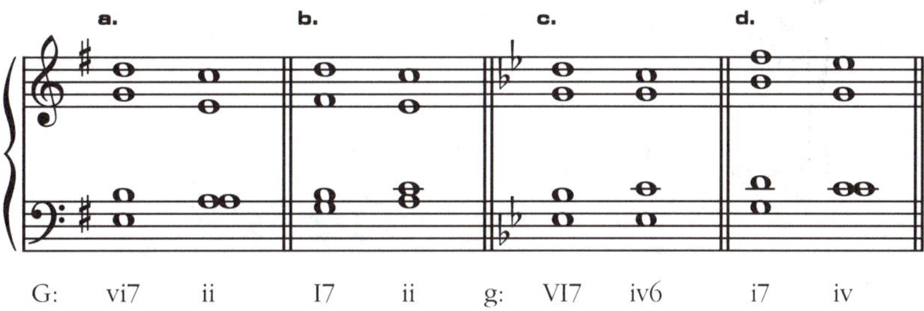


The mediant seventh and minor dominant seventh chords in group 5 and the subtonic seventh chord in group 6 are relatively rare. The progressions and voice leading resemble those in other chord groups where a fifth or step between roots influences the part writing. Sample resolutions are given in example 13-13. In example 13-14a the progression VI7–V7 appears in an instrumental setting, which allows some freedom in the voice leading. Example 13-14b uses both the i7 and $VII^{6}_{5}$ chords. In example 13-15, the composer places several seventh chords in succession and in different inversions.

**EXAMPLE 13-13.** Resolutions of iii7, III7, and v7 chords

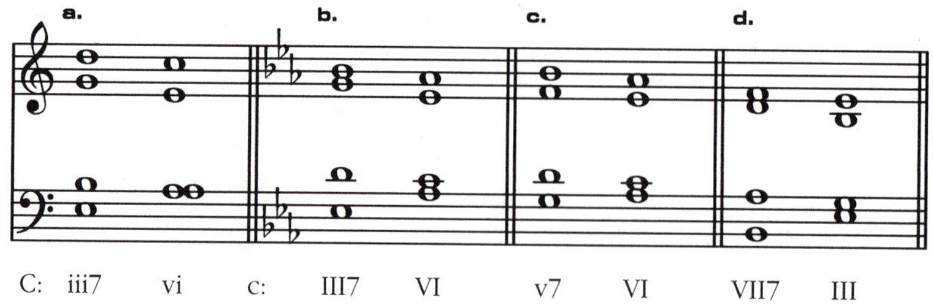


**EXAMPLE 13-14.** Examples of the resolutions of iii7, III7, and v7 chords

**a.** Beethoven: Cello Sonata, op. 69, first movement

**b.** J. S. Bach: *Wer weiß, wie nahe mir*

**EXAMPLE 13-15.** Schumann: *Dichterliebe* op. 48, no. 7, "Ich grolle nicht"

Sometimes composers write a sequence with a "chain" of seventh chords in which each chord resolves to a chord whose root is a fifth below but the resolution contains a seventh that must resolve to another chord whose root is again a fifth below, and so forth, as seen in example 13-16. Note that every other seventh chord omits the fifth.

**EXAMPLE 13-16.** A chain of seventh chords

In some circumstances, a passage may be analyzed either as containing a seventh chord or a nonharmonic tone. If faced with this choice, use these guidelines: First look for the analysis that makes the most normal progression; second, look for the analysis that uses fewer chords and more nonharmonic tones. Of course, these are only guidelines. The ear is often the best judge, since the purpose of the analysis is to describe what the listener hears. Example 13-17 shows an application of these guidelines. Analysis c is preferred.

**EXAMPLE 13-17.** J. S. Bach: *Nun freut euch*

## SUMMARY

Diatonic seventh chords other than the dominant provide harmonic variety yet follow many of the principles previously established for the treatment of other chords. Nondominant sevenths offer variety in chord quality but have several related features and similarities in their treatment. Since all seventh chords have four tones, there is usually no need for doubling in a four-voice setting. The chord's seventh resolves downward one scale degree, while the other tones resolve conservatively but differently, depending on circumstances.

All seventh chords and their inversions have the same figured bass symbols and abbreviations. They resolve with conservative voice leading and do not usually omit tones. Normally all seventh chords resolve to a chord in the next lower-numbered chord group. Viewing nondominant sevenths in chord groups emphasizes their normal usage in progressions and part writing.

CHAPTER FOURTEEN

# Harmonic Tension

armonic tension, arising from the factors of harmonic rhythm, progressions, and sonority, makes a strong contribution, along with melody, to the crest of tension within the phrase.

## IDENTIFYING PHRASES

When we first identified phrases the musical context consisted of only a single melody. Now we are able to consider identifying phrases in which an accompaniment is used and harmony is an added consideration. The initial criteria for locating phrases in a melody are still important: (1) normal length, (2) strength of cadence, (3) contrast in the content of phrases, and (4) reappearance of opening figures. The evidence for the cadence is primarily in the melody; however, harmonic features must also be taken into account now, as well as the possibility that the accompaniment may clarify or obscure the cadential effect.

There are five types of harmonic cadences, and these must be considered together with the melodic evidence for a cadence. A phrase may end with either a perfect authentic cadence, an imperfect authentic cadence, a half cadence, a plagal cadence, or a deceptive cadence. The harmony at the end of the phrase will use one of these types of cadences. In example 14-1 the upper voice in measures 1–5 is unified by a recurring motive. Contrast appears in measure 6. In these same measures the accompaniment reveals a similar unity and contrast. There is a supertonic chord in measure 6, so a normal harmonic cadence is not possible there. The phrase must end in measure 4, where an imperfect authentic cadence may be found. The arrow indicates this. The first phrase displays the normal four-measure length; however, the second phrase does not. While the use of a cadential six-four chord in measure 7 leads to a possible deceptive cadence in measure 8, this has the disadvantage of leaving an unacceptably short two-measure phrase at the end of the example (shown here as a definite cadence). But if we recognize these last two measures as an extension, we will have a six-measure phrase that again uses a cadential six-four chord, leading this time to a perfect authentic cadence.

The accompaniment may be treated in ways that clarify or obscure the phrase structure. Like the melody, the accompaniment may strengthen the cadential effect with an agogic accent. In example 14-2a the bass provides a strong agogic accent with longer tones and rests in measure 4 and again in measures 12–13. The end of the phrase is clearer in the bass than in the upper voice alone, where interlocking is found. In example 14-2b the accompaniment doubles the melody in the first phrase but then changes to a clear chordal pattern in the second phrase. The slurred figure in measure 10 is perceived, like the same figure in measures 8 and 11, as leading to and belonging with the measure that follows it. In measure 13 the fourth phrase begins with an interlocking cadence, which is seen in the melody as the leading tone in the soprano resolves and the initial theme returns.

**EXAMPLE 14-1.** Mozart: Cantata "Die ihr unermesslichen Weltalls," K. 619

**EXAMPLE 14-2.** Accompaniment clarifies the phrase by agogic accent (a) or by doubling (b)

**a.** Mozart: *Six Country Dances,* K. 606, no. 2

**EXAMPLE 14-2.** (continued)

**a.**

**b.** Mozart: Allegro einer Sonate, K. 312

## HARMONIC FACTORS

To assess the impact of harmony on the tension pattern within a melodic phrase, it is necessary to review the three main harmonic factors: (1) harmonic rhythm, (2) chord progressions, and (3) sonority.

### Harmonic Rhythm

As harmonic rhythm increases in activity, tension increases. Harmonic rhythm may confirm or oppose the metric rhythm and may do so mildly or strongly. Opposition to the established meter increases tension, and when the harmonic and metric rhythms finally coincide, the release of tension is greater than if there were no opposition at all. Agogic accents make particularly strong contributions to the increase and decrease of tension.

In example 14-3, the harmonic rhythm is marked below the Roman numerals with note values indicating the duration of each chord. The harmonic rhythm reinforces the meter because the chords change on strong pulses. Tension is not increased by this harmonic rhythm.

**EXAMPLE 14-3.** Mozart: Eight Minuets with Trios, K. 315g, no. 3

G: I V7 I V I

If the durations of the various harmonies are different, agogic patterns may arise. These are often found in positions that strengthen the meter; that is, the thesis of the agogic pattern will fall on a metrically strong pulse. Within the harmonic rhythm, the relative strength of the agogic accents and the tension level will vary depending on the length of the thesis, the length of the arsis, and the degree of activity in the arsis.

In the harmonic rhythm of example 14-4, a clear agogic accent appears on the downbeat of the second and fourth measures. Notice that the more active harmonic rhythm in measure 3 strengthens the final thesis so the tension level is increased leading to measure 4.

**EXAMPLE 14-4.** Muffat: *Rigaudon*

When agogic and metric accents do not coincide in the harmonic rhythm, the tension that is generated is released the next time they do coincide. Note the agogic accent on the second beat of measure 2 of example 14-5. The cadence in measure 3 is strengthened by the agogic and metric accents at this point.

**EXAMPLE 14-5.** J. S. Bach: *Nun lob', mein Seel', der Herren*

## Chord Progressions

A harmonic cycle may consist of as few as two chords, for example, V–I, or it may consist of many. The overall length of the cycle is a factor in tension production: The longer the cycle, the greater the tension. Table 14-1 shows how tension relates to harmony. As a progression moves through the cycle towards the I chord, tension increases, to be released with the arrival of the tonic chord.

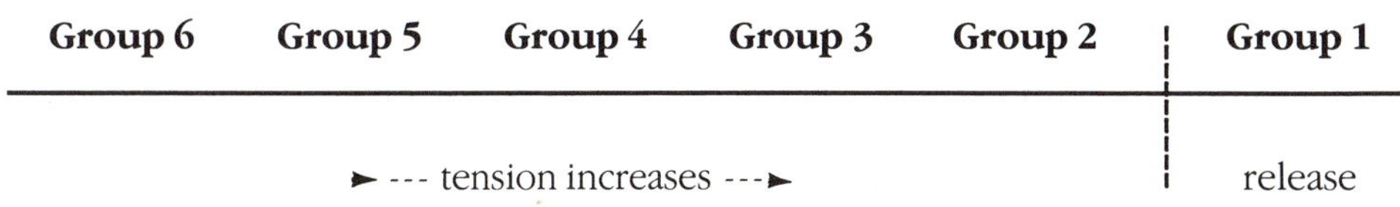

| Group 6 | Group 5 | Group 4 | Group 3 | Group 2 | Group 1 |
|---|---|---|---|---|---|
| | | ► --- tension increases ---► | | | release |

**TABLE 14-1.** Tension in normal chord progressions

Departures from the normal progression patterns may represent an increase in tension if they present a chord that is new to the phrase. When a chord appears for the first time, it brings an increase in tension, just as the appearance of a new emergent tone does. This does not apply to the tonic chord, which always represents a decrease of tension.

The phrase in example 14-6 consists of one harmonic cycle, with time divided evenly between chords that produce tension (ii and V) and chords that release tension (I). The progression follows the normal course, resulting in an increase in tension throughout measures 2 and 3, with the crest reached in measure 4, as the tension releases with the arrival of the I chord.

**EXAMPLE 14-6.** Tension and release

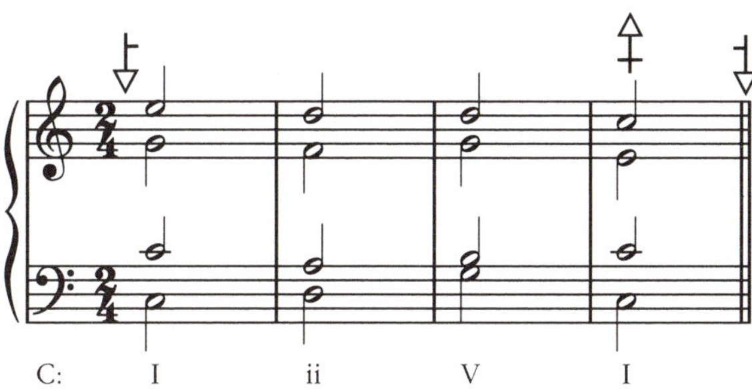


The quality of "newness" may extend beyond a single cycle. The appearance of a chord not heard before (or for a long time) may bring a considerable increase in tension, as in example 14-7. There are three cycles, but the fresh IV chord makes the second cycle have greater tension.

The relative duration of tension-producing chords is another important factor in assessing the overall tension pattern: The longer a harmonic cycle remains in the tension-producing portion of the progression, the greater the accumulated tension. This is a matter of total time, not the number of chords involved, as in example 14-8. The repeated V chord in measure 3 creates greater tension that is released thereafter.

**EXAMPLE 14-7.** Tension and newly used chords

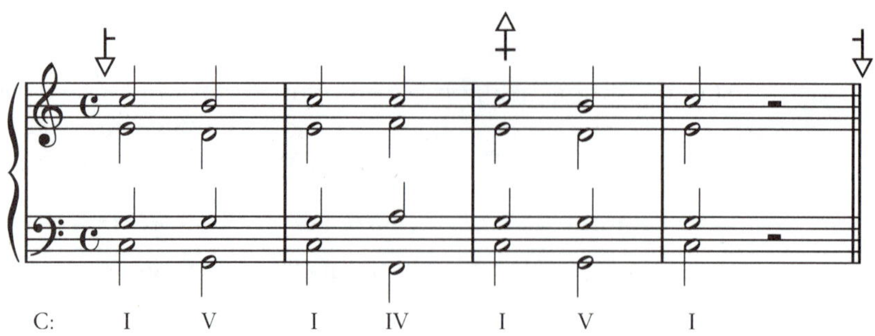


**EXAMPLE 14-8.** Length of harmonic cycle and tension

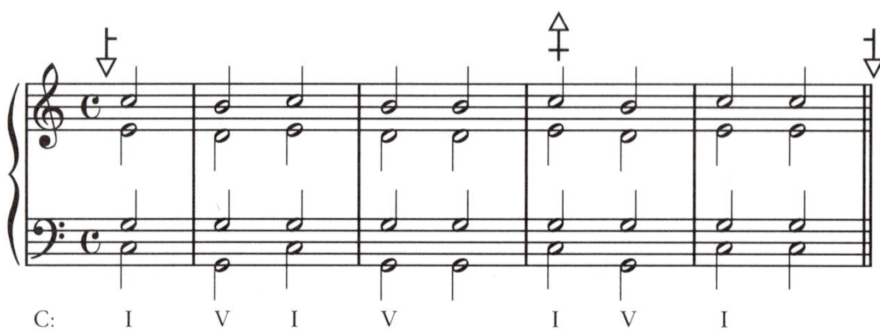


## Sonority

Some chords have greater potential than others for developing tension. The greater instability and complexity of different triads, seventh chords, and dissonance from nonharmonic tones develop tension.

### Triads

There will of course be differences of opinion about which chords are more tense than others. The general listing in table 14-2 is suggested. The most stable chords are at the top of the list.

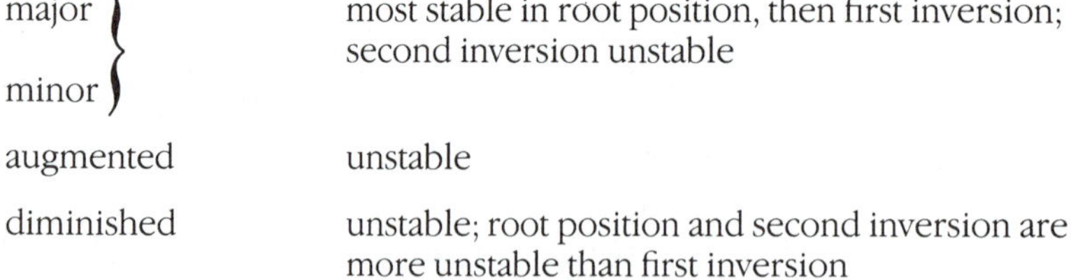

| | |
|---|---|
| major, minor | most stable in root position, then first inversion; second inversion unstable |
| augmented | unstable |
| diminished | unstable; root position and second inversion are more unstable than first inversion |

**TABLE 14-2.** Relative stability of triads

## Seventh Chords

It is difficult to assess the relative tension of various seventh chords; they are all unstable. The major-minor seventh has been singled out for its unique sonority and significance to the tonality. In general, inverted seventh chords are more tense than the same chords in root position. The voicing of the chord is important here; however, if the chord is set so that it contains seconds rather than sevenths, the dissonance is greater and the tension rises.

## Nonharmonic Tones

These are important in assessing tension patterns. Metrically accented nonharmonic tones are more tense than unaccented ones; the greater the dissonance, the greater the tension.

In example 14-9a, the second cycle creates increased tension through seventh chords, while in example 14-9b, the second cycle yields greater tension from nonharmonic tones with dissonance.

**EXAMPLE 14-9.** Tension and nonharmonic tones

a.

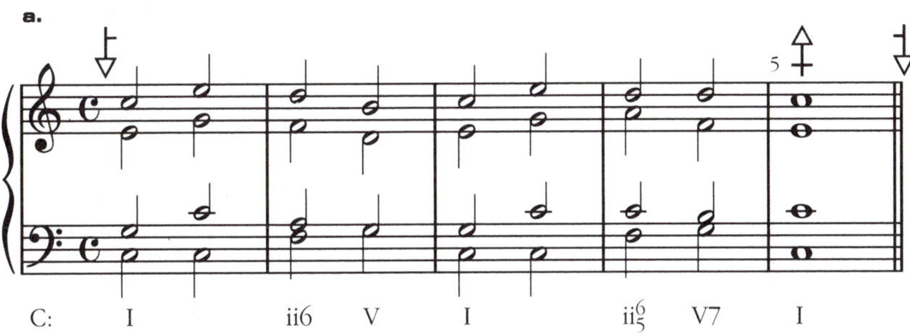


b.

## THE CREST OF THE PHRASE: HARMONY AND MELODY

As a final step, the analyses of harmony and melody are combined to locate the crest of the phrase, the point where tension reaches its peak and begins to release. In example 14-10, the melodic line contains one agogic pattern with the principal thesis on the last note. The contour is also very clear, with a dramatic stepwise rise to the cadence. The crest for the phrase appears to be on the third beat of measure 2.

**EXAMPLE 14-10.** J. S. Bach: *Meinen Jesum lass' ich nicht*

The chord progression consists of five chords with one harmonic cycle culminating on the last chord. The harmonic rhythm, shown in example 14-11, contains a principal agogic pattern with the thesis on the last chord. The fourth chord (V7) has the thesis of a subordinate agogic pattern. The harmonic sonorities are primarily traditional chords, the nonharmonic tones being relatively unremarkable. Tension increases gradually until the V7 and releases with the final I.

**EXAMPLE 14-11.** Harmonic rhythm of example 14-10

The melodic rhythm and contour and the harmonic progression all point to the third beat of measure 2 as the crest. Only the harmonic rhythm suggests that the thesis on the first beat of measure 2 might be the crest. The most tense sonority is the V7, which resolves at the point where the melody and the chord progression peak. The conclusion, as shown in example 14-12, is that this point, beat 3 of measure 2, is the crest for the phrase.

**EXAMPLE 14-12.** J. S. Bach: *Meinen Jesum lass' ich nicht*

In example 14-13, the strongest events in the melody are the three agogic accents: a brief one on the second beat, but strong agogic accents in the last measure on the first and third beats. The bass has similar agogic accents in the last bar. The harmonic rhythm has agogic accents in the last measure as well. There are three harmonic cycles, the first and last having the longest duration. The chord that is the freshest is the IV6, following the V6 in an irregular progression. The strongest sonorities are the $V^4_2$ and the suspension in the last measure. The general effect is of more activity in the first six beats and less in the last four. The final decision is to place the crest on the first beat of the last bar.

**EXAMPLE 14-13.** J. S. Bach: *Freu' dich sehr, o meine Seele*

The conflict between the tension in the salient line and the harmony in example 14-14 becomes quite exaggerated. In measure 8, tension in the harmony reaches a peak and begins to decrease on the first beat with the arrival of the I chord, but the melody builds beyond this level to create an even higher crest on the high $a^2$.

**EXAMPLE 14-14.** Offenbach: *Orphée aux enfers*

## TENSION AND INTERPRETATION

Throughout this book we have called attention to those elements in music that cause tension to grow and decline. A detailed examination has been made of the technical means by which tension has been created and shaped to serve the expressive purpose of the composer. Having located those points in the music where tension accumulates, reaches a crest, or begins to decline, the performer alone can use this information to bring life to his or her performance.

Knowledge of how tension has been created is of enormous value to the performer since it can be made the basis for interpretive decisions for particular situations. Of course, a good performer is one who has a fine intuition for the direction, impact, and style of a piece. The best performers have the capacity to enhance the tension patterns the composer created. This enhancement is accomplished by the use of expressive techniques or devices at the disposal of the performer only. Often these techniques are too subtle to be notated by the composer. The delicate lengthening of a tone or a slight crescendo is often left to the intelligence and intuition of the performer. The composer cannot issue absolutely complete instructions for the performance.

While this is not a textbook on interpretive techniques, it may be useful to list some of the most important musical resources that the performer may employ; how these are employed depends on the judgment and skill of the performer.

1. Rhythm: accelerating, retarding, slight changes of tempo, rubato, pauses, and timing not specifically notated by the composer (called agogic interpretation);
2. Dynamics: crescendo, diminuendo, minor changes of dynamics, such as echo effects on repeated passages (called dynamic interpretation);
3. Articulation: accents of various types depending on the medium, portamento;
4. Timbre: changes in tone color for special effect or contrast, vibrato, organ stops.

It is impossible to list all the combinations of these and other devices that may be conceived. The point is that the performer brings a formidable array of techniques and resources with which to enhance the music. Just which of these resources to use at a particular point and the degree to which it should be used is a matter of great sensitivity and artistry, much of which is beyond verbalization and certainly beyond the scope of this text. But students who find that their analytical studies prove of little value in their performance may not have sufficiently considered the sources of tension in the music to see how the resources at their disposal may best be utilized to enhance the desired musical effect.

## SUMMARY

Harmonic tension makes a strong contribution, along with melody, to the crest of tension within the phrase. To assess the impact of harmony on the tension pattern within a melodic phrase, it is necessary to review three main factors: harmonic rhythm, chord progressions, and sonority. As harmonic rhythm increases in activity, tension increases.

The overall length of the cycle is a factor in tension production: The longer the cycle, the greater the tension. The chart of normal chord progressions shows how tension relates to harmony. As a progression moves through the cycle towards the I chord, tension increases, to be released with the arrival of the I. The greater instability and complexity of different triads, seventh chords, and dissonance from nonharmonic tones develops tension. The analyses of harmony and melody are combined to locate the crest of the phrase, the point where tension reaches its peak and begins to release.

## CHAPTER FIFTEEN

# Texture and Two-Voice Homophony

**Terms Introduced in This Chapter**

- texture
- vertical placement
- density
- salient line
- recessive line
- implied lines
- rhythmic coupling
- full coupling
- heterophony
- melody with accompaniment
- broken chord

he emphasis on four-voice homophony in previous chapters can now be broadened with a more detailed consideration of texture and a study of various possibilities for homophonic texture with two voices.

# TEXTURE

**texture**

*Texture* is the combined effect of the simultaneous component lines in music. It is among the most basic aspects of music; changes in texture have a strong impact on the listener. The study of texture requires an examination of the relative placement of pitch, the component lines of the music, the quantity and quality of the individual melodic lines, and their interrelationships. Those features will be reflected in the system of textural analysis presented in this chapter. The terms melody, voice, and line will be used interchangeably.

## Relative Placement of Pitch

A basic feature of music is the relative placement of pitch in terms of high and low, the vertical placement of the lines; and thick and thin, the density of the texture.

### Vertical Placement

**vertical placement**

*Vertical placement* refers to the pitch level of a musical line. Most music lies in the most familiar range in the gamut of available sounds, that is, in the middle register. If one or more voices are notably high or low in tessitura, this fact is readily noted by the listener. In deciding where to place a particular line, the composer will naturally consider the practical range of the medium (voice or instrument). In addition, the psychological effect of a line in the middle, high, or low register is different, and radical changes in vertical placement may have a dramatic impact on emotions.

### Density

**density**

*Density* refers to the distance between component lines and the number of lines present. Major changes in the density of the music, like vertical placement, may be very dramatic.

## Types of Lines

There are essentially two types of lines, "salient" and "recessive," distinguished by the degree of prominence and melodic interest.

### Salient Line

**salient line**

A *salient line* is a melodic line with a sufficiently high level of melodic interest to sustain the listener's attention. This is the primary component of all textures. Sometimes a texture consists of a solitary salient line, as in monophony. The letter S is the abbreviated designation for a salient line and is placed below the staff (see ex. 15-1).

**EXAMPLE 15-1.** Telemann: Fantasie for Violin, No. 7

### Recessive Line

**recessive line**

A *recessive line* is a melodic line with a sufficiently low level of melodic interest that, of itself, does not sustain the listener's attention. The recessive line is not independent. Except for brief introductory passages that are immediately perceived as accompanimental, a recessive line almost never occurs except in support of a salient line. Most often the recessive line lies below the salient, but the reverse is not uncommon. The letter R is the abbreviated designation for a recessive line. In the analysis, the abbreviations will not show the relative vertical placement of the lines in the texture; the R is written below the S as $\frac{S}{R}$ (see ex. 15-2a–c).

## Identifying Lines

In studying texture, it is of major importance to identify the distinct and separate lines that are the components of the texture so they may be evaluated for their role in the texture as a whole. These lines may or may not be clear as they appear in the texture.

**EXAMPLE 15-2.** Notating salient and recessive lines

**a.** Scarlatti: Larghetto

**b.** Haydn: Piano Sonata in D Major, Hob. XVI:19, second movement

**c.** Mozart: Menuetto, K. 15qq

## Clear Lines

In most cases, the number of lines is very clear, as in four-voice writing. The voices are listed in a column of Ss and Rs. A single salient line accompanied by three recessive lines would be indicated $\begin{smallmatrix}S\\R\\R\\R\end{smallmatrix}$ or $\begin{smallmatrix}S\\3R\end{smallmatrix}$. A texture of two salient and two recessive lines would be designated $\begin{smallmatrix}S\\S\\R\\R\end{smallmatrix}$. For convenience, several similar lines may be combined with a single number to the left of the line designation, for example, $\begin{smallmatrix}2S\\2R\end{smallmatrix}$.

## Variable Lines

The number of recessive lines may vary irregularly. Voices may appear and disappear, particularly in keyboard writing, without much impact on the broader texture. If a specific number of lines cannot be fixed, vR indicates a variation in the number of R lines, as in example 15-3.

**EXAMPLE 15-3.** Schubert: Piano Sonata in B-flat Major, D. 960, first movement

## Implied Lines

**implied lines**

A single line may incorporate, or comprise, two or more *implied lines.* Analysis indicates this with the number of the implied lines in parentheses to the left of the R or S. Example 15-4 illustrates this, the staff below each music example showing the individual implied lines.

**EXAMPLE 15-4.** Implied lines

**a.** Telemann: Fantasie for Violin No. 7

**b.** Haydn: Ländler, Hob. IX:12

## Variable Implied Lines

Sometimes it is difficult to determine exactly when and where implied lines begin and end and exactly how many voices are implied. In example 15-5, the analysis indicates that the number of implied lines varies. The v in parentheses (v) to the left of the capital letter indicates this.

**EXAMPLE 15-5.** Johann Christian Bach: Piano Sonata No. 10, op. 5, no. 3, second movement

As with other implied lines, broken chord accompaniment figures are sometimes difficult to reduce to a specific number of voices. The use of (v) in measure 4 of example 15-6 is preferable to counting all the implied lines.

**EXAMPLE 15-6.** Beethoven: Piano Sonata, op. 13, second movement

## The Relationships between Lines

Lines may be independent of each other, contrast with each other, or be combined in various kinds of groupings, of which coupling and doubling are the most common.

### Contrasting Lines

When the lines are independent and not grouped in any associative way, the letters S and R are given without any other indications. This is a common texture in two-voice homophony.

### Rhythmic Coupling

**rhythmic coupling**

*Rhythmic coupling* exists when lines move with the same rhythm but not the same pitch classes. In analysis this is shown with brackets to the left of the letters indicating the voices that are rhythmically linked. The bracket may be extended to each letter with short horizontal lines to indicate exactly which letters (melodic lines) are coupled, as illustrated in example 15-7. The rhythms need not be exactly identical at all times in the passage. The same basic texture is found in examples 15-7a and b, though the recessive lines show more activity due to the nonharmonic tones in example 15-7b. Example 15-8 shows the rhythmic coupling of two accompanimental lines.

**EXAMPLE 15-7.** Rhythmic coupling

**a.** J. S. Bach: *Nimm von uns, Herr*

**b.** J. S. Bach: *Ich ruf' zu dir, Herr Jesu Christ*

**EXAMPLE 15-8.** Mozart: Piano Sonata, K. 333, third movement

Depending on the purpose of the analysis, it may not be necessary to write a separate designation for each line. As mentioned above, several lines may be combined and the number of such parts shown by a number written to the left of the line designation. Thus [R R R may be abbreviated [3R. This is especially useful for chordal passages, where individual recessive lines may have minimal melodic interest (see exx. 15-9a–c).

**EXAMPLE 15-9.** Notating rhythmic coupling

Example 15-10 is particularly interesting from the standpoint of texture. One might almost argue that it is interesting only from that perspective since melodic interest is minimal and harmonic interest almost nonexistent.

**EXAMPLE 15-10.** Haydn: String Quartet, op. 76, no. 5, first movement

## Full Coupling

**full coupling**

When a salient and a recessive line are linked in contour as well as rhythm, they are said to be *fully coupled.* This texture resembles doubling at an interval other than the unison or octave. To designate a fully coupled line, we use a double bracket below the two lines, as seen in example 15-11.

**EXAMPLE 15-11.** J. S. Bach: Invention No. 8, BWV 779

## Doubling

Doubling here refers to melodic doubling, in which lines are the same, either in unison or in octaves. When a part is melodically doubled, the analysis shows an x after the line designation. If it is useful to be more precise, the number of octaves in which a particular line is sounding may be shown as x2 (sounding in two octaves), x3 (sounding in three octaves), and so on. In an orchestral work with many parts, the number of octave doublings may not be important or it may vary. In these cases, use Sxv, the v indicating "variable." Some of these options are shown in example 15-12.

**EXAMPLE 15-12.** Use of notation for doubling

**a.** Telemann

**b.** Johann Christian Bach: Piano Sonata No. 10, op. 5, no. 3, second movement

**c.** Schubert: Der Erlkönig, D. 328

**d.** Beethoven: Piano Sonata, op. 13, third movement

## Heterophony

**heterophony** When two or more lines present simultaneous variants of the same melody, the result is called *heterophony*. It is most common in song accompaniments and in orchestral writing (especially in concertos when the soloist plays an elaborated version of the orchestral melody). In example 15-13 the voice has the salient melody while the upper line in the piano presents a simpler recessive version of the same melody.

**EXAMPLE 15-13.** Schumann: *Frauenliebe und Leben,* op. 42, no. 8, "Nun hast du mir"

## Procedure for Textural Analysis

There are three steps in the analysis of texture: (1) determine and mark the salient line or the most important line if there is more than one; (2) determine and mark the other lines, salient or recessive; (3) determine and mark relationships between the lines. Some abbreviation or consolidation of lines may be incorporated in the last stage.

Example 15-14 shows some of the problems encountered in textural analysis. In example 15-14b, the cello is above the viola, but the analysis does not reflect the vertical placement of parts.

This analytical system is designed to point out important features of texture, not to reduce the music to a simple formula. It is important to keep in mind the degree of detail that is desired in an analysis. Slight changes in texture may be important for one purpose, but unessential for another.

Example 15-15 is a short piece consisting of three six-bar phrases. At the beginning of each subphrase there is a change of texture.

**EXAMPLE 15-14.** Textural analysis

**a.** Haydn: Piano Sonata in C Major, Hob. XVI:10, first movement

**b.** Haydn: String Quartet, op. 74, no. 2, second movement

**c.** Schubert: *Der Erlkönig,* D. 328

**d.** Beethoven: Piano Sonata, op. 26, first movement

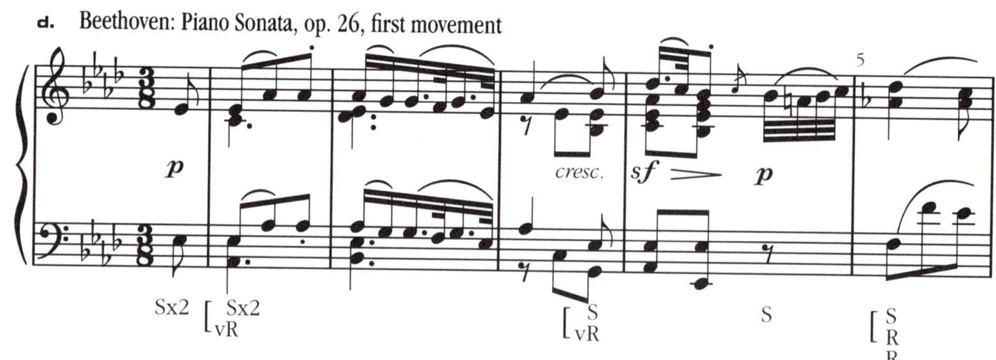

**EXAMPLE 15-15.** Telemann: Bourrée

# TWO-VOICE HOMOPHONY

The concentration in part writing thus far has been on four voices, as this offers the best combination of harmonic fullness and smooth voice leading. Nonetheless, textures of fewer than four parts are very common in all periods of music. Two-part music is very flexible, the voices easily maintaining their identity. The two types of homophony, chordal homophony and melody with accompaniment, may both be represented with two voices; however, the thinness of the texture creates different kinds of problems in providing harmonic content and implications.

## Chordal Homophony

Treatments of texture, chord representation, and part writing in chordal homophony are different for two voices than for four. In chordal homophony with two voices, the soprano is typically the salient voice and the bass is recessive. The two voices are coupled rhythmically, but the usual goal is to maintain the same kind of restrained independence that is sought in four-voice writing where the limits on voice leading maintain subordination with some degree of melodic identity. Particular attention is needed for chord representation in two voices since it differs markedly from that for four voices.

### Chord Representation in Two-Voice Chordal Homophony

Since a triad has three tones, how can a satisfactory harmonic sonority be achieved with only two? As seen earlier, a triad may be represented by only two tones, the fifth of the chord being omitted. The V7 chord has four tones but may also be represented by fewer. Example 15-16 shows possible chord representations with two voices. These combinations apply to all triads. Strictly speaking, two tones sounding together form an interval, not a triad, so it is necessary to speak of harmony in terms of implied chords.

**EXAMPLE 15-16.** Two-voice representation of triads

| Voice | Root position | | | 1st inversion | 2nd inversion |
|---|---|---|---|---|---|
| upper | third | fifth | root | root | root |
| lower | root | root | root | third | fifth |

Some of the combinations in example 15-16 are used only in special cases. For instance, octaves and unisons are usually found only at the beginning or end of a phrase. If the progression is quite normal, a triad may even be represented by the combination of a third and a fifth, as seen in example 15-17, where the second interval is heard as a tonic six-four chord rather than as an irregular iii6 chord. In analyzing an ambiguous passage, always choose the most normal progression.

**EXAMPLE 15-17.** Analysis of a two-voice passage

Dominant seventh and leading tone triad cannot always be distinguished in two-part writing, but since they function the same way as members of chord group 2, there is usually no need to be specific. The possible combinations for seventh chords are shown in example 15-18. Combinations that omit the root or seventh will be interpreted as triads.

Remember that the lowest sounding part acts as bass, even if it is actually the alto voice. In a duet for soprano and alto, the alto part determines the inversions.

**EXAMPLE 15-18.** Two-voice representation of seventh chords

| Voice | Root position | 3rd inversion |
|---|---|---|
| upper | seventh | root |
| lower | root | seventh |

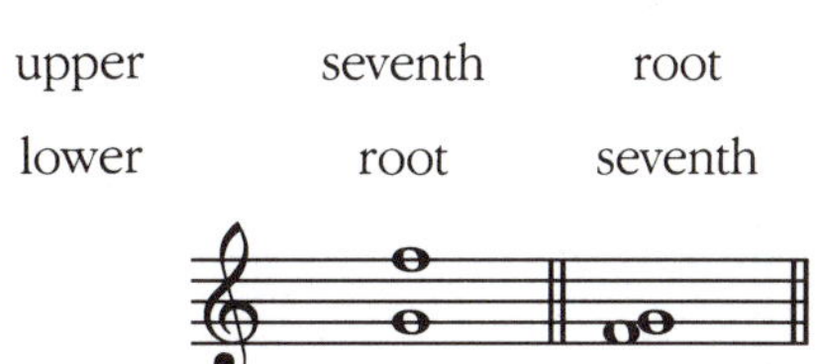

## Part Writing in Two Voices

The discussion of part writing in two voices begins with simple combinations of two tones, using cadences as models, and then proceeds to the "harmonizing" of melodic phrases with the soprano given. Cadence patterns combine chord representation with part writing based on principles previously established.

Notice in examples 15-19 and 15-20 that the large skips are usually confined to the lower (bass) part. Most often, one part moves by step, the other by step or skip. Both voices rarely skip at the same time.

**EXAMPLE 15-19.** Conclusive cadences

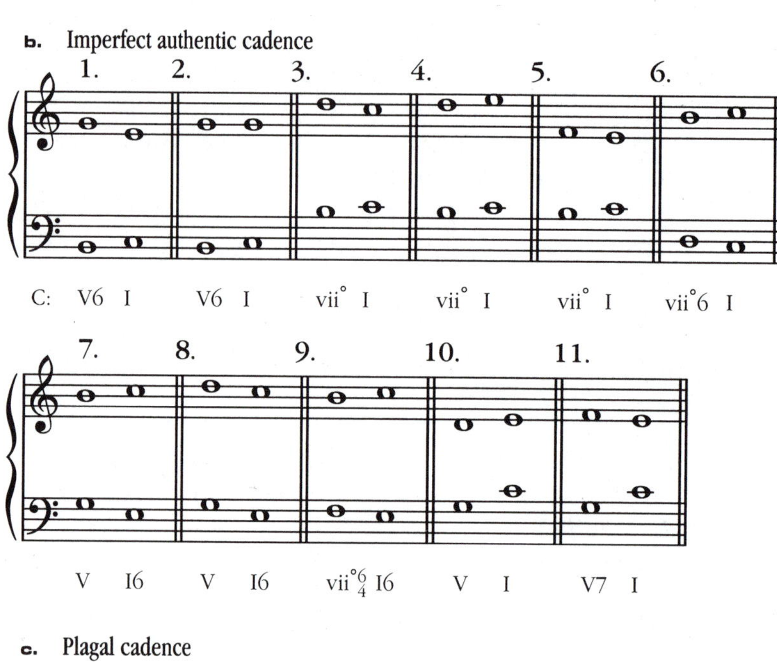

**EXAMPLE 15-20.** Inconclusive cadences

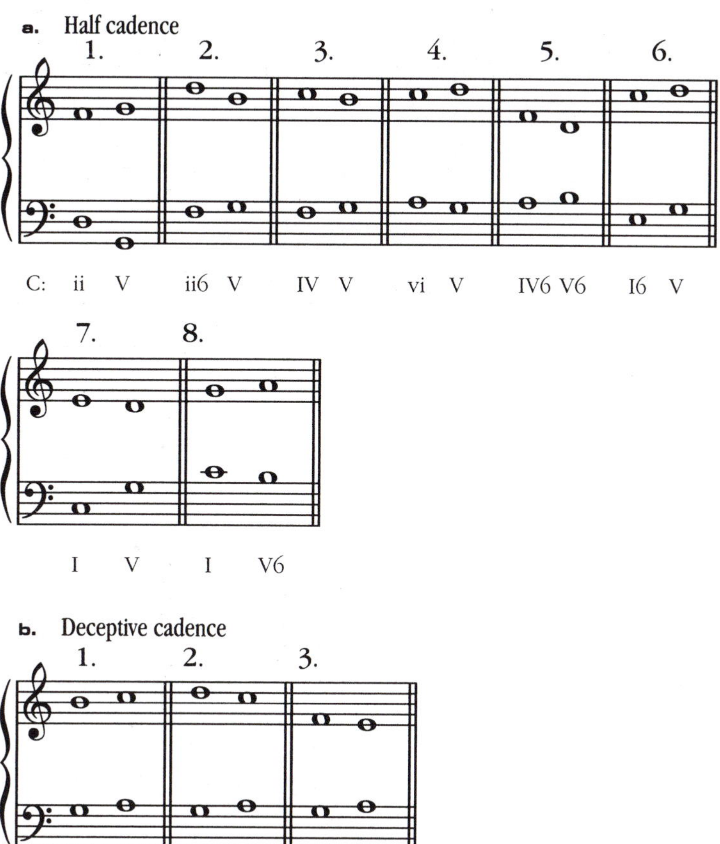


In further developing an understanding of chordal homophony, a coupled recessive line (bass) is added to a given salient line (soprano). Texture is controlled by the nature of the second (recessive) part, that is, by the degree of "competition" offered by the recessive line. The melody in example 15-21a is provided with Roman numerals below the staff; the numerals reflect an initial selection of chords. Example 15-21b shows these chords in root position, providing a starting point for creating a bass line.

A judicious use of inversions can produce a bass line that is more melodic, at the same time giving each chord a clear representation. The version in example 15-22 uses more thirds and sixths and is less disjunct.

Previously discussed limitations on part writing must be maintained. Note the errors in example 15-23.

**EXAMPLE 15-21.** Two-part chordal homophony

a.

b.

**EXAMPLE 15-22.** Adding inversions to two-part chordal homophony

**EXAMPLE 15-23.** Errors in two-part writing

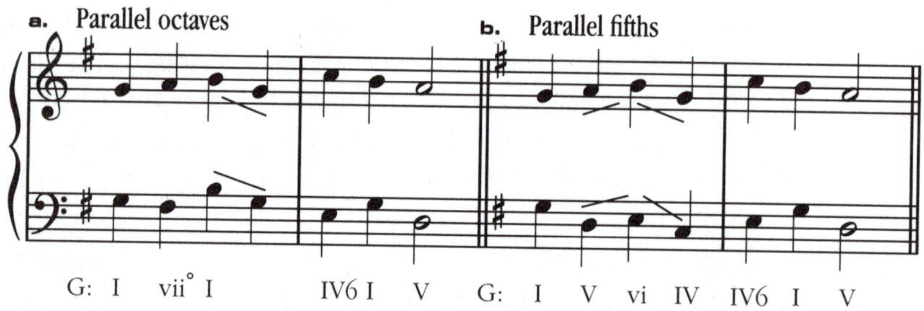


To be considered a chordal homophonic texture, the recessive voice does not have to be completely tied to the salient voice. In example 15-24, the soprano and bass have a few nonharmonic tones and brief decorative chord tones. Notice that the nonharmonic tones do not interfere with the harmonic progression. The nonharmonic tones occur at different times in the two voices, although cases where nonharmonic tones occur simultaneously in both voices can also be found. Care must always be exercised to avoid a clouding of the harmony.

**EXAMPLE 15-24.** Two-part chordal homophonic texture

## Melody with Accompaniment

**melody with accompaniment**

Another very common type of homophony, *melody with accompaniment,* is a group of textures that includes a wide range of possibilities for relating two voices to one another and to the harmony. In fact, it is by far the most commonly used texture in all types of music since about 1750.

It might at first seem that greater rhythmic activity in a salient line would guarantee interest, as in example 15-25a, but the opposite can also be true, as in example 15-25b. While the recessive line has three implied lines, the most interesting line is in the slower-moving upper part. The key to capturing the listener's interest lies in the strength of a line's contour and rhythm.

**EXAMPLE 15-25.** Melody with accompaniment

**a.** Leopold Mozart: Andante

**b.** Wolfgang Mozart: Piano Sonata, K. 545, first movement

The rhythmic activity may be greater or less in the salient line, but the salient line will always have the strongest melodic contour. If the voices should reach the point of competing for the listener's attention the texture is not homophony, but polyphony, since by definition homophony has only one salient line and polyphony has two or more.

## Broken Chord Accompaniments

**broken chord**

In two-voice examples of melody with accompaniment, one of the common techniques used in keyboard writing is the *broken chord.* This includes a multitude of possible chordal patterns in which the recessive voice is very active, moving quickly to touch on various chord tones.

Broken chord accompaniments usually have these traits: (1) rhythm that moves faster than the salient line, (2) uniform rhythmic values, (3) pitch selection implying the harmony, (4) conjunct motion in the implied lines (part writing), and (5) contour unified by a repeated pattern. Example 15-26 shows a few such patterns that were often used beginning about 1750. The pattern in example 15-26a is sometimes called the "Alberti bass."

**EXAMPLE 15-26.** Examples of broken chord accompaniment

Broken chord patterns often produce implied lines. These skeletal lines usually move as if they were simple recessive lines. They follow good voice-leading principles; that is, they move predominantly stepwise, usually with the accented note as the most important. Note the implied nonharmonic tones in example 15-27.

**EXAMPLE 15-27.** Mueller: Serenade

When a chord appears in arpeggiated form, the bass (and hence the inversion) is determined by several factors. Usually the lowest note in the pattern is placed in a prominent metric position, making the bass line prominent. This can be seen in example 15-27 and example 15-28.

**EXAMPLE 15-28.** Determining the bass in an arpeggiated pattern

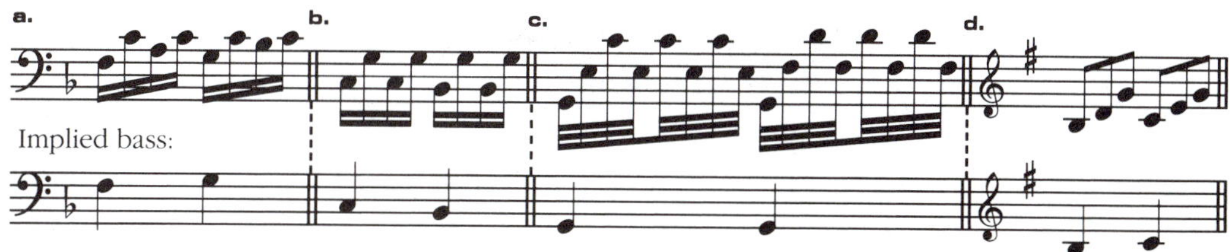


Recognizing that chords may be represented or implied by particular intervals, and that the effect of the chord is quite valid even if the chord is incomplete, you should be able to understand the harmonies implied in example 15-29, which is typical of the Classical era.

In example 15-29b, the effect of the $V^4_3$ is quite clear, even though the third, F-sharp, is missing. Notice also that the ear easily handles the rather harsh dissonances formed by the parallel sevenths in the last beat of measure 1. This is because the V7 is fused into a single chord and is not heard as a succession of individual notes. This "horizontalization" of a chord through broken chord patterns is extremely important in maintaining interest with a slow harmonic rhythm.

**EXAMPLE 15-29.** Examples of implied chords

**a.** Beethoven: Piano Sonata in D Major, op. 10, no. 3, first movement

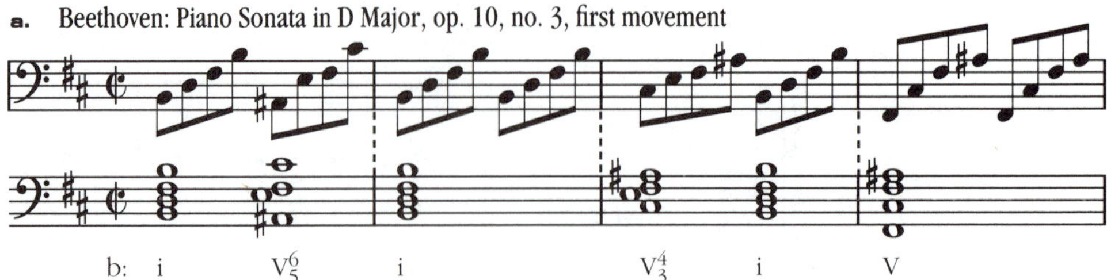


**b.** Mozart: Piano Sonata, K. 545, second movement

**Andante**

G: I V4/3 I

## Less Active Accompaniments

For comparison with the above examples, in which the recessive line was more active than the salient line, example 15-30 illustrates simpler recessive lines. The examples are in strong contrast with the more active accompaniments seen earlier. These passages may seem at first to be chordal, but the rhythm of the recessive voice is consistently less active than that of the salient line.

## Alternating Roles

Generally speaking, a piece of music will establish a particular texture for an extended period of time, but the pattern may change when the voices exchange their roles briefly, so that a recessive line temporarily becomes salient during less active moments in the salient line. The change often occurs at the cadence, when the supporting voice comes forward for a brief moment, as in example 15-31a. In example 15-31b, the broken chord pattern and the salient melody change parts, allowing a smooth transition to a slower moving accompaniment.

**EXAMPLE 15-30.** Less active accompaniments

**a.** Wolfgang Mozart: Duet, K. 487

**b.** Leopold Mozart: Andante

**EXAMPLE 15-31.** Alternating roles of voices at cadences

**a.** J. S. Bach: *Notebook for Anna Magdalena,* BWV Anh. 115, Menuet

**b.** Haydn: Piano Sonata in G Major, Hob. XVI:8, fourth movement

## SUMMARY

The study of texture requires an examination of the relative placement of the music, the component lines of the music, the quantity and quality of the individual melodic lines, and their interrelationships. Two aspects of texture are prominent in the listening experience: the vertical placement of the lines and the density of the texture.

There are essentially two types of lines, salient and recessive, distinguished by degree of prominence and melodic interest. A salient line is a melodic line with a sufficiently high level of melodic interest to sustain the listener's attention. A recessive line is a melodic line with a sufficiently low level of melodic interest that, of itself, does not sustain the listener's attention.

In studying texture, it is of major importance to identify the distinct and separate lines that are the components of the texture so they may be evaluated for their role in the texture as a whole. The lines may be independent of each other, contrast with each other, or be combined in various kinds of grouping, of which coupling and doubling are the most common.

Three steps in the analysis of texture are: (1) determine and mark the salient line or the most important line, if there is more than one; (2) determine and mark the other lines, salient or recessive; (3) determine and mark relationships between the lines.

A particular set of symbols is used in textural analysis. These are as follows:

| | |
|---|---|
| S | salient line |
| R | recessive line |
| ( ) | implied lines |
| v | variable number of parts |
| (v) | variable number of implied lines |
| [ [ | rhythmic coupling (2 parts, 3 parts) |
| ⟦ ⟦ | full coupling (2 parts, 3 parts) |
| [3R | three rhythmically coupled recessive lines |
| ⟦ S/R | a salient and a recessive line fully coupled |
| x | doubled in octaves, or unison |
| x3 | three lines in octaves |
| [ [ | heterophony (2 parts, 3 parts) |

Chordal homophony as well as melody with accompaniment may be represented with two voices; however, the thinness of the texture creates different kinds of problems in providing harmonic content and implications. The treatments of texture, chord representation, and part writing in chordal homophony are different for two voices than for four. Melody with accompaniment is a group of textures including a wide range of possibilities in relating two voices to one another and to the harmony.

## CHAPTER SIXTEEN

# Two-Voice Polyphony

**Terms Introduced in This Chapter**

counterpoint

contrapuntal

differentiated polyphony

unified polyphony

imitation

leader

follower

delay

interval of imitation

strict imitation

free imitation

Polyphony refers to musical textures in which there are two or more salient lines, two-voice polyphony being the simplest polyphonic texture. The term *polyphony* is often used in opposition to homophony; that is, while the second voice in homophony (a recessive line) adds support to the salient line, the second voice in polyphony (a salient line) competes for the listener's attention. It would be rare, however, to find a pair of lines of absolutely equal interest at every moment. In fact, the listener's attention in most cases skips back and forth between the lines, focusing first on one, then on the other.

There is a full spectrum of polyphonic types, ranging from passages with two parts vying constantly for dominance to cases where one part is clearly superior throughout. The latter type, of course, borders on becoming homophonic, and there are many situations where it is difficult to decide how to classify a particular texture.

**counterpoint**

**contrapuntal**

From the beginning of polyphony (perhaps in the ninth century) another term, *counterpoint,* has been associated with it. The terms *polyphonic* and *contrapuntal* are really synonymous, although some writers use the term *polyphony* to refer to music from earlier periods (say from 900–1600) and the term *contrapuntal* to refer to music from the Baroque period on.

## TYPES OF POLYPHONY

Polyphonic textures may be categorized by the degree of contrast or unity between the melodic lines. On this basis, two types may be identified: differentiated and unified.

### Differentiated Polyphony

**differentiated polyphony**

A polyphonic passage composed of salient lines that have independent or unrelated motives is called *differentiated polyphony.* This texture is characterized by high contrast between parts, as seen in example 16-1. In example 16-1 the upper voice moves entirely by step, the lower entirely by skip. Quick-moving eighth notes in the upper voice contrast with half notes and quarter notes in the lower, and repeated note figures oppose arpeggiated chords.

Example 16-2 shows a lower level of contrast. The lower voice consists mostly of eighth notes moving by skip, while the upper moves in stepwise sixteenth notes. The upper voice has greater salience, but the lower voice has its own clear shape and direction. The voices complement each other rhythmically, producing a steady stream of sixteenths.

**EXAMPLE 16-1.** Mozart: Piano Sonata, K. 570, first movement

**EXAMPLE 16-2.** J. S. Bach: *Goldberg Variations,* BWV 988

## Unified Polyphony

**unified polyphony**

In contrast to differentiated polyphony, *unified polyphony* is composed of two or more salient lines that share rhythmic or melodic motives. The degree of unification will vary, of course, but a texture is considered unified if the voices deal with identical or related motives.

In example 16-3, the voices share motives in a pattern of alternating activity; the sixteenth notes are associated with conjunct motion, the eighth notes with disjunct. The first two beats of this example may lead one to consider this differentiated polyphony, but as the music progresses, it becomes clear that the voices are dealing with the same material.

The feeling of both parts dealing with the same material is even stronger in example 16-4, which is very tightly knit. Looking at the parts separately, the independence is clear, but the shared elements of rhythm and contour are also obvious.

**EXAMPLE 16-3.** J. S. Bach: French Suite II, BWV 813, Air

**EXAMPLE 16-4.** J. S. Bach: Invention No. 9, BWV 780

## WRITING TWO-VOICE COUNTERPOINT

Writing two-voice counterpoint will begin with a given soprano, to which a polyphonic bass will be added. The writing can be done in four stages.

First, a tentative chord selection is made. This is shown in example 16-5, but keep in mind that the V chords may become vii° in later stages.

**EXAMPLE 16-5.** Chord selection

Second, a tentative decision is made about the nature of the pitch and rhythm of the line to be added. A choice must be made between differentiated and unified polyphony. In selecting differentiated polyphony the goal will be to have contrast in rhythm, contour, and motives. In this case, the second line will be mostly conjunct and will use the motive ♩ ♫ or ♫ ♪.

Third, a few notes of the added melody are sketched at selected places where a desirable relationship can be anticipated. As shown in example 16-6, pitches are chosen that provide good chord representation, a contour that complements the given melody, and allow for good voice leading when the details are added. It is useful to consider moments when the activity could alternate between the voices. To be independent, voices should not have similar contours. An independent line is sketched in example 16-6.

**EXAMPLE 16-6.** Sketch of an independent lower voice

Fourth, the final line is completed with some adjustments and altering of plans. Note that the chords in example 16-7 are somewhat different from those originally planned in example 16-5.

**EXAMPLE 16-7.** Completed two-voice counterpoint

## IMITATION

**imitation**

**leader**

**follower**

One of the most effective techniques for unifying independent lines is *imitation,* the repetition of melodic material in a different voice, entering after some delay while the initial voice continues. The first voice to state the melody is called the *leader,* and the answering or imitating voice is called the *follower.* These are indicated by the letters L and F, as shown in example 16-8.

**EXAMPLE 16-8.** J. S. Bach: *Notebook for Anna Magdalena,* BWV Anh. 120, Menuet

## Basic Concepts

**delay**

**interval of imitation**

Two important aspects of imitation are the *delay* before the appearance of the follower and the *interval of imitation,* that is, the interval between the first notes of the leader and the first notes of the follower.

Delay is the time elapsed between the statement by the leader and the entrance of the follower. In reckoning this distance, one must count the time (in measures or beats) between the initial attacks of each of the entries.

If the imitating voice enters on the same pitch as the leader, we speak of "imitation at the unison." If the follower enters at a different pitch we refer to imitation at the interval between the starting pitch of the leader and the starting pitch of the follower, for example, "imitation at the octave below," "at the fifth above," and so on.

## Analysis of Imitation

An analysis of imitation consists of: (1) a dash-line bracket showing the length of the imitation from the beginning of the leader to the point where the follower ceases to imitate; (2) a description of the interval of imitation and the delay; and (3) the letters L and F, showing the entry of the leader and the follower. In example 16-9, the imitation is at the octave below, with a delay of one eighth note, as the description indicates. Pinpointing the end of the imitation is important; the bracket should be marked very carefully

**EXAMPLE 16-9.** Mozart: Piano Sonata, K. 576, first movement

## Strict Imitation

**strict imitation**

Imitation in which the follower imitates the leader exactly throughout the length of the imitation is called *strict imitation.* Example 16-10 shows this in measures 1, 8, and 10, but it may be difficult to locate the instances when they occur in the middle of a work, as in example 16-11, measure 8. The interval and delay changes are marked in the usual manner in the analysis.

**EXAMPLE 16-10.** Telemann: Fugue

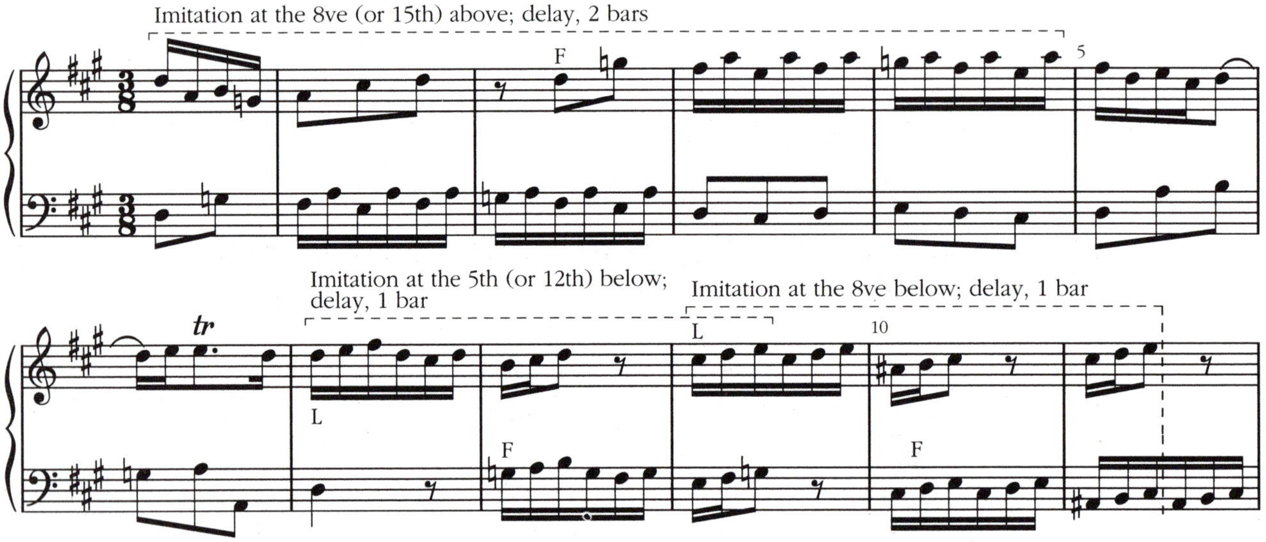


## Free Imitation

**free imitation**

*Free imitation* is imitation in which one or a few durations are changed or tones appear at a slightly different pitch than strict imitation would require. Usually the changed pitches are only a step above or below what would have been expected. In example 16-11, there are three instances of imitation: The first two are strict imitation and the third is free. The tones that have been adjusted are circled and are a step lower than expected.

Such adjustments are common and especially noticeable at the beginning of an imitative passage, where the relationships between leader and follower is most apparent, and where it is most important to tonality and harmonic background. In example 16-12, the follower is a fifth (twelfth) below the leader most of the time. But the harmony at the moment the follower enters is intended to be a tonic chord, making the first note of the second voice a step too high to fit the chord. The extra staff shows the tone changed to the fifth below.

**EXAMPLE 16-11.** J. S. Bach: English Suite I, BWV 806, Bourrée

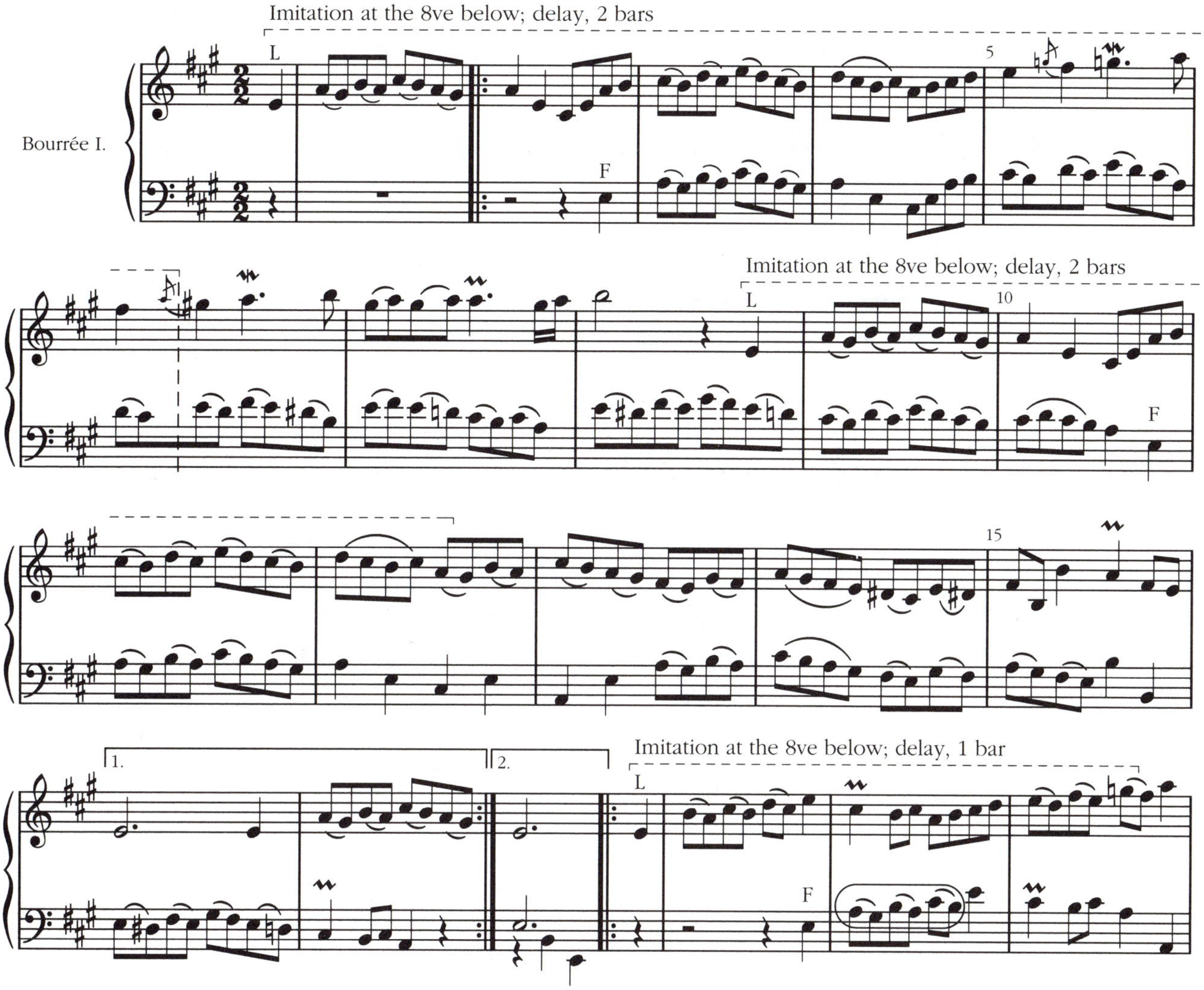
Imitation at the 8ve below; delay, 2 bars
L
5
Bourrée I.
F
Imitation at the 8ve below; delay, 2 bars
L
10
F
15
1.
2.
Imitation at the 8ve below; delay, 1 bar
L
F

**EXAMPLE 16-12.** J. S. Bach: French Suite II, BWV 813, Gigue

Imitation at the P5 below; delay, 1 bar
L
5
F
c: i ii°6 V i6 iv6 V i
etc.

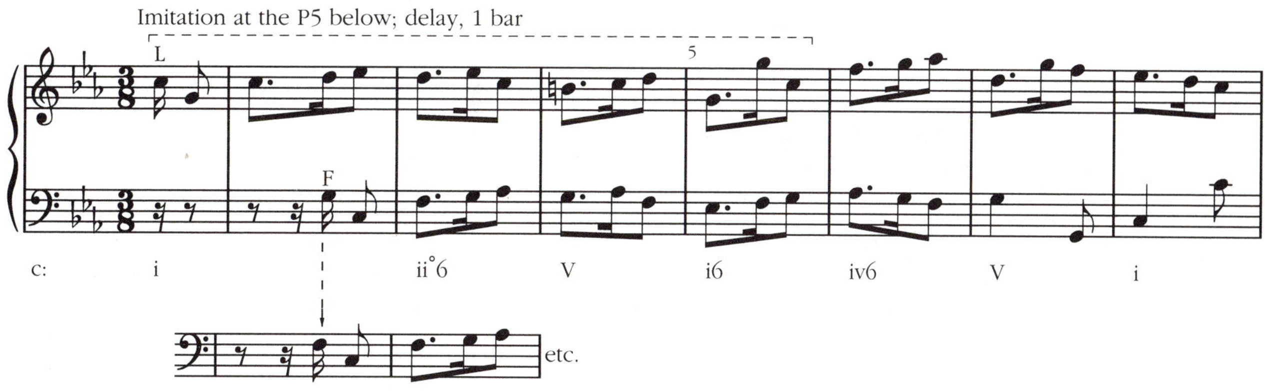

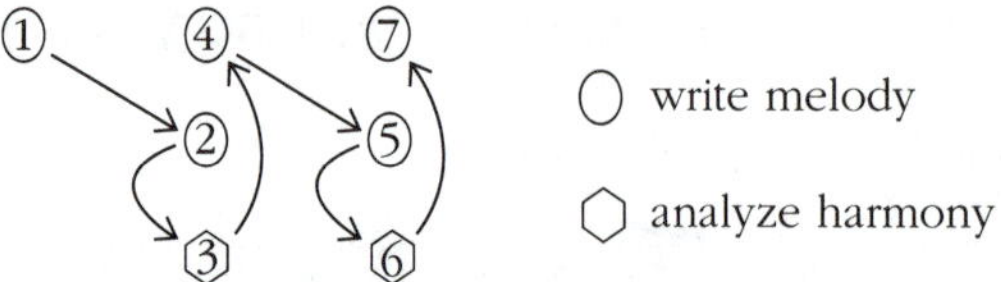


**FIGURE 16-1.** Steps in writing imitation

## Writing Imitation

The procedure for writing imitation is necessarily quite systematic:

1. Write the leader, up to the entry of the follower.
2. Copy the follower at the desired interval.
3. Determine the underlying harmonic background.
4. Write the continuation of the leader in accordance with this harmony.

5–9. Continue by repeating steps 2, 3, and 4 until the imitation is completed (see fig. 16-1).

Example 16-13 illustrates the steps shown in figure 16-1 applied to the opening of a gigue by J. S. Bach.

**EXAMPLE 16-13.** J. S. Bach: English Suite I, BWV 806, Gigue

**a.** Write the leader ①.

**b.** Copy the follower ② and analyze the harmony ③ .

**EXAMPLE 16-13.** (continued)

c. Continue the leader by writing new counterpoint ④.

d. Copy the continuation of the leader ⑤. Analyze the harmony ⑥ (note that the harmonization of the follower may be different from the harmonization of the leader).

e. Continue the leader by writing new counterpoint ⑦.

## SUMMARY

Polyphony refers to musical textures in which there are two or more salient lines, two-voice polyphony being the simplest polyphonic texture. Polyphonic textures may be categorized by the degree of contrast or unity between the melodic lines. On this basis, two types may be identified: differentiated and unified. A polyphonic passage composed of salient lines that have independent or unrelated motives is called differentiated polyphony. In contrast to differentiated polyphony, unified polyphony is composed of two or more salient lines that share rhythmic or melodic motives.

When writing a polyphonic bass with a given soprano, four steps are needed:

1. A tentative chord selection is made.
2. A tentative decision is made about the nature of the pitch and rhythm of the line to be added.
3. A few notes of the added melody are sketched at places where a desirable relationship can be anticipated.
4. The final line is completed with some adjustments and altering of plans.

One of the most effective techniques for unifying independent lines is imitation, the repetition of melodic material in a different voice, entering after some delay while the initial voice continues. Two important aspects of imitation are the delay before the appearance of the follower and the interval of imitation. The analysis consists of (1) a dash-line bracket showing the length of the imitation from the beginning of the leader to the point where the follower ceases to imitate, (2) a description of the interval of imitation and the delay, and (3) letters L and F, showing the entry of the leader and the follower.

CHAPTER SEVENTEEN

# Modulation

**Terms Introduced in This Chapter**

- common chord
- closely related key
- remote key
- distant key
- pivot chord
- harbinger chord
- harbinger tone
- direct modulation

The value and importance of modulation, or change of key, is reflected in the frequent and varied use of this technique by virtually every composer in the period of common practice. This chapter will deal with modulation and modulation techniques.

## BASIC CONCEPTS

The organization of modulation is markedly affected by two important factors: how smoothly the change of key will be made and the relationship or distance between the new and old keys. The establishment of tonality and subsequent modulations have a significant impact on the effect of a musical work.

### Smoothness of Modulation

**common chord**

Modulations may be organized for either a smooth or abrupt change of key. Keys may have chords in common as well as other features that allow for easy modulation from one to the other. A *common chord* is a chord that is found with the identical root and chord type in two different keys. For instance, the C major triad appears in both the key of C and the key of F. If a modulation uses a common chord and carefully prepares the arrival of new pitches, the change of key can be very smooth. Most modulations take advantage of these common areas, but, if a sharp break is desired, the composer may deliberately juxtapose conflicting or contradictory elements so that one is keenly aware that a new key has come to the fore. The smoothness of a modulation depends largely upon the degree of relatedness between the keys.

### Key Relationships

**closely related key**

**remote key**

**distant key**

Those keys that have identical pitch complements (such as a major key and its relative minor) and those whose complements differ by only one pitch are said to be *closely related keys,* while all others are considered to be *remote* or *distant keys.* Another way to view this is that keys whose signatures differ by no more than one sharp or one flat are closely related.

The degree of relatedness of keys can be shown more fully with the circle of fifths. Figure 17-1 shows major and minor keys together, that is, with relative keys sharing the same position on the circumference. Those keys that lie adjacent to each other are said to be closely related.

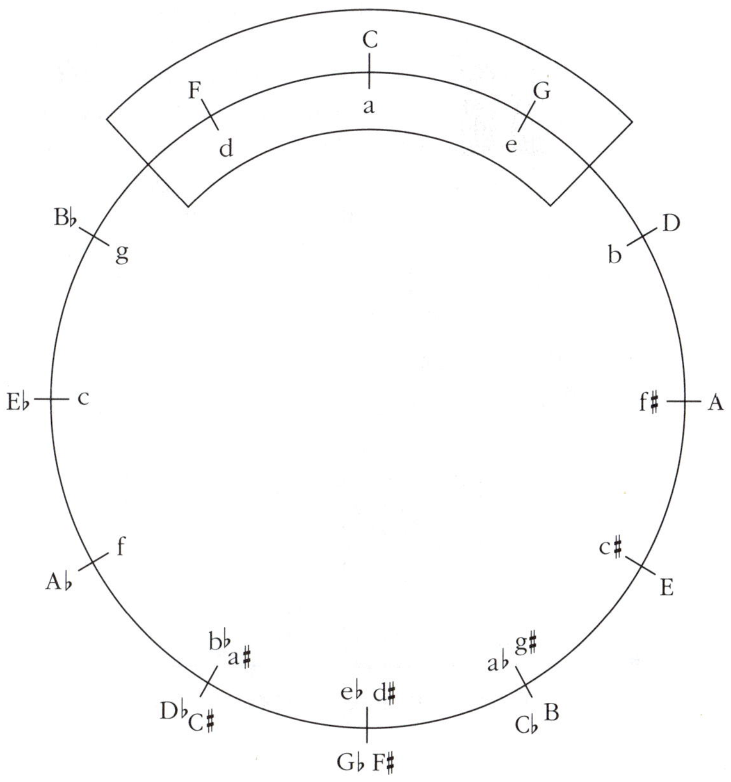


**FIGURE 17-1.** Circle of fifths

In figure 17-1, C major is bracketed with its five closely related keys, two major and three minor keys. Keys that are further apart along the circumference of the circle are distant or remote; keys opposite each other on the circle have the most remote relationship. The degree of relatedness between two keys can also be seen in the number of common chords. Example 17-1 shows the chords common to the keys of C and F major.

**EXAMPLE 17-1.** Chords common to C major and F major

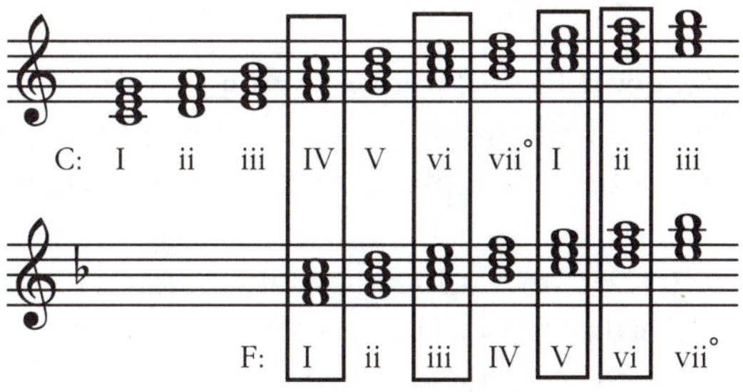

Moving beyond the range of the closely related keys, the keys of C and D major have only two chords in common, as seen in example 17-2. Going still further, the keys of C and A major have no chords in common. This does not mean that one cannot modulate from C to A; any modulation is possible, but not by a common diatonic chord. (Other means of getting from one key to another include using a chromatically altered chord, an approach through some less distantly related key, or a direct modulation—one in which no common chord is used.) If common chords are not used in a modulation, the two keys are set in greater opposition because their differences have been emphasized, not their similarities.

**EXAMPLE 17-2.** Chords common to C major and D major

C: I ii iii IV V vi vii° I ii

D: I ii iii IV V vi vii° I

## COMMON-CHORD MODULATION

Common-chord modulation is by far the most often used and the smoothest way to modulate. Just as a progression is smoothed by retaining common tones, a modulation can be smoothed by a common chord, that is, a chord that is common to both the original key and the new key. To understand how a modulation is effected, it is necessary to see how the common chord is used.

### The Four Stages of Modulation

To establish a new key fully and smoothly requires a four-stage process. If not all of the stages are observed, the modulation may be only suggested, not fully realized.

In stage 1, the first key is established. This usually requires, as a minimum, the I and the V chords.

**pivot chord**

In stage 2, the *pivot chord* appears. A pivot chord is a common chord that appears as the last chord in the old key and the first chord in the new key.

**harbinger chord**

In stage 3, the *harbinger chord* appears, heralding the approach of the new key. The harbinger chord is the first chord that belongs in the new key of a modulating passage and does not belong in the old key. One or more tones in the harbinger chord belong to the new key and not to the old, tones that may be called *harbinger tones*.

**harbinger tone**

In stage 4, the new key is confirmed by one of the following methods: (1) a cadence that includes V(7) I; (2) a melodic passage that reveals the pitch complement of the new tonality; or (3) an additional harmonic cycle in the new key.

Example 17-3 illustrates the four stages of a common-chord modulation. Stage 1 is accomplished in measures 1–5, where the key of E-flat is well established. Stage 2, determining the pivot chord, is accomplished by looking ahead to the first chord not in the original key, then seeing if the preceding chord is common to both keys. In figure 17-2, which diagrams the chords from example 17-3, the pivot chord appears in measure 5. The pivot chord is assigned a Roman numeral in both the original and the new keys. Thereafter, beginning in measure 6, the Roman numerals refer to the new key, B-flat major.

**EXAMPLE 17-3.** Mozart: Minuetto, K. 15qq

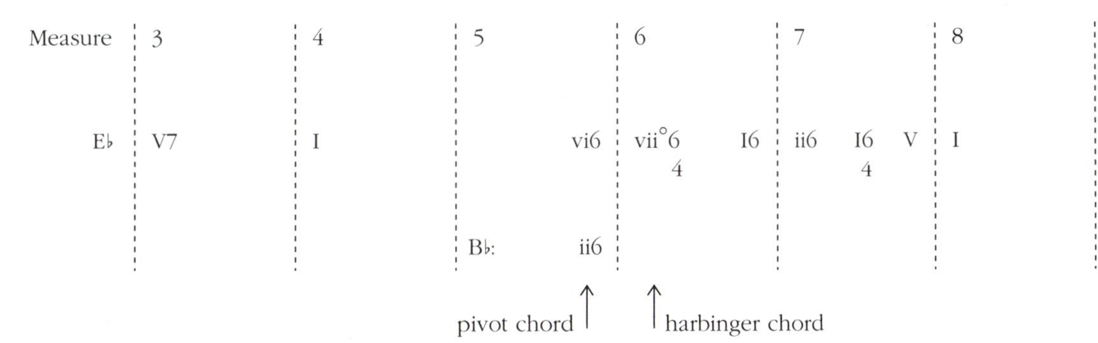


**FIGURE 17-2.** Diagram of chords in example 17-3, mm. 3–8

Stage 3 is reached in measure 6. The A diminished chord, with the A-natural, is the harbinger chord, announcing the arrival of the key of B-flat. The A-natural, the harbinger tone, is first introduced here; A-natural replaces A-flat from here on. This chord makes clear that the pivot chord is the chord just before it. Stage 4 takes place in measures 6–8. Once the key of B-flat has been announced, it is reaffirmed by two completed harmonic cycles.

The four stages may be reviewed further in example 17-4. Stage 1: The original key is established with the first three chords. Stage 2: The pivot chord is the I in measure 2. When it is first heard, the listener has no idea a modulation is about to take place.

Stage 3: The harbinger chord is the D-major triad in measure 2. Because it contains a note (F-sharp) not in the complement of C major, it announces that a modulation is taking place. From this point on the F is sharped.

Stage 4: After the harbinger chord, the new key is confirmed by the appearance and reassertion of the new dominant and tonic (mm. 3–5).

**EXAMPLE 17-4.** J. S. Bach: *Weg, mein Herz*

## Establishing New Keys

A new key is established by a new pitch complement and harmonic progression leading to a cadence. The most common modulation during the period of common practice was to the dominant key, if the piece began in a major key. Knowing this, one can scan the music and look for accidentals that indicate that the modulation is taking place. If the piece begins in minor, the most common modulation in the period of common practice was to the relative major. In this case, the visual clue that the modulation is taking place is the absence of the leading tone of the old key. The presence or absence of accidentals is not sufficient evidence of a modulation; the new key must be established by evidence that continues beyond the harbinger chord, often including a cadence in the new key.

In example 17-5 there is a suggestion in measure 6 that a modulation to D major is under way because the A-sharp is no longer used. These chords all fit within B minor, though, and the phrase ends in B minor. The situation is different in measure 14, where the A-natural returns and remains, while a harmonic cycle in D major is completed at the cadence.

**EXAMPLE 17-5.** J. S. Bach: French Suite III, BWV 814, Menuet

One must not be misled by false clues into thinking a modulation has taken place when it has not. Example 17-6 includes several accidentals that do not point to a modulation. The G-sharp in measure 3, the D-sharp in measure 8, and the A-sharp in measure 13 are merely chromatic nonharmonic tones. Of course, they have an impact on the pitch complement, but their importance is lessened by the fact that they do not reappear consistently. The C-sharp, however, appears first in measure 7 (as a chord tone) and remains until the cadence in measure 14.

A tonic six-four chord often appears in the cadence following a modulation. This is because of its strong key-defining role. In such cases, the tonic six-four should be viewed as a prolonging decoration of the V that follows. Do not consider the tonic six-four to be a pivot chord, even if the following chord is the harbinger. The tonic six-four is so distinctive in cadences that it becomes the harbinger. Thus, in example 17-7, the analysis places the tonic six-four in the new key, but not in the old. In example 17-8, the harbinger appears in measure 4. The F-sharp remains consistently in the melody from then until the cadence, when an implied tonic six-four chord appears, strengthening the new tonality. The modulation relies on the melodic treatment and the cadential pattern for clarity.

**EXAMPLE 17-6.** Haydn: Piano Sonata in G Major, Hob. XVI:27, second movement

**EXAMPLE 17-7.** The tonic six-four in modulations

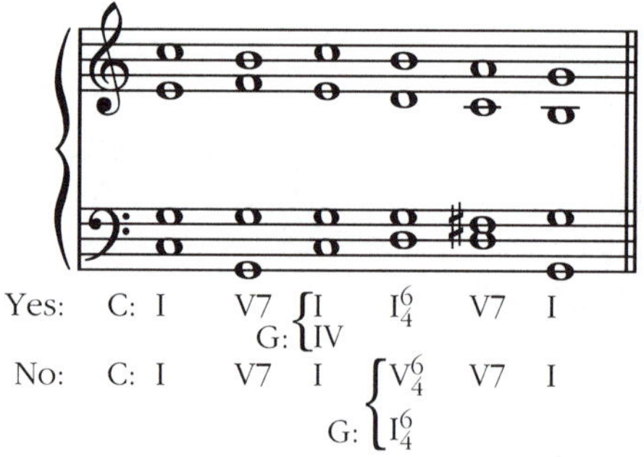

**EXAMPLE 17-8.** Haydn: Piano Sonata in C Major, Hob. XVI:3, third movement

## DIRECT MODULATION

**direct modulation**

Occasionally one encounters a modulation in which there is no common chord and in fact little attempt before the harbinger to smooth the transition from one key to the next. This is called *direct modulation,* a change of key in which there is no pivot chord. The elements of difference between the two keys are set in sharp conflict; there is a feeling of contradiction. There are only three stages in direct modulation: the establishing of the first key, the harbinger chord, and the establishing of the new key.

In example 17-9a, the composer has been careful to provide a very smooth voice leading to lessen the shock of the new key: Notice the common tone in the soprano, the half-step chromatic alteration in the alto, and the small intervals in the tenor and bass. In example 17-9b, the opposite purpose has been served: The two keys are placed in strong contrast with each other.

In both example 17-9a and b the direct modulation took place at the beginning of a new phrase. This is a common location for this device. Having the new phrase in the new key emphasizes its impact on the form. It is less common to find direct modulation in the middle of a phrase, as in example 17-10. Likewise, the direct modulation to a remote key in example 17-11 is abrupt and startling.

**EXAMPLE 17-9.** Direct modulation

**a.** J. S. Bach: *Sei Lob und Ehr'*

**b.** J. S. Bach: *Christus, der ist*

**EXAMPLE 17-10.** J. S. Bach: *Du grosser Schmerzensmann*

**EXAMPLE 17-11.** Beethoven: Rondo a Capriccio, op. 129

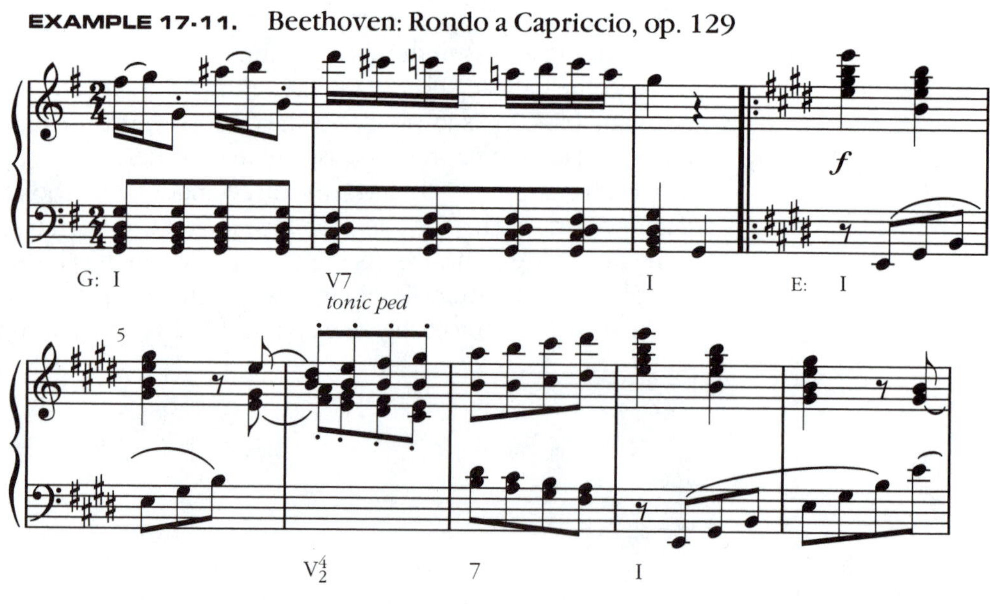

## ANALYSIS OF MODULATION

One analyzes the stages of modulation in a different order than the listener perceives. In analysis one first observes the establishment of the initial key (stage 1), but the next evidence of modulation will be the harbinger chord (stage 3), after which one can determine the pivot chord in retrospect (stage 2) and finally establish the new key (stage 4). Note in example 17-12 the modulation to the dominant key, illustrating this process: In modulations to the dominant key, the harbinger chord is frequently V or vii° in the new key. The four stages are summarized as follows:

Stage 1: establishment of the first key

Stage 3: harbinger chord

Stage 2: pivot chord

Stage 4: establishment of the new key

**EXAMPLE 17-12.** Stages in modulating

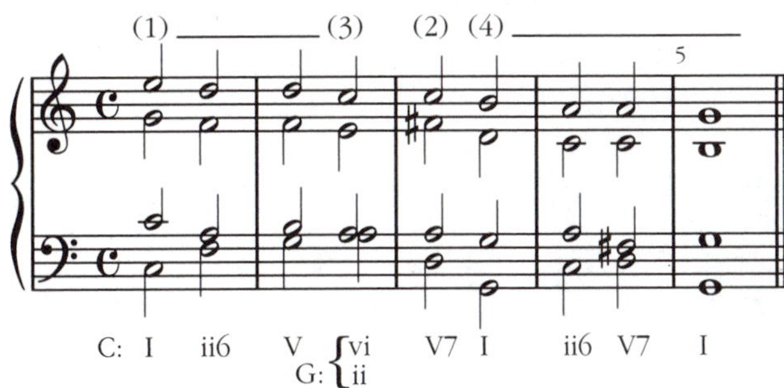


If no common chord appears as a pivot before the harbinger, the modulation is a direct modulation. The pitch complement of a new key may be evident in a new key signature, but it is usually shown by the consistent use of new accidentals or the departure of accidentals previously used.

Be wary of key signatures; they do not always give clear evidence of the tonality, especially in the middle of a piece. Pay careful attention to accidentals, which give better clues about the tonality. The harbinger chord, when it signals a return to the original tonic key of a piece, as in example 17-13, will not usually require accidentals, but previous accidentals will no longer be used.

In minor keys, remember that a raised note is likely to be an indication of the dominant chord, not the tonic. When a piece in a minor key begins to modulate to its relative major, the raised $\hat{7}$ will drop out in favor of a lowered version of that note. This note is the $\hat{5}$ in the relative major. As such, it will be a harbinger note, but without an accidental. If an analysis seems to require frequent use of III and VII in a minor key, one should check to see if perhaps there has been a modulation to the relative major. There are no cadences on III or VII; an analysis that ends a phrase with these chords is in error. In example 17-14, the key of G minor should be dropped before the F-sharp gives way to F-natural in measure 8. The I and V in B-flat major make a simpler, more logical explanation than the remote and unconventional $VII^6_4$ and III.

**EXAMPLE 17-13.** J. S. Bach: *O Haupt voll Blut und Wunden*

**EXAMPLE 17-14.** Bellini: *Norma*

**EXAMPLE 17-14.** (continued)

## WRITING MODULATIONS

When writing modulatory progressions, one follows the four stages in the original order: (1) establish the first key; (2) select the pivot chord, the last common chord before the new key; (3) be sure that the harbinger chord follows the pivot chord; and (4) confirm the new key in all the chords including and following the harbinger. If one goes beyond the harbinger chord using only chords that are common to both keys, the pivot may not be the last common chord before the true harbinger.

When harmonizing a melody that modulates there are two issues to consider: first, determining the keys, old and new; and second, locating the best place for the pivot chord. In the melody in example 17-15 there is a likely modulation from F to C major. The most practical way to determine the placement of the pivot is to see where to put a harbinger, probably the new dominant chord. Locating the V at point (a) allows the new I to fall on a strong agogic accent. Placing it at (b) makes the modulation less conspicuous.

The melody in example 17-15 could also have modulated to the key of A minor, but the melody in example 17-16 is more clearly aimed in that direction. The new V might appear as early as (a), but it is more practical at (b).

A similar melody in the minor mode is given in example 17-17. If it ends in F major, this would be a change of mode, not a modulation. Change of mode requires no pivot chord.

In example 17-18, the clue that a modulation has occurred is the absence of the raised leading tone (E-natural). There are several points at which a modulation to A-flat major could take place.

**EXAMPLE 17-15.** Placement of the harbinger chord, F major to C major

**EXAMPLE 17-16.** Placement of the harbinger chord, F major to A minor

**EXAMPLE 17-17.** Change of mode

**EXAMPLE 17-18.** Modulation from F minor to A-flat major

## SUMMARY


A variety of techniques for modulation are organized around the basic concepts of common chord and direct modulation. The organization of modulation is markedly affected by two important factors: how smoothly the change of key will be made and the degree of relatedness between the new and old keys. Modulations may be smoothly executed by means of a common chord, a chord that is found with the identical root and type in two different keys. Those keys that have identical pitch complements (such as a major key and its relative minor) and those whose complements differ by only one pitch are said to be closely related keys, while all others are considered to be remote or distant keys. Just as a progression is smoothed by retaining common tones, a modulation can be smoothed by the use of a common chord. To fully and smoothly establish a new key requires a four-stage process:

Stage 1: establishment of the first key;

Stage 2: pivot chord;

Stage 3: harbinger chord;

Stage 4: establishment of the new key.

A modulation in which there is no pivot chord before the harbinger is called a direct modulation.

One analyzes the stages of modulation in a different order than the listener perceives them.

Stage 1: establishment of the first key;

Stage 3: harbinger chord;

Stage 2: pivot chord;

Stage 4: establishment of the new key.

When writing modulatory progressions, one follows the four stages in the original order: (1) establish the first key; (2) select a pivot chord that is common to the old and the new keys; (3) be sure that the harbinger chord follows the pivot chord; and (4) confirm the new key.

CHAPTER EIGHTEEN

# Secondary Dominants

**Terms Introduced in This Chapter**

altered chord

secondary dominants

secondary leading tone

secondary tonic

tonicize

**altered chord**

**secondary dominants**

The possibility of suggesting a new key without actually modulating is often very useful, particularly in extended pieces in which variety in the tonality is desired. The suggestion of a new key introduces chromatic alterations into the music. A chord containing a tone foreign to the prevailing scale, a chromatic alteration, is called an *altered chord.* Some of the most common altered chords are those that result from dominant-like chord types and relationships applied to chord groups 3, 4, 5, and 6. These are known as *secondary dominants,* which function in most respects like regular dominant chords.

In example 18-1, the chord marked * does not fit in G major; it is the dominant of the D-major chord that follows. There is a brief suggestion of a modulation to D major, but the music continues thereafter entirely in G.

**EXAMPLE 18-1.** J. S. Bach: *Von Himmel hoch, da komm' ich her*

**secondary leading tone**

**secondary tonic**

**tonicized**

The A-major chord in example 18-1 is a secondary dominant. Because the chord contains a tone that is not part of the complement of G major, it is considered an altered chord. The altered tone, the C-sharp, may be called the *secondary leading tone,* as it is the leading tone in the brief "secondary" or "temporary" key of D major. D major may be said to be a *secondary tonic.* A triad (other than the tonic) that is preceded by its dominant is said to be *tonicized,* that is, a secondary tonic.

The characteristics of a secondary dominant are:

1. It is an altered chord, that is, one that uses one or more tones not in the established key.
2. The chord is either a major triad or a Mm7, a chord type typical of normal dominants. The chord may thus serve as V or V7 in some key.
3. The chord moves to a chord whose root lies a perfect fifth lower (or a fourth above), resembling a progression of V7–I in a new key.

The difference between a passage involving a secondary dominant and one involving a modulation is that in a modulation (1) the new key is established by a clear cadence and (2) there are usually more than one or two chords that belong only to the new key.

Notice that in example 18-1 the secondary tonic is a supertonic, Mm7 chord. It is the secondary dominant that contains the altered note and will therefore require some special identification. This is done in relation to the secondary tonic; that is, the chord marked * is acting as the dominant of the V chord. It is therefore named V/V ("five of five").

## SECONDARY DOMINANTS IN MAJOR AND MINOR KEYS

Secondary dominants are like regular dominants in every regard except that they appear in chord groups 3, 4, 5, and 6. They may be used in major and minor keys. They may be inverted, the doubling and voice leading is identical to that found in any V–I progression, and they may have a seventh added to become V7. Table 18-1 illustrates how a triad or seventh chord may become a secondary dominant (or a secondary dominant seventh) in major keys. Notice that each of these chords requires an altered tone. In some cases a secondary dominant is not possible: A Mm7 built on the subdominant in major would lead to a chord that is outside the original key.

| Chord group | Triad or seventh chord | Uses this altered scale degree | To form this secondary dominant |
|---|---|---|---|
| 3 | ii(7) | $\sharp\hat{4}$ | V(7)/V |
| 4 | vi(7) | $\sharp\hat{1}$ | V(7)/ii |
| | I7 | $\flat\hat{7}$ | V7/IV |
| 5 | iii(7) | $\sharp\hat{5}$ | V(7)/vi |
| 6 | vii°(7) | $\sharp\hat{2}, \sharp\hat{4}$ | V(7)/iii |

**TABLE 18-1.** Secondary dominants in major keys

In major keys, triads that are normally minor (ii, iii, and vi) become secondary dominants if they are changed to major triads. Thus, if ii becomes II, it should be understood as V/V. Triads that are normally major, for example, I in major and III in minor, must have the seventh added if they are to be altered chords and heard as secondary dominants. That is, V/IV in major will be heard as I, and V/VI in minor will be heard as III. In example 18-2, secondary dominants in a major key are shown.

**EXAMPLE 18-2.** Secondary dominants in major keys

| Chord group | Triad or seventh chord | Uses this altered scale degree | To form this secondary dominant |
|---|---|---|---|
| 3 | ii°(7) | ♯$\hat{4}$, ♯$\hat{6}$ | V(7)/V |
| | iv(7) | ♯$\hat{6}$ | V(7)/VII (rare) |
| 4 | i(7) | ♯$\hat{3}$, ♭$\hat{7}$ | V(7)/iv |
| 5 | III7 | ♭$\hat{2}$, ♭$\hat{7}$ | V(7)/VI |
| 6 | VII(7) | ♭$\hat{7}$ | V(7)/III |

**TABLE 18-2.** Secondary dominants in minor keys

Table 18-2 illustrates secondary dominants in minor keys. Since the raised $\hat{7}$ is more frequently used, ♭$\hat{7}$ is shown in table 18-2 as if it were an altered scale degree. In example 18-3, secondary dominants in a minor key are illustrated in notation.

**EXAMPLE 18-3.** Secondary dominants in minor keys

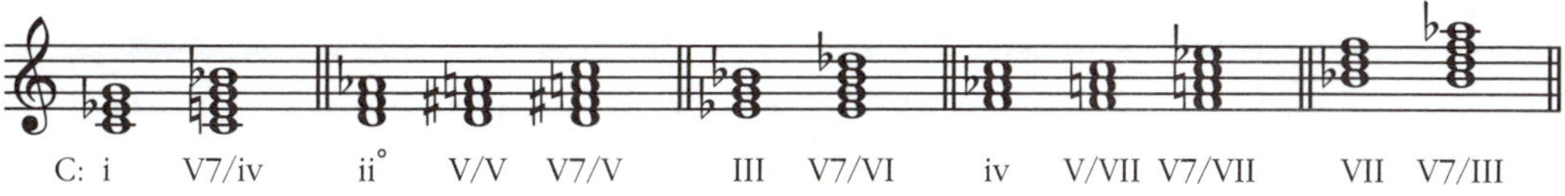

## NORMAL TREATMENT OF SECONDARY DOMINANTS

The usual treatment of secondary dominants follows the normal progression and conventional voice leading and doubling.

### Secondary Dominants in the Normal Progression of Chords

Figures 18-1 and 18-2 show the use of secondary dominants in normal progressions. Figure 18-1 shows major keys; figure 18-2 shows minor keys. Secondary dominants are shown in their chord groups, and the standard diatonic chords are shown in parentheses.

Group 6
Group 5
Group 4
Group 3
Group 2
Group 1
V7/iii
(iii)
(vi)
(ii)
(V)
V7/vi
V7/ii
V7/V
I
(I7)
(IV)
(vii°)
V7/IV

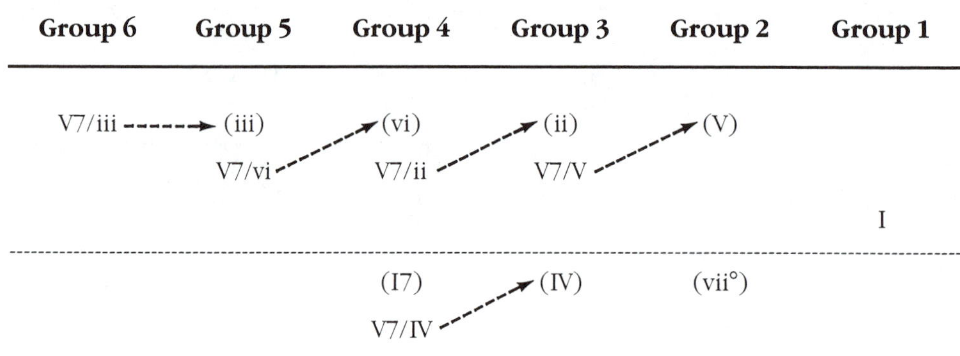

**FIGURE 18-1.** Secondary dominants in normal progressions (major keys)

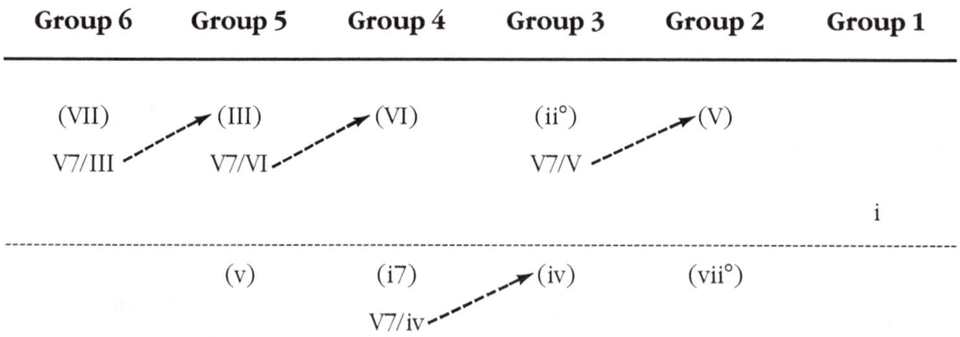

Group 6
Group 5
Group 4
Group 3
Group 2
Group 1
(VII)
(III)
(VI)
(ii°)
(V)
V7/III
V7/VI
V7/V
i
(v)
(i7)
(iv)
(vii°)
V7/iv

**FIGURE 18-2.** Secondary dominants in normal progressions (minor keys)

Secondary dominants usually resolve to the chord written after the slash. These progressions are viewed as normal since they each represent V–I in a new key. The frequency with which the various secondary dominants occur is reflected in the position of the chord in the chart of normal progressions. Chords in the lower-numbered groups are encountered more frequently.

Secondary dominants and dominant sevenths are treated the same as ordinary V and V7 chords as regards voice leading. Each secondary dominant has a secondary leading tone that will tend to move up to the secondary tonic. The seventh of a secondary dominant seventh chord will resolve by moving down a step. Comments made earlier about the handling of tritones apply to secondary dominants as well.

The least-used option for doubling in a major triad is the third of the chord. This is especially true in the case of a dominant chord, where the third is the leading tone. Because it has such a strong drive to resolve, the leading tone is a very prominent tone; it should not be doubled.

## Secondary Dominants in Root Position

Examples 18-4 and 18-5 show secondary V and V7 chords in root position in typical resolution patterns. Concerning voice leading, doublings, and omissions, the resolutions are comparable to those of V or $V^7$ in chord group 2; however, $V^7/V$ is shown resolving to V, $V^7$, and a tonic six-four chord, which delays the resolution to V.

**EXAMPLE 18-4.** Secondary dominants in major keys

a. C: V/V V — b. V7/V V — c. V7/V V7 — d. V7/V $I^6_4$ V — e. V/ii ii — f. V7/ii ii

g. V7/IV IV — h. V/vi vi — i. V7/vi vi — j. V/iii — k. V7/iii iii

**EXAMPLE 18-5.** Secondary dominants in minor keys

Examples 18-6–18-8 are typical examples of secondary dominants in root position. Example 18-6 illustrates V7/V, the most common of all secondary dominants. In example 18-7 the tonic chord becomes a secondary dominant (V7/iv) while the bass holds a G. The listener must revise his or her perception of the chord; first it is tonic and stable, then it becomes dissonant and unstable. The resolution is quite normal. In example 18-8, a V/ii appears between the IV and ii chords. The resolution and the succeeding progression are normal.

**EXAMPLE 18-6.** Bellini: *Norma*

**EXAMPLE 18-7.** Verdi: *La Traviata*

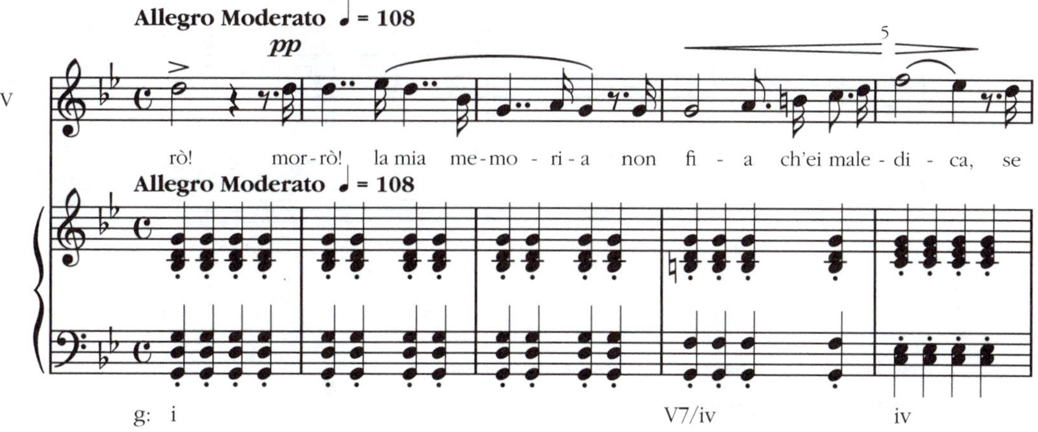


**EXAMPLE 18-8.** Beethoven: *Lied aus der Ferne,* WoO 137

## Inversions of Secondary Dominants

The inversions of secondary dominants are treated exactly the same as inversions of V and V7. The same figured bass numbers used for inversions of seventh chords apply to secondary dominants. Example 18-9 shows V7/V in all inversions; the same treatment would apply to any secondary dominant. Note the insertion of the cadential six-four in examples 18-9b and d, just as it would appear in a normal cadence pattern.

**EXAMPLE 18-9.** Resolutions of inversions of secondary dominants

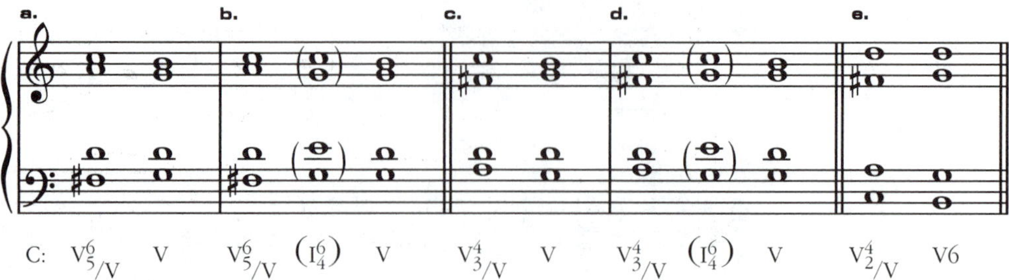


## First Inversions

The use of inversions adds new melodic possibilities for the bass. In example 18-10, an arpeggio-like figure appears in the bass. Chord groups are shown below the Roman numerals with Arabic numbers in circles. Note how normal the progression is.

**EXAMPLE 18-10.** Schubert: *Tischlerlied,* D. 274

## Second Inversions

Example 18-11 shows secondary dominants in first and second inversions. Note how chromatic the music may become when many secondary dominants are used, yet the basic tonality is always clear.

## Third Inversions

Just as $V^4_2$ resolves to I6, the third inversion of a secondary dominant must resolve to a first inversion triad. Example 18-12 takes the V7/IV through various inversions, all resolving normally.

**EXAMPLE 18-11.** Mendelssohn: *Elijah,* "Sei stille dem Herrn"

**EXAMPLE 18-12.** Verdi: *La Traviata*

## LESS COMMON RESOLUTIONS AND SUCCESSIONS OF SECONDARY DOMINANTS

Thus far the emphasis has been on the similarities between ordinary dominants and secondary dominants, but the resolution of secondary dominants may follow an alternate or irregular resolution in some instances. Just as the dominant may resolve "deceptively" (V(7)–vi), so may a secondary dominant. In the deceptive resolution, the root of the V moves to a chord whose root is a step above, instead of down a perfect fifth or up a perfect fourth. This is seen in example 18-13, where the relationships are the same as the normal deceptive resolution of V7.

**EXAMPLE 18-13.** Donizetti: *Don Pasquale,* Sinfonia

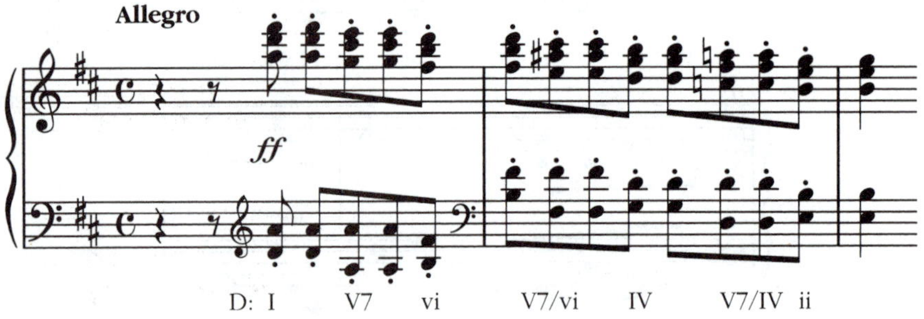

Allegro

*ff*

D: I V7 vi V7/vi IV V7/IV ii

More striking is example 18-14, in which the progressions are not regular. The smoothness of the voice leading, especially when the voices move by half steps, adds a logic to this passage that overrides the irregular progressions.

Because secondary dominants are such attractive chords, they have been used by composers with considerable imagination and ingenuity and are occasionally handled in somewhat irregular ways, which may pose difficulties in analysis. It is generally advisable to label as a secondary dominant any Mm7 chord with altered tones, provided it could have a reasonable secondary tonic in the established key. This advice is valid even in cases where the resolution to the secondary tonic does not follow immediately. It is possible for a secondary tonic to make a delayed appearance, as in example 18-15a, or even to appear before the secondary dominant, as in example 18-15b. In some instances, as in example 18-15c, the secondary tonic is not present.

**EXAMPLE 18-14.** Mendelssohn: *Elijah,* "So ihr mich von ganzem Herzen suchet"

**EXAMPLE 18-15.** Unusual uses of secondary dominants

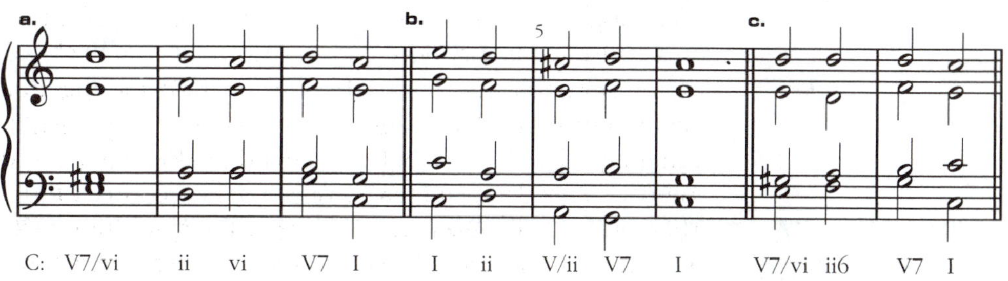


Secondary dominants may resolve to other secondary dominants in a normal progression by fifths, each chord leading to the next in a series or chain of Mm7 chords. This progression leads to a succession of tritones between two of the voices. The chords are alternately complete or incomplete, with the fifth omitted, as in example 18-16.

In example 18-17, a chain of dominants appears in a five-voice texture, which allows all chords to be complete. The progression moves by fifths from chord group 6 to group 1.

**EXAMPLE 18-16.** A chain of secondary dominants

**EXAMPLE 18-17.** Chopin: Mazurka, op. 33, no. 3

## ANALYSIS

In analysis, secondary dominants must conform to the correct and normal standards for the analysis of diatonic chords, cadences, and modulations; that is, the simplest, most normal option for analysis is preferred. A diatonic chord should not be called a secondary dominant since a secondary dominant must be an altered chord. In minor keys, if the tonic becomes a major chord and moves to iv, it is heard as V/iv. On the other hand, VII resolving to III may appear as though it were V/III, and some theorists prefer this analysis. These options are shown in example 18-18; however, we prefer the analysis VII–III, since the VII is not altered.

**EXAMPLE 18-18.** Schubert: *Die schöne Müllerin,* D. 795/18: "Trockne Blumen"

In analyzing passages with secondary dominants it is important to keep in mind that cadences must end on I, V, vii°, or vi. Therefore, a secondary dominant cannot be used as a cadence chord. This may require a modulation in the analysis. In example 18-19, the cadence must be E: V, not A: V/V.

**EXAMPLE 18-19.** J. S. Bach: *Ach Gott, wie manches Herzeleid*

In examples 18-20, 18-21, and 18-22, the distinction between a modulation and a secondary dominant should be very clear. Example 18-20 does not modulate, although it moves toward the dominant at the strong cadence in measure 8. This progression might be considered a modulation, but the modulatory effect does not continue past measure 8, and only one chord uses the B-natural. In this case the analysis would show a half cadence preceded by a secondary dominant (V6/V).

**EXAMPLE 18-20.** Haydn: Piano Sonata in F Major, Hob. XVI:9, third movement

In example 18-21, the dominant key is evident before and after the double bar. Also, a substantial portion of the music before the double bar gives evidence of the new key. Since there is a modulation in measure 4, rather than a secondary dominant at the cadence, there is a perfect authentic cadence in measure 8. The effect is totally different from the same type of cadence at the end of the piece since the key in measure 8 is the dominant, not the primary key of the piece. Compare the emphasis on the dominant at the double bar, measure 8 of example 18-21, with the effect of the secondary dominant at the cadence in measure 8 of example 18-20, where less emphasis is placed on the dominant.

Our sense of tonal center is highly developed and quite subtle. Secondary dominants have the wonderfully paradoxical quality of being both "in" and "out" of a key at the same time. They add valuable color to the palette of diatonic harmony and expand the range of harmonic possibilities within the realm of a single tonality.

**EXAMPLE 18-21.** Mozart: Menuetto, K. 15pp

## SUMMARY

A chord containing a tone foreign to the prevailing scale, a chromatic alteration, is called an altered chord. Some of the most common altered chords are those that result from dominant-like relations applied to chord groups 3, 4, 5, and 6. These are known as secondary dominants. Secondary dominants are like regular dominants in every regard except that they appear in chord groups 3, 4, 5, and 6. The voice leading in secondary dominants and dominant sevenths is the same as in ordinary V and V7 chords. Similarly, the inversions of secondary dominants are treated exactly the same as inversions of V and V7. The same figured bass numbers used for inversions of seventh chords apply to secondary dominants.

The resolution of secondary dominants may follow alternate or irregular resolutions in some instances. The secondary dominant may have a deceptive resolution with the root of the secondary dominant, like the actual dominant, moving to a chord whose root is a step above, instead of down a perfect fifth or up a perfect fourth.

In analysis, secondary dominants must conform to the correct and normal standards for the analysis of diatonic chords, cadences, and modulations; that is, the simplest, most normal option for analysis is preferred.

CHAPTER NINETEEN

# Secondary Leading-Tone Chords

**Terms Introduced in This Chapter**

secondary leading-tone chord

type 1 secondary diminished seventh chord

type 2 secondary diminished seventh chord

he chords in group 2 are the dominant and the leading-tone: V, V7; vii°, viiø7, and vii°7. Like the dominant, leading-tone chords may be used in secondary relationships.

## LEADING-TONE CHORDS

To gain a better perspective of secondary leading-tone chords, a brief review of the chord types and part writing principles for leading-tone chords will be useful.

### Types of Leading-Tone Chords

Any of the three types of leading-tone chords (and their inversions) may be used in a secondary role, that is, as a secondary leading-tone triad or seventh chord. The three types of leading-tone chords are: the diminished triad (d); the fully diminished seventh chord (dd7, "diminished seventh chord"); and the half-diminished seventh chord (dm7). Example 19-1 illustrates these.

**EXAMPLE 19-1.** The three types of leading-tone chords

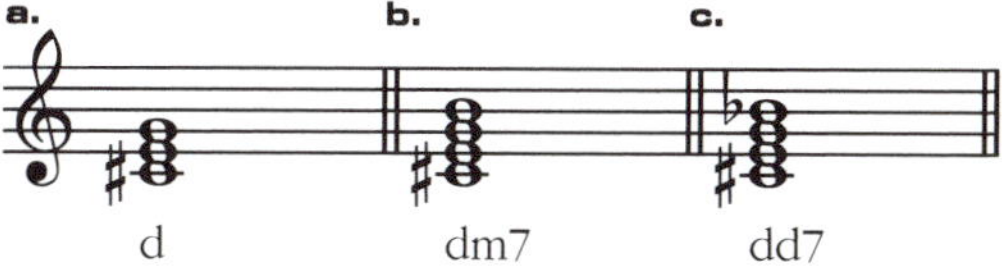


The fully diminished seventh chord (dd7) may be used as a leading-tone chord (vii°7) progressing to I in a major key. In other words, example 19-1c may be found in the key of D major as well as D minor. The half-diminished seventh (dm7) is not used as a leading-tone chord (viiø7) in a minor key. All inversions are possible; however, the diminished triad is most often used in first inversion.

## Part Writing

These reminders should be helpful regarding the part writing of leading-tone chords:

1. The root of the chord usually ascends a half step while the seventh descends by step (in the viiø7) or half step (in the vii°7).
2. When possible, the fifth resolves downward by step to resolve the tritone that includes the leading tone.
3. In the diminished triad, the third is usually doubled.
4. In four-part writing, the full and half-diminished seventh chords are usually found with all four tones present.

# SECONDARY RELATIONSHIPS

**secondary leading-tone chord**

A *secondary leading-tone chord* is an altered chord that has as its root a leading tone belonging to a major or minor chord in chord group 2, 3, 4, 5, or 6. Recall that secondary dominants were reckoned in relation to a secondary tonic. The same is true for secondary leading-tone chords. Once the secondary tonic and its leading tone are determined, the tones of the secondary leading-tone chord are altered as necessary to create the desired leading-tone chord type on the scale degree. In example 19-2, the secondary tonic is V and the leading tone is F-sharp. The chord vii°7/V requires F-sharp and A-natural. The vii°7/V resolves quite regularly to V.

**EXAMPLE 19-2.** Beethoven: Piano Sonata, op. 13, first movement

The fully diminished seventh chord illustrated in example 19-2 contains two tritones. The characteristic instability of this sonority will be familiar to you. It was a favorite of nineteenth-century composers for suggesting fear, danger, and other tension-filled situations. The chord is complete, and the resolution accommodates the interval of the d7 between the root and the seventh in the outer voices.

In contrast, example 19-3a–c shows the secondary diminished triad, without the seventh. Not only is the chord thinner, but the entire texture is more open and transparent. In example 19-3a, the secondary vii° is used in root position leading to ii. The resolution is delayed by the suspensions in the upper voices, but the voice leading in the resolution is quite regular. Example 19-3b shows the secondary vii° in root position leading to iv and in the commonly used first inversion leading to V. Example 19-3c shows a smooth, chromatic bass with a second-inversion secondary diminished triad leading to iv and the secondary diminished seventh leading to V.

**EXAMPLE 19-3.** Examples of the vii° chord

**a.** Haydn: *The Creation,* Hob. XXI:2

**b.** Mozart: Piano Sonata, K. 457, third movement

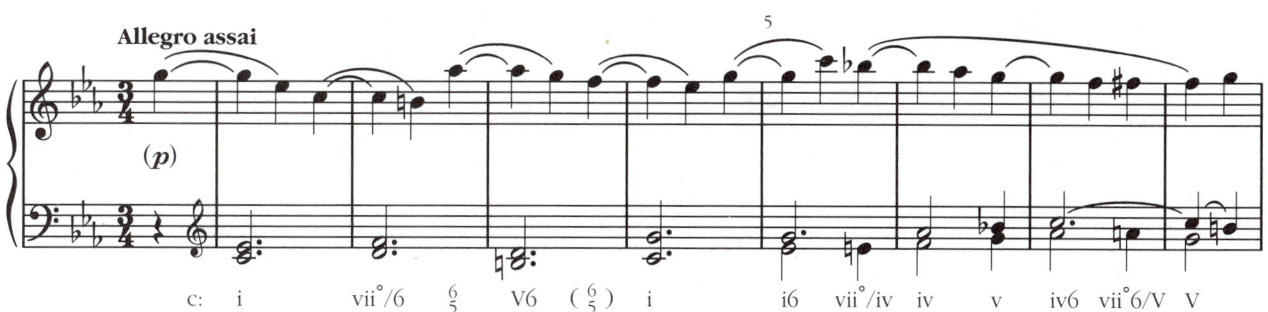


**c.** J. S. Bach: *Herr Jesu Christ, du höchstes Gut*

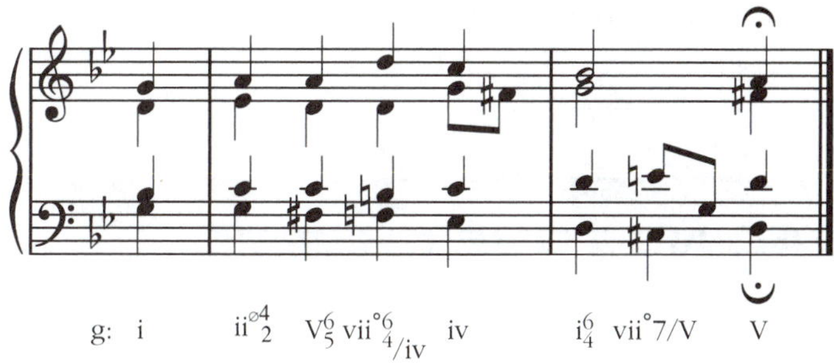

Example 19-4 contains a secondary half-diminished seventh chord. The unique sonority of this chord makes it quite special and relatively easy to identify. With only three voices present, the third is omitted. This example shows a delicate use of the secondary dominant and leading-tone chords without slowing up the harmonic flow or overpowering the melody with harmonic color.

**EXAMPLE 19-4.** Brahms: *Sonntag,* op. 47, no. 3

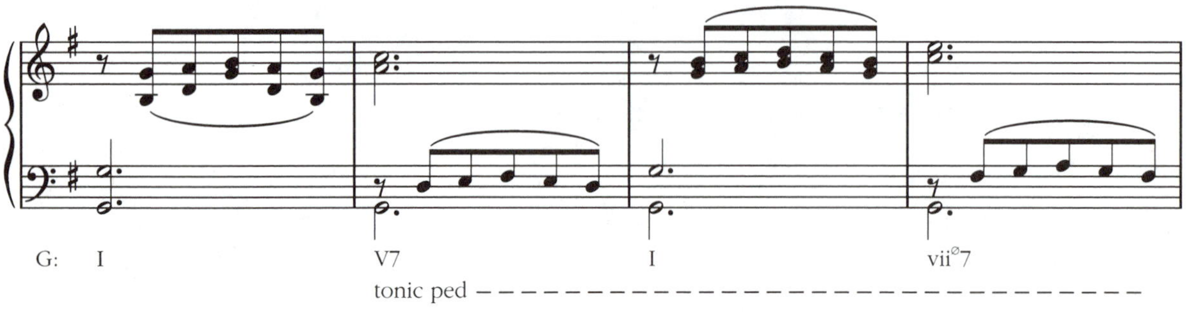


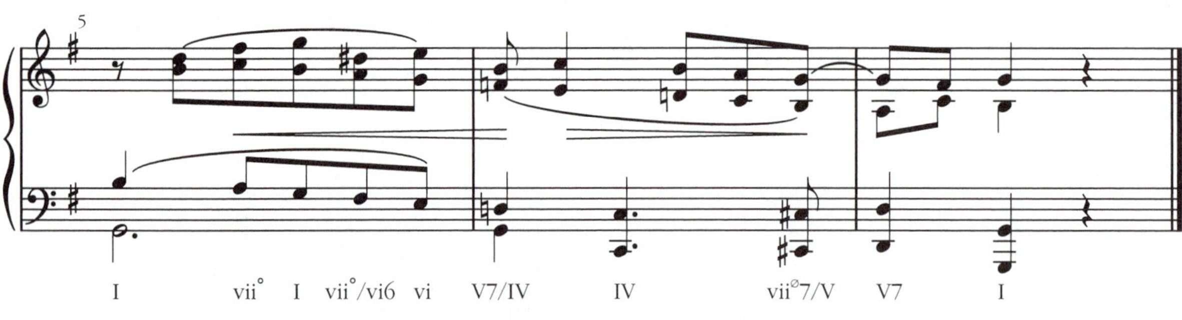


In summary, these points may be made regarding examples 19-2 through 19-4: These examples contain altered chords using the leading-tone chord in a secondary role, that is, a half step below the secondary tonic. These chords function similarly to secondary dominants: They represent a temporary fluctuation in the tonality, a "leaning" towards a secondary tonic, a tonicized chord. They are colorful extensions of the range of available chords within a key.

## POSSIBLE SECONDARY LEADING-TONE CHORDS

Table 19-1 illustrates the possible secondary leading-tone chords in major keys. Note that secondary leading-tone chords do not lead to vii° because its instability as a diminished triad prevents it from acting as a secondary tonic. Although it is listed, IV (in a major key) is rarely used as a secondary tonic for these chords, probably because the tone a half step below it is a diatonic tone. Musical illustrations are given in example 19-5.

| Chord group | Possible secondary leading-tone chords | Chord type | Root (scale degree) |
|---|---|---|---|
| 3 | vii°/V | d | ♯4 |
| | vii$^{ø}$7/V | dm | ♯4 |
| | vii°7/V | dd | ♯4 |
| 4 | vii°/ii | d | ♯1 |
| | vii°7/ii | dd | ♯1 |
| 4 | vii°/IV | d | 3 |
| | vii$^{ø}$7/IV | dm | 3 |
| | vii°7/IV | dd | 3 |
| 5 | vii°/vi | d | ♯5 |
| | vii°7/vi | dd | ♯5 |
| 6 | vii°/iii | dd | ♯2 |
| | vii°7/iii | dd | ♯2 |

**TABLE 19-1.** Secondary leading-tone chords in major keys

**EXAMPLE 19-5.** Secondary leading-tone chords in major keys

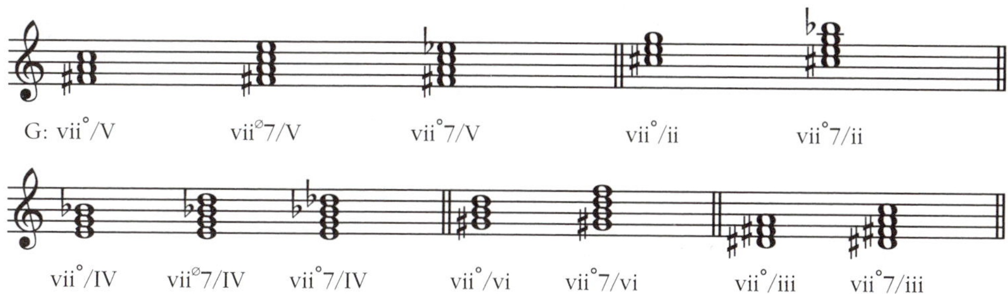


A comparable table of secondary leading-tone chords in minor keys presents special problems (table 19-2). The vii° chord is omitted as a secondary tonic for the same reason given earlier, but ii° is also unstable and omitted. Only one secondary leading-tone chord leads to III because the other possibilities have simpler explanations as diatonic chords: vii°/III is better analyzed as ii° and vii$^{ø}$7/III as ii$^{ø}$7. The subtonic, VII, is shown as a secondary tonic, although this is very rare. Example 19-6 shows musical examples of these chords.

| Chord group | Possible secondary leading-tone chords | Chord type | Root (scale degree) |
|---|---|---|---|
| 3 | vii°/V | d | ♯4 |
| | viiø7/V | dm | ♯4 |
| | vii°7/V | dd | ♯4 |
| 4 | vii°/iv | d | ♮3 |
| | vii°7/iv | dd | ♮3 |
| 5 | vii°/VI | d | 5 |
| | viiø7/VI | dm | 5 |
| | vii°7/VI | dd | 5 |
| 6 | vii°7/III | dd | 2 |
| 7 | vii°/VII | d | ♮6 |
| | viiø7/VII | dm | ♮6 |
| | vii°7/VII | dd | ♮6 |

**TABLE 19-2.** Secondary leading-tone chords in minor keys

**EXAMPLE 19-6.** Secondary leading-tone chords in minor keys

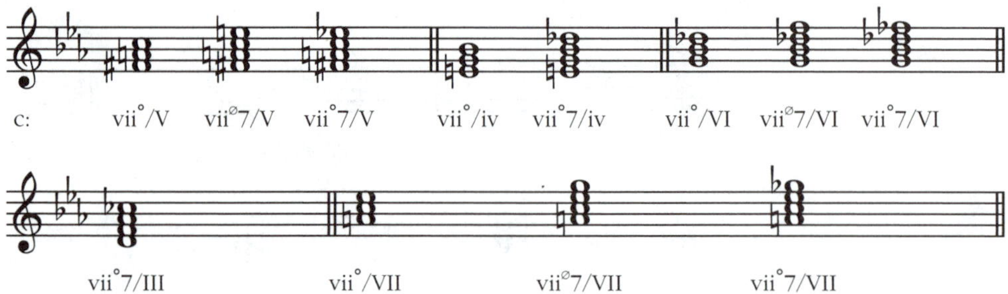


## PROGRESSIONS

Secondary leading-tone chords usually follow the normal progression and are included in tables 19-3 and 19-4. Not all of these chords are used with equal frequency. Those to the right side of the tables are the more commonly used. The tables have evolved considerably from the time they were introduced. Diatonic chords are shown in parentheses. In these tables vii°7 represents not only the diminished seventh chord but also the half-diminished seventh and the diminished triad, wherever these might be used.

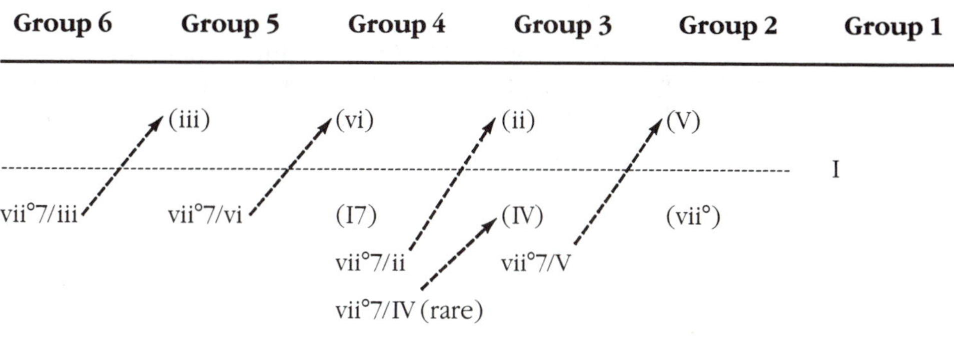


**TABLE 19-3.** Normal chord progressions for major keys

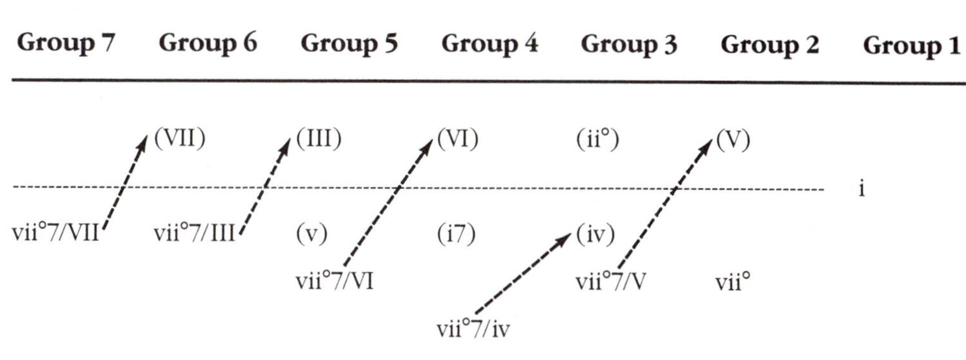


**TABLE 19-4.** Normal chord progressions for minor keys

## RESOLUTIONS OF SECONDARY LEADING-TONE SEVENTH CHORDS

Secondary leading-tone chords resolve like their diatonic counterparts; however, the secondary diminished seventh (dd7) is more frequently used and has greater diversity in its resolution. Basically, there are two patterns of resolution to be observed when secondary diminished sevenths resolve. In type 1, the diminished seventh chord moves to the next lower-numbered chord group. In type 2, a chord group is skipped, and the diminished seventh moves two chord groups to the right in the chart of normal progressions.

## Type 1

**type 1 secondary diminished seventh chord**

The most common type of resolution for a diminished seventh chord is comparable to the progression vii°7–i, chord group 2 moving to group 1. *Type 1 secondary diminished seventh chords* also resolve to the next lower-numbered chord group. A feature of this resolution is that the diminished seventh chord contains a tone that lies a half step below the root of the chord of resolution. As in example 19-7, the progression resembles vii°7–i, and the diminished seventh chord is usually spelled consistent with the key.

**EXAMPLE 19-7.** J. S. Bach: *Valet will ich dir geben*

If the vii°7/V moves to a tonic six-four, the resolution is still type 1, with a delayed resolution. This is seen in example 19-8.

**EXAMPLE 19-8.** Weber: *Oberon*

## Type 2

**type 2 secondary diminished seventh chord**

The *type 2 secondary diminished seventh chord* progression resembles vii°7/V–I, in which a chord group is skipped. The characteristic of this resolution is that the diminished seventh contains a tone that is the same as the root of the chord of resolution. Do not confuse this with the progression from the vii°7/V to the tonic six-four chord mentioned above. In example 19-9, the diminished seventh of vi (vii°7/vi) omits chord group 4 to progress to IV, whose root (D) is a common tone with the diminished seventh chord.

**EXAMPLE 19-9.** Schubert: *Who Is Sylvia?* D. 891

There is one other possible resolution, in which the diminished seventh moves to a chord in the same chord group, analogous to vii°7–V7. When this happens with a secondary leading-tone seventh chord and a secondary dominant, one of the tones in the progression usually acts as a nonharmonic tone, leaving only one chord to deal with. In example 19-10a, one hears either vii°7/V or $V^6_5$/V. In example 19-10b, a similar passage is analyzed so the diminished seventh on the beat is acknowledged and the off-beat is considered nonharmonic.

Example 19-11 illustrates resolutions of various secondary leading-tone chords in four voices. Note that the altered tones only occasionally appear in the soprano. When the altered tone is in the soprano, it may be the root, possibly requiring an inverted chord for the harmonization.

**EXAMPLE 19-10.** Type 2 secondary diminished seventh chords

**a.** J. S. Bach: *Lass, o Herr, dein Ohr sich neigen*

**b.** J. S. Bach: *Wer nur den lieben Gott*

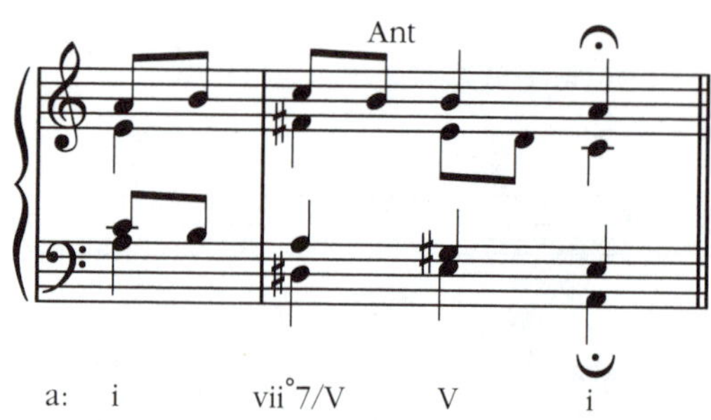


**EXAMPLE 19-11.** Resolutions of secondary leading-tone chords

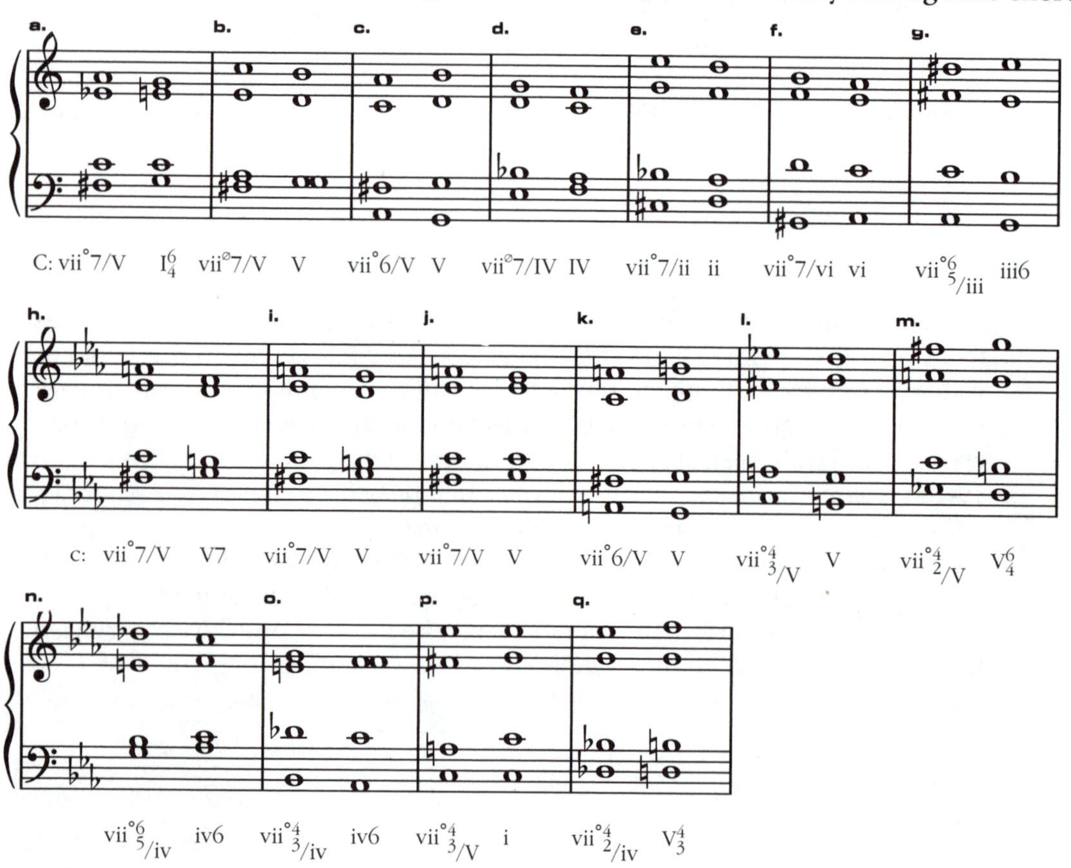

## PROBLEMS IN ANALYSIS

In analyzing progressions with leading-tone chords, first determine the type of chord (is it fully diminished? is there a seventh? and so on), and then determine the resolution. If it is a diminished seventh chord, look at the resolution to see which of the two types discussed above is involved. Be especially careful if the chord of resolution is a tonic six-four moving to a V. In this case, the six-four chord should be viewed as a decoration to the V; that is, the six-four chord and the V are both in the same chord group.

A series of what appear to be secondary chords that repeatedly refer to the same secondary tonic should be considered as a possible modulation. For example, if the analysis shows V7/V–V–vii°7/V–V, one might consider if there has not, in fact, been a modulation to the key of the dominant. If the passage ends with what might be seen as an authentic cadence on V, the case may be even stronger that a modulation has occurred.

Diminished seventh chords can be used as pivot chords in modulation, but that will be studied later. When it is possible and logical to do so, it is preferable to use a diatonic chord as a pivot chord in modulation.

In example 19-12, there may be differences of opinion about the best place to locate the pivot chord. The modulation has begun in measure 11. The diminished seventh moves to the six-four in measure 12 in a type 1 progression, as one would expect in approaching a cadence, vii°7/V leading to V. The preceding chord is therefore chosen as the pivot. The establishment of the new key, however, does not take place as expected in measure 13. Instead, the passage is repeated, arriving solidly at the tonic in measure 17.

### Enharmonic Spelling

The interval structure of the diminished seventh chord is unique: Composed of superimposed minor thirds, it contains no perfect intervals. One curious result of this is that aurally the chord has no root; it has the same aural effect in all inversions. Since the chord itself is so unstable, it often relies on the chords surrounding it to clarify its relationship to the tonality. The chord is sometimes spelled irregularly so that the relationship of the chord to the key and the normal progression is not immediately apparent from the notation. Such passages may arise from a preference for good voice leading over correct chord spelling, as in example 19-13. In analyzing such a passage, first determine the succeeding chord (this will necessitate looking ahead by several chords or measures in the passage), then use the analysis that employs the lowest-numbered chord groups and is the most normal in its progression.

In example 19-13, a vii°7/V (spelled as a vii°7/iii) moves to a tonic six-four chord in a major key. The voice leading makes E-sharp more convenient than F-natural. The F-natural would be the normal spelling and would be practical if it moved

**EXAMPLE 19-12.** Mozart: Horn Concerto No. 2, K. 417, second movement

directly to the F-sharp in the tonic six-four chord. This analysis results in a very normal progression. The chord at x presents a more difficult situation. It appears literally as vii°$^{4}_{2}$/vii, an improbable explanation. Using enharmonic spelling (B-sharp = C) it could be considered vii°$^{4}_{3}$/ii, but this would progress irregularly to V7. The preferred analysis is to consider the D-sharp and B-sharp as nonchord tones. This preserves normalcy in the progression.

**EXAMPLE 19-13.** Schumann: *Liederkreis,* op. 24, no. 9, "Mit Myrten und Rosen"

## Successive Diminished Sevenths

Occasionally one encounters a succession of diminished sevenths in a characteristically chromatic descent. As there are only three different-sounding diminished sevenths, the progression must repeat. Typically all voices descend by half steps, so the voice leading is quite smooth. The analysis shown in example 19-14a includes an irregular, type 2 resolution, as chord group 2 moves to group 4. Another, less detailed approach is taken by some analysts, who prefer to analyze such passages by indicating the chord type dd7, for the first of a series of diminished seventh chords, and giving a functional Roman numeral analysis only for the last one, as shown in example 19-14b.

**EXAMPLE 19-14.** Mozart: Sonaten-Finalsatz, K. 15v

## SUMMARY

Leading-tone chords may be used in secondary relationships in which altered chords of the type used for leading-tone chords are related to diatonic chords other than the tonic. The three types of leading-tone chords are the diminished triad, the fully diminished seventh chord, and the half-diminished seventh chord.

Secondary leading-tone chords in a major key may be found in relation to all diatonic chords except vii° and I but are rarely found in relation to IV. In a minor key, secondary leading-tone chords are found in relation to all diatonic chords except vii°, i, and ii°. Secondary leading-tone chords usually follow the normal progression and are included in a version of the table for normal progressions (see tables 19-3 and 19-4). Secondary leading-tone chords resolve like their diatonic counterparts; however, the secondary diminished seventh (dd7) is the most frequently used and has the greatest diversity in its resolution.

The most common type of resolution (type 1) for a diminished seventh chord is comparable to the progression vii°7–i, chord group 2 moving to group 1, so the secondary diminished seventh chord resolves to the next lower-numbered chord group. The less common progression for a secondary leading-tone chord (type 2) resembles vii°7/V–I, in which a chord group is skipped. In analyzing progressions with leading-tone chords, first determine the type of chord and then determine the resolution. Because of a preference for good voice leading in the resolution over correct chord spelling, the chord is sometimes spelled differently than its function implies.

CHAPTER TWENTY

# Borrowed Chords

**Terms Introduced in This Chapter**

borrowed chord

Picardy third

**borrowed chords**

An important category of altered chords is known as *borrowed chords.* These are chords that use only those alterations that are derived from the parallel major or minor of the given key. In a minor key, V and vii° fall in this category, but since they are accepted as normal diatonic chords in minor, they are not considered altered or "borrowed."

Compare the major and minor scales shown in example 20-1. Of the seven degrees in these scales, four are the same in major and minor. The difference in mode is determined by the remaining three degrees: $\hat{3}$, $\hat{6}$, and $\hat{7}$. If these tones are exchanged, or borrowed, singly or in combination, many altered chords will result. In this chapter only the most commonly used of these will be explored. Conventional principles of voice leading and doubling apply to these chords. In deciding the doubling for root position or inverted borrowed chords, the same concepts are applied as for diatonic chords. The progression of chords remains the same as in the table of normal progressions, regardless of alterations. In reading figured bass, accidentals written next to Arabic numbers refer to that interval above the bass. Accidentals before a Roman numeral indicate that the root of the chord has been altered (♭VI, ♭III, ♯vi°, etc.).

**EXAMPLE 20-1.** C-major and C-minor scales

## BORROWED CHORDS IN MAJOR KEYS

Several chords result from the borrowing of lowered $\hat{3}$, $\hat{6}$, and $\hat{7}$ in major keys. These very colorful chords are to be found in chord groups 1 through 5.

### Chord Group 1

By borrowing the lowered $\hat{3}$ in major, a minor tonic chord will result; however, this may appear with a change of the mode to the parallel minor key. In example 20-2a, the tonic chords alternate between I and i. If $\hat{3}$ were consistently lowered, the key would be considered minor, as in example 20-2b.

**EXAMPLE 20-2.** Use of the lowered $\hat{3}$ in major

**a.** Verdi: *Aida*

**b.** Mozart: *Don Giovanni,* K. 527

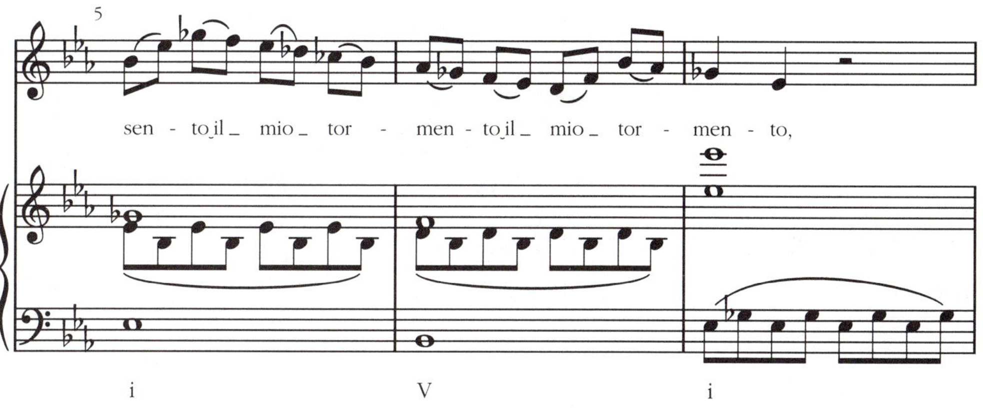


## Chord Group 2

In this chord group, the only borrowed chord is the fully diminished vii°7. The chord uses the lowered $\hat{6}$, which usually descends to $\hat{5}$. This chord is treated exactly the same as vii°7 in minor. In example 20-3, a famous example appears over a tonic pedal; the effect is dissonant, but pleasant.

**EXAMPLE 20-3.** Tchaikovsky: *The Nutcracker,* op. 71, "Waltz of the Flowers"

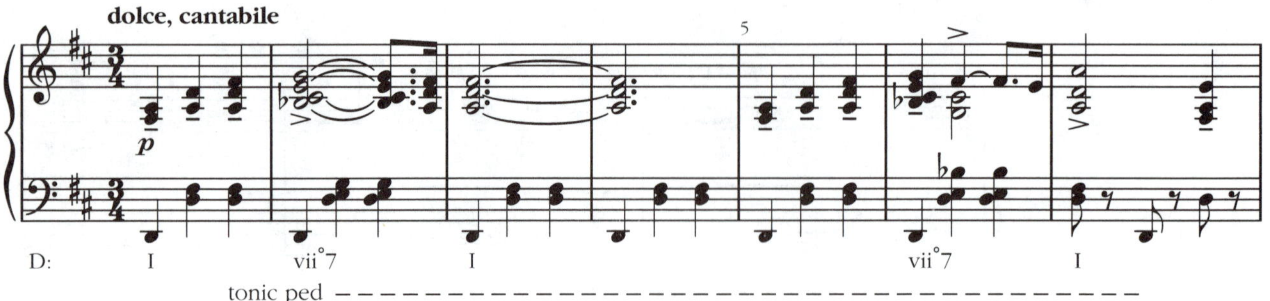


## Chord Group 3

The tone most commonly borrowed from minor to major, the lowered $\hat{6}$, affects both the subdominant and supertonic chords. Its half-step relationship to $\hat{5}$ gives it an "upper leading tone" effect. It almost always resolves downward, as seen in examples 20-4, 20-5, 20-6, and 20-7. The borrowed tones bring about very colorful changes in the quality of the chords. IV changes to iv, ii changes to ii°. These borrowed chords are "darker," more serious-sounding, than the normal diatonic chords they replace.

### The Supertonic Chord

The borrowed diminished supertonic chord is most often used as the foundation of a half-diminished seventh chord. Example 20-4 illustrates the borrowed diminished triad in second inversion with the lowered $\hat{6}$ moving strongly to $\hat{5}$ in the bass.

The half-diminished supertonic seventh chord is a borrowed chord much favored by the Romantic composers. In example 20-5, the borrowed chord allows the tenor to descend chromatically. In example 20-6, the lowered $\hat{6}$ descends to $\hat{5}$, but the resolution is an octave higher (see m. 4).

### The Subdominant Chord

In example 20-7a, the minor iv progresses normally to the dominant. The lowered $\hat{6}$ resolves down to $\hat{5}$ in the dominant chord in these examples. In example 20-7b, a smooth bass leads to iv$^6_4$ and ii$^{ø4}_{2}$, both borrowed chords.

**EXAMPLE 20-4.** Verdi: *Macbeth*

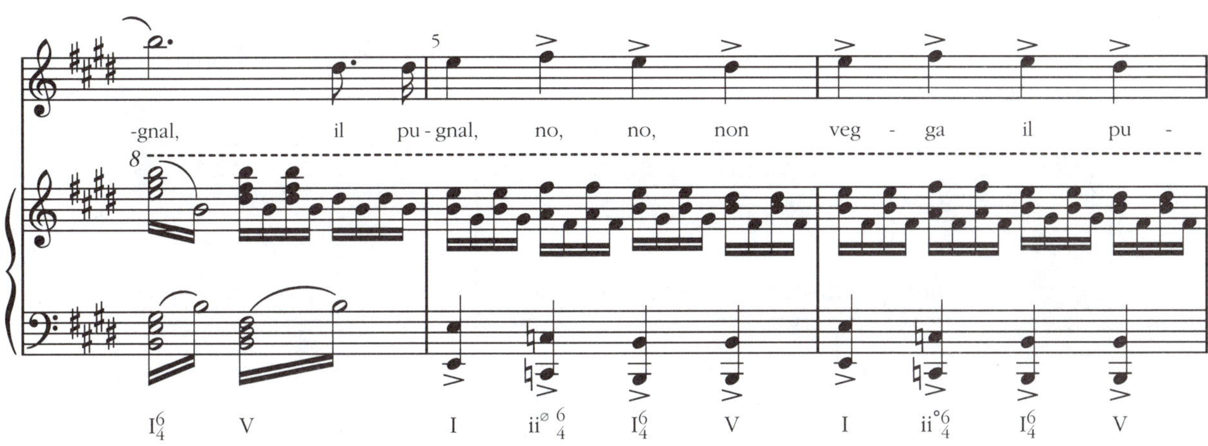

**EXAMPLE 20-5.** Beethoven: *Sechs Lieder von Gellert,* op. 48, no. 2, "Die Liebe des Nächsten"

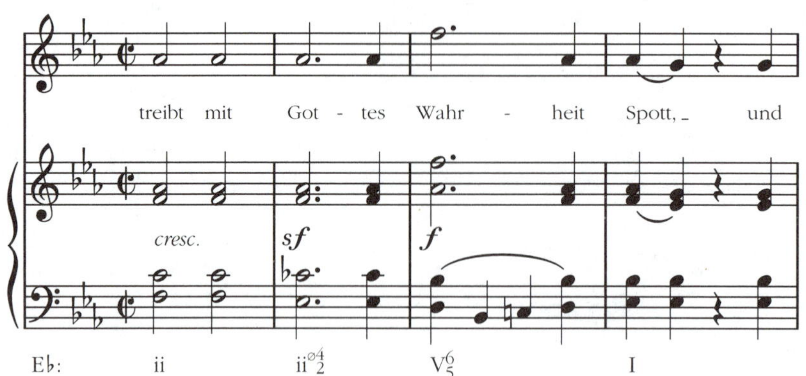


**EXAMPLE 20-6.** Tchaikovsky: *The Nutcracker,* op. 71, "Dance of the Mirlitons"

**EXAMPLE 20-7.** The subdominant chord

**a.** Beethoven: Symphony No. 5, fourth movement

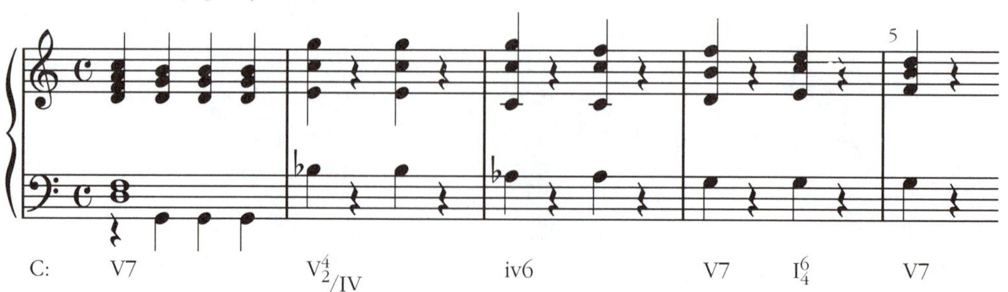

**EXAMPLE 20-7.** (continued)

**b.** Mozart: Piano Sonata movement, K. 400

## Chord Group 4

This group contains only one borrowed chord: ♭VI. Using the lowered $\hat{3}$ and $\hat{6}$ together produces this major triad, a half step above $\hat{5}$. In example 20-8a, ♭VI is followed by another borrowed chord (from group 3) that also employs the lowered $\hat{6}$ and then continues to move normally through V to I. As in this case, ♭VI usually is followed by other borrowed chords in group 3. Because it is a major triad, it adds a bright, fresh quality to the passage. Example 20-8b shows the ♭VI in a dramatic deceptive cadence. The impact of the ♭VI is strengthened by the change from the preceding monophony to full chordal treatment.

## Chord Group 5

The major triad on ♭III is the only borrowed chord in this group. Because it replaces the leading tone and combines two altered notes, it is quite removed from the tonality. It is brilliant and strong, like ♭VI, but is so far from the tonic that it is usually followed by other borrowed chords as it works its way back to the tonic. Example 20-9 shows how remote from the tonic these borrowed chords may become in an extended passage. One almost feels that this music has gone to the minor mode and then returns to its original key.

**EXAMPLE 20-8.** The ♭VI chord

**a.** Verdi: *Macbeth*

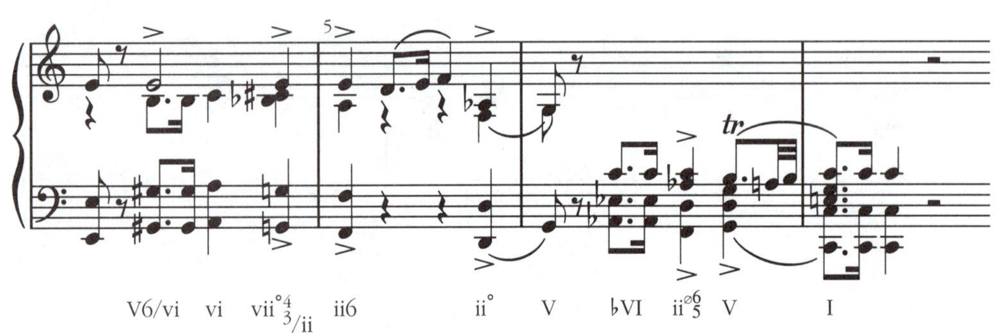


**b.** Beethoven: Piano Sonata, op. 2, no. 3, first movement

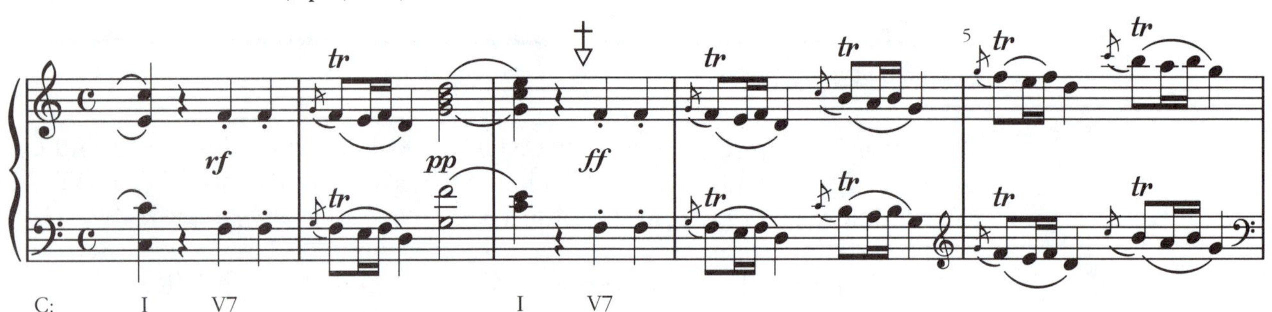

**EXAMPLE 20-9.** Verdi: *Il Trovatore*

## BORROWED CHORDS IN MINOR KEYS

There are fewer borrowed chords in minor keys since the possibilities in chord group 2 are considered diatonic. Like the chords in group 2, borrowed chords in a minor key often come about from melodic considerations. Raising the $\hat{6}$ in minor is usually done for melodic purposes in conjunction with raising the $\hat{7}$, as in the melodic minor. With the lowered $\hat{7}$, the raised $\hat{6}$ causes a half-step that weakens the tonality. The location of the tritones in a scale is another factor. The tritone in a major scale resolves to $\hat{1}$ and $\hat{3}$ (ex. 20-10a). By using the raised $\hat{7}$, the same tritone resolution is found in minor (ex. 20-10b). But raising the $\hat{6}$ creates a tritone whose resolution to the lowered $\hat{7}$ does little to confirm the tonic in a minor key (ex. 20-10c).

**EXAMPLE 20-10.** Tritone resolution

## Chord Group 1

Altering the minor tonic to become major (I) does not change the mode of the passage. A major tonic in a minor key may be a secondary dominant of iv or a special device used at final cadences.

**Picardy third**

For centuries after the beginning of the development of harmony (around the ninth century), the final chord in a piece never included the third at all. Only the octave and perfect fifth were considered consonant enough for the conclusion. Later, the major third was included, even if the entire piece was in a mode that used the minor third. The raised $\hat{3}$ at the end of a piece in minor is called the *Picardy third* (*tierce de Picardie*), a cadence formula whose use and fame spread over a much greater geographical area than the name suggests. The chord is seen in example 20-11.

**EXAMPLE 20-11.** Scheidt: *Nun komm der Heiden Heiland*

There are no borrowed chords in group 2 since the V and vii° are considered part of the standard array of diatonic chords in the minor mode.

## Chord Group 3

Borrowed chords in this group are rather rare, although the chords that result from using the raised $\hat{6}$ in minor do not seem very unusual: IV and ii. These chords are found in passages where their origin seems more melodic than harmonic. In example 20-12a, the chromatically descending bass moves through the raised $\hat{6}$, briefly producing IV. In example 20-12b, the ii6 is the result of the melodic minor pattern in the soprano.

**EXAMPLE 20-12.** Use of the raised $\hat{6}$ in minor

**a.** J. S. Bach: Sinfonia No. 9, BWV 795

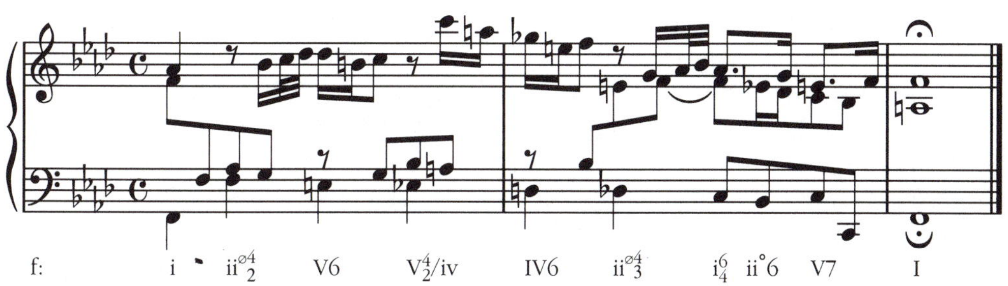


**b.** J. S. Bach: *Goldberg Variations,* BWV 988, Variation 15

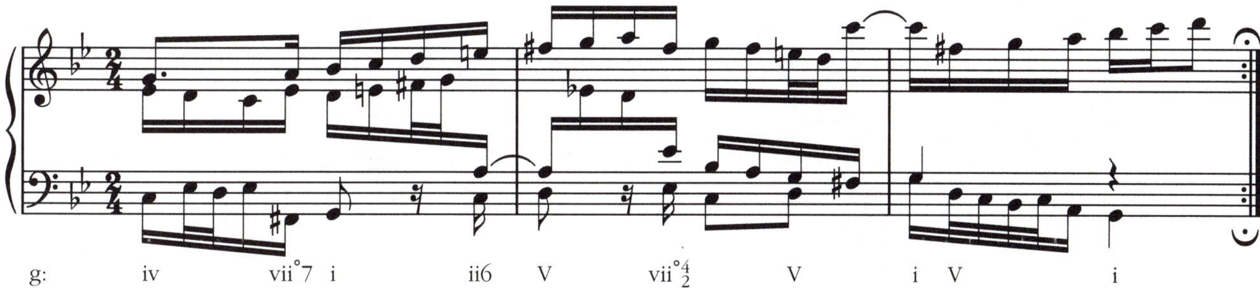


# PROBLEMS IN ANALYSIS

The concept of tonality established with diatonic chords in chapter 4 is expanded enormously with the use of secondary chords and modulation. Example 20-13 illustrates a borrowed chord in measure 3, along with other chromatically altered chords throughout. This example is complicated by a few chromatic nonharmonic tones. The harmony appears to go further and further from the tonic (B-flat major), only to be wrenched back rather violently after the diminished seventh (vii°7/V). Although ♭VI is consonant (that is, a major triad), it is remote from the tonic.

**EXAMPLE 20-13.** Mozart, Piano Sonata, K. 333, third movement

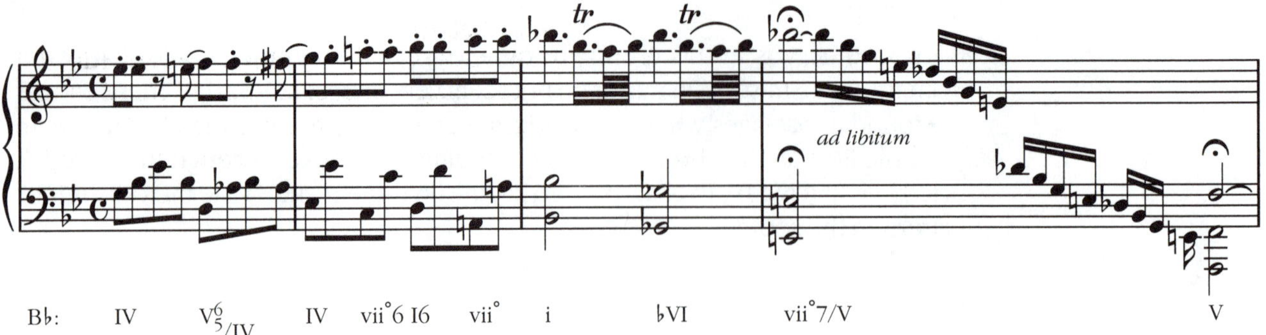


As one becomes more familiar with altered chords one gains facility in identifying the sources of the accidentals. For instance, in example 20-14, the A-flat is borrowed from minor, while the F-sharp is part of a secondary leading-tone chord.

Music becomes quite chromatic when secondary dominants and secondary leading-tone chords are used in conjunction with borrowed chords. It is sometimes hard to determine the key, that is, to decide whether an analysis is simpler showing a modulation than another approach. Generally, it is advisable to stay as long in one key as a reasonable analysis will allow, even if this requires labeling many chromatic chords. The ultimate test is whether the passage can be heard in the way it has been analyzed.

**EXAMPLE 20-14.** Brahms: Intermezzo, op. 119, no. 3

## SUMMARY

A piece in a major key sometimes uses chords using the $\hat{3}$, $\hat{6}$, and $\hat{7}$ as they normally occur within the scale pattern of the natural minor mode, and vice versa. These altered chords are treated with the same techniques of part writing and doubling as diatonic chords. Each borrowed chord remains in the same chord group as it was originally in the tables of normal progressions.

| Groups | Normal diatonic chords | Borrowed chords |
|---|---|---|
| Group 1 | I | i |
| Group 2 | V, V7 | |
| | vii°, viiø7 | vii°7 |
| Group 3 | ii, ii7 | ii°, iiø7 |
| | IV, IV7 | iv |
| Group 4 | vi, vi7 | ♭VI |
| | I7 | |
| Group 5 | iii, iii7 | ♭III |

**TABLE 20-1.** Borrowed chords in a major key

| Groups | Normal diatonic chords | Borrowed chords |
|---|---|---|
| Group 1 | i | I |
| Group 2 | V, V7 | |
| | vii°, vii°7 | |
| Group 3 | ii°, iiø7 | ii |
| | iv, iv7 | IV |
| Group 4 | VI, VI7 | |
| | i7 | |
| Group 5 | III, III7 | |
| | v, v7 | |
| Group 6 | VII, VII7 | |

**TABLE 20-2.** Borrowed chords in a minor key

CHAPTER TWENTY-ONE

# Form: Higher Structural Units

**Terms Introduced in This Chapter**

- first-level unit
- formal unit
- period
- second-level unit
- antecedent
- consequent
- unit relationship
- parallel phrase construction
- contrasting phrase construction
- similar phrase construction
- symmetrical units
- asymmetrical units
- extended phrase
- shortened phrase
- phrase extension
- third-level units
- double period
- overlapping phrases
- quasi-cadence

**first-level unit**

**formal unit**

The phrase, as the principal unit of musical structure, is the basis for understanding larger units. There is, therefore, a hierarchy of units: The phrase is called the lowest or *first-level unit;* units of structure larger than a phrase are referred to as higher units or levels. The term *formal unit* refers to a unit of structure on any level.

## HIGHER STRUCTURAL LEVELS IN MELODY

Phrases, the first structural level, group together to form a larger unit, a second-level unit, and these units group together to form third-level units. These may be succinctly illustrated with melodic examples.

### Second-Level Structural Units: Periods

**period**

A group of two or three phrases is called a *period.* Periods may be described by the unit relationships of the component phrases.

#### Periods of Two Phrases

A typical period consists of two phrases. The factors causing phrases to group into periods are: (1) similarity of content and (2) the tendency of the last cadence to be the most conclusive. The two phrases of example 21-1 have almost identical content. The cadence of the first phrase is inconclusive, while the cadence of the second phrase is conclusive. The second cadence not only ends that phrase but the entire period as well.

**EXAMPLE 21-1.** Mozart: Piano Quartet, K. 478, Rondo

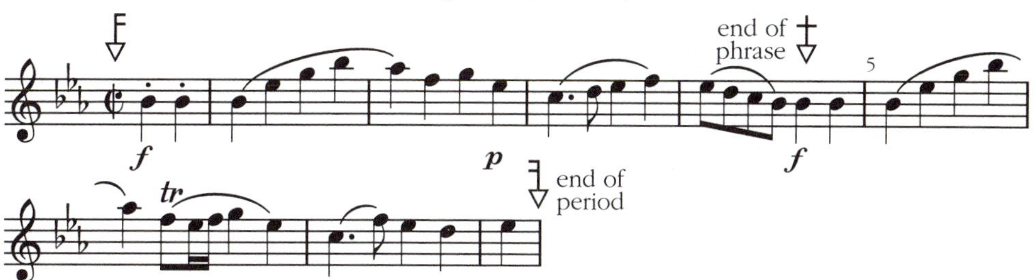

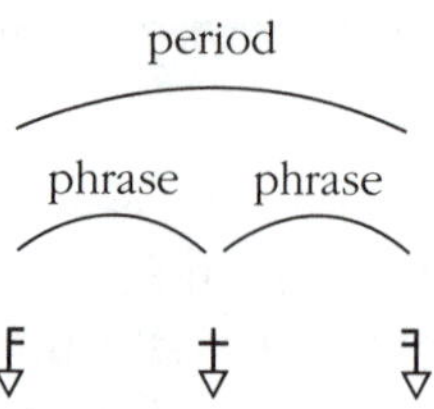


**FIGURE 21-1.** The second-level unit

**second-level unit**

**antecedent**

**consequent**

Notice in example 21-1 that the arrows at the beginning and ending have two slashes. The first slash indicates the end of the first-level unit (the phrase), while the second slash shows the end of the *second-level unit* (the period). The second slash is added to the beginning so that the analysis shows from the outset just what level of structural complexity is present in the music under consideration. (Later more slashes will be added to show higher levels of organization.)

Most often phrases group in pairs, the first phrase called the *antecedent* and the second called the *consequent* (see fig. 21-1). The consequent phrase may closely resemble the antecedent, as in example 21-1, or be contrasting.

## Unit Relationships

**unit relationship**

**parallel phrase construction**

**contrasting phrase construction**

**similar phrase construction**

To express *unit relationships,* that is, to show how phrases compare with one another, we will use a letter identification system similar to the one employed for identifying motives, namely, a, b, b′, b″, and so on. Thus, the unit relationship for two phrases will consist of two letters. If the second phrase is a variant of the first phrase, the letters a a′ are used. If the second phrase differs substantially from the first it is described with the unit relationship a b.

When paired phrases employ the same materials (motives and patterns), especially at the beginning of the phrase, the term *parallel phrase construction* is used (see ex. 21-2). If different materials are used, the term *contrasting phrase construction* is applied (see ex. 21-3a). There are, of course, many cases that fall between these clear categories; some texts use the term *similar phrase construction* for such variants, as in example 21-3b. Example 21-3c also illustrates similar phrase construction.

**EXAMPLE 21-2.** Schumann: *Album for the Young,* op. 68, no. 6, "Poor

**EXAMPLE 21-3.** Phrase construction

**a.** Mozart: Piano Concerto, K. 488, first movement (contrasting phrase construction)

**b.** Schumann: *Liederkreis,* op. 39, no. 7, "Auf einer Burg" (similar phrase construction)

**c.** Schubert: *Schwanengesang,* D. 957, no. 5, "Aufenthalt" (similar phrase construction)

**symmetrical units**

**asymmetrical units**

**extended phrase**

**shortened phrase**

**phrase extension**

The term *symmetrical unit* is applied to successive structural units of equal length. Symmetrical phrase relationships, such as those found in all of the melodies in example 21-3, are more common than those of unequal length, called *asymmetrical units.* Usually the listener anticipates that the consequent phrase will be the same length as the antecedent, but sometimes the consequent is *extended* or *shortened. Phrase extension* refers to a portion that is added to make the phrase longer than the length previously established. One only knows that a phrase has been shortened or extended by comparing it with its antecedent phrase or another earlier appearance. For instance, in example 21-4a, the cadential effect in measure 12 has been repeated in measures 13 and 14, adding two bars to the consequent phrase. In example 21-4b, the consequent phrase begins with a dramatic shift to the upper octave in measure 4, but the consequent is cut short, to only three measures.

Though four-bar lengths are extremely common, other lengths do occur and need not be treated differently. Example 21-5 shows a five-bar phrase pattern.

**EXAMPLE 21-4.** Symmetrical units

**a.** Mozart: Piano Sonata, K. 332, first movement

**b.** Beethoven: Piano Sonata, op. 2, no. 1, first movement

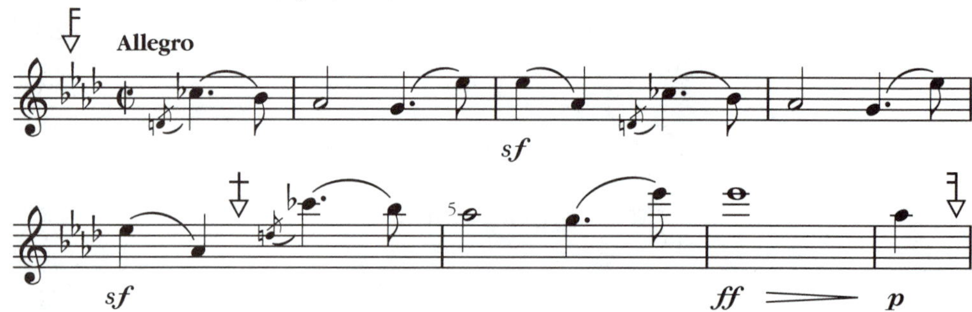

**EXAMPLE 21-5.** Brahms: Intermezzo, op. 117, no. 3

## Periods of Three Phrases

Less commonly a period is composed of three phrases. (Some texts refer to this as a "phrase group.") Example 21-6 shows such a period. Notice that the cadences of the first two phrases are not conclusive, while the last cadence brings the entire period to a full close. The cadence in measure 8 deliberately smooths the entry of the third phrase, bringing the three phrases together into a single unit.

**EXAMPLE 21-6.** Mendelssohn: *Song without Words,* op. 19b, no. 1

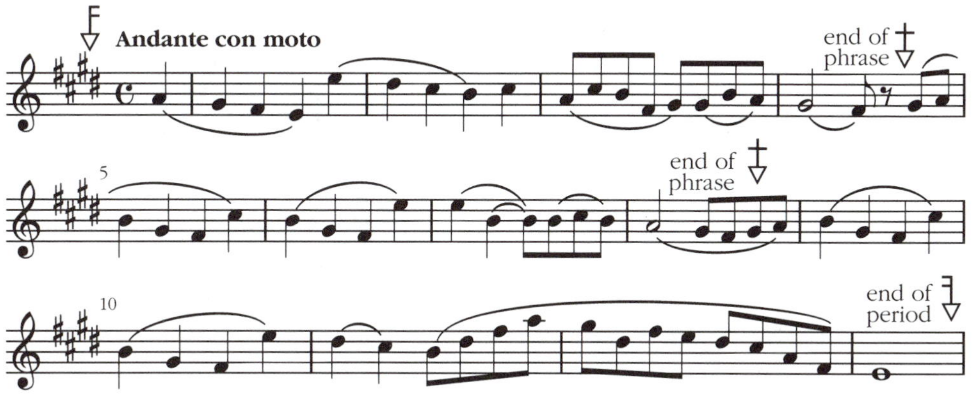


## Third-Level Units

**third-level units**

**double period**

Just as phrases group to form a period, periods may group to form a larger unit. Since groups of phrases are called second-level units, groups of periods are called *third-level units.* A third-level unit consisting of two periods is known as a *double period.* The same forces that caused phrases to group are still at work here: Periods will group as a result of similarity in content and from the tendency for the last cadence to be the most conclusive. A third-level structure is shown in example 21-7. Note the strong cadence at the end and the similarities between all phrases, particularly the first and third phrases.

**EXAMPLE 21-7.** Purcell: *The Fairy Queen,* "Dance"

The three slashes at the beginning and end of the double period in example 21-7 indicate that the structure of this example consists of three levels. Both periods exhibit contrasting phrase construction, but clearly the recurrence in measure 9 of the opening material binds the two periods very tightly.

As explained earlier, a period may contain three phrases. Such periods may also combine with other periods composed of either two or three phrases. Thus, there are many possible combinations for third-level units. Further, a third-level unit may consist of three periods grouped together; however, there is no traditional term for this compared to that for the double period. Figure 21-2 shows the unit relationships for some common double-period patterns. Capital letters indicate the periods, while small letters indicate the phrases. In numbers 4 and 5 the pattern A A′ shows that the second period uses half or more of the material from the first period. Number 3 shows a double period in which each period has three phrases. Many other combinations are possible.

Formal structure may be symbolized with a system of arcs or brackets that show the relationships between structural levels, as shown in figure 21-3.

| 1) | | 2) | | 3) | | 4) | | 5) | |
|---|---|---|---|---|---|---|---|---|---|
| A | B | A | B | A | B | A | A′ | A | A′ |
| a b | c d | a a′ | b b′ | a a′ b | c d b | a b | a c | a b | c b |

**FIGURE 21-2.** Unit relationships for some common double-period patterns

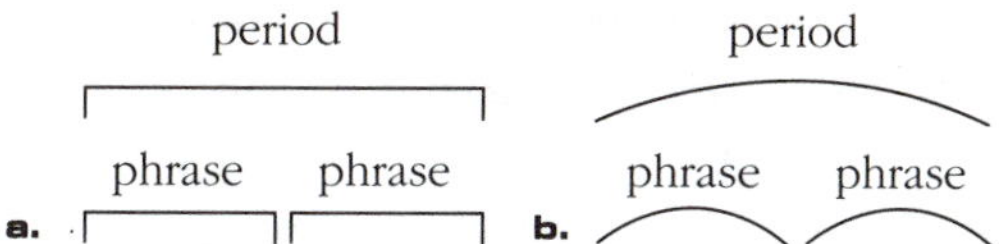


**FIGURE 21-3.** Diagrams indicating structure

Figure 21-4 combines the system of arrows with the brackets. The first and last arrows in the piece (or passage) always have the largest number of slashes, as these represent the piece as a whole.

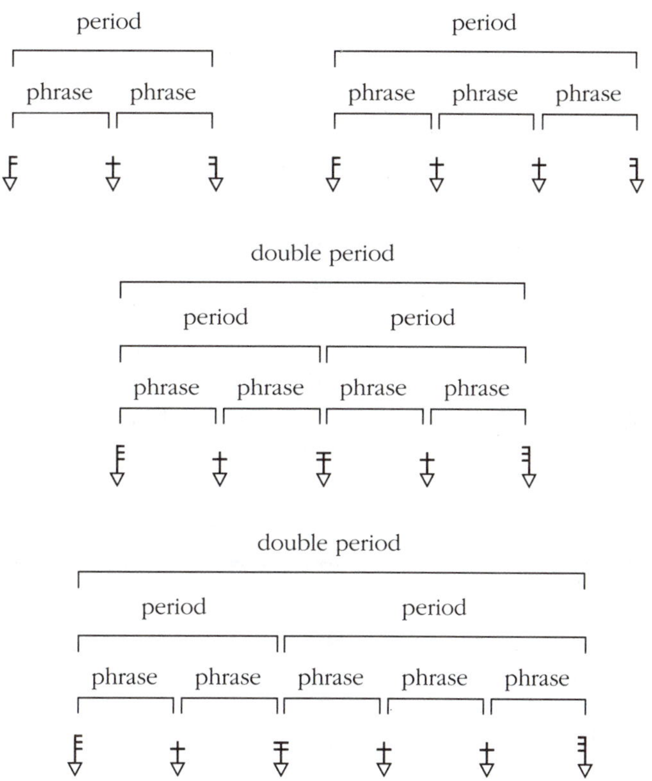


**FIGURE 21-4.** Grouping of units

## Units above the Third Level

The same principle of grouping operates for larger structural units, above the third level. While there are traditional terms for most of the possible units at the lower three levels, there is no accepted term for units at the fourth structural level and above. Third-level units group together to form fourth-level units. We will refer to these higher structural units by the number of their structural level. The concept of grouping small units to create larger units is extended upward indefinitely. Figure 21-5 illustrates a typical idealized structure in which units are grouped in pairs up to a fourth level. The appropriate arrows that would be put in the music are also shown.

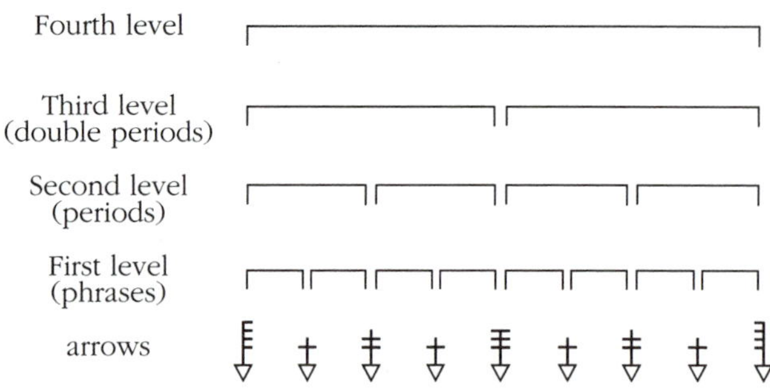


**FIGURE 21.5.** Typical fourth-level structure

Based on the assumption that each phrase in figure 21-5 will be four measures long, typical lengths of various structural units are shown in table 21-1.

| Units | Length in measures |
|---|---|
| Fourth-level unit | 32 |
| Each third-level unit (double period) | 16 |
| Each second-level unit (period) | 8 |
| Each first-level unit (phrase) | 4 |

**TABLE 21-1.** Typical lengths of structural levels

## HIGHER STRUCTURAL LEVELS WITH THE COMPLETE TEXTURE

The concepts of form apply to higher structural levels, where the complete musical experience is taken into account, including melody, texture, and harmony.

### Second-Level Structural Units

The phrases in second-level units may be clear or obscured in various ways through interlocking, overlapping, or atypical treatment of the internal cadence.

#### Clear Cadences

Differences in agogic accents make the period clear in example 21-8. The agogic accent in measure 8 is very strong, and the agogic pattern in measure 4 does not clarify the cadence. The beginning of the second phrase is clearly indicated by the reappearance of opening material.

**EXAMPLE 21-8.** Corelli: Violin Sonata No. 8, Sarabande

Largo

d: i iv i6 V$^6_5$ i iv7 V i VI6 VII7 v VI7 iv6 V

#### Interlocking Phrases

The internal cadence of a period may be obscured through interlocking in the primary melodic line as in example 21-9. The second phrase begins with a motive related to the motive that begins the first phrase; however, this is smoothly connected with continuous melodic activity.

**EXAMPLE 21-9.** Handel: Suite in G minor, HHA iv/1,61, second movement

## Overlapping Phrases

**overlapping phrases**

Two or more voices may begin or end the phrase at different times, a situation termed *overlapping phrases.* This is seen in example 21-10, where the second phrase begins earlier in the upper voice than in the lower one. In measure 4, the upper voice actually begins the new phrase with the second beat while the lower voice begins the second phrase in measure 5, causing the phrases to overlap. This overlapping is indicated by the dashed line.

**EXAMPLE 21-10.** Mozart: Eight Minuets with Trios, K. 315a, no. 7

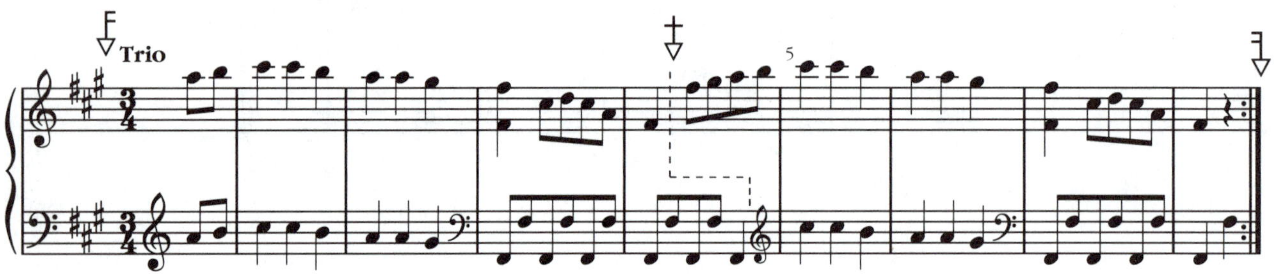


Slight differences do not greatly affect our perception of the phrase, but in example 21-11, the composer extends the phrase in the voice (by repeating the words) while the new phrase begins with a new accompanimental motive. The accompaniment ends two bars later, alone, completing three phrases while the voice performs only two. The difference in cadence points is marked with the dashed line.

**EXAMPLE 21-11.** Schubert: *Der Entfernten,* D. 350

## Quasi-Cadences

There are cadences that do not fall into the established categories listed, but they are quite uncommon. These should not obscure the overriding importance of the established cadence types. Occasionally one may find an abnormally long phrase, in which a normal cadence does not appear at the appropriate time, so a unit of about eight measures is heard. This may involve a *quasi-cadence* after four bars, at which time there may be a clear melodic cadence, but it is not accompanied by a normal harmonic cadence at the same time. On rare occasions the quasi-cadence may end with a chord such as IV. An instance of this may be found in the song "Auld Lang Syne," example 21-12. The melodic cadence must be strong and create a normal phrase length but, as in example 21-12, without a normal harmonic cadence formula. The quasi-cadence is designated by an arrow in parentheses ( ⇟ ).

**quasi-cadence**

**EXAMPLE 21-12.** Auld Lang Syne

In example 21-13, the melody in measure 4 seems to indicate a cadence for three reasons: (1) the agogic accent; (2) the rest, which suggests a "breathing point"; and (3) the figure at the beginning of measure 5 is new, although related to material in measures 1–4. But Beethoven uses a very slow harmonic rhythm, which "lags" so far behind the pace of the melody that at the expected cadence point the progression has only arrived at a ii chord, causing a quasi-cadence. The second phrase is extended to six bars, and the first clear, normal cadence arrives only at measure 10.

## Unit Relationships

In homophonic music the relationships between the antecedent and consequent of a period may show several different kinds of phrase construction, with the melodic content being the main aspect determining the type. Contrasting phrase construction is illustrated in example 21-14, with the unit relationship a b. The close relationships of the phrases in example 21-15 are represented as a a′, producing parallel phrase construction.

**EXAMPLE 21-13.** Beethoven: Violin Sonata, op. 24, first movement

**EXAMPLE 21-14.** Beethoven: *Kleine Clavierstück, WoO 54*

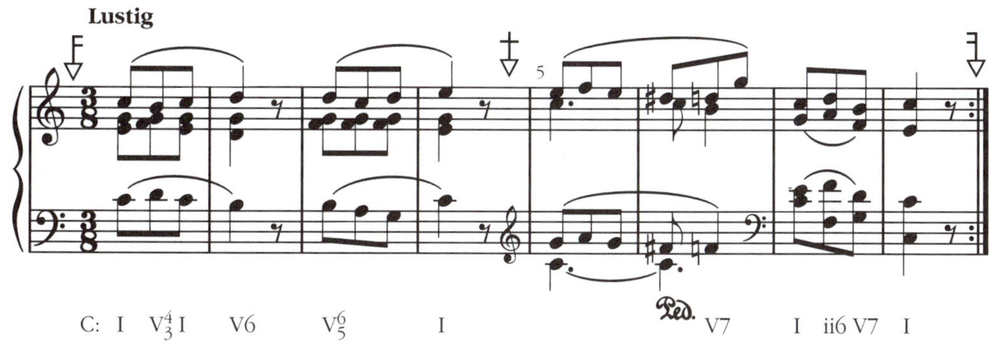


**EXAMPLE 21-15.** Rameau: *Pieces de Clavecin* (1724), Suite No. 1, Musette

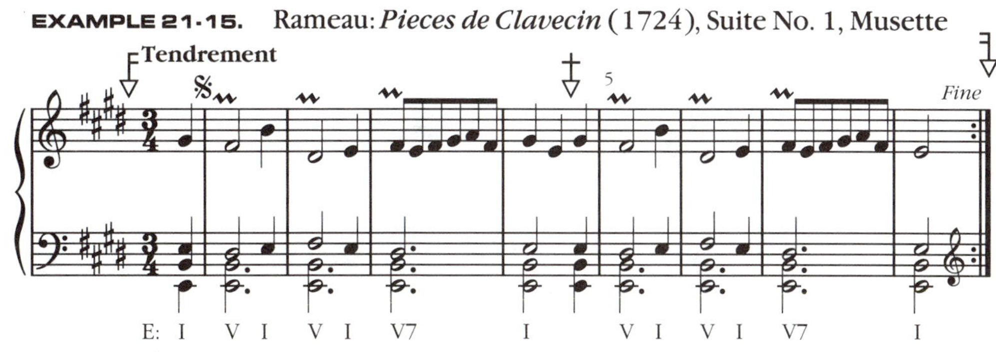

Several different instances of similar phrase construction are seen in example 21-16. The unit relationships for these are a a′; however, the second phrase is not as closely related to the first as in the case of parallel construction. These examples also illustrate asymmetrical phrase relationships: In example 21-16a there are phrase lengths of 4 + 5 measures and in example 21-16b 4 + 6. Symmetrical five-bar phrases are seen in example 21-16c. A period with three phrases appears in example 21-17 with phrase lengths of 4 + 6 + 4 measures and unit relationships of a b c.

**EXAMPLE 21-16.** Similar phrase construction

**a.** Haydn: Piano Sonata in F major, Hob. XVI:9, first movement

**b.** Haydn: Piano Sonata in C Major, Hob. XVI:3, third movement

**EXAMPLE 21-16.** (continued)

**c.** Haydn: Piano Sonata in E-flat Major, Hob. XVI:16, third movement

**EXAMPLE 21-17.** Haydn: Piano Sonata in B-flat Major, Hob. XVI:2, third

## Third-Level Structural Units

The combination of periods to form a double period is often the means of organizing a complete small piece. Example 21-18 is such a case. The division of this piece into two periods is revealed by the rhythm of the lowest voice where agogic accents mark the end of the first second-level unit and divide the piece into two periods.

**EXAMPLE 21-18.** Mozart: Menuetto, K. 15

The cadences are actually made clearer by the lower voice, which sets forth a very regular progression leading to a melodic cadence formula first seen in the fourth bar. The upper voice delays the cadence somewhat with $e^1$, a retardation; this pattern occurs at every cadence in the piece.

## SUMMARY

Units of structure larger than a phrase are referred to as higher units or levels in a hierarchy of relationships in which the phrase is called the lowest or first-level unit. The term *formal unit* refers to a unit of structure on any level. Phrases group together to form larger, second-level units, and these group together to form third-level units.

A group of two or three phrases is called a period. Periods may be described by the unit relationships of the component phrases. To express unit relationships, a system of letter identification is used. The terms *parallel phrase construction, contrasting phrase construction,* and *similar phrase construction* are used for the most common relationships between phrases in a period. The term *symmetrical* refers to successive structural units of equal length, and, in periods, symmetrical phrase relationships are the most common. Groups of periods are called third-level units. A third-level unit consisting of two periods is known as a double period. Higher structural levels are formed as the grouping process is continued to a fourth level and above.

The concepts of form at higher structural levels apply to the complete musical experience, including the melody, texture, and harmony. The phrases in second-level units may be clear or obscured in various ways through interlocking, overlapping, or atypical treatment of the internal cadence. Overlapping phrases are phrases that two or more voices begin or end at different times. A quasi-cadence consists of a clear melodic cadence that is not accompanied by a normal harmonic cadence at the same time. In the complete texture, the melodic content is the main element determining the unit relationships and phrase construction. The combination of periods to form a double period is often the means of organizing a complete small piece.

CHAPTER TWENTY-TWO

# Two-Part Forms

**Terms Introduced in This Chapter**

- two-part form
- binary form
- tonal arch
- parallel beginning
- parallel ending
- recapitulation
- rounded binary form
- internal cadence

**two-part form**

The classification of two-part forms includes a vast number of pieces from the Baroque and Classical eras, with many examples before and since that period. To fall within the classification, the structure of a piece at the highest level must reveal a division into two parts. The term *two-part form* is used to describe pieces that divide into two main portions, whether they are symmetrical or asymmetrical, contrasting or highly unified.

## SIMPLE TWO-PART FORMS

The simpler versions of two-part form may lack one or more of the features associated with the more sophisticated versions: modulation in both parts, motivic unity, and close relationships between the two parts. In example 22-1, the first part ends with a perfect authentic cadence in the tonic key, and the second part, very similar to the first, also ends with a perfect authentic cadence. The two parts are sufficiently alike that they may be described as A A′.

**EXAMPLE 22-1.** Beethoven: *Ecossaise,* WoO 86

**EXAMPLE 22-1.** Part 2 (continued)

Example 22-2 uses contrasting motives in the two parts to create an A B relationship. The cadence ending each part resembles those in example 22-1; however, part 2 modulates to F major and then reestablishes the tonic D minor at the end. This is an asymmetrical two-part form. In example 22-3, the second half is somewhat different from the first, offering a degree of change without modulation or strongly contrasting motives. The form is A A′.

**EXAMPLE 22-2.** Handel: Suite in D minor, HHA iv/1,18 *Air*

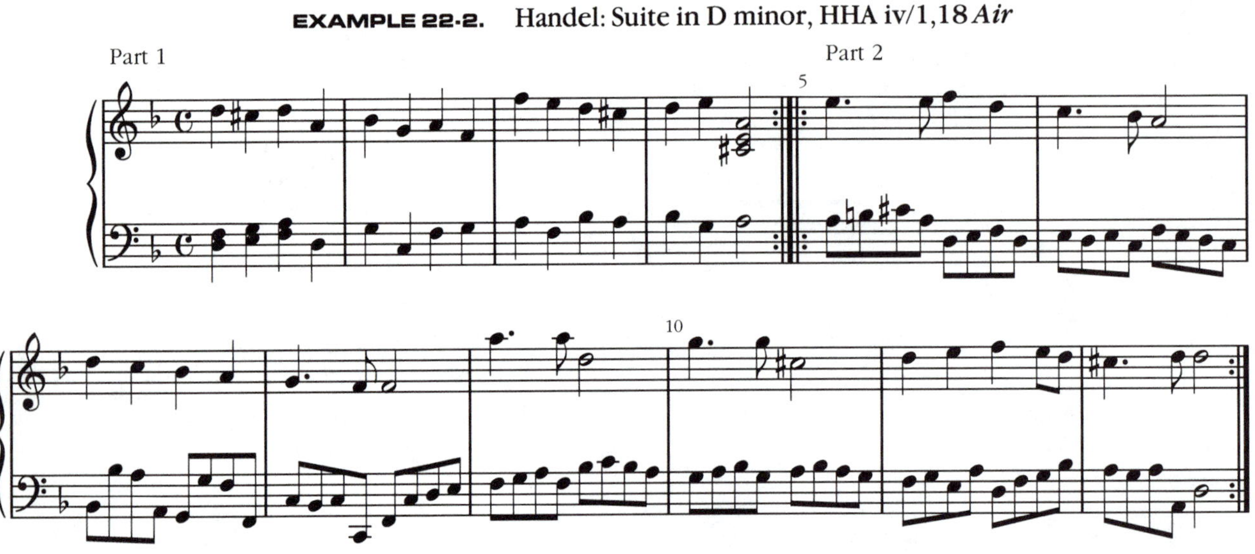

**EXAMPLE 22-3.** Beethoven: Waltz, WoO 85

## BINARY FORM

**binary form**

Within the broad classification of two-part forms there is a special subgroup known as *binary form.* It was most popular in the Baroque period and further developed during the early Classical era (around 1750) into the sonata; hence, it has been a form of great interest to many composers.

## Tonal Arch

**tonal arch**

One of the chief characteristics of the binary form is the *tonal arch,* which consists of the establishing of a particular tonality at the beginning of a piece, departing from that tonality to one or more new keys, and then returning to the original key at the end. In binary forms there are also the following expectations.

> Part 1: The tonic major key modulates to the dominant key, while the tonic minor goes to the relative major.
>
> Part 2: From the key at the end of part 1 there are modulations to other closely related keys before returning to the original key. In short pieces the other keys may be omitted or only suggested with secondary dominants.

Example 22-4 begins in C Major and during part 1 modulates to G major in measures 6–8. In part 2 it returns to C major in measure 11 after a secondary dominant, $V_7/V$ in measures 9 and 10. Note in example 22-5 that the key changes from D minor to the relative major in part 1, then returns to D minor in part 2.

**EXAMPLE 22-4.** Haydn: Piano Sonata in C major, Hob. XVI:15, third movement

**EXAMPLE 22-5.** J. S. Bach: *Notebook for Anna Magdalena*, Polonaise

## Continuity

Another very important feature of the binary form is the continuity of the melodic and motivic material throughout the piece. The second part of the piece (often marked off visually by the repeat sign) may evidence a *parallel beginning* if it begins very much the same as the opening of the first part. Example 22-5 shows this in measures 1 and 9. Other pieces in binary form may also have *parallel endings*, in which the two parts end with very similar material. Example 22-6 illustrates this with measures 7–8 resembling measures 15–16.

**parallel beginning**

**parallel ending**

The binary form has been called "continuous," with a close relationship between the parts, smooth changes of key, and generally uniform texture. In noncontinuous forms the component parts are more sectionalized and separated by more sharply contrasting and differentiated motives and by contrasts in texture and tonality. Example 22-7 demonstrates in a larger work the closely related melodies, uniformity of texture, and tonal arch characteristic of a binary form. Keys are indicated below the staff, and the first statements of important motives are shown with brackets and letters.

**EXAMPLE 22-6.** Haydn: Piano Sonata in G Major, Hob. XVI:8, second movement

**EXAMPLE 22-7.** J. S. Bach: French Suite No. 5, BWV 816, Courante

**EXAMPLE 22-7.** (continued)

Also illustrated in example 22-7 are parallel beginnings and endings, the motivic unity of the piece, and greater tension in the second part. In measure 24 there is a melodic inversion of the opening theme, which is explored or developed for the following two measures. The two-voice texture is maintained through much of the piece with the exception of a few measures where an added voice appears rather unobtrusively.

| Part 1 | | | Part 2 | |
|---|---|---|---|---|
| 𝄆 | | 𝄇𝄆 | | 𝄇 |
| Beginning theme | | Ending theme | Beginning theme | Ending theme |
| Tonic key | modulates | Dominant key | Dominant and/or other keys | Tonic key |

**FIGURE 22-1.** Typical pattern of binary form

Figure 22-1 shows the typical pattern of the binary form. This pattern is, of course, only a stereotype; it is frequently used but not universally required. The name attached to the form of a particular piece is useful only for communicating ideas about how the piece compares with other pieces; not all binary pieces will display identical characteristics.

## Binary Form without Repeats

A "double bar" is a good visual clue about the structure of the music, but it does not directly affect the analysis of the form. An exact repetition of a section does not constitute an additional part in the form. Many examples of binary form have double bars and repeats for both parts, but this is not essential. Even though the double bar is "missing" in example 22-8, an analysis of the structure will reveal two parts for the piece. Although the key signature has three sharps, the piece begins and ends in E major. The second part begins in the dominant and in measure 8 modulates to C-sharp minor. The return to the tonic key begins in measure 10.

Note that the bass line here is a figured bass, a continuo part for a bass instrument (violone) and keyboard instrument (cimbalo), which will be realizing the harmony with middle voices.

**EXAMPLE 22-8.** Corelli: Violin Sonata XI, Preludio

## Rounded Binary Form

**recapitulation**

Example 22-9 shows a somewhat later stage in the evolution of the binary form. Although the piece does not have clear parallel beginnings or endings, the opening material does return in the middle of the second part, in the tonic key (in measure 17). This is called a *recapitulation,* or restatement of the first part, with necessary changes, such as in measure 23, to allow the piece to end in the tonic key instead of modulating, as in measure 8. This recapitulation of the opening material at the point where the tonic key returns is of great significance, as it links the return of the melodic starting point with the return of the tonal staring point. This offers possibilities for dramatic presentation, which composers have used with great effect. A binary form that contains a recapitulation of the opening material in the second part is called a *rounded binary form.* This was used only occasionally by J. S. Bach but very often by Haydn, Mozart, and other composers of the Classical period.

**rounded binary form**

**EXAMPLE 22-9.** Haydn: Piano Sonata in G Major, Hob. XVI:27, second movement

It was mentioned that asymmetry is common between the two parts of the binary form. The important issue is not simply the number of measures but the number of phrases and differences in the structural levels in the two parts. Note the slashes on the arrows in the analysis of example 22-10. Figure 22-2 shows a graphic summary of the structure of this piece. As the slashes indicate, part 1 consists of a second-level unit, a period. Part 2, on the other hand, consists of two periods combined to form a third-level structure (a double period). Although the piece contains three periods, it does not divide into three parts because of the cadences.

**EXAMPLE 22-10.** Handel: Suite in D Minor, HHA iv/17,60, Sarabande

Part 1 Part 2

**FIGURE 22-2.** Analysis of example 22-10

One of the main forces causing phrases to group is the tendency for a later cadence to be more conclusive. Compare the cadences at measures 8, 16, and 24. The cadence at measure 8 is rhythmically stronger, but the key is F, the relative major of D minor. The cadence at measure 16 is in A minor; the strong agogic accent in the upper voice is weakened by the activity in the lower voice in this measure. Only the cadence in measure 24 is strong rhythmically and is conclusively in the tonic key. Further, notice the transitory and unsettled quality of the material at measure 17. The instability at this point is evidence that the second part is still in development. It is a characteristic of the binary form that the strongest *internal cadence,* that is, a cadence other than the final cadence of the piece, comes at the close of the first part.

**internal cadence**

To briefly review the explanation of the slashes, the stem of the arrow represents the point of separation. The slashes on the left of the stem indicate the level of the unit completed at that point ( ↓ ) and the slashes on the right, the level for the unit beginning at this point ( ↓ ). Thus, the asymmetry of design of example 22-10 is most clearly shown by the arrow at the end of part 1 (m. 8). An arrow at the beginning or ending of a piece has slashes on only one side, while an internal cadence has slashes on both sides.

The lowest level of formal structure is the phrase. Cadences separating these units are marked with a single slash. The second level indicates the grouping of phrases (into periods); these groupings are indicated by arrows with two slashes on the stem. The grouping of periods is the third level, marked with three slashes. In example 22-10, the piece as a whole is a fourth-level structure, as shown in figure 22-3.

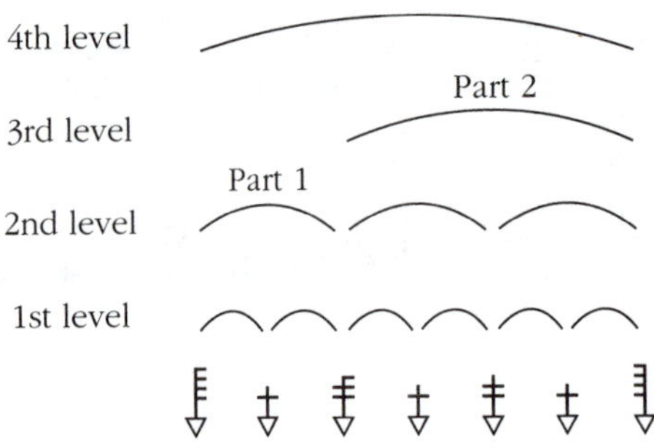


**FIGURE 22-3.** Structural analysis of example 22-10

It should be apparent from this analysis that there is considerable asymmetry between the two parts of this piece. Part 1 comprises a second-level structure, but part 2 has another layer or level of structure. To grasp the analysis of this piece quickly, one would look first at the number of slashes on the arrow at the beginning or ending of the piece, in this case, four slashes. Next, a cadence with three slashes is located, at measure 8; however, since this arrow has an unequal number of slashes, one concludes that the piece is asymmetrical at this level of structure; that is, a more elaborate structure is found in the section after measure 8 than before.

The system of arrow analysis is designed to indicate the location and grouping of the units (phrases, periods, and larger units) that make up a piece of music. The system does not undertake to show the thematic relationships, although such relationships may exist.

## SUMMARY

Two-part form is the general category for pieces that, at the highest structural level, divide into two parts. Binary form is a specific type of two-part form, one of the most frequently used. The essential feature of two-part form is the division of the work into two parts at the highest structural level. Additional features typical of binary form are:

1. a tonal arch;
2. the strongest internal cadence at the end of part 1;
3. melody and texture relatively unified throughout.

Features of binary form that are occasionally found are:

1. asymmetric structure between the two parts;
2. a double bar separating the parts;
3. modulations in part 2, other than to the tonic;
4. parallel beginnings and endings;
5. rounding.

CHAPTER TWENTY-THREE

# Three- and Four-Part Forms

**Terms Introduced in This Chapter**

- three-part form
- ternary form
- reprise
- da capo
- trio
- extended ternary form
- introduction
- transition
- coda
- codetta
- ritornello
- strophic song
- bar form
- four-part form
- through-composed
- two-voice framework
- key cycle

Two-, three-, and four-part forms are often found in vocal music, hence they are sometimes referred to as song forms and described as "sectional" in that the principal sections are relatively independent and generally end conclusively. Many unit relationships are possible; however, we will consider only the most frequently used of these forms.

## THREE-PART FORMS

**three-part form**

A musical structure which at its highest level divides into three parts is known as a *three-part form.* Such pieces may be of great length, with each of the three parts being in itself quite complex, or they may be very short, with parts that may consist of nothing more than a phrase. Just as one may distinguish between the general two-part forms and binary form (as a specific type), one may distinguish between three-part forms and the more specific ternary form, ABA.

In three-part forms it is customary to use letters to describe the unit relationships of the main parts. To refer to the binary form as AB may give the false impression that the parts are very different, when a chief feature of the binary form is that the A and B sections are closely related; however, in the case of the three-part forms, the parts usually exhibit clear relationships of recurrence or contrast.

### Ternary Form

**ternary form**

The most common of the three-part forms is *ternary form.* The first and third parts are essentially the same; the typical pattern is ABA. Sometimes the return of A is varied to the point where ABA′ is a more accurate description; so long as the first and third parts are heard as essentially the same, the piece may be considered a ternary form.

The treatment of melody and tonality in ternary form is distinctive and differs from that of binary form. In ternary form the first part usually ends with a conclusive cadence in the tonic key. The middle part usually has contrasting melodic content and, except for very brief works, usually is in a new key. The middle part usually ends with a clear cadence, either in the new key or a half cadence in the original key.

Binary form, on the other hand, does not have such a sharp separation of sections: The first part does not normally end in the original tonic key, and the second part does not clearly contrast in melodic content and tonality. The sections of ternary form are often the same length or similar in length. Common variants of the form include a more extensive treatment of the initial A material than of the other sections. This may appear as AA′BA′ or AA′BA″. The first two sections are paired as though A′ were simply a repetition of A. Since repeats are not considered to affect the overall form, AA′BA or AA′BA″ may be taken as almost the same as AABA and both reduce to ABA. All these variants are considered ternary forms.

A relatively simple example of ternary form is shown in example 23-1. The A section consists of an eight-measure period beginning and ending in A major. The section is devoted to a single chordal theme; the final cadence is clear and conclusive. The middle section is also an eight-bar period, in D major, ending conclusively; the texture is melody with accompaniment. The bass line in section B is more active and independent than it was in section A. Though there are some common elements—for example, the rhythm ♩. ♬ ♩ ♩ | ♩, the chords in the right hand, the octaves in the left, and so on—the B is quite different from the A. The return of A (recapitulation or *reprise*) is exactly the same as the first statement. The repeat sign for the B section has no effect on the overall form. A summary of the form, sectional relationships, keys, and cadences is given in figure 23-1. The measure numbers indicate the bars in which the cadences occur.

**reprise**

**EXAMPLE 23-1.** Schumann: *Scenes from Childhood,* op. 15, no. 6, "An Important Event"

**EXAMPLE 23-1.** (continued)

**FIGURE 23-1.** Analysis of example 23-1

**da capo**

**trio**

Short pieces in dance forms (minuets, gavottes, and others) were often presented in pairs in which, for instance, the first would be called Minuet I and the second called Minuet II. Minuet II was usually followed by a D.C., *da capo* (an indication in the music to return to the beginning), repeating Minuet I, making an overall ternary form, ABA. Because the second part (or Minuet II) was sometimes written in a three-voice texture, this part was called the *trio.* A trio is simply another dance of the same kind as the first part. Later the term *trio* was used in marches and scherzos. In the Baroque period, vocal solos and ensemble pieces in operas, cantatas, and oratorios often used similar da capo indications for ternary forms. The term *da capo aria* is sometimes given to such movements.

In example 23-2, the whole piece is a ternary form, while the component parts (A and B) are each two-part forms. The recurrence of part A is not written out but is indicated by the words *Menuetto da capo,* or Menuetto D.C. It is true that the repeats are often omitted in these da capo forms, but the da capo recapitulation must not be omitted, for this will drastically alter the form of the piece. In example 23-2, part A is in C major while part B is in F major. The return of part A in the da capo is needed to bring the piece to a conclusion in the tonic key. Sometimes the Italian word *fine* ("end") is written at the end of part A, but frequently it is omitted, as in example 23-2, and it is understood that the movement ends after the recapitulation of part A (measure 16).

**EXAMPLE 23-2.** Mozart: Duet for Two Woodwind Instruments, K. 487, no. 9

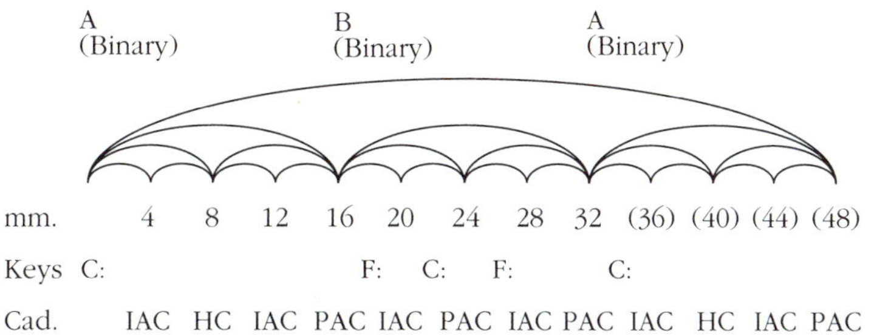


**FIGURE 23-2.** Analysis of example 23-3

**extended ternary form**

One interesting expansion of the ternary principle is the *extended ternary form,* ABABA. This was used by a few composers, notably Beethoven in the third movement of his Seventh Symphony and the second movement of his cello sonata, opus 69.

Example 23-3 is a modified ternary form with the pattern AA′A: the middle part is practically identical to the first A, except for the changes of texture and tonality. Because the piece is clearly heard in three sections, with some degree of contrast in the middle section and a return to section A for the third part, it can be considered an unusual ternary form.

**EXAMPLE 23-3.** Schumann: *Album for the Young,* op. 68, no. 8, "Wild Rider"

**EXAMPLE 23-3.** (continued)

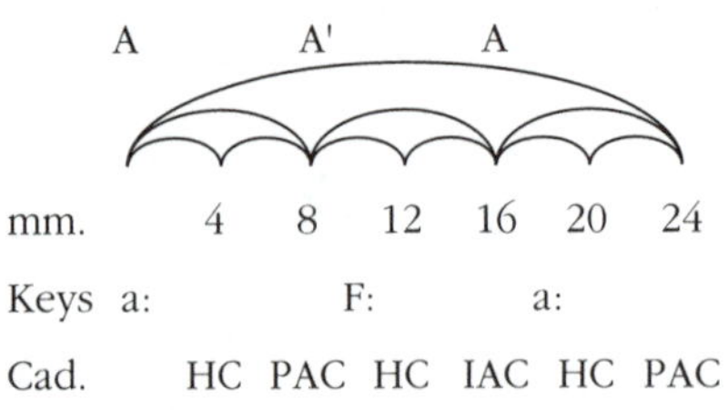


**FIGURE 23-3.** Analysis of example 23-3

There is continuing debate among theorists regarding the use of the term *ternary*. Larger ternary forms in which the component parts themselves consist of binary or ternary forms are sometimes referred to as "compound ternary." Some authors prefer to use the term *incipient ternary* instead of rounded binary. The form called extended ternary is sometimes called a type of rondo. Rondo form will be discussed in more detail in volume 2.

## Introductions, Transitions, and Codas

**introduction**

**transition**

**coda**

**codetta**

**ritornello**

Additional structural features may appear adjacent to the principal units without changing a basic form such as ternary. These additional units are usually short in relation to the rest of the work, but not smaller than a phrase in length, and perform one of several fairly clear functions: introduction, interlude or transition, or closing unit. An *introduction* prepares the listener for the first main section of the work and may be related or contrast with it. A *transition* is a passage that smoothly connects one section with another and often involves a change of key. A closing unit at the end of a piece, after the last main section, is called a *coda;* an internal closing unit, that is, not at the end of the piece but at the end of a section, is called a *codetta.* Occasionally the same music will be used for several of these functions. This "returning" passage is called a *ritornello* in music from the Baroque period.

In example 23-4, the ternary form includes an introduction and coda that are almost identical. The specific form of this piece is AA′BA″, a common variant of ternary form. The key of section B, G major, is remote in relation to the initial B major of section A. It is entered and left by direct modulation. Note the irregular cadences in section B, ii7–I6, that are listed as a variant of a plagal cadence, since ii7 is in the same chord group as IV. Notice the cadence in measure 40 where the voice has the salient line, ending the phrase on the chord third while the uppermost line, a recessive line in the piano, ends on the chord root. We recommend that the salient voice should take precedence over the recessive in deciding the cadence in such a case. We therefore call the cadence IAC, not PAC (see fig. 23-4).

**EXAMPLE 23-4.** Schumann: *Liederkreis,* op. 24, no. 3, "Ich wandelte unter den Bäumen"

**EXAMPLE 23-4.** (continued)

**EXAMPLE 23-4.** (continued)

**EXAMPLE 23-4.** (continued)

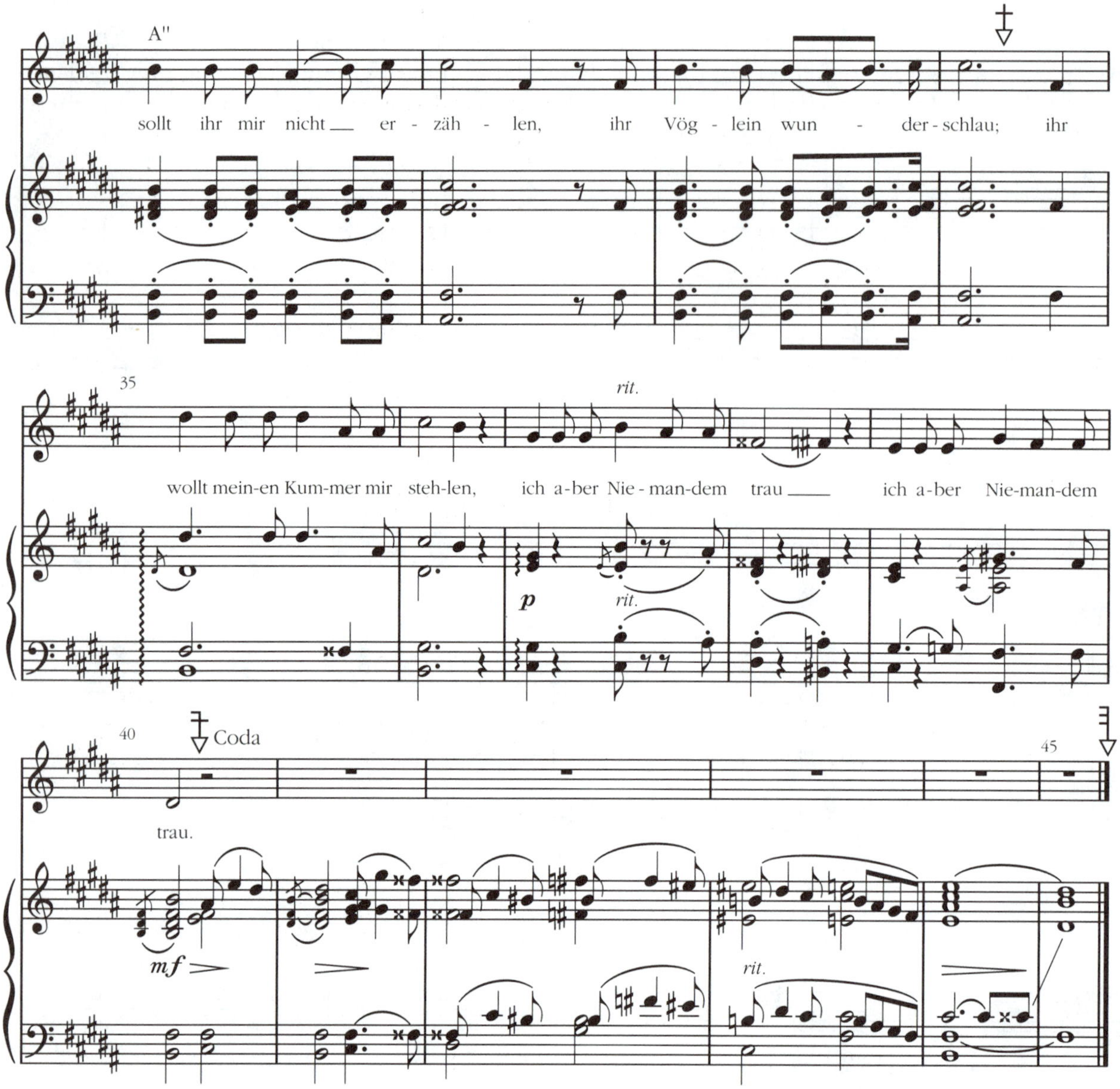

A''
sollt ihr mir nicht___ er - zäh - len, ihr Vög - lein wun - der - schlau; ihr
35
wollt mein-en Kum-mer mir steh-len, ich a-ber Nie - man-dem trau___ ich a-ber Nie-man-dem
rit.
p
rit.
40
Coda
trau.
45
mf
rit.

Intro A A' B A'' Coda
mm. 4 8 13 17 22 26 30 34 40 45
Keys B: G: B:
Cad. HC HC HC HC HC PC PC HC IAC IAC

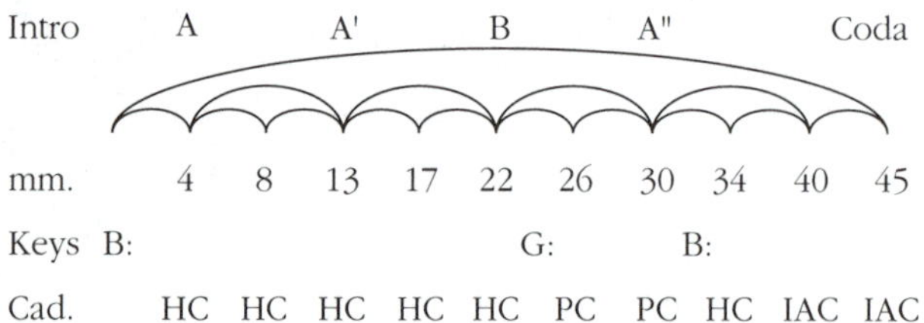

**FIGURE 23-4.** Analysis of example 23-4

Notice the slash marks on the arrow in measure 4. The slash on the left side of the arrow indicates that a phrase has ended; the two slashes on the right side indicate that a period is beginning. In measure 40 the two slashes on the left side indicate that a period has ended; the slash on the right indicates that only a single phrase follows. The final arrow has three slashes to indicate the three structural levels of the piece as a whole.

Example 23-5 includes a returning or ritornello passage in a work by Bach. This passage serves as an introductory and concluding passage for section A. This is a da capo aria from the Baroque period. It was not unusual for an initial passage preceding section A to be used several times thereafter. As in example 23-5, the initial passage may also appear as a codetta at the end of section A. Then, with the da capo, the ritornello passage appears twice more, four times in all, throughout the piece. In such works a fermata is often used as a marker or sign: It indicates the end of section A and serves as an ending point for the whole movement.

**EXAMPLE 23-5.** J. S. Bach: Cantata No. 7, "Christ unser Herr zum Jordan kam," BWV 7, Aria

**EXAMPLE 23-5.** (continued)

**EXAMPLE 23-5.** (continued)

**EXAMPLE 23-5.** (continued)

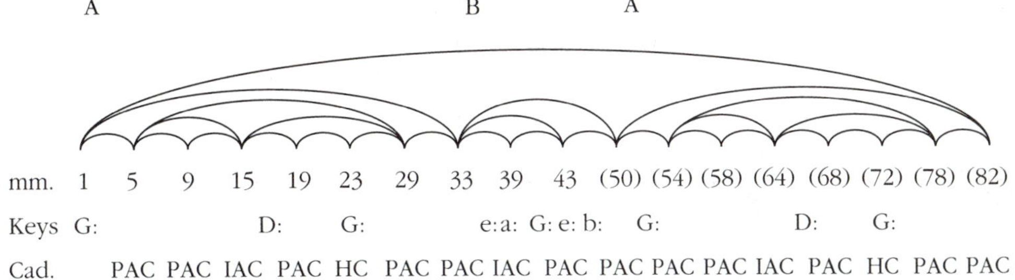


**FIGURE 23-5.** Analysis of example 23-5

## Other Three-Part Forms

The pattern ABC is most often found in rather short pieces; for longer works composers have found the ternary pattern more satisfactory. In example 23-6, each part consists of a period, the part C including a final phrase for a large ensemble. This is a *strophic song* in that the music is repeated exactly with different words. The words of only the first verse are shown here.

**strophic song**

**EXAMPLE 23-6.** Beethoven: *Kriegslied der Österreicher,* WoO 122

**EXAMPLE 23-6.** (continued)

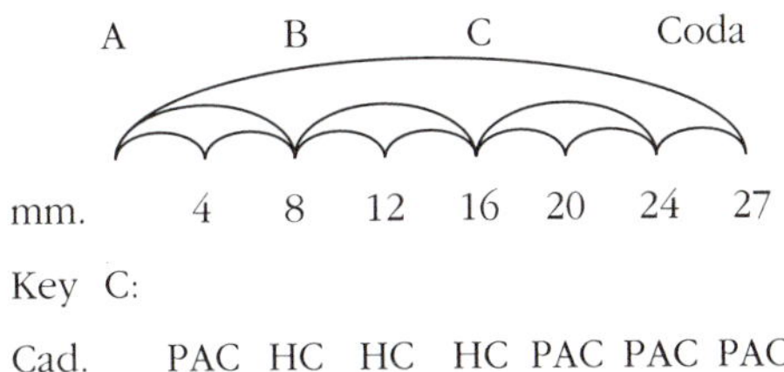


**FIGURE 23-6.** Analysis of example 23-6

Example 23-7 uses the form ABB′. This is a relatively rare pattern that has the proportions of a three-part form, but the close relationship of the last two sections strongly suggests an extremely asymmetrical AB.

**EXAMPLE 23-7.** Beethoven: *Abschiedsgesang,* WoO 121

**EXAMPLE 23-7.** (continued)

**EXAMPLE 23-7.** (continued)

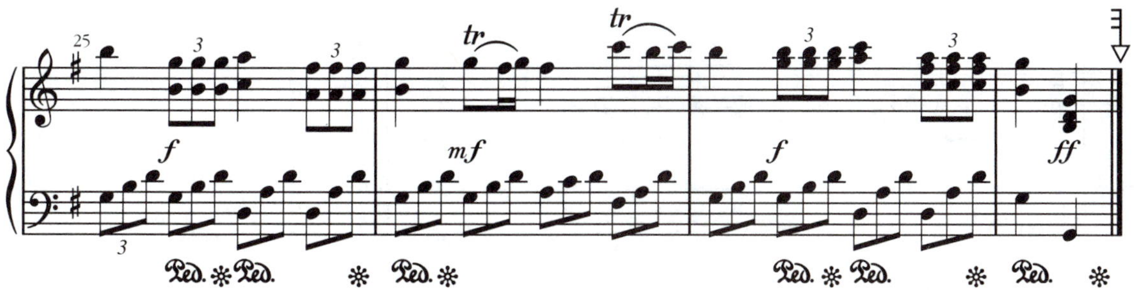


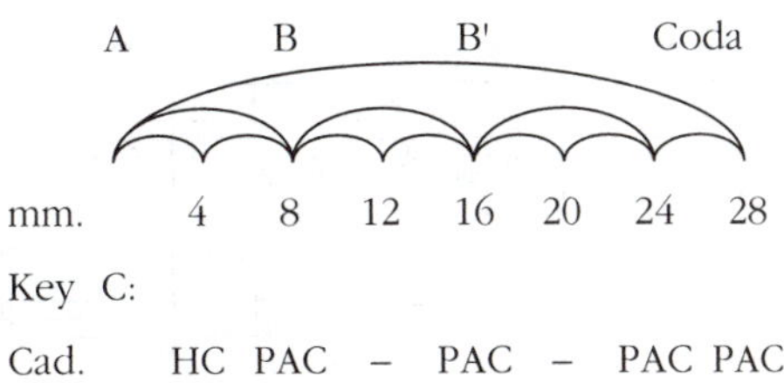


**FIGURE 23-7.** Analysis of example 23-7

**bar form**

The pattern AAB is sometimes known as *bar form.* This was a form employed by the Minnesingers and Meistersingers of medieval Germany in their monophonic songs. The AAB description of bar form is deceptive. As the pattern was usually applied, the result was really a two-part form, since the repeat of A does not constitute a new part. Many Bach chorales are basically in two parts, AB, with a double bar indicating that A should be repeated. Although this repeat usually means new text would be sung, from a purely musical standpoint these songs are best classified as two-part. This is illustrated in example 23-8.

**EXAMPLE 23-8.** J. S. Bach: *O Haupt voll Blut und Wunden*

**FIGURE 23-8.** Analysis of example 23-8

## FOUR-PART FORMS

**four-part form**

A *four-part form* is divided into four divisions at the highest structural level. Whereas two- and three-part forms abound in the literature, four-part forms are relatively rare. One of the problems is that with four sections there is a tendency in some instances for the parts to group into pairs and actually be a two-part form.

In example 23-9, the pattern ABCA′ is used. This particular piece exhibits four clear sections, each composed of a period. Because of the change of key in section C, there is a feeling that perhaps the piece falls into three unequal parts, but each part seems different enough from adjacent parts to warrant classification as a four-part form. This is a strophic song. Note the D. S. (dal segno, return to the sign 𝄋) marked in measure 42.

**EXAMPLE 23-9.** Beethoven: *Sechs Lieder von Gellert,* op. 48, no. 4, "Die Ehre Gottes aus der Natur"

**EXAMPLE 23-9.** (continued)

**EXAMPLE 23-9.** (continued)

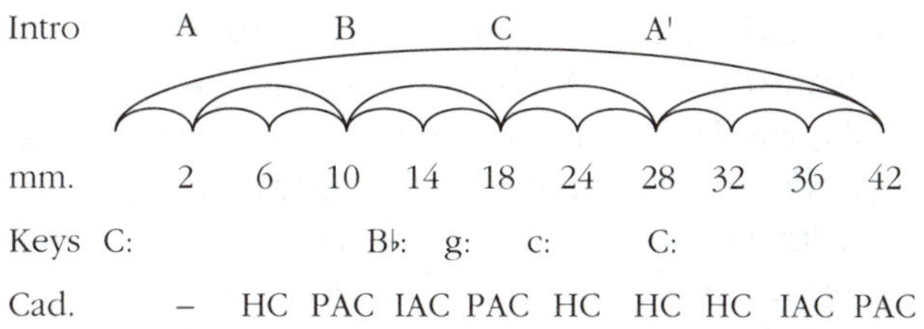


**FIGURE 23-9.** Analysis of example 23-9

**through-composed** Another possibility for a four-part form, ABCD, is rarely found. Forms such as this, which do not recapitulate any part, are sometimes known as *through-composed,* or "composed throughout," from the German term *durchkomponiert.* A characteristic of the remaining possibilities for four-part forms is, as stated earlier, a tendency to group the parts into two pairs, thus reducing the piece to a basic two-part structure (AA′ or AB): ABAB, AA′BB′, ABAC, ABCB, ABCC. These patterns are more frequently found in songs than in instrumental music. In vocal music the text may offer formal possibilities that make certain structures reasonable which in instrumental music might seem illogical.

## TONAL COHERENCE

After completing the study of the basic forms it is valuable to integrate aspects of tonal organization that build coherence. Many of the factors that lend coherence to a work have been examined. Several of these factors must be brought together to gain an overview of the tonal coherence that underlies traditional music. Of course, it is understood that a piece in G normally will start and end in that key, possibly with excursions to other tonalities related to the central key. Now, some of the analytical techniques developed in this text may be applied in a summary analysis to gain a picture of the cohering elements at work in a particular piece. The analysis of tonal coherence will include four parts: the two-voice framework, step progressions, harmonic cycles, and key cycles. The *two-voice framework* consists of the emergent tones of the two most prominent voices: The primary melodic line (usually the soprano) and the bass.

**two-voice framework**

### Two-Voice Framework

The first step in the procedure is to identify the essential features of a two-voice framework. The criteria for selecting emergent tones are the same as before. One begins by considering agogic and metric accents, then examining the contour to find other features that might bring tones into prominence.

A formal analysis must be made, locating the structural units and marking cadences with downward arrows and the appropriate slashes. For illustrative purposes, a portion of a work is shown in example 23-10. In an analysis, the emergent tones are written in whole notes on a grand staff, separating the phrases by bar lines. In example 23-11, the emergent tones for the first two phrases are shown in a two-voice framework.

**EXAMPLE 23-10.** J. S. Bach: French Suite No. 5, Courante

**EXAMPLE 23-11.** First two phrases of example 23-10, with emergent tones indicated

## Step Progressions

The emergent tones identified in the two-voice framework draw our attention from measure to measure, providing short-term coherence. To gain a broader perspective it is necessary to discover step progressions that connect these tones into lines covering a greater span of music. For practical purposes we will indicate those step progressions that: (1) lie entirely within the confines of a single phrase or (2) extend to the highest level, possibly the entire length of the piece. Notice the step progressions in the first four phrases in the Bach Courante, as seen in example 23-12. As before, special value is given to those tones that conclude a step progression, particularly if these tones are the first, third, or fifth scale degrees. A step progression that concludes with a cadence tone will also be of special interest. Surveying the emergent tones in the two-voice framework, one should note any pitches that repeat or recur frequently throughout the work. These tones play a major role in adding coherence to the music.

Notice in example 23-12 that in the second phrase, the F-sharp in the soprano is not a part of the step progression within the phrase, but it becomes part of a larger step progression that extends over a much larger span.

The entire movement is given in example 23-13, and a step progression analysis of that is provided in example 23-14. The analysis in example 23-14 reveals broad relationships. Notice the overall pattern in the step progression for the upper voice of the two-voice framework. It moves to $\hat{5}$ at the end of the first section and finally to $\hat{1}$ at the end. Through seven phrases, the step progression at the higher level for the bass ascends toward $\hat{5}$, after which the final $\hat{5}$ skips to the tonic ($\hat{1}$) at the end.

**EXAMPLE 23-12.** Step progressions of example 23.10

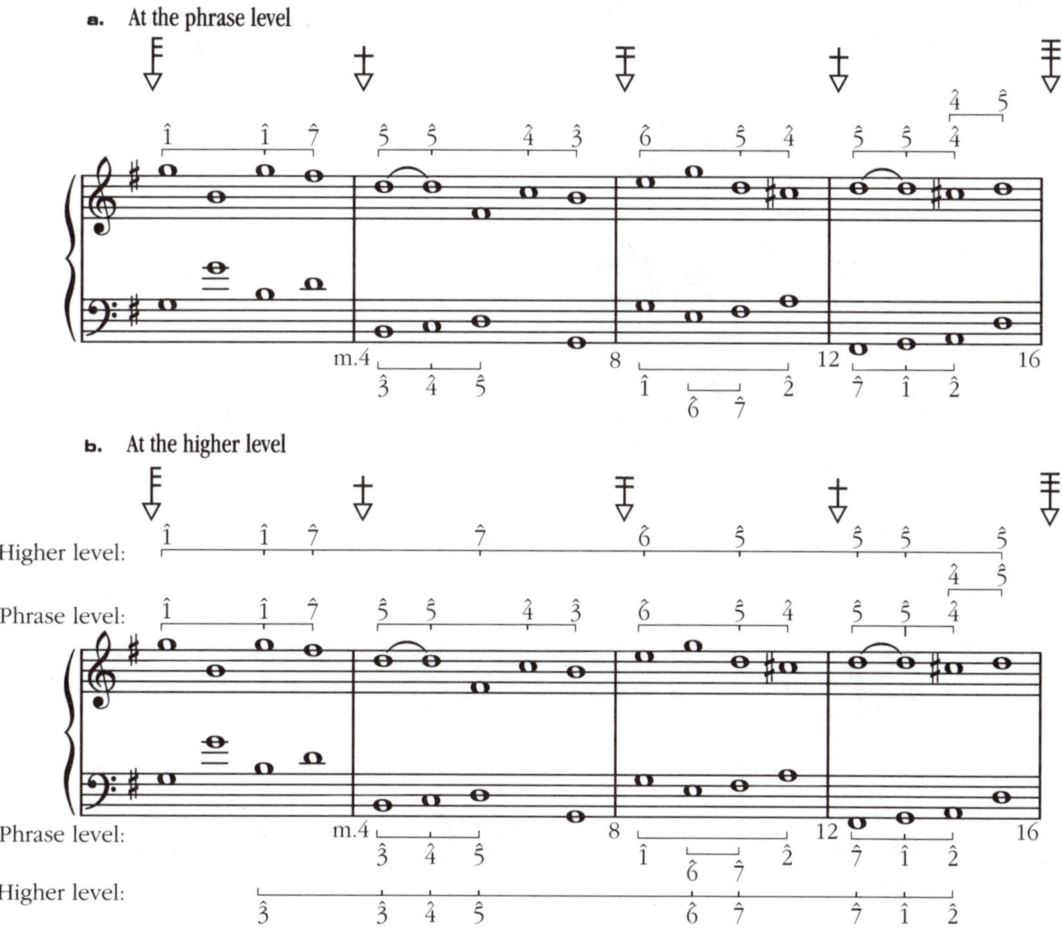


**EXAMPLE 23-13.** J. S. Bach: French Suite No. 5, Courante

**EXAMPLE 23-13.** (continued)

**EXAMPLE 23-14.** Step progressions of example 23-13



## Harmonic Cycles

In analyzing music with particularly interesting harmony it may be useful to identify every chord, but for most pieces it will suffice to identify the harmonic cycles and the key changes. A harmonic cycle begins with the tonic, moves to other chords, and ends with the return to the tonic chord. The end of each harmonic cycle will be marked on the analysis with a I (or i) below the emergent tones with which the tonic chord is reestablished, as seen in example 23-14. Coherence is further expressed by indicating the initial tonic before the first harmonic cycle begins. A bracket is begun under the first emergent tone that begins the cycle, and the bracket ends with the first appearance of the tonic chord that concludes the cycle. In some cases there will be a blank space between brackets. These spaces result from prolonged tonic chords and therefore represent points or areas of no harmonic movement, hence these are areas of high stability. Harmonic cycles for the whole movement are indicated in the space below the staff in example 23-15.

**EXAMPLE 23-15.** Harmonic cycles of example 23-13

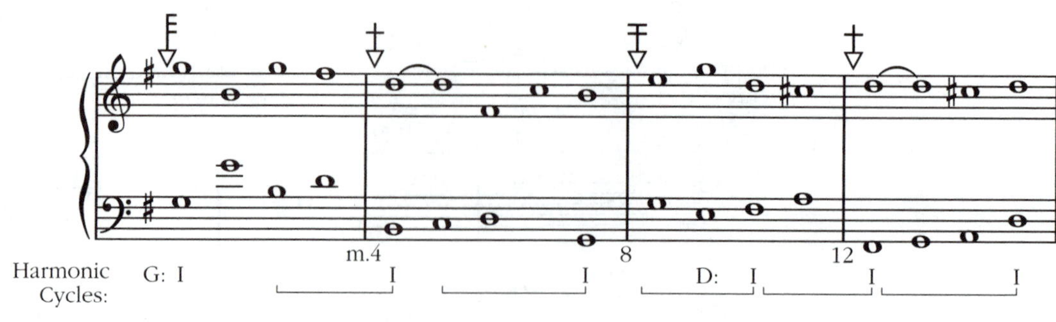


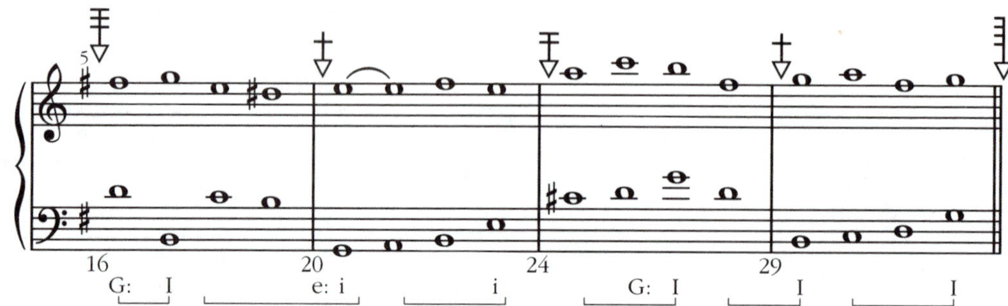


## Key Cycles

**key cycle**

*Key cycle* is the term used to describe the initial establishment of a key, followed by one or more new keys and a return to the initial key. The keys to which the piece modulates are shown as Roman numerals relating to the initial tonality.

In example 23-16, the key cycles are indicated below the harmonic cycles. The Roman numeral that represents the key is placed directly under the first tonic of the harmonic cycle that presents that key. Key cycles are marked with brackets that start just before the Roman numeral for the recurrence of the initial key and end with the returning tonic key. Note: A return to the tonic key that is not confirmed by a cadence is indicated in parentheses and does not suffice to end a key cycle. In example 23-16, the fifth phrase analysis illustrates this. It should also be noticed that the analysis of key cycles is similar to harmonic cycles in that the empty space appearing around the brackets is meaningful as a reflection of the emphasis on the tonic key and the absence of changes of tonality.

An additional analysis of tonal coherence is shown in examples 23-17 and 23-18, a ternary form from the Classical period. This work includes small binary forms within each section. Almost every aspect of the analysis of this work differs from the work by Bach previously examined.

**EXAMPLE 23-16.** Key cycles of example 23-13

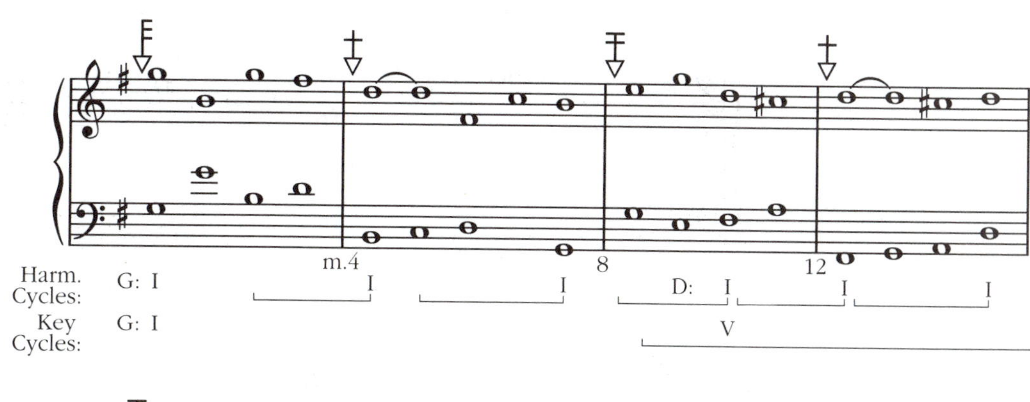


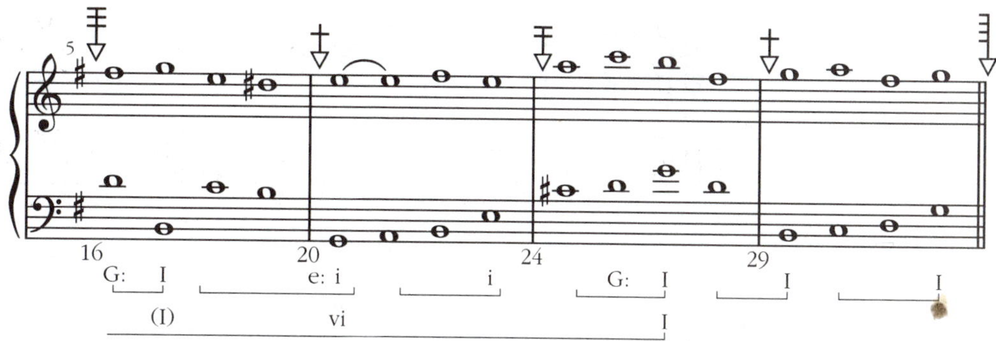


The degree of coherence will differ depending on the treatment of the main factors in the analysis. Three of the main factors are step progressions, harmonic cycles, and key cycles.

The larger the span of a work that is covered by a step progression, the greater will be the linear coherence. From the lowest structural level to the highest, the step progression is one of the most powerful forces for coherence in music. The repetition of tones within the step progression not only emphasizes those tones but also lends further coherence and importance to the step progression itself. In general, step progressions present the greatest coherence when they include fewer scale degrees. Step progressions ending on $\hat{1}$, $\hat{3}$, or $\hat{5}$ lend more coherence to the piece than those ending on other scale degrees.

The more time devoted to the tonic chord within the harmonic cycles, the greater the coherence in a work. Extended passages built entirely on the tonic are not unusual at the beginning or ending of a piece. The process of establishing or confirming the tonic is an essential element in developing coherence. In general, shorter harmonic cycles lend greater coherence than long cycles since a brief cycle will bring a return to the tonic sooner. More frequent assertions of the tonic will, of course, add coherence.

The more time devoted to the tonic key, the greater will be the coherence within the work. The length of time in the tonic key is a more critical factor than the length of the key cycle. Several short key cycles will emphasize the tonic and strengthen coherence if the length of time in the tonic is greater than in other keys.

**EXAMPLE 23-17.** Mozart: Duet for Two Woodwinds, K. 487, No. 9

**EXAMPLE 23-18.** Analysis of example 23-17

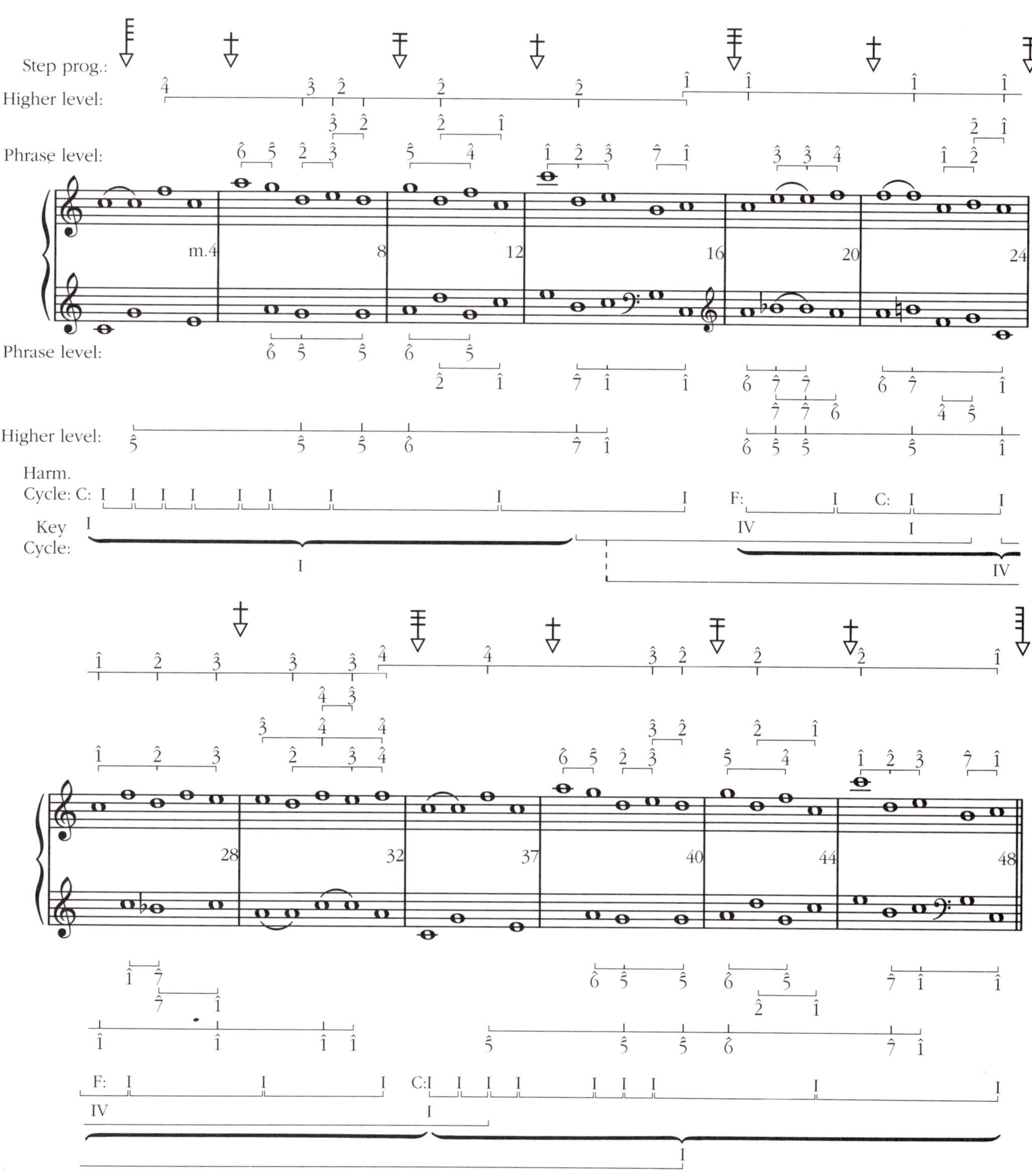

## SUMMARY

Three- and four-part forms, often used for vocal music, are sometimes included in the category of song forms and are usually considered to be sectional due to the independence and conclusive endings of the sections. Three-part forms divide into three parts at the highest structural level and may be found with various unit relationships; however, ternary form, ABA, is the most important type. Ternary form is sectional in that the first section normally ends with a conclusive cadence in the tonic key, the middle section contrasts in key and melodic content, and the third section is usually identical or very similar to the first part. A common variant of ternary form is AA′BA′. Extended ternary form follows the pattern ABABA. Other three-part forms are ABC and ABB′ and the rare bar form, AAB. Introductions, codas, and codettas may be found in three-part forms.

Four-part forms are relatively rare since many possible combinations give the effect of a two-part structure. The patterns ABCA and ABCD may be clear four-part forms; however, other patterns, such as ABAB, AA′BB′, ABAC, ABCB, and ABCC result in two-part structures of AA′ or AB.

Tonal coherence, coherence resulting from tonal organization, is analyzed in four parts: the two-voice framework, step progressions, harmonic cycles, and key cycles. The emergent tones in the primary melodic line and the bass constitute the two-voice framework, and the step progressions found in this are judged to be of special importance in establishing coherence. Harmonic cycles provide an emphasis on the tonic chord that engenders coherence and stability. In key cycles the emphasis on the tonic key has a comparable effect in developing coherence.

CHAPTER TWENTY-FOUR

# Tension in Homophonic Music

The earlier discussions of tension largely dealt with melody and harmony at the phrase level. This chapter considers how the other musical elements contribute to tension and how the tension patterns of the component phrases relate to shape the crest of the larger structural units.

## SOURCES OF TENSION

It is useful to review how tension develops in melody and harmony to assist in formulating concepts about the development of tension in texture, dynamics, and timbre.

### Melodic Tension

The main sources of melodic tension are found in the categories of rhythm and pitch. In order of importance, these are: in rhythm—agogic accents, metric accents, and motivic changes; in pitch—contour, newness of emergent tones, and motivic changes.

Tension in a melodic line is generated by the rhythmic and pitch activity. The more important sources of rhythmic tension are agogic accents, metric accents, and differences in rhythmic patterns. The strongest of these are the agogic accents, in which differences in the amount of tension depend on the length of the thesis and the length and amount of activity in the arsis.

The more important notes, the emergent tones, arise from the prominence of rhythmic and melodic factors: prominence in the contour, special location in the phrase, the newness of the emergent tone, the culmination of a step progression, and newness in pitch patterns. Most often there is agreement between pitch and rhythm concerning the location of the crest, which is the point with the greatest level of tension and where the release of tension begins. Frequently, of course, the situation is less apparent, and a solution is based on an assessment of the tension-producing factors, which at times can neither be quantified nor clarified by a priori "rules." In ambiguous and uncertain situations the option that occurs last in the phrase is frequently the best choice for locating the crest. When focusing on homophonic music our main attention will, of course, be on the salient melodic line, but the impact of harmony and other factors previously discussed always plays a role in the final decision.

### Harmonic Tension

The main sources of harmonic tension are harmonic rhythm, chord progressions, and harmonic sonority.

## Harmonic Rhythm

In harmonic rhythm the agogic accents are the most important, as in the case of melodic rhythm. Harmonic rhythms may vary in tension, depending on the characteristics of the agogic patterns, such as the length of the arsis and thesis, and so on. Metric accents may be important if there are no agogic accents for substantial periods.

## Chord Progressions

Tension is developed as harmonic progressions present new chords within the "nontonic" portion of the harmonic cycle. The arrival of the tonic chord releases harmonic tension. Longer harmonic cycles generate more tension, but the length of time devoted to the tension portion of the cycle is the most significant. A passage with altered chords will have more tension than a comparable passage without them. Modulation creates more tension than a nonmodulating passage. A cadence confirming a modulation retains some degree of tension; it does not produce the same release of tension as a similar cadence in the original key.

## Harmonic Sonorities

Harmonic sonorities in traditional tonal music may be categorized in two groups: chords and sonorities created by nonharmonic tones. One can understand the range of possibilities best if one first considers the simpler components that both these categories have in common: harmonic intervals. In some situations it may be necessary to compare the relative tension of certain intervals or chords. Such a list can be roughly drawn, based on common practice. The most stable interval is the perfect octave, followed by the perfect fifth, and so forth. Similarly, lists of chords, based on relative stability, have been presented earlier, but it is better to make such an ordering based on the style of the particular piece being studied rather than to assume a standard of consonance or stability that might not hold true for all works of a given period or even of a given composer.

# Tension from Texture

The main sources of textural tension are textural changes and the relative complexity of texture. In example 24-1, the texture throughout is melody with accompaniment; however, the nature of the coupling changes as the phrase progresses. The melodic and harmonic elements both point towards the same possible crest for the phrase: the first beat of the fourth measure. The effect is particularly strong in the melodic rhythm, harmonic rhythm, and harmonic sonorities. The textural analysis corroborates this. The changes in texture are shown in figure 24-1, along with the harmonic analysis. Note the principles that are demonstrated.

**EXAMPLE 24-1.** Mozart: String Quartet, K. 428, fourth movement

First, changes in texture generate tension. Usually changes in texture take place between phrases; however, within this phrase three different textural arrangements occur. The first lasts two bars, while the other two last one bar each—the increase in textural activity develops more tension.

Second, the more complex the texture, the greater the tension that is developed. The texture becomes more complex when two different recessive lines appear in measure 3. The release of tension appears in the texture as some of the recessive lines are coupled with the salient line, leaving only one differentiated recessive line. The tension in the texture increases through the first three measures and releases in measure 4, paralleling the other elements and reinforcing the idea that the crest of the phrase is on the first beat of measure 4.

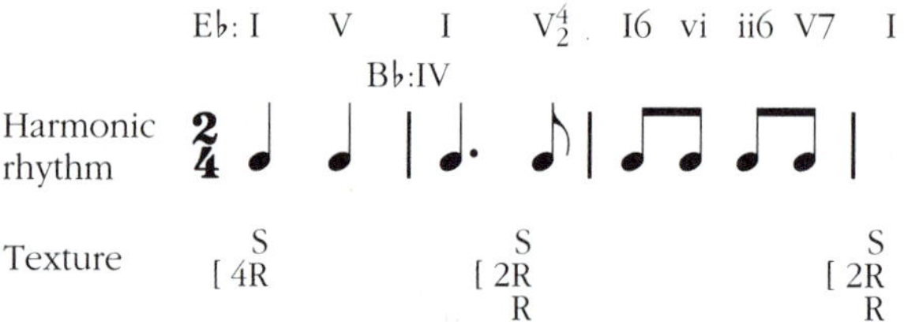


**FIGURE 24-1.** Analysis of example 24-1

## Tension from Dynamics

Dynamics have often been used to reinforce and emphasize the patterns of tension that other musical elements create. Example 24-2a illustrates the customary close relationship of louder dynamics with increases in tension resulting from other aspects. In examples 24a and b, the dynamics support the melodic tension but ignore the harmonic tension, which increases through the altered chords in the last four measures.

**EXAMPLE 24-2.** Two passages from Schumann: *Carnaval,* op. 9, no. 4, Valse noble

Reversed dynamics occur when the material with greater tension, even the crest of the phrase, is softer than the preceding material. Example 24-3 shows an increase in tension as the melodic line moves through the eighth notes and the higher notes of the phrases. The melodic and harmonic activity increases in tension as the crescendo increases in measures 1 and 2. As the crest arrives in the third measure, the dynamics suddenly become softer. The impact of the radical change in dynamics emphasizes the crest.

**EXAMPLE 24-3.** Beethoven: String Quartet, op. 18, no. 3, third movement

## Tension from Timbre

Changes in timbre also increase tension. Frequently, changes in timbre occur from phrase to phrase rather than within the phrases, hence they are more important when considering the relationships between phrases in structural units above the phrase.

Example 24-4 illustrates how timbre may be a factor in the growth of tension within the phrase. The treatment of timbre explores the color possibilities of the three voices: flute, violin, and viola.

The colors vary as the voices are doubled and coupled in different ways. The doubling and coupling change frequently, and each of the phrases develops more tension because of these shifts in color. Notice these color effects: flute alone, measures 1–2; violin and viola doubled with a fragmentary doubling in the flute, measure 3; flute, violin, and viola all doubled, measure 4; solo viola alternating with coupled violin and flute, measures 9–11; all three doubling, measure 12. Notice that the alternating colors shift more rapidly in measure 11 as the cadence of the second phrase is approached. Another important factor is the shift of color in measure 7, from the first beat. The first beat of this measure interlocks the two phrases and serves as the last, strongest agogic accent of the earlier phrases. The shift in color makes this phrase ending vivid.

In general, the treatment of timbre serves in both phrases to maintain a relatively high level of tension throughout the passage. Melodic, rhythmic, harmonic, and textural aspects are also active and are more critical in the determination of the exact, detailed placement of the crests of the phrases.

**EXAMPLE 24-4.** Beethoven: Serenade, op. 25, Entrata

## TENSION AT HIGHER STRUCTURAL LEVELS

The crest of a period, or any higher level structural unit, is the crest of the component phrase that develops the greatest tension.

## Melodic Tension in Higher Structural Levels

In considering tension in higher structural units, the criteria must be adapted and adjusted to the broader perspective, in which unit relationships are important.

### Criteria for Locating Higher-Level Crests

The criteria for locating the crests of higher units will be similar to those for the crests of phrases, with some shift in emphasis. The analytical tool that is most useful for determining the crests of larger units is the system for comparing the content of phrases, unit relationships. The letters used represent a summary of the thematic relationships between phrases and other formal units. The greater the difference between units, the greater the tension produced by the later unit. Thus, in the unit relationship a a′ or a b, one expects the greater tension in the second phrase. The last different unit tends to produce more tension, so that in the unit relationship a b c one expects the tension to be greater in phrase c. The degree of difference is a stronger factor in this case than the occurrence of the last different unit. In a b a′, the greater tension is probably in phrase b. These are only probabilities, not certainties, since a contrasting phrase might be benign and lacking in tension by comparison with its predecessor. To make a more definitive judgment one must examine the details of rhythm and contour.

Other criteria are important if their treatment is very strong or if the main criterion, unit relationships, is unclear. Such criteria might include tonality, texture, dynamics; or, in melody, the criteria might include the agogic accents, contour, newness of emergent tones, and culmination of step progression.

### The Second-Level Crest

In example 24-5, a melody of two phrases appears with the relationship a b. This relationship suggests that the tension will be greater in the second phrase. Rhythmically, the second phrase is more active; the numerous eighth notes serving to set up the half-note F with a very strong agogic and metric accent. The rhythmic activity makes the second phrase considerably more agitated, helping to confirm our expectation that the crest for the period would occur in the latter half.

**EXAMPLE 24-5.** Verdi: Requiem, Dies Irae

With the same reasoning used earlier in the analysis of larger units, the upward arrows indicate the crest not only of each phrase but of the larger unit as well. Since the second phrase was more tense overall than the first, the crest of the second phrase will serve as the point of greatest tension release for the second-level unit (period). This is indicated by the second slash on the stem of this arrow. (For a complete review of analytical symbols used in this book see the Guide to Analytical Symbols, p. 399.)

## The Third-Level Crest

This same approach may be applied to higher structural units. Our judgments about the component formal units to be grouped become broader. The letters summarizing larger unit relationships (A, A′, B, etc.) are generalizations that may cover a relatively complex set of smaller relationships. As larger units are considered, it becomes increasingly important to view details in perspective and identify the more significant features that relate to the development of tension and not become lost in a consideration of details. Example 24-6 is a third-level structure, a double period comprising two phrases. The unit relationship then is ${}_{a}{}^{A}{}_{b}\ {}_{a'}{}^{B}{}_{c}$. This leads one to anticipate that the crest for the whole unit will appear in the fourth phrase. Phrases 2 and 4 are the most active; the long passage in sixteenth notes in the last phrase is the most active in the example. By far the strongest agogic accent occurs in the last phrase. Generally the first and third phrases have the stronger skips, the second and fourth phrases relying on quicker conjunct motion to generate tension. The shift to the higher register substantially increases tension in the fourth phrase.

**EXAMPLE 24-6.** Mozart: Piano Sonata, K. 333, first movement

The analysis of pitch, and most especially rhythm, in example 24-6 confirms several typical expectations: The crest of the first period is in the second phrase, and the crest of the second period—and the entire example—is in the fourth phrase. (Note the number of slashes on the upward arrows in the example.) This placement of the crest was anticipated by the unit relationship and borne out by the analysis. The treatment of the rhythm is the most influential factor in shaping the tension.

## Tension in Higher Structural Units of Homophonic Music

Analyzing the tension in homophonic music at higher structural levels requires emphasis on the melodic element, but other sources or elements must also be taken into account. The sources for tension within the component phrases of a higher structural unit need to be compared and a judgment made regarding the relative amounts of tension. If there is ambiguity in the tension from the separate musical elements, the unit relationships between the phrases are the dominant forces in determining the stronger phrase. The last different (new or modified) structural unit is the most tense in such cases.

Example 24-7 shows two phrases that form a period. The analysis shows structural units and crests. The melodic lines of the two phrases of the example are virtually identical. Only the last notes are changed. The chords are also the same except that the inversions have been changed, creating a new tension-building emphasis of B-flat in the bass in the second phrase. The unit relationship is a a′; therefore, the crest of the second phrase is the crest for the period, due to the changes in the material.

**EXAMPLE 24-7.** Mozart: String Quartet, K. 428, fourth movement

Example 24-8 adds two more phrases to those of the preceding example, yielding the third-level unit that begins this movement. The analysis of the structural units and crests is shown.

**EXAMPLE 24-8.** Mozart: String Quartet, K. 428, fourth movement

The tension in the melodic line of the third phrase is less clear since it consists of continuous sixteenth notes. The contour has its highest point after the first beat of measure 10. The harmonic rhythm in this measure has a strong agogic accent. In measures 11 and 12, the texture becomes thinner since there are only two tones rather than five sounding simultaneously. The dynamics have also changed from the forte of measures 9 and 10 to piano, the dynamic level of the previous two phrases. Measures 11 and 12 have some tension, particularly in the harmony and texture. The harmony is much more active, with rapid harmonic rhythm, including an agogic accent on the second beat of measure 12, which coincides with the agogic accent in the melodic rhythm of the recessive line. Note also the series of perfect fourths between the violins on the beats of these last two bars. The texture here is somewhat more complex in that the recessive line in measures 11 and 12 is melodically stronger and more competitive with the salient line than the recessive voices in measures 8 and 9.

Summarizing the relationships in this phrase, one might come to two different conclusions: The crest is in measure 10 (due to melodic contour and harmonic rhythm) or in measure 12 (due to harmonic progressions, sonorities, and texture). The analysis shown favors measure 10 for the crest of this phrase.

At higher levels, the last two phrases may be compared to determine the crest of the period. The strong and active texture and harmony plus the clear agogic accent in the melody cause the crest of the second phrase (m. 16) to have much more tension than the first phrase of the pair. The crest of the third-level unit will be either the crest in measure 8 or that in measure 16. The great increase in melodic activity and the considerable increase in both textural changes and harmonic events after measure 8 raise the level of tension substantially. Note also that the key has changed from E-flat major to B-flat major for the strong crest in measure 16. The strong dissonance on the first beat of measure 16 is especially prominent, confirming this as the location of the crest for this third-level unit.

A special problem is raised in some cases when material recurs sometime later in a different structural unit, for instance, if the material of one phrase recurs in a phrase of a different period later in a form. This happens in rounded binary forms in particular. Generally, the greater the amount of recurrence, the more important is the material in shaping the crest of the later structural unit. If the recurrence is only fragmentary, then more of the later structure will contain new or modified material, hence more tension will be developed. If the recurrence is complete or extensive, the tension will be less. In the rounded binary form seen in example 24-9, there are six phrases, of which the last two (beginning in m. 17) are very similar to the first two. This is important to consider when the crest for the third-level unit is determined. At that stage of the analysis the crest for the second period (b) is to be compared with the crest for the third period (c).

Because of the different treatment and new aspects of the material in the second period in comparison with the recurring older material in the third period, one must conclude that the crest for the second period involves more tension than that for the third period. For this reason the crest at (b) will be given three slashes; it is the crest for the third-level unit. Next, one must find the crest for the entire structure, the fourth-level unit. To do this, one must compare the crests of the component units, that is, at (a) and at (b). The difference and the newness of material in several respects lead one to select (b). In example 24-10, four slashes are written on the arrow at (b), matching the four at the beginning and end of the piece.

**EXAMPLE 24-9.** Haydn: Piano Sonata in G Major, Hob. XVI:27, second movement

It should be noted that there are some instances where the modifications in recurring material may be so strong that they generate more tension than is found in the preceding unit with which it is grouped. For instance, example 24-11 contains six phrases grouped into a period (the first part of a binary form) and a double period (the second part of the binary). The phrase relationships can be summarized as: a a′ b c a″ a‴.

When phrase a recurs in the last period (m. 19) the texture is thickened, the range broadened, the dynamics raised, and, in the last phrase (m. 23), altered chords are added. An unusually long agogic pattern in the melodic material appears at the same time as a long agogic pattern in the harmonic rhythm, cadencing on a very long thesis on the tonic chord. The last phrase is remarkably long because of these modifications and tension-building devices. The crest for the whole example is in the last phrase, after the rounding, rather than before, as is usually the case.

**EXAMPLE 24-10.** Haydn: Piano Sonata in G Major, Hob. XVI:27, second movement

**EXAMPLE 24-11.** Brahms: *Variations on a Theme by Haydn,* op. 56b

EXAMPLE 24-11. (continued)

## Procedure for Formal Analysis

The formal analysis may include two categories for the procedure: the structural analysis for structural units and tension analysis for crests.

### Structural Analysis

1. Determine the phrases. Write downward arrows in the score: ⇣.
2. Determine the unit relationships. Express phrase relationships with lower case letters, for example, a b.
3. Determine the second-level structures (periods). Add downward arrows with two slashes: ⇣.
4. Determine the unit relationships. Express period relationships with upper case letters, for example, A B.
5. Determine the third-level structure. Indicate third-level structures with three slashes: ⇣.

### Tension Analysis

1. Determine the crest of each phrase. Write upward arrows with one slash in the score: ⇡.
2. Determine the crest of each period. Give upward arrows two slashes: ⇡.
3. Determine the crest of the third-level units. Give upward arrows three slashes: ⇡.

## TENSION AND INTERPRETATION

Some of the many alternatives for interpretation will now be reviewed in more detail. In the discussion of tension and interpretation in chapter 14 four areas for interpretation were listed: rhythm, dynamics, articulation, and timbre. The two categories that will be considered here are dynamic and agogic (rhythmic) interpretation, the most important for detailed and varied treatment.

### Dynamic Interpretation

Louder dynamics are usually associated with greater tension; however, the use of reversed dynamics may also be applied in interpretation. This provides interest and may be quite strong in its effect; however, the performer must make a judgment about the appropriateness of this device for the specific passage. If the material near the crest is emotionally suited to the more gentle and restrained effect of reversed dynamics, it can be a useful alternative.

### Agogic Interpretation

Subtle changes in tempo tend to increase tension, and crests may be enhanced through an interpretation that explores this resource, rubato. The approach to the crest may be retarded, with a return to the original tempo at the crest, or the retard may be continued past the crest, the original tempo being reinstated later. Yet another possibility is to retard and then accelerate during the approach to the crest. The more change in tempo, the greater the tension produced, but judgment must be used to avoid distortion. A phrase may consist of subdivisions, each having a crest. In Romantic music especially, the performer may interpret these crests with dynamic and agogic modifications. One would expect the crest of the phrase to be stronger in comparison with the crests of the subdivisions. As a rule, more extreme changes are expected at the crests of higher-level units than at lower levels.

The performer has a range of possibilities at his or her disposal; these can be used with subtlety and restraint or in a rather obvious fashion. The style of the piece will dictate which approach is suitable. It is impossible to list all the combinations of these and other devices that may be conceived. The point is that the performer brings a formidable array of techniques and resources with which to enhance the music. Just which of these resources to use at a particular point, and the degree to which it should be used, is a matter of great sensitivity and artistry, much of which is beyond verbalization and certainly beyond the scope of this text.

## SUMMARY

Tension and tension patterns in phrases and higher-level structural units are understood through an analysis of all the musical elements. Tension in texture, dynamics, and timbre must be considered in addition to that in melody and harmony. The main sources of melodic tension are found in the categories of rhythm and pitch. The main sources of harmonic tension are harmonic rhythm, chord progressions, and harmonic sonority. The main sources of textural tension are textural changes and the relative complexity of texture. Dynamics have often been used to reinforce and emphasize the patterns of tension that other musical elements create. Changes in timbre also create increases in tension; however, changes in timbre often occur from phrase to phrase rather than within the phrases, hence they are more important when considering the relationships between phrases in structural units above the phrase.

The crest of a period or higher-level structural unit is the crest for the component phrase that develops the greatest tension, but the criteria for such a crest must be augmented with a consideration of unit relationships as the most important initial factor. Analyzing the tension in homophonic music at higher structural levels requires emphasis on the melodic element, but other sources or elements must be taken into account. In any case, the unit relationships between the phrases are the dominant force in determining the stronger phrase.

The procedure for the formal analysis is divided into two categories: the structural analysis that identifies structural units and the tension analysis for crests. For the structural analysis:

1. Determine the phrases.
2. Determine the unit relationships.
3. Determine the second-level structures (periods).
4. Determine the unit relationships.
5. Determine the third-level structure.

For the tension analysis:

1. Determine the crest of each phrase.
2. Determine the crest of each period.
3. Determine the crest of the third-level unit.

The performer uses information about the crests and tension in the music to bring life to his or her performances. Dynamic and agogic interpretation are the most important avenues for interpretation. For dynamic interpretation, the performer may associate higher dynamics with higher tension (the obvious association), or this may be reversed. Agogic interpretation includes subtle changes of tempo (rubato) for expressive purposes.

APPENDIX A

# Aspects of Acoustics

Acoustics, the science of sounds, encompasses some important concepts that are valuable for the study of basic theory. Sound consists of vibrations perceptible by the ear. As musical tones, these vibrations have four attributes: (1) frequency, (2) duration, (3) tone color or timbre, and (4) amplitude or loudness. Of concern here is a consideration of the attributes of musical pitch and the subject of tuning. Exercises related to material on acoustics are found in the appendix of the workbook.

## VIBRATION

Sound is produced by vibrations, which may be started by striking the vibrating material, forcing air past it, plucking it, or using other physical means. From its position of rest, the vibrating body moves to a position of greatest displacement in one direction. Its natural resilience will draw it back toward its starting position, but it moves past that to the opposite extreme position, from which it returns to its starting position. This entire process constitutes one full cycle. This vibrating process has several aspects: frequency and the resonance of tone; overtones, which are perceived as tone color or timbre; and amplitude, which is considered as loudness.

### Frequency

The number of cycles completed within one second is known as *frequency*. To a musician, a change of frequency is heard as a change of pitch; higher frequencies produce higher pitches. These vibrations occur at surprisingly rapid speeds. For example, $c^1$, or middle c on the piano, has a frequency of 261.1 cps (cycles per second). Cycles are measured in hertz, for example, 261.1 Hz. Vibrations are audible to humans within the range of 16 to 20,000 Hz. As people age, they often lose some of their ability to hear higher frequencies. For instance, the average person of fifty can hear up to only 15,000 Hz.

The pitch of a vibrating body depends upon several factors: the length of the vibrating body, the density of the material, the tension, the temperature, and the thickness. Music theorists since ancient Greece have paid particular attention to the relationship between the length of a vibrating body and its pitch. Comparing the pitch of a string eighteen inches long with the pitch of an identical string thirty-six inches long, under equal tension, finds them an octave apart. The mathematician Pythagoras, in the sixth century B.C., was able to make this measurement and conclude that the ratio of 2 to 1 produced the octave. Later, when the actual frequencies could be measured, it was found that the same ratio applies. Thus, if $c^1$ is 261.1 Hz., then $c^2$ (an octave higher) will be 522.2 Hz.

## Resonance

Another vital factor in musical instruments is *resonance,* the transmission of vibrations from one vibrating body to another. This is important because ultimately the vibrations must be transmitted to the air around the instrument and thence to the listeners. In some instruments the resonators are obvious, such as the piano sound board or the body of the guitar or violin. In other instruments the resonator may be less obvious. In brass instrument the players' lips supply the vibrations, and the length of the tube is altered to provide resonance at the various pitches. A few percussion instruments have no resonators, for example, triangle and cymbals. These are instruments that do not produce a definite pitch. The glockenspiel, or orchestral bells, is a percussion instrument with definite pitch that also does not have resonators.

## Overtones and Timbre

The vibration of a musical tone usually consists of a complex pattern in which the fundamental cycle contains smaller, faster cycles within it that are considered as an overtone series and that account for differences in tone color or timbre.

Vibration is not a simple swinging from side to side. Vibrating bodies vibrate in many segments simultaneously. For example, when the cello C string vibrates as a whole (fig. A-1), it produces the pitch shown in example A-1. But in fact the string does not vibrate only as a whole. It also vibrates in halves, thirds, fourths, fifths, and so on up to infinity (or at least up to the limits of flexibility for the vibrating string; see fig. A-2).

**FIGURE A-1.** Vibrating cello C string

**EXAMPLE A-1.** Pitch produced by cello's C string

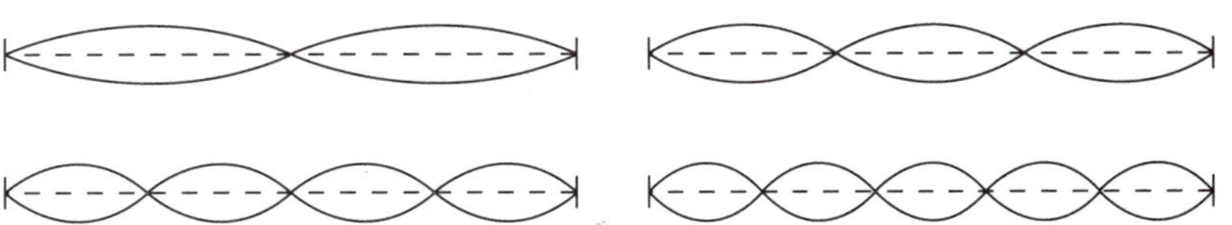

**FIGURE A-2.** Vibrating cello string

Such a complex pattern of motion is almost impossible to visualize, but in fact these vibrations do take place simultaneously. Since segments vary in length, a shorter segment produces a tone higher than the string vibrating as a whole (the fundamental). These higher tones are known as *overtones.* Overtones get increasingly faint as they get higher and further from the fundamental. Although the overtones extend to infinity, only the first fifteen are significant to most music theorists. Shown in example A-2 are the tones produced by an instrument sounding the fundamental C. This is called the *overtone series* or *harmonic series.* The term *harmonic* refers to the fundamental tone as well as to the overtones. The numbers in example A-2 indicate harmonics; thus, the fundamental is designated 1, the first overtone is designated 2, and so on.

**EXAMPLE A-2.** Harmonic series (Notes marked with an x are lower in pitch than corresponding sounds on the piano)

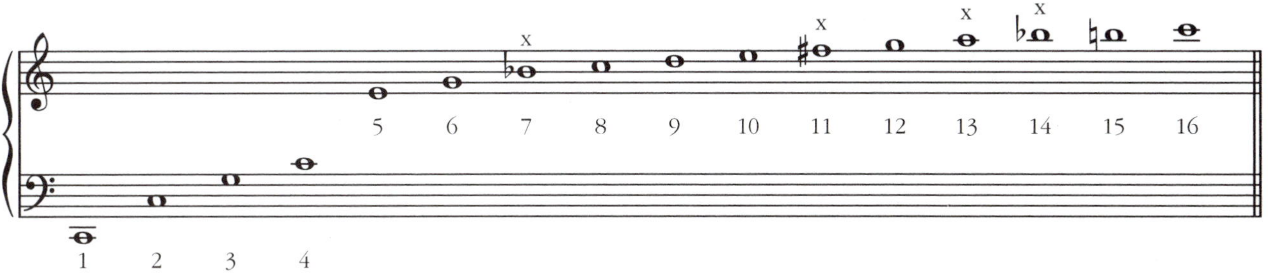

Several important observations can be made from this harmonic or overtone series. First, intervals get smaller and smaller as the series ascends. This is because the vibrating segments become increasingly shorter. Second, notice that harmonics 7, 11, 13, and 14 are significantly out of tune: They do not fit well into our system of tuning. Third, the numbers for the harmonics (or *partials* as they are sometimes called) show not only the order of the harmonics but the ratios that correspond to particular intervals. Thus, 2:1 represents the ratio of frequencies for tones an octave apart, 3:2 represents the ratio for the perfect fifth, 4:3 the perfect fourth, and so on. These ratios can be seen to work throughout the series. For example, the ratio between harmonic 6 and harmonic 12 is 2:1, an octave.

The acoustical basis for differences in tone color can be found in the overtones, for each vibrating body will produce a characteristic pattern of stronger and weaker partials. The varying prominence of one overtone or another will give each instrument its particular tone color (timbre). Other factors of course enter into the characteristic acoustical aspects of voices and instruments, such as the way in which the vibrations are initiated, but it is not possible to consider all these issues in detail here.

### Loudness

Loudness varies with the amplitude of the vibrating body. When the vibrating body is displaced to a greater degree the tone produced will be louder. An interesting phenomenon operates here, for human ears are far more sensitive to high sounds than to low. Obviously, a guitar string vibrating as a whole has a greater amplitude, that is, moves further and displaces a correspondingly larger amount of surrounding air, than the vibrations of any of the upper partials of the same string. This explains why the higher one goes in the overtone series the fainter are the sounds produced.

## TUNING AND TEMPERAMENT

As noted above, some of the intervals in the harmonic series do not fit into our tuning system. The interval from harmonic 7 to harmonic 8 is too large to be heard as a whole step, yet it is smaller than a minor third. The problem arises because our tuning system is a human construct while the harmonics are natural phenomena. The problem of reconciling these pitches has fascinated and plagued musicians for centuries. Pythagorus was able to calculate exactly the size of the discrepancy between the intervals that appear in nature and our system that attempts to divide the octave into twelve half steps.

The most perfect interval is the octave, but if we begin with any pitch and then tune the octave above and below it, we have not made any progress toward a system of tuning. In order to tune a new pitch we may turn to the next most perfect interval, the perfect fifth, with a ratio of 3:2. If we begin with a pitch, and from it tune new pitches using the ratio 3:2, we will indeed obtain all twelve tones of the chromatic scale (twelve half steps). For example, beginning with A-flat: A-flat, E-flat, B-flat, F, C, G, D, A, E, B, F-sharp, C-sharp, G-sharp.

Since G-sharp is the enharmonic equivalent of A-flat, it would seem that this is an ideal way of tuning the chromatic scale. Unfortunately, this G-sharp is not the same as A-flat. When one begins on A-flat and calculates the twelve perfect fifths at the ratio of 3:2 and transposes the final G-sharp into the same octave as original A-flat, one finds a discrepancy of 128:129.746 or 24/100 of a minor second (approximately one-fourth of a half step). This discrepancy can easily be heard and is quite sufficient to render this method of tuning impractical for most music performed today. The discrepancy is known as the *Pythagorean comma;* it has troubled musicians and instrument builders for centuries.

It may seem this discussion is abstract and somewhat divorced from the practical concerns of a performing musician, but this is not the case. When musicians sing or play instruments on which the pitch may be adjusted, they use "pure" intonation, that is, they place each tone as closely in tune as possible. The perfect fifth will be very close to the 3:2 ratio. The sensitive musician makes constant adjustments to keep each successive chord and interval in tune. But when one tries to tune all twelve pitches at once, as on a keyboard instrument, one is faced with the decision of whether to have the fifths in tune or the octaves, but one cannot have both at the same time. Obviously, out-of-tune octaves would be intolerable, and so we must resort to a system of *temperament,* which is a process of accommodating various intervals to the unavoidable conflict between a human tuning system and the intervals as they appear in nature.

Many attempts were made to solve the dilemma. The final compromise, gradually adopted in the eighteenth and nineteenth centuries, is known as *equal temperament.* In equal temperament, the octave is the only interval that is truly in tune; the Pythagorean comma is equally divided between all twelve tones. Each fifth is slightly smaller than the "pure" perfect fifth. To get a useable picture of how the pitches in the Pythagorean tuning system compare with equal temperament, it will be easiest to use the *cent* system, in which the equal-tempered half step is divided into 100 parts. Thus, an interval of a minor second would be 100 cents; a major second, 200 cents; and so on.

Table A-1 shows the Pythagorean method of calculating each interval. The perfect fifth in the Pythagorean scale is equal to 702 cents, slightly larger than the perfect fifth in equal temperament (700 cents). As one adds fifths above C the discrepancy or comma increases until one reaches 24 cents, the full Pythagorean comma. It will appear that the equal-tempered scale is more regular and "correct," but in fact neither scale can resolve the dilemma of good intonation and regular-sized intervals.

| Tone | Adding perfect fifths (3:2) in the Pythagorean system P5 = 702 cents | Corresponding tone in equal temperament | Difference in cents |
|---|---|---|---|
| A♭ | 0 | 0 | 0 |
| E♭ | 0 + 702 | 700 | 2 |
| B♭ | 702 + 702 = 1404 − 1200 = 204 | 200 | 4 |
| F | 204 + 702 = 906 | 900 | 6 |
| C | 906 + 702 = 1608 − 1200 = 408 | 400 | 8 |
| G | 408 + 702 = 1110 | 1100 | 10 |
| D | 1110 + 702 = 1812 − 1200 = 612 | 600 | 12 |
| A | 612 + 702 = 1314 − 1200 = 114 | 100 | 14 |
| E | 114 + 702 = 816 | 800 | 16 |
| B | 816 + 702 = 1518 − 1200 = 318 | 300 | 18 |
| F♯ | 318 + 702 = 1020 | 1000 | 20 |
| C♯ | 1020 + 702 = 1722 − 1200 = 522 | 500 | 22 |
| G♯ | 522 + 702 = 1224 | 1200 | 24 |

**TABLE A-1.** Comparison (in cents) of pitches in the Pythagorean and equal-tempered scales

APPENDIX B

# Guide to Analytical Symbols

**Structural Analysis**

First-level unit (phrase) Chapter 3

Interlocking phrases Chapter 3

Overlapping phrases Chapter 21

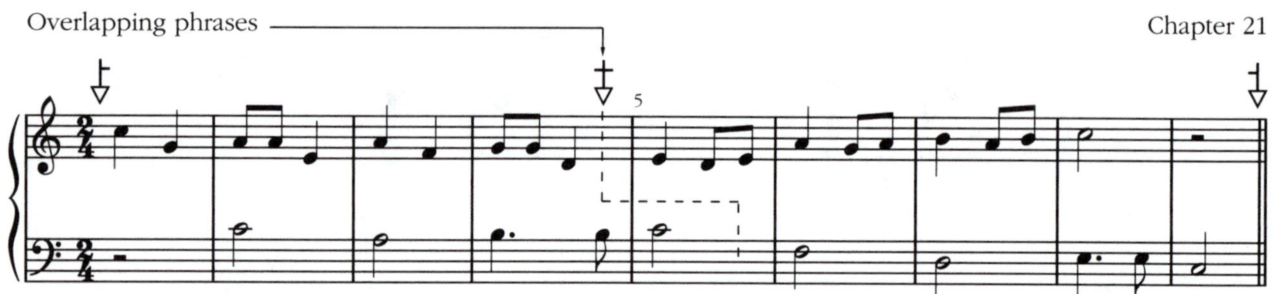

Higher-level units Chapter 21

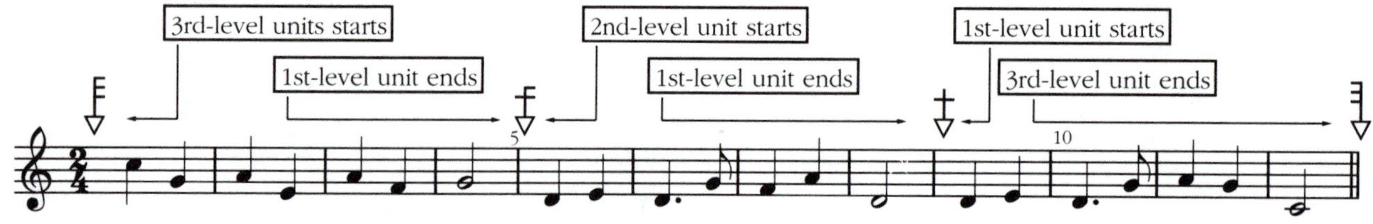


**Rhythmic and Melodic Analysis** Chapter 2

Agogic accents Metric accents Emergent tones

**Tension Analysis**

Crests of phrase at first level

Chapter 3

Crests of higher-level units

Chapter 24

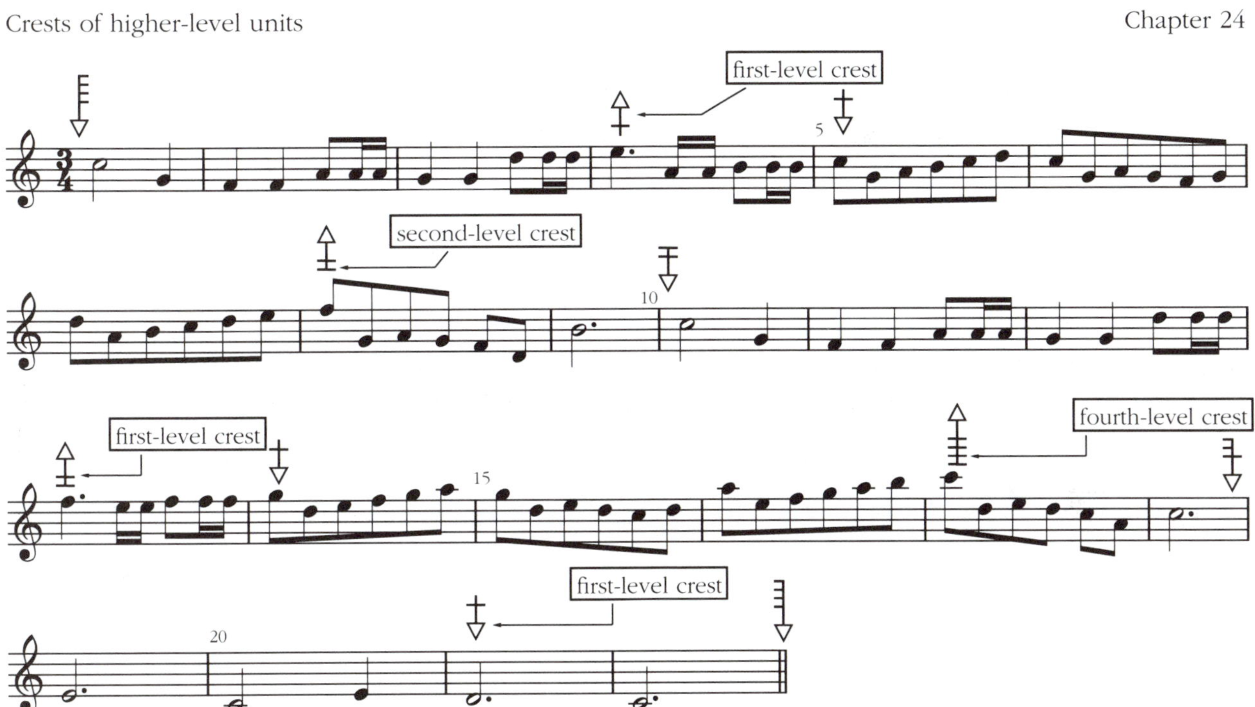


**Textural Analysis**

Chapter 15

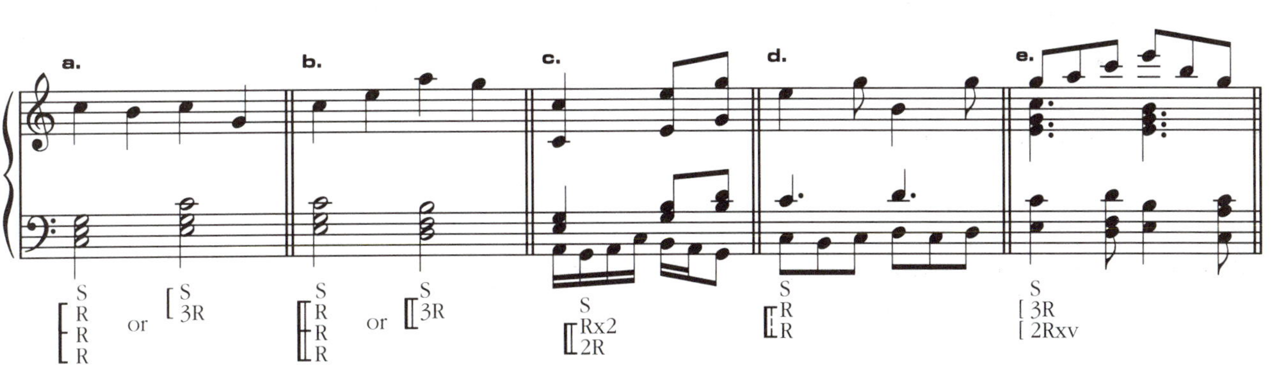

# GLOSSARY

This glossary includes the most important terms from the lists of new terms given at the beginning of each chapter. Not included are terms that are assumed to be already in the students' vocabulary from previous training but only reviewed in this text, terms that are synonymous with other more commonly used terms, terms of incidental interest, and terms whose meanings are not limited to usage in music.

**AGOGIC ACCENT:** The psychological emphasis that accrues to a tone that is preceded by one or more shorter tones.

**AGOGIC PATTERN:** A group of durations ending with the longest and including all the preceding shorter durations. The last tone is called the thesis; the shorter note or notes are termed the arsis. Agogic patterns within an arsis are called subordinate agogic patterns.

**ALTERNATE PROGRESSION:** A progression that does not appear in the table of normal progressions but that occurs with such frequency that it cannot be considered irregular, that is, IV–I, V–vi, vi–V, iii–IV.

**ANTECEDENT:** The first of a pair of phrases that group to form a period.

**ARSIS:** See agogic pattern.

**ATONALITY:** Absence of tonality; implying that a tonal center has not been established.

**AUGMENTATION:** The reappearance of a motive with the note values increased by a specific amount, often doubled.

**BASIC DURATION (BD):** The duration of a beat considered as the time elapsing between pulses.

**BEAT GROUP:** A group of two or three beats (basic durations) in which the first beat is either a primary or secondary accent within a meter. In meters with two or three beats, the whole measure is a beat group, and meters with four or more beats contain two or more beat groups of two or three beats each.

**BORROWED CHORDS:** Chords that contain tones borrowed from another mode, for example, in a major key, a chord that uses one or more tones found in the parallel minor key, such as minor iv.

**CHORD:** A simultaneous sounding of three or more different tones. Certain combinations of tones produce chords that are heard as consonant, while others are heard as dissonant. Chords may be implied when the tones are played in arpeggiated fashion, so that the tones are sounded successively, not simultaneously.

**CHORD GROUP:** In the table of normal progressions all chords are assigned to a group that bears a particular relationship to the tonic. Chords within a particular group usually progress to a chord in the next lower-numbered group.

**CHORD TONE:** A tone that is a member of the chord sounding at a particular moment.

**CONJUNCT MOTION:** Melodic motion in which each tone moves to the nearest available tone in the scale, avoiding any skips (disjunct motion).

**CONSEQUENT:** The second of a pair of phrases grouped to form a period.

**CONTINUO:** In ensemble music of the Baroque era, the bass part, which was usually played by a bass instrument along with a keyboard player who improvised the chords normally indicated by figures (Arabic numbers) written by the composer.

**COUPLING:** Two or more simultaneously sounding parts with identical melodic contour or rhythmic content. The coupling may be rhythmic, meaning the lines have identical rhythms, or the coupling may be full, in which case the lines have identical rhythm and contour. The contours may be any interval apart except unison or one or more octaves, in which cases the relationship is termed doubling.

**CREST OF TENSION:** The point in a phrase or higher structural unit at which the tension reaches its highest level and the release of tension begins.

**DA CAPO:** The Italian instruction ("from the head") to return to the beginning of the piece and perform the first section again. Between the first and second performances of the first section lies a middle part, producing the overall unit relationship ABA. Da capo forms are common in dance and dance-influenced pieces.

**DELAY:** In imitation, the time elapsing between the initial statement by the leader and the appearance of the follower. The delay is usually measured in beats or measures.

**DIATONIC MODES:** Any of the seven patterns that are possible within the diatonic system, that is, the patterns that arise if one begins on a particular tone in the system and includes all diatonic tones within an octave.

**DIATONIC SYSTEM:** The pattern of tones with relationships as represented in the white keys of the piano keyboard. A scale may begin on any of the seven tones within an octave. All such scales are called diatonic, and may be transposed to any pitch.

**DISJUNCT MOTION:** Melodic motion by skip, that is, motion in which the melody does not move to the nearest available tone, but leaps to a more distant tone. Most melodies combine disjunct and conjunct motion.

**DISSONANCE:** A sounding of two or more tones that are not heard as part of the same chord. The result is a perception of disagreement or tension. A dissonance in traditional music requires a resolution, a movement by one or more of the tones to a tone perceived as consonant with the surrounding tones.

**DYNAMIC ACCENT:** The psychological emphasis brought to a tone by playing or singing it louder than surrounding tones.

**EMERGENT TONE:** A tone in a melody that achieves special prominence through its rhythmic location, duration, contour, or other feature.

**FIGURED BASS SYSTEM:** In the Baroque era, a method of indicating along with the bass line through Arabic numbers the appropriate chords to be improvised by a keyboard player. This shorthand system has been used for teaching harmony up to the present time.

**FIRST-LEVEL UNIT:** A phrase, which is the basic unit of musical form. The analytical method used in this text indicates the point between phrases by a downward arrow with single slashes.

**FORMAL UNIT:** A unit of musical structure. The smallest such unit is the phrase. Phrases combine to form periods, which group to form ever-larger units, allowing the creation of huge musical works. Each unit is set off by the ending (cadence) of the preceding unit. Sometimes called structural unit.

**HARBINGER CHORD:** In a modulation, the first chord that is clearly not in the original key. This harbinger signals the approach of the new key.

**HARMONIC CADENCES:** The harmonic characteristics at the end of a phrase. Conventionalized types are used to achieve varying degrees of conclusiveness and inconclusiveness at the end of the phrase.

**HARMONIC CYCLE:** A chord progression extending from one appearance of the tonic chord to the next. It may include one or many intervening chords.

**HARMONIC RHYTHM:** The rhythm created by the changes of harmony.

**HETEROPHONY:** The simultaneous sounding of two differing versions of a melody.

**IMPLIED LINE:** The perceived division of a melodic line into two or more component lines, creating the illusion of simultaneous parts. Monophony can be heard as polyphony through this device. Usually the lines are projected through disjunct motion.

**INTERVAL ROOT:** In any interval, one tone is perceived as dominating. This is the root of the interval.

**MELODIC DOUBLING:** The reinforcing of a melodic line by another voice or instrument sounding the same melody in unison or octaves.

**MELODIC INVERSION:** The reappearance of a melodic line with the directions reversed, that is, those intervals that at first were ascending are later heard descending, and vice versa.

**METRIC ACCENT:** Accent points ascribed to the meter.

**MODULATION:** A change of tonal center or of key. The establishing of a new tonic.

**MUTATION:** A change of mode, as from major to minor or vice versa, without a change of tonic.

**NONHARMONIC TONE:** A tone that is not a member of the chord sounding at a particular time.

**NORMAL PROGRESSION:** A progression that has been traditionally used so often that it can be considered normal or expected. These are reflected in the table of normal progressions. Harmony that uses predominately normal progressions is said to be functional.

**QUASI-CADENCE:** A cadence effect created by any of various elements, such as contour or rhythm, but not reflected in the harmony.

**RECAPITULATION:** The return of a section of music heard earlier, usually the first part of a piece returning toward the end.

**RECESSIVE LINE:** A melodic line that is perceived as secondary or less important than the salient line or lines.

**ROUNDED BINARY FORM:** A binary form in which the opening material returns toward the middle of the second part. The return is in the tonic key.

**SALIENT LINE:** A melodic line that captures the primary attention of the listener.

**SECONDARY DOMINANT:** A chord (other than V) that has been altered to have the relationship of dominant to a chord that is not tonic, for example, the dominant of the supertonic chord (V/ii).

**SEQUENCE:** In melody, the repetition of a motive on a new pitch level. In harmony, a progression that presents chords in recurring interval relationships, such as a progression with the bass moving by thirds: I–vi–IV–ii.

**STEP PROGRESSION:** Step-wise relationship between emergent tones of a melody. Other emergent and non-emergent tones may intervene.

**SUBPHRASE:** A structural unit that forms a component division of a phrase. Not all phrases have subphrase units. In the Classical period subphrase units were often two measures in length.

**TERNARY FORM:** A formal pattern consisting of the unit relationship ABA. This pattern is often used in shorter works and in numerous da capo forms.

**TONAL ARCH:** A pattern of key organization in which the initial key of a work returns at the end after modulating to other keys.

**TRIAD:** A particular type of chord, consisting of three tones, or members. The basic form of the triad is built on a tone called the root. A third above the root lies a second tone, and a fifth above the root lies the last tone. The members of the triad need not appear in this order at all times.

**UNIT RELATIONSHIP:** The thematic relationship of one formal unit to another. These relationships are expressed by letters of the alphabet. Two phrases that are identical would have a unit relationship of aa or, if quite different, ab. If they were similar they might be called aa′. Unit relationships are also seen in higher structural levels, in which case capital letters are used, for example, ABA.

# INDEX


**A**

accents 31, 34, 53, 69
  agogic, see agogic accent
  dynamic, see dynamic accent
  metric, see metric accent
  strongest, determining 69–70
accidentals 13–14
accompaniment 229–234
  broken chord 230–232
  less active 232
acoustics 393–398
aeolian mode 48–49, 50
agogic accent 31, 53, 198, 201, 202, 207, 259, 322, 374–375, 380
  assessing strength of 69–70
agogic pattern 31, 55, 56, 201, 206, 385
  principal 33
  subordinate 33
Alberti bass 230
altered chord 263, 280, 294
alternate progressions 90
alternating roles 232
amplitude 393, 396
answer, tonal and real 241, 242
antecedent 308
anticipation 162, 168, 172
appoggiatura 165, 168, 171, 172, 174
arpeggiated six-four chord 150–151
arrows, downward 63–67, 308, 312–314, 318, 334, 336, 349, 362, 389, 391
arrows, upward 68, 381–382, 384
arsis 31, 375
  degree of activity in 70
  length 69
arsis group 32
asymmetrical units 310, 320
atonal 44
attack 31
augmentation 57
augmented triad 76–77
authentic cadence 92–94, 126
  perfect and imperfect 157, 158, 198

**B**

bar 4
bar form 357
basic duration (BD) 4–7
basso continuo, see continuo
beaming 8
beat 4–8
beat groups 6–8
binary form 327–337, 339, 385
  continuity in 329
  parallel beginnings and ending 329
  rounding 334, 337
  summary of characteristics 337
borrowed chords 294–305
  analysis of 303–304
  in major keys 294–301
  in minor keys 301–303
  summary list of 305
broken chord 230–232

**C**

cadences 36, 64, 67
  conclusive and inconclusive 64
  reappearance of opening figure 66
  harmonic 91, 94, 157–158
  harmonic, authentic 92–94, 126, 157, 158
  harmonic, conclusive 92–94, 126, 158, 159, 226, 307
  harmonic, deceptive 92–94, 158, 198, 227, 298
  harmonic, half 92, 94, 198, 227
  harmonic, imperfect authentic 157, 158, 198, 226, 345
  harmonic, inconclusive 92–94, 126, 158, 159
  harmonic, perfect authentic 157, 158, 198, 226, 345
  harmonic, phrygian 157–158
  harmonic, plagal 92–94, 126, 158, 198, 226, 345
  internal 335
cadential six-four chord 145–148, 198
cent 397–398
change of mode 51, 53, 260
chord 75
  identification by letter name 77, 81
  open and close position 98
  soprano position 99
chord groups 85–89, 91, 188–196
chord members 75–76, 79

chord progression 85, 202, 375
chord representation 186, 224, 225
chord roots 75–76
chord tones 119
chordal homophony 103, 224–229, 234
circle of fifths 28–29, 249
clefs 12
close position 98
closely related keys 248, 249
coda 345–348
codetta 345, 349
coherence 55
  tonal, see tonal coherence
common chord 249
common chord modulation, see modulation
common tones 106, 110
conjunct motion 37–38
consecutive fifths and octaves, see parallel fifths and octaves
consequent 308–309
consonance 75
continuo 130
contour 36
contrary motion 105
contrasting phrase construction 308, 323
counterpoint, writing two-voice 239–240
coupling, full 219, 234
  rhythmic 217, 234
crest 68, 71–72, 73, 203, 374, 377
  in higher structural levels 279–389, 390
  in phrases with melody and harmony 206–208
  location of 71–72
crossed voices 96, 105–106
cycle, harmonic 91, 94, 126, 127, 203, 251, 252, 367, 368, 369, 372, 375

**D**

da capo forms 341–342, 349
deceptive cadence 92–94, 158, 198, 298
delay, in imitation 240, 241
density 212, 234
diatonic modes 48–50, 53
diatonic seventh chords 81–83
diatonic system 17, 29, 48, 53
  scales (modes) 48–50, 53
differentiated polyphony, see polyphony
differentiation 55
diminished seventh chord 81, 189, 279–280
diminished triads 76, 78, 79, 151–152, 279–280
  doubling in 137
diminution 57, 58
direct modulation, see modulation
disjunct motion 37–38
dissonance 75, 144
distant key 248, 249
divisions of beats 4
dominant seventh chord 82–84, 111, 115–116
dominant seventh chords, inversions 152–156
dorian mode 49
dotted rests 3
double neighbor group 167, 168, 172, 176
double period 311–313, 322, 323, 334
doubling 98, 134, 139–140, 145
  melodic 219, 234
durations, articulation 31
  notation of 29
dynamic accents 31, 53
dynamics 16–17, 377
  changes 17

**E**

emergent tone 39–43, 46, 51, 53, 70–72, 362, 364, 367, 372, 374, 380
enharmonic equivalent 15
equal temperament 397–398
escape tone 162, 168, 171
extended phrase, see phrase

**F**

figured bass, altered tones in 131, 152, 154
  realization 130, 132
  summary of figures 184
  system 130
first-level unit 307, 323
follower 240
form 55, 73
formal unit 307, 323
formal analysis 386–389, 391
forms, bar form 357
  binary form 327–337, 339, 385
  binary form, rounded 334, 337
  four-part forms 358–362
  ternary, da capo forms 341–342, 349
  ternary form 339–344, 372
  ternary form, extended 343, 372
  three-part forms 339–358, 372
  two-part forms 325–337, 339, 357
four-part forms 358–362
free imitation, see imitation
frequency 393
full coupling 219, 234
functional harmony 90, 94
fundamental 394, 395

**G**

great staff 12

**H**

half cadence 92, 94, 158, 198
half-diminished chord 81, 191, 279–280
half step 31, 17
harbinger chord 250–253, 255, 257, 259–260
harbinger tone 250, 257
harmonic cycle 91, 94, 126, 187

harmonic minor scale 26–27
harmonic rhythm 123, 125, 127
 agogic accents in 375
harmonic tension 197–210, 374
harmonics 395, 396
harmonization 124–127, 139–142
hearing range, human 393
hertz 393
heterophony 221, 234
hidden octaves and fifths 108
Hindemith, P., interval roots 44
homophonic music 75, 384–388, 390
homophony, chordal 103, 224–229, 234

**I/J**

imitation 240–245
 follower 240
 free 242
 interval of 240
 leader 240
 strict 241
 writing 244–245
implied lines 215, 234
incipient ternary form 345
incomplete chord 98
interlocking phrases 67, 198, 315–316, 323
internal cadence 335
interpretation 67
 agogic 390, 391
 dynamic 389, 391
 tension in 209, 389–390
interval of imitation 240
intervals 18–22
 augmented 19
 compound 21
 contraction and expansion 59
 diminished 19
 inversion of 20–21
 major 19
 minor 19
 roots 44
 simple 21
 summary of 22
introductions 345–353
inversion, harmonic 227
 melodic 59
 of intervals, see intervals
 of secondary dominants 270–271, 277
 of seventh chords 80, 132–142
 of triads, first inversions 76
 of triads, second inversions 76
ionian mode 48–49

**K**

key cycle 368, 370, 372
key relationships 248, 249
key signatures 24, 27–28

**L**

leader (imitation) 240
ledger lines 13
locrian mode 48–49
loudness 393, 396
lydian mode 49

**M**

major seventh chord 81
major triad 76–77, 78, 79
measure 4
melodic analysis 42–43, 55–73
melodic cadences 64, 67
melodic doubling 219, 234
melodic inversion 60
melodic minor scale 26–27
melodic motion 37–38
melodic sequence 58–59
 leg (member) 58–59
melodic motives 57–62, 66, 68, 73
 interval contraction and expansion 59, 62
 inversion 59
modified recurrence 60
 recurrence 57, 60
 repetition 57
 retrograde 59–60
 sequence 58–59
melodic tension, tension crest 68–73
melodies, writing 52–53
melody, prominence through change of direction 38, 42
 prominence through disjunct motion 38, 42
 prominence through location 39, 42
 prominence through recurrence 39, 42
melody with accompaniment 103, 229–233, 234, 340
melody and harmony, relationship of 230
meter 4–11
 duple 5
 quadruple 5
 signatures 4
 simple and compound 4–6
 triple 5
metric accent 31, 34, 53, 69, 202, 375, 380
 relative strength of 6
minor mode 50, 51, 53
minor scales, harmonic 26–27
 melodic 26–27
 natural 25, 26, 27
minor seventh chord 81
minor triad 76–77, 78, 79
mixed choir 96
mixolydian mode 49
modes, diatonic 48–50, 53
modulation 51, 53, 249–261, 264, 275–277, 325, 375
 analysis of 257–259

common (pivot) chord 248, 249, 250–255, 257, 259–261, 289
direct 255–257, 261
establishing new key in 252–255, 261
harbinger chord 250–252, 255, 257, 259–260
six-four chord in 253–254
stages in 257
writing 259–260, 261
monophonic music 75
motion, contrary 105
oblique 105
parallel 104
relative 104–105
similar 5
motives 55, 66, 68, 73
augmentation 57
diminution 57
fragmentation 56, 57, 58
interval contraction and expansion 59, 62
inversion 59
melodic 57–62, 68, 73
modified recurrence 60
recurrence 55, 57, 60
repetition 55, 57
retrograde 59, 60
rhythmic 55–57
sequence 58–59
variants 56
motivic analysis 56, 57, 61–62
motivic change, effect on agogic accents 70–71
mutation 51

## N

natural minor scale 25, 26, 27
neighbor six-four chord 145–148
neighbor tone 120, 162, 168, 172, 174–175
nonchord tones (see nonharmonic tones)
nonfunctional harmony 90, 94
nonharmonic tones 119–122, 124, 126–128, 161–170, 172, 183, 205, 228, 230, 287
anticipation 162, 168
appoggiatura 165–166, 168, 172, 175
chromatic 169, 172, 253
consonant 168–169
double neighbor tone 167–168, 172, 176–177
escape tone 162, 168, 172, 175
in figured bass 177–183
neighbor tone 120, 161, 168, 174–175
passing tone 119–120, 161, 168, 172, 174, 182
pedal tone 166, 168, 172, 177
preparation 119, 161, 172
resolution 119, 161, 172
retardation 165, 168, 172, 176
simultaneous 169
suspension 164–165, 168, 172, 176, 178–182
normal progression 85–89, 90, 94, 203, 210, 266, 284–285, 289
notation, pitch 11–15
rhythmic, grouping 7–11
note, dotted 3
tied 2, 9
note names 12
note values 3

## O

oblique motion 105
octave designations 16
octave signs 13
open position 98
overlapping 105–106, 316–317, 323
overtone series 395
overtones 394–396

## P

parallel beginnings and endings 329
parallel fifths 108, 117, 127, 128
parallel motion 104
parallel octaves 108, 117, 127
parallel phrase construction 308–309, 320, 323
parallel scales, major 26, 51
minor 26, 51
part writing 103, 226–229
partials 396
passing six-four chord 149
passing tone 119–120, 161–168, 174, 182
pedal point 166, 168, 172, 177
period 307, 311, 312, 313, 315–321, 323, 334, 336, 359
phrase 36, 62–73, 307, 313, 323, 336
phrase, construction 308–309, 320, 323
contrasts in content 65, 198
phrase and cadences 36, 307
phrase extension 198
phrase grouping 307, 311, 313, 323, 335
phrase length 63, 198
phrygian cadence 157–158
phrygian mode 49
Picardy third 302
pitch, names, see note names
pitch, notation, see notation
pitch class 15
pitch complement 46–48, 50, 51, 53, 252, 253, 257, 261
pivot chord 250, 251, 253, 255, 257, 259–261, 289
plagal cadence 92–94, 158, 198, 345
polyphonic music 75, 236, 245
polyphony, differentiated 236, 245
unified 237, 245
preparation of nonharmonic tone 119, 172
progressions, alternate 90, 94, 272
chord 124
irregular 90, 94, 272
normal 85–89, 90, 94, 203, 210, 266, 284–285, 289

tension in 202–204, 210
pulse 4
Pythagorean comma 397
Pythagorus 393, 396

**Q**

quasi-cadence 318, 323

**R**

range of a melody 36–37
ranges of voices 96
realization, figured bass 130, 132
recapitulation 333
recessive line 213, 214, 217, 218, 227, 228, 229, 234, 376
relative motion 104–105
relative scales, major 25, 26
minor 25, 26
release 31
remote key 248, 249
repeat signs, significance in analysis 339, 340
repeated sections 339
repetition of tones 41
reprise 340
resolution of nonharmonic tones 119, 172
resolution of dominant seventh 115–116, 152–156
resonance 394
rests 2, 3, 10–11
retardation 168, 172, 174, 322
retrograde motion 59–60
rhythmic analysis 31–35
rhythmic coupling 217, 234
rhythmic motives 55–57
augmentation 57
diminution 57
fragmentation 56
recurrence 55
repetition 55
variants 56
rhythmic notation, see notation
ritornello 345, 349
Roman numerals 77–78, 83
root position 76
rounded binary form 334

**S**

salient line 207, 213, 214, 221, 227, 229, 230, 232, 234, 245, 345, 376
SATB 96
scale 23–28, 46–50, 53
diatonic 48–50, 53
major 22–24, 29, 47–48, 50
minor 25–28, 29, 47–48, 50
writing a major 24
scale degree names 23, 28
scale degrees 23, 27, 29, 44–45
variable 26–27, 50
second-level unit 307–311, 315–321, 323, 334, 336
crest of 380–381
secondary dominants 263–277
analysis of 274–277
characteristics 263–264, 277
inversions of 270–271, 277
irregular resolution 272–273, 277
normal treatment 266–271, 277
regular resolution of 267–269, 277
successive (chains of) 273–274
secondary leading tone 263
secondary leading tone chords 278–292
analysis 289–291, 292
characteristics 280, 292
enharmonic spelling of 289, 292
progressions 284–288, 292
resolution 291
successive
secondary metric accents 6
secondary tonic 263, 280, 282, 283
sequence 58
diatonic (tonal) 59
exact 58
leg 58
member 58
modified 59
seventh chords 79, 83
in major keys 81, 186–187
in minor keys 82–83, 186–187
inversions 152–156, 187
members of 79
types of 80–81, 83, 186–187
shortened phrase, see phrase
similar motion 104
similar phrase construction 308–309, 320, 323
six-four chords 144–159, 225, 253, 267, 286, 287, 289
arpeggiated 150–151
cadential 145–148, 198
passing and neighbor 149–150
sonorities, tension in 204
soprano position 99
spacing of voices in chords 97
staff 12
great 12
stem direction 14, 15, 97
step progression 40–43, 46, 51, 53, 72, 364, 369, 374, 380
culmination of 40, 51
role in unification 66
strict imitation, see imitation
strophic song 353, 359
structural analysis, cadences 315
downward arrows 63–67, 308, 312–314, 318, 334, 336, 349, 362, 389, 391
unit relationships 307–311, 323
structural units, first-level units 307, 323
higher levels 307–323

period 307
phrase 307
second-level units 307–311, 315–321, 323, 334, 336
third-level units 311–313, 322, 323, 334, 336
typical lengths 314
subdivisions of beats 7
subphrase 63, 221
subtonic 28, 88, 283
successive diminished seventh chords 291
successive secondary dominants 373–374
suspensions 164, 168, 171, 174, 177–182
successive (chain) 180
symmetrical units 310, 320, 323
syncopation 52

**T**

temperament 396–397
tempo 4
tension, at higher structural levels 379–389, 390
crest 68, 71–72, 73, 203, 206–208
dynamics as sources 377–378
harmonic sources 202–205, 210, 374–375
in agogic patterns 35–36, 53
increase and decline 68
melodic 68–73, 374
melodic sources 374
sources of 374–379, 390
textural sources 375–376
timbre as source 378–379
tension analysis, upward arrows 68, 71, 381, 389, 391
ternary form 339–344, 372
extended 343, 372
incipient 345
tessitura 37
textural changes 212
texture 375
analysis 212–234, 375
analysis, symbols used in 234
thesis 31, 55, 201, 375
length 69
third-level units 311–313, 322, 323, 334, 336
crest 381–382
thoroughbass, see continuo
three-part forms 339–358, 372
through-composed 362–372
tie, see note
tierce de Picardie 302
timbre 378, 393–396
time signatures, see meter
tonal arch 328–329
tonal center 44
tonal coherence 362–372
tonal melodies 45–46
tonality, changes in 51, 53
tone 2, 31
attributes of 393
tonic 23, 29, 44
how established 45–46
tonicized 263, 282
transitions 345
triads 75, 83
first inversion 132–142
in major keys 77–78
in minor keys 78–79
incomplete 98, 114–115, 116
members of 75–76
second inversion 144–151
types of 76
trio 341
tritone 44–45
resolution 111, 115
tuning 396
two-part forms 325–337, 339, 357
two-voice framework 362–364
two-voice music, cadences in 226–227
chord representation in 224

**U**

unified polyphony, see polyphony
unit relationships 308–312, 318, 320, 323, 339, 380

**V**

variable implied lines 216, 234
variable lines 214, 234
vertical placement 212, 221, 234
vibrating strings 394–395
voice leading 103, 106–112, 124, 230
voices, ranges 96
relative motion of 104–105
voicing 96

**W/X/Y/Z**

whole step 13